be returned on or before
below.

GOODS AND SERVICES IN EC LAW

Goods and Services in EC Law

A Study of the Relationship Between the Freedoms

Jukka Snell

Oikeust. kand. (Helsinki), LL M, PhD (London)
Lord Slynn Foundation Fellow
Fellow in European Law, British Institute of International
and Comparative Law
Lecturer, University of Wales Swansea

OXFORD
UNIVERSITY PRESS

OXFORD

UNIVERSITY PRESS

Great Clarendon Street, Oxford OX2 6DP

Oxford University Press is a department of the University of Oxford.
It furthers the University's objective of excellence in research, scholarship,
and education by publishing worldwide in

Oxford New York

Auckland Bangkok Buenos Aires Cape Town Chennai
Dar es Salaam Delhi Hong Kong Istanbul Karachi Kolkata
Kuala Lumpur Madrid Melbourne Mexico City Mumbai Nairobi
São Paulo Shanghai Singapore Taipei Tokyo Toronto

with an associated company in Berlin

Oxford is a registered trade mark of Oxford University Press
in the UK and in certain other countries

Published in the United States
by Oxford University Press Inc., New York

© J. Snell 2002

The moral rights of the author have been asserted

Database right Oxford University Press (maker)

First published 2002

British Library Cataloguing in Publication Data

Data available

Library of Congress Cataloging in Publication Data

Snell, Jukka.
Goods and services in EC law: a study of the relationship
between the freedoms/Jukka Snell.
p. cm
Includes bibliographical references and index.
1. Free trade—European Union countries. 2. International and municipal law—European
Union countries. 3. Proportionality in law—European Union countries. I. Title.
KJE5177.S64 2001   341.7′543′094—dc21   2001055473

ISBN 0–19–925009–X

1 3 5 7 9 10 8 6 4 2

Typeset by Hope Services (Abingdon) Ltd.
Printed in Great Britain
on acid-free paper by
T. J. International Ltd., Padstow, Cornwall

Foreword

Law students probably begin their studies of substantive EC law by looking at the four freedoms: goods, services, persons, and capital. Judges may well begin their consideration of EC law with a case involving what used to be Articles 30 and 36 (now Articles 28 and 30)—freedom of movement of the goods. Both will find that there are very many cases dealing with free movement of goods from the earliest days and as time went on with free movement of services and freedom of establishment. To a considerable extent these various freedoms have been looked at in separate compartments. Yet there are common factors, and if regard is had to the purposes of the four freedoms and to their link with other aspects of Community law—competition law, preventing discrimination—these common factors and the link between the freedoms needs to be considered.

The Advocate General and the Court have done this from time to time; it is hardly suprising that national courts should stick to the case and the Article directly in point before them. They, and at times the Court, had more than enough to do in deciding whether items were or were not goods or services—waste, television signals.

And so it is largely for academic writers to analyse the basis of and the link between the freedoms and particularly the link between the other three freedoms and services since the latter are defined as not being covered by the Treaty rules concerning the free movement of goods, persons, and capital.

Dr Jukka Snell has set out to do that. His aim is primarily one of analysis of principle but he combines the more abstract general questions with frequent references to judgments of the Court in looking in the first place at three questions—what constitutes a restriction on the free movement of goods and services, who is bound by or entitled to the benefit of the freedoms, and how a limit on the restriction on free movement of goods and services can be justified. To all of these his discussion on the role of proportionality is important.

He lays much emphasis on economic market cosiderations but ultimately his guiding light is that for the lawyer—as he puts it 'the building of a coherent and transparent European legal system demands a common approach that is based on generally accepted principles, not on dubious distinctions'. It follows in his thesis that the approach to freedom of goods and services should be the same. All, however, has to be seen in relation to the division of power between the Community and Member States and what is decided will have its effect on whether we are moving to a unitary or to a decentralised federal system in the Community.

This is not a book to be read in a hurry when looking at Cassis and Keck at Torfaen or at Alpine Investment, cases which may be very familiar to the reader, or when he is discussing the more abstract questions which arise—why should there be a difference between goods and services, are private parties to be treated differently, what should be the influence of constitutional opinion on the development of the law in what is essentially a practical commercial area?

Very clearly and well written with a remarkable range of references to the writings of others, this book is in my view both a challenge and a significant contribution to the jurisprudential analysis which the author thinks, rightly, is important particularly at this stage of development of Community law. Inevitably not everyone will agree with his approach or his conclusions. The more, however, I read of the book the more I realised the importance of coming back to read it again. It would be a valuable addition to every university law library as well as to the library of those who want to see where Community law could or should be going in this area.

Slynn of Hadley

Preface

This book is based on research for a PhD conducted at King's College London under the supervision of Dr Mads Andenas and Professor Piet Eeckhout. Earlier versions of parts of it have been or will be published as articles in European Business Law Review, and in M. Andenas and W.-H. Roth (eds), *Services and Free Movement in EU Law* (Oxford University Press, forthcoming 2002). Chapter 3 is partly based on a paper presented to the UKAEL conference 'The Right to Provide Services in EC Law—Toward a Unified Freedom Jurisprudence' in May 1999.

I wish to express my gratitude in particular to Mads Andenas who has given me strong support throughout my research and also at the beginning of my academic career. Piet Eeckhout has shown dedication beyond the call of duty and his many incisive comments have been invaluable. Kelyn Bacon of Brick Court Chambers has been kind enough to read through the whole manuscript making numerous suggestions and saving me from many errors. I also wish to thank David Vaughan QC for introducing me to the practical side of Community law, all participants in several PhD Seminars at King's College London for their constructive criticism, Lord Slynn of Hadley for the honour of being awarded the very first Lord Slynn Fellowship, and Professor Miguel Poiares Maduro and Damian Chalmers for acting as my PhD examiners. They, as well as the two anonymous readers appointed by Oxford University Press, have also contributed to the book by their perceptive comments. The substantial financial backing of King's College London Association, Olga ja Kaarle Oskari Laitisen Säätiö, Merita Pankin Säätiö and Helsingin Sanomain 100-vuotissäätiö is also gratefully acknowledged. On a more personal note, I wish to thank my parents for their ever present support, and my wife, Alison, who has not only supported me personally but also read the draft for this book commenting on the substance and revising my English. Finally, this book is dedicated to Frederick Snell, whose imminent arrival helped me to finish it in a timely fashion.

JS
April 2001

Contents

Table of Abbreviations

AG	Advocate General
AJCL	American Journal of Comparative Law
CDE	Cahiers de Droit Européen
CLR	Commonwealth Law Reports
CMLR	Common Market Law Reports
CMLRev	Common Market Law Review
COM	Communication
DL	Defensor Legis
EBLR	European Business Law Review
EC	European Community
ECLR	European Competition Law Review
ECR	European Court Reports
ECSC	European Coal and Steel Community
EEC	European Economic Community
EIPR	European Intellectual Property Review
ELJ	European Law Journal
ELRev	European Law Review
EU	European Union
EUI	European University Institute
EuR	Europarecht
Euratom	European Atomic Energy Community
Fordham Int LJ	Fordham International Law Journal
GATS	General Agreement on Trade in Services
GATT	General Agreement on Tariffs and Trade
GRUR	Gewerblicher Rechtsschutz und Urheberrecht
Harvard Int LJ	Harvard International Law Journal
ICLQ	International and Comparative Law Quarterly
IJEL	Irish Journal of European Law
ILO	International Labour Organisation
JCMS	Journal of Common Market Studies
JEL	Journal of Environmental Law
JWT	Journal of World Trade
LIEI	Legal Issues of European Integration
LM	Lakimies
LQR	Law Quarterly Review
Michigan LR	Michigan Law Review
MJ	Maastricht Journal of European and Comparative Law
MLR	Modern Law Review

OJ	Official Journal of the European Communities
OJLS	Oxford Journal of Legal Studies
QJ Econ	Quarterly Journal of Economics
RMUE	Revue du Marché Unique Européen
RTDE	Revue Trimestrielle de Droit Européen
SEW	Sociaal Economische Wetgeving
TEU	Treaty on European Union
Univ of Chicago LR	University of Chicago Law Review
VAT	Value added tax
WTO	World Trade Organisation
Yale LJ	Yale Law Journal
YEL	Yearbook of European Law
ZHR	Zeitschrift für das gesamte Handelsrecht und Wirtschaftsrecht

Table of Cases

Court of First Instance of the European Communities

Commission decisions

Australia

Denmark

Germany

United Kingdom

United States

Table of Legislation

Australia

United States

1

Introduction

1. The free movement of goods and services in the scheme of the EC Treaty

The free movement of goods and the freedom to provide services form a central part of the original common market and the new internal market.[1] Together with the free movement of persons and capital they are at the heart of the EC Treaty.

Free movement of goods and services can bring about great economic benefits producing positive static and dynamic welfare effects, especially by increasing competition and allowing economies of scale.[2] In addition, the four freedoms create possibilities for competition between legal orders, which may result in superior regulation.[3]

The freedoms are just a tool, however, merely a means to an end. Article 2 of the EC Treaty states that the task of the Community is 'to promote throughout the Community a harmonious, balanced and sustainable development of economic activities, a high level of employment and of social protection, equality between men and women, sustainable and non inflationary growth, a high degree of competitiveness and convergence of economic performance, a high level of protection and improvement of the quality of the environment, the raising of the standard of living and quality of life, and economic and social cohesion and solidarity among Member States'. The common market is mentioned in the same provision as one of the methods used in pursuit of the tasks.

Thus, the question is how to harness the freedoms so that they best contribute to the achievement of these objectives? The issue is not how to maximise the freedoms but how to use the freedoms and their beneficial effects to reach the aims of the EC Treaty. How to bring about the economic efficiencies, ensure proper scope for competition between legal orders and

---

[1] See P.J.G. Kapteyn and P. VerLoren van Themaat, *Introduction to the Law of the European Communities. From Maastricht to Amsterdam* (3rd edn by L.W. Gormley London 1998) 123 on the distinction between these two concepts. On the development from the common market to the internal market see K. Mortelmans, 'The Common Market, the Internal Market and the Single Market, What's in a Market' (1998) 35 CMLRev 101 at 102–107.

[2] See generally W. Molle, *The Economics of European Integration* (3rd edn Aldershot 1997) 79–154.

[3] See Chapter 2 section 1 below.

make sure that the freedoms do not paradoxically undermine the objectives set out in Article 2?[4]

Two different idealised readings of the Treaty can be adopted to solve this puzzle. The first one sees the free movement rules as aimed against state protectionism. This reading might result in an approach where all directly or materially discriminatory national measures are caught by the relevant Treaty provisions, as discrimination is the main tool of protectionism, but a Member State may justify its rules as long as they are in the general interest and are suitable and necessary.[5] This way the European Court of Justice ('the Court') could examine all national measures having a disparate impact to determine whether they are motivated by protectionism. I call this an anti-protectionism reading.[6] This approach maximises Member State discretion but it has the obvious weakness that it may not be sufficient to bring about a truly single market.[7]

The second reading departs from the idea that the internal market is based on unhindered trade, is connected to economic liberalism, and gives intrinsic value to free movement. The issue is not protectionism or discrimination but simply whether a national measure makes trade more difficult. This reading might result in an interpretation according to which all national measures having any kind of adverse effect on trade fall within the relevant EC Treaty provisions. However, to protect other legitimate interests, the Court could balance the Community interest in free trade against the national interest in regulation. This way free trade is protected but does not automatically trump all other interests. I call this an economic freedom reading.[8] This approach maximises free trade but it has a clear weakness in that it gives the Court an impossibly wide role.[9]

Both readings are hermeneutically perfectly feasible[10] and seem to have been adopted by the Court at different times for different freedoms. The

[4] For example, a wide reading of free movement rules might invalidate national environmental regulations thereby endangering the achievement of 'a high level of protection and improvement of quality of the environment'.

[5] Suitability and necessity tests are needed to weed out national measures purportedly seeking a legitimate aim but in reality pursuing a protectionist purpose. See Chapter 4 section 4b below.

[6] See M. Poiares Maduro, *We The Court. The European Court of Justice and the European Economic Constitution. A Critical Reading of Article 30 of the EC Treaty* (Oxford 1998) 58–60. This approach has traditionally dominated American commerce clause analysis. See C.R. Sunstein, 'Protectionism, the American Supreme Court, and Integrated Markets' in R. Bieber, R. Dehousse, J. Pinder and J.H.H. Weiler (eds), *1991: One European Market? A Critical Analysis of the Commission's Internal Market Strategy* (Baden-Baden 1988) 129–131.

[7] See eg L. Gormley, *Prohibiting Restrictions on Trade within the EEC* (Amsterdam 1985) 14.

[8] See Poiares Maduro (n 6 above) 58–60. See also Sunstein (n 6 above) 129–131. This approach has traditionally enjoyed a wide support in the doctrine in Europe.

[9] See eg Poiares Maduro (n 6 above) 59.

[10] See J.H.H. Weiler, 'The Constitution of the Common Market Place: Text and Context in the Evolution of the Free Movement of Goods' in P. Craig and G. de Búrca (eds), *The Evolution of EU Law* (Oxford 1999) 351–360.

Court's approach has not been set in stone, however, but has varied, reflecting the tension between the readings.

Both approaches are *capable* of catering for different levels of public intervention in the marketplace although the economic freedom reading tends to produce a more *laissez-faire* approach. In the anti-protectionism model the Member States, or the Community legislator, are free to set the desired level of state intervention as long as it is not done for protectionist purposes. In the economic freedom model the permitted level of intervention depends on the value the Court gives to other legitimate interests, on the activities of the Community legislature, and on judicial review of Community acts.[11]

The tension between the two readings masks an even more fundamental issue, the division of power between Member States and the Community. The approaches produce a widely differing vertical distribution of power. The anti-protectionist reading is decentralised and leaves important competences in the hands of Member States. It is a federal model. As long as Member States do not pursue a protectionist purpose, they are free to regulate as they see fit. The economic freedom approach is centralised and concentrates power to the Community. It is a unitary model. National regulation can always be struck down under central rules by a central organ if it disagrees with the cost-benefit analysis of the Member State. Therefore, the readings can only be assessed in the light of the desired level of centralisation. Only after the proper division of power between Member States and the Community has been determined, can an approach be assessed. The economics of federalism has to play a crucial part in the decision on the interpretation of the free movement rules.

The two readings also produce different institutional solutions.[12] In the first model, legislatures decide on the desired level of public intervention. In the second model a court is empowered to determine the correct balance between trade and other values. Therefore, strengths and weaknesses of institutions have to be taken into account when assessing the models.[13] The question is which institution is better suited for making these decisions.

The tension between the two readings, anti-protectionism and economic freedom, and, more fundamentally, centralisation and decentralisation, is reflected throughout this work. When a particular approach is criticised, it is usually due to the economics of federalism or because of the weaknesses of the institutional choice, and the suggested course tends to fall somewhere between the two models.

Whatever the solution, a further question has to be answered. Is the same approach optimal for both the free movement of goods and services? A

---

[11] If the Court tends to value the non-trade interests highly, or if there are interventionist Community measures not invalidated by the Court, the second model does not necessarily produce a *laissez-faire* result.

[12] In both readings the Community legislature may have an important part to play.

[13] The institutional comparison approach was used very successfully by Poiares Maduro (n 6 above) to analyse the free movement of goods.

freedom-specific approach would depart from the fact that the freedoms appear in differently worded EC Treaty provisions, and would seek to analyse each in isolation. A uniform approach would take as its starting point the idea that the freedoms form a part of a coherent system and have to be governed by the same principles.

2. Subject matter

a) Goods

In this section I present the subject matter of the study. I examine the meaning given to the notions of 'goods' and 'services' in the context of the EC Treaty.

The provisions of Part III Title I of the EC Treaty deal with the free movement of goods. They seek to eliminate customs duties and quantitative restrictions between Member States and to set up a common customs tariff. The concept of goods is not defined but has the same meaning in all of these provisions, and the words 'goods' and 'products' are used interchangeably.[14]

The point of departure for the European Court of Justice has been that goods are material objects.[15] In the case *Commission v Belgium* (Wallonian waste)[16] the Court referred to '*objects* which are shipped across a frontier'[17] when determining the subject matter of Article 28 (ex 30) EC. In the same manner the Court held in *Sacchi*[18] that the transmission of television signals fell, by reason of its nature, under the ambit of services, while trade in material recordings and films was subject to the provisions on the free movement of goods. The judgment was confirmed in *Debauve*,[19] where the transmission of television signals by cable was held to come within the rules relating to services. In contrast, however, the Court has held that electricity falls within the scope of the free movement of goods.[20] This seems to be a special case and serves to put gas, oil and electricity under the same provisions.[21]

In *Commission v Italy* (Art treasures)[22] the Court defined goods as 'products which can be valued in money and which are capable, as such, of forming the

---

[14] See Kapteyn and VerLoren van Themaat (n 1 above) 590, and P. Oliver, *Free Movement of Goods in the European Community* (3rd edn London 1996) 8–9.
[15] See also the Opinion of AG Fennelly in Case C-97/98 *Peter Jägerskiöld v Torolf Gustafsson*, judgment of 21 October 1999, para 30.
[16] Case C-2/90 *Commission v Belgium* [1992] ECR I-4431.
[17] ibid, para 26 (emphasis added).
[18] Case 155/73 *Giuseppe Sacchi* [1974] ECR 409 paras 6–7.
[19] Case 52/79 *Procureur du Roi v Debauve* [1980] ECR 833 para 8.
[20] Case 6/64 *Costa v Enel* [1964] ECR 585, and Case C-393/92 *Gemeente Almelo et al v Energiebedrijf Ijsselmij NV* [1994] ECR I-1477.
[21] AG Fennelly in Case C-97/98 *Peter Jägerskiöld v Torolf Gustafsson*, judgment of 21 October 1999, para 20.
[22] Case 7/68 *Commission v Italy* [1968] ECR 423.

subject of commercial transactions'. This definition was loosened in *Commission v Belgium* (Wallonian waste),[23] which concerned shipments of waste across national borders. The problematic issue was the treatment of non-recyclable and non-reusable waste, which has only negative value. The Court no longer mentioned the 'valued in money' criterion and stated that 'objects which are shipped across a frontier for the purposes of commercial transactions are subject to Article 30 [now 28], whatever the nature of those transactions' thus bringing all waste within the ambit of the free movement of goods provisions.

The line between goods and means of payment was drawn in *Thompson*.[24] The Court held that coins which were legal tender in a Member State did not fall within Articles 28 to 31 (ex 30 to 37) EC. The same applied to South African Krugerrands, as they were treated on the money markets of the Member States as being equivalent to currency. In contrast, British silver alloy half-crowns minted before 1947, which were no longer legal tender but could be exchanged at the Bank of England, were held to be goods. The same principles seem to apply also to other valuables such as jewellery and paintings, which means that their transfers do not fall under the rules on the free movement of capital but under the provisions on the free movement of goods.[25]

Naturally, the EC Treaty rules on the free movement of goods do not apply to all objects falling within the definition of goods. According to Article 23(2) (ex 9(2)) EC the provisions of the Chapter on Prohibition of Quantitative Restrictions apply only 'to products originating in Member States and to products coming from third countries which are in free circulation in Member States'. Quantitative restrictions are being eliminated between Member States, not between the Community and third countries.[26]

The nationality of the owner of products is irrelevant to the application of the provisions on the free movement of goods. As long as the goods originate in a Member State or are in free circulation, they stand to benefit. The status of the goods is important, not the status of the owner.[27]

Activities of private individuals, as well as traders, are covered.[28] As Advocate General Warner noted in *Henn and Darby*,[29] if an individual moves with his possessions from one Member State to another, he is not subjected to customs duties, and if an individual brings his possessions into the Community from outside, it is the Common Customs Tariff that applies, not the original tariff of a Member State. Based on this, he supported a similar interpretation of Article 28 (ex 30) EC.

---

[23] See n 16 above. [24] Case 7/78 *R v Thompson, Johnson and Woodiwiss* [1978] ECR 2247.
[25] See Oliver (n 14 above) 27. [26] On this issue see Oliver (n 14 above) 15–22.
[27] Joined Cases 2 and 3/69 *Sociaal Fonds voor de Diamantarbieders v SA Ch Brachfeld and Sons and Chougol Diamond Co* [1969] ECR 211.
[28] Case 215/87 *Schumacher v Hauptzollamt Frankfurt-am-Main-Ost* [1989] ECR 617.
[29] Case 34/79 *R v Henn and Darby* [1979] ECR 3795.

Articles 28 (ex 30) EC *et seq.* apply to goods in transit as well as to goods passing from one Member State to be sold in another.[30]

Finally, some goods are governed by specific rules,[31] or fall under the ECSC or the Euratom Treaties.[32]

b) Services

Services are a wide and diverse category of economic activities. For example, GATT Secretariat's Services Sectoral Classification List, which was used during the Uruguay Round trade negotiations, contains the following broad sectors, each divided into sub-sectors: business services; communication services; construction and engineering services; distribution services; educational services; environmental services; financial services; health-related services and social services; tourism and travel-related services; recreational, cultural and sporting services; and transport services. In addition, there is a residual category of 'other services'.

Given the great variety of services, it is not surprising that the definition of services has created problems in the context of international trade. Many of the attempted definitions have concentrated on the non-storable nature of many services as they require the simultaneity of provision and use.[33] These definitions have been criticised as it is possible to find services that do not fall under this classification. For example, pension management is a service which is not provided and consumed simultaneously.[34] Nicolaides has therefore suggested that services may be thought of as a process, and can be defined as 'an agreement or undertaking by the service-provider to perform now or in the future a series of tasks over a specified period of time towards a particular objective'.[35] Be that as it may, the General Agreement on Trade in Services (GATS) does not contain a definition of services.[36]

The EC Treaty has a separate Chapter, consisting of Articles 49 to 55 (ex 59 to 66) EC, on services. Services are defined negatively as not being covered by the Treaty rules concerning the free movement of goods, persons and capital.

[30] See Art 30 (ex 36) EC, and Case 266/81 *SIOT v Ministry of Finance* [1983] ECR 731.

[31] Agricultural products, drugs, counterfeit money, weapons, and strategic goods. See Kapteyn and VerLoren van Themaat (n 1 above) 591, and the footnotes therein.

[32] See Annex I to the ECSC Treaty, and Annex IV to the Euratom Treaty.

[33] See T.P. Hill, 'On Goods and Services' (1977) 23 *Review of Income and Wealth* 315 at 337, and J. Bhagwati, 'Services' in J.M. Finger and A. Olechowski (eds), *The Uruguay Round. A Handbook on the Multilateral Trade Negotiations* (Washington 1987) 208.

[34] See P. Nicolaides, *Liberalizing Service Trade. Strategies for Success* (London 1989) 7–9, and D. Chalmers and E. Szyszczak, *European Union Law. Volume II. Towards a European Polity?* (Aldershot 1998) 352–353.

[35] Nicolaides (n 34 above) 9–10.

[36] On the potential difficulties caused by the lack of definition see P. Eeckhout, 'The General Agreement on Trade in Services and Community Law' in S.V. Konstadinidis (ed), *The Legal Regulation of the European Community's External Relations after the Completion of the Internal Market* (Aldershot 1996) 111.

As an example of services, Article 50(2) (ex 60(2)) EC lists activities which are of industrial or commercial character and activities of craftsmen and the professions. Examples from the case law of the European Court of Justice include medical, education and business services, and invisible transactions by telecommunications.[37]

The particular nature of certain services, such as the provision of manpower, does not remove them from the scope of the Chapter on services.[38] According to Article 51 (ex 61) EC special rules apply in the transport sector, and the liberalisation of banking and insurance services connected with movements of capital is to be effected in step with the liberalisation of movement of capital.[39]

The morally questionable character of an activity does not remove it from the scope of the free movement of services as long as the service is provided legally in a Member State. The Court does not substitute its moral assessment for that of the legislature of the Member State where the service activity is legal. Thus, in *Grogan*[40] the Court held that the termination of pregnancy, which was lawfully practised in several Member States, was a service within the meaning of the Treaty. In *Schindler*[41] the Court observed that lotteries, even though subject to regulation and control in various Member States, were not totally prohibited, and even in the United Kingdom, where the case originated from, small-scale lotteries were permitted. Therefore, lotteries could not be regarded as activities whose harmful nature causes them to be prohibited in all the Member States, and, thus, they fell within the scope of the free movement of services.[42]

The negative definition of services implies that they are a residual category and that Articles 49 to 55 (ex 59 to 66) EC are only relevant if no other Treaty provisions apply. Correspondingly, the Court has held, for example in *Gebhard*,[43] that the Treaty Chapters on the free movement of workers, the right of establishment, and services are mutually exclusive and that the provisions relating to services can be only used if the right of establishment is not applicable.

[37] See Joined Cases 286/82 and 26/83 *Luisi and Carbone v Ministero del Tesoro* [1984] ECR 377 para 16, and Case C-353/89 *Commission v Netherlands* [1991] ECR I-4069. The identification of services has not always been easy in the Community context either. See eg Case 352/85 *Bond van Adverteerders v Netherlands* [1988] ECR 2085, where the parties, the intervening governments, AG Mancini, and the Court held widely diverging views on how many and what services were in issue.

[38] Case 279/80 *Criminal Proceedings Against Alfred John Webb* [1981] ECR 3305 para 10.

[39] For a brief overview of these sectors see D. Martin and E. Guild, *Free Movement of Persons in the European Union* (London 1996) 88–90.

[40] Case C-159/90 *Society for the Protection of the Unborn Child v Grogan* [1991] ECR I-4685 paras 16–21.

[41] Case C-275/92 *Her Majesty's Customs and Excise v Gerhart Schindler and Jörg Schindler* [1994] ECR I-1039 paras 31–32.

[42] The element of chance inherent in a lottery did not remove it from the scope of Art 49 (ex 59) EC either. Ibid, para 33.

[43] Case C-55/94 *Reinhard Gebhard v Consiglio dell'Ordine degli Avvocati e Procuratori di Milano* [1995] ECR I-4165 paras 20 and 22.

The mere fact that other freedoms might be relevant does not always render the Treaty provisions on services non-applicable, however. The Court has held that in the event of transactions involving both movement of goods and services the rules concerning services are relevant if the supply of goods is not an end in itself but is incidental to the provision of services.[44] Thus, if the movement of goods is purely ancillary to the movement of services, Articles 49 to 55 (ex 59 to 66) EC apply and the rules on goods are excluded.[45] This approach is sound as it brings the whole transaction under a single set of rules.[46]

The ruling of the Court in the case of *Svensson and Gustavsson*[47] appears to diverge further from the view of services as a subsidiary category. In that case the Court held that Luxembourg legislation infringed both the Treaty provisions on the free movement of services and on the free movement of capital.[48] The decision is difficult to reconcile with the judgment given by the Court two weeks later in *Gebhard*[49] and with the wording of the EC Treaty.

Ambry[50] is another decision where the Court ignored the residual nature of the free movement of services.[51] The case concerned French rules which required a person applying for a licence to operate as a travel agent to produce evidence of financial security, covering the cost of repatriation of travellers in the case of insolvency. The security could be provided by a credit institution or an insurance company. However, if the body providing the security was situated in another Member State, it had to enter into an agreement with a credit institution or an insurance company located in France, making the security available for immediate payment. The Court held that the rules were contrary to Article 49 (ex 59) EC as well as to various directives. It then stated: 'In the view of the foregoing, it is not necessary to examine whether such rules are also contrary to Article 73b [now 56] of the Treaty'.[52] The Court's approach seems impossible to reconcile with the wording of the Treaty on the residual nature of the free movement of services. On a literal reading, the Court ought to have first examined whether the situation was governed by the provisions on the free movement of capital. Only if the rules

---

[44] Case C-55/93 *Criminal Proceedings Against J G C van Schaik* [1994] ECR I-4837 para 14, and *Schindler* (n 41 above) para 22. See also Case C-97/98 *Peter Jägerskiöld v Torolf Gustafsson*, judgment of 21 October 1999, paras 30–39 where the Court decided that fishing rights and spinning licences are not goods even though evidence of the right may be provided by a tradable physical document.

[45] cf however Case 45/87 *Commission v Ireland* (Dundalk pipeline) [1988] ECR 4929.

[46] V. Hatzopoulos, 'Case C-275/92, *Her Majesty's Customs and Excise v Gerhart and Jörg Schindler*, [1994] ECR I-1039' (1995) 32 CMLRev 841 at 846. See generally P. Oliver, 'Goods and Services: Two Freedoms Compared' in M. Dony and A. De Walsche (eds), *Mélanges en hommage à Michel Waelbroeck* (Bruxelles 1999) 1381–1382.

[47] Case C-484/93 *Svensson, Gustavsson v Ministre du logement et de l'urbanisme* [1995] ECR I-3955.

[48] See at paras 10–12.

[49] See n 43 above.

[50] Case C-410/96 *André Ambry* [1998] ECR I-7875.

[51] See, however, the Opinion of AG Mischo, ibid, para 10.

[52] ibid, para 40.

on capital had been inapplicable, should Article 49 (ex 59) EC have become relevant.[53]

How is the borderline between services and other freedoms to be drawn? Services can be distinguished from goods by virtue of their non-material character. The Court held in *Sacchi*[54] that the transmission of television signals falls within the Treaty rules relating to services while material such as films and other products are goods.[55]

The free movement of services may involve movement of persons as either the provider or the recipient of the service moves to another Member State for the service to be performed. This aspect of services is closely related to the free movement of workers and the right of establishment, as these freedoms envisage the movement of natural or legal persons as well.

Article 50(3) (ex 60(3)) EC stipulates that a provider of services may temporarily pursue his activity in a state other than the state of his establishment. This temporary nature of activities distinguishes services from establishment.[56] According to the Court's judgment in *Steymann*,[57] if a national of a Member State establishes his primary residence in another Member State to provide or receive services there for an indefinite period, his activities are covered by the rules on either the free movement of workers or the right of establishment. The Court held in *Gebhard*[58] that the temporary nature of activities is determined in the light of the duration, regularity, periodicity or continuity of the activity. The mere fact that the provider of the service has equipped himself with some infrastructure[59] in the host state does not mean that he is established there.[60] Accordingly, the Court ruled that the stable and

[53] See also Case C-118/96 *Jessica Safir v Skattemyndigheten in Dalarnas Län* [1998] ECR I-1897 where the Court found that Swedish tax law infringed the right to provide services, and, therefore, did not feel it was necessary to determine whether the legislation was incompatible with the free movement of capital. See further P. Cabral and P. Cunha, 'The Internal Market and Discriminatory Taxation: Just How (Un)steady is the Ground?' (1999) 24 ELRev 396 at 401. The refusal of the Court to give primacy to the free movement of capital serves to reduce the impact of the problematic rule in Art 58(1)(a) (ex 73d(1)(a)) EC, which allows Member States to discriminate on the basis of residence for tax purposes. See V. Hatzopoulos, 'Case C-484/93, *Svensson, Gustavsson v Ministre du logement et de l'urbanisme, Judgment of 14 November 1995, [1995] ECR I-3955*' (1996) 33 CMLRev 569 at 579.

[54] Case 155/73 *Giuseppe Sacchi* [1974] ECR 409 paras 6–7.

[55] See also Case 52/79 *Procureur du Roi v Debauve* [1980] ECR 833, and Joined Cases 60 and 61/84 *Cinéthèque v Fédération Nationale de Cinemas Francaises* [1985] ECR 2605 paras 10–11.

[56] See generally on the distinction between establishment and services A. Arnull, *The European Union and its Court of Justice* (Oxford 1999) 332–335.

[57] Case 196/87 *Udo Steymann v Staatssecretaris van Justitie* [1988] ECR 6159 paras 15–17.

[58] Case C-55/94 *Reinhard Gebhard v Consiglio dell'Ordine degli Avvocati e Procuratori di Milano* [1995] ECR I-4165 paras 25–28.

[59] In Case 205/84 *Commission v Germany* (Insurance) [1986] ECR 3755 para 21, the Court held that an office managed by the undertaking's own staff or by an independent person authorised to act on a permanent basis for the undertaking would amount to establishment. It seems that after *Gebhard* an undertaking may maintain an office with some personnel in a Member State without becoming automatically established, though in most cases this will probably still indicate a sufficiently stable participation in the economic life of the host state.

[60] Correspondingly, the requirement by the host state that the service provider must maintain some infrastructure in the country does not deprive Arts 49–55 (ex 59–66) EC of all substance.

continuous activities of Mr Gebhard, his established professional base, and the fact that he also served nationals of the host country, brought the situation under the rules concerning the right of establishment.[61] However, a service provided on a lasting basis from the home state does not fall under the provisions on establishment if it does not involve the movement of the service provider.[62]

The Court's case law does contain hints that the permanency of the activity is the decisive factor also in distinguishing the freedom to provide services from the free movement of workers. In his Opinion in *Bosman*[63] Advocate General Lenz stated that 'the essential criterion for distinguishing between Article 48 [now 39] and Article 59 [now 49] is that the latter only covers activities which are "temporarily" pursued in another Member State'.

It is true that permanent activities can never fall under the free movement of services. This does not mean that temporary activities cannot be governed by Article 39 (ex 48) EC, however. The Court's definition of a worker in *Lawrie-Blum*[64] does not contain any reference to non-temporary duration of employment. Recitals of Regulation 1612/68[65] on freedom of movement for workers within the Community state that 'such a right must be enjoyed without discrimination by permanent, seasonal and frontier workers and by those who pursue their activities for the purpose of providing services'. The reference to seasonal workers and to those pursuing their activities for the purpose of providing services, such as employees of a firm providing services across borders, show that the temporary nature of the employment does not remove the activity from the ambit of the free movement of workers. Support for this can be easily found in the case law of the Court.[66]

Thus, the fundamental criterion for distinguishing between the free movement of workers and the freedom to provide services is the nature of the relationship between the person performing the activities and the person for whom the activities are performed. Only in the former case does an employment relationship exist between them. The key factor in determining this is

---

[61] See Case C-190/95 *ARO Lease BV v Inspecteur der Belastingdienst* [1997] ECR I-4383 paras 15–22 for an example, in the context of the Sixth VAT Directive (n 82 below), of the difficulty of determining whether a company has a fixed establishment in a Member State.

[62] Case C-56/96 *VT4 Ltd v Vlaamse Gemeenschap* [1997] ECR I-3143. See also Commission Interpretative Communication on freedom to provide services and general good in the insurance sector [2000] OJ C43/3, 7–8.

[63] Case C-415/93 *Union Royale Belge des Sociétés de Football Association ASBL and others v Jean-Marc Bosman* [1995] ECR I-4921, the Opinion of AG Lenz, para 201.

[64] Case 66/85 *Lawrie-Blum v Land Baden-Württemberg* [1986] ECR 2121 para 17.

[65] [1968] OJ Spec Ed L257/2, 475.

[66] See Case 279/80 *Criminal Proceedings Against Alfred John Webb* [1981] ECR 3305 para 10, the Opinion of AG Jacobs in Case 66/85 *Lawrie-Blum v Land Baden-Württemberg* [1986] ECR 2121, 2133, the Opinion of AG van Gerven in Case C-113/89 *Rush Portuguesa Lda v Office national d'immigration* [1990] ECR I-1417 para 14, Case C-106/91 *Ramrath v Ministère de la Justice* [1992] ECR I-3351 para 25 and the Opinion of AG Jacobs, paras 9 and 13, and the Opinion of AG Tesauro in Case C-43/93 *Raymond Vander Elst v Office des Migrations Internationales* [1994] ECR I-3803 para 20.

the right of direction. If the activities are performed under the direction of another person, the rules concerning workers apply,[67] but if the activities are performed in a self-employed capacity, either the right of establishment or the free movement of services becomes relevant.

Article 49 (ex 59) EC reserves the right to provide services to nationals of Member States, nationality being determined by national law. In this respect the free movement of goods differs from the free movement of services. Once a product has been put in free circulation within the Community, the provisions on the free movement of goods apply irrespective of the nationality of the owner.[68] In contrast, a service provider established in a Member State does not benefit from the free movement provisions unless he is a national of a Member State.

By virtue of Articles 55 and 48 (ex 66 and 58) EC some companies and firms may also benefit from the free movement of services. Non-profit-making entities are excluded and the company or firm must have been formed in accordance with the law of a Member State and have its registered office, central administration or principal place of business within the Community.

Free movement of services applies only to persons established within the Community. The meaning of establishment may not necessarily be the same as in Article 43 (ex 52) EC. It is clear, for example, that an auditor working as an employed person in one country is able to provide, independently of his employer, temporary auditing services to customers in another Member State as a self-employed person.[69]

Article 49 (ex 59) EC requires that the provider and the recipient of services be established in different Member States. Thus, wholly internal situations, where all relevant aspects are confined within a single Member State, fall outside the scope of the Treaty.[70] The existence of an inter-state element is a question of fact and for the national court to decide.[71] The cross-border element does not have to be present from the beginning of the relationship between a provider and a recipient as long as the activities meet the criterion at some stage.[72] The prior existence of identifiable recipients is not a condition for the application of Article 49 (ex 59) EC.[73]

This cross-border aspect of the free movement of services can be contrasted with a recent judgment in the field of the free movement of goods. In *Pistre*,[74] 7 May 1997, the Fifth Chamber of the Court ruled, against the arguments of

---

[67] See n 64 above para 17.   [68] See section 2a above.

[69] See in general Case C-106/91 *Ramrath v Ministère de la Justice* [1992] ECR I-3351, especially paras 23–28, and Martin and Guild (n 39 above) 71. See also Case 143/87 *Christopher Stanton and SA belge d'assurances L'Étoile 1905 v Inasti* [1988] ECR 3877, especially paras 12–13.

[70] Case 52/79 *Procureur du Roi v Debauve* [1980] ECR 833 para 9.

[71] Case C-41/90 *Klaus Höfner and Fritz Elser v Macrotron GmbH* [1991] ECR I-1979 para 37.

[72] Case 15/78 *Société Générale Alsacienne de Banque v Koestler* [1978] ECR 1971 para 3.

[73] Case C-384/93 *Alpine Investments BV v Minister van Financiën* [1995] ECR I-1141 para 19.

[74] Joined Cases C-321/94, C-322/94, C-323/94 and C-324/94 *Criminal Proceedings Against Jacques Pistre* [1997] ECR I-2434 paras 41–45.

the French government, the Commission, and the Opinion of Advocate General Jacobs,[75] that Article 28 (ex 30) EC was available even though all the facts of the case were confined to a single Member State. It stated that the application of the national measure may at least potentially hinder intra-Community trade even if restricted to domestic producers, in particular when the measure facilitates the marketing of goods of domestic origin.[76] In contrast, in its judgment in *Sodemare*,[77] 17 June 1997, the Full Court stated that the Treaty provisions concerning freedom to provide services cannot be applied to activities which are confined in all respects within a single Member State.[78]

According to Article 50 (ex 60) EC, services fall within the scope of the Treaty only in so far as they are normally provided for remuneration. Therefore, services are economic activities.[79] This corresponds to the economic character of the original EC Treaty[80] and the provision has not been altered despite the changes brought to other areas.

Remuneration constitutes consideration for the service, and is usually agreed between the provider and the recipient of the service.[81] It may be noted that in the context of the Sixth VAT Directive[82] the Court interpreted the concept of 'the supply of services effected for consideration' as not including activities of a street musician. The musician received donations from passers-by but there was no agreement between the parties and no necessary link between the performance and the donation. The passers-by did not request the music and their payments did not depend on the musical service but on subjective motives.[83] Remuneration does not need to be monetary but may be in kind.[84] The Court has made it clear in *Bond*[85] that remuneration does not need to flow directly from the recipient of services to the provider. It has to be noted that the phrase '*normally* provided for remuneration' in Article 50(1)

[75] ibid, paras 32–42 of his Opinion.
[76] On the interpretation of this judgment see P. Oliver, 'Some Further Reflections on the Scope of Articles 28–30 (ex 30–36) EC' (1999) 36 CMLRev 783 at 786–788, and E. Spaventa, 'Casenote on TK-Heimdienst' (2000) 37 CMLRev 1265 at 1270–1271.
[77] Case 70/95 *Sodemare SA et al v Regione Lombardia* [1997] ECR I-3435 para 38.
[78] See also Case C-108/98 *RI.SAN Srl v Comune di Ischia et al*, judgment of 9 September 1999, and Case C-97/98 *Peter Jägerskiöld v Torolf Gustafsson*, judgment of 21 October 1999, paras 42–45. See in more detail on this case law, Oliver (n 46 above) 1388–1391.
[79] See also Case C-363/89 *Danielle Roux v Belgian State* [1991] ECR I-273 para 9.
[80] Similarly Art 48 (ex 58) EC excludes non-profit-making companies and firms from the scope of the right of establishment and the Court has demanded, eg in Case 53/81 *Levin v Staatssecretaris van Justitie* [1982] ECR 1035 para 17, that the worker must be engaged in genuine economic activity in order to benefit from rules relating to the free movement of workers.
[81] Case 263/86 *Belgian State v René Humbel and Marie-Thérèse Humbel née Edel* [1988] ECR 5365 para 17.
[82] Sixth Council Directive 77/388/EEC of 17 May 1977 on the harmonisation of laws of the Member States relating to turnover taxes; common system of value added tax; uniform basis of assessment [1977] OJ L145/1.
[83] Case C-16/93 *R.J. Tolsma v Inspecteur der Omzetbelasting* [1994] ECR I-743 para 17. The case is interesting as a point of reference and comparison; it is not suggested that the same necessary applies to services within the meaning of the EC Treaty.
[84] Case 196/87 *Udo Steymann v Staatssecretaris van Justitie* [1988] ECR 6159.
[85] Case 352/85 *Bond van Adverteerders v Netherlands* [1988] ECR 2085 para 16.

(ex 60(1)) EC shows that a service may fall within the scope of the free movement of services even if it is provided for free in the particular instance.

The requirement of remuneration disqualifies some public services. If public services provided below cost were covered by the free movement of services, the result could be 'public service tourism'. Persons from countries with a low tax rate and poor public services could travel to a country with high taxes and take advantage of the ensuing good public services, taking a free ride on the tax-payers of the latter state.[86]

In *Humbel*[87] the Court was confronted with the question whether courses taught in a technical institute which formed a part of the secondary education provided under the national education system constituted services within the meaning of Article 50(1) (ex 60(1)) EC. The Court noted that the state was not seeking to engage in gainful activity but was fulfilling its duties towards its own population in the social, cultural and educational fields, and that the system was generally funded from the public purse even though the pupils or their parents sometimes had to pay teaching or enrolment fees to contribute to the operating expenses. Thus, the Court held that the courses could not be regarded as services for the purpose of Article 49 (ex 59) EC.[88] The judgment was confirmed in *Wirth*.[89] The Court added, however, that establishments of higher education financed essentially out of private funds and seeking to make a profit were aiming to offer services for remuneration within the meaning of Article 50(1) (ex 60(1)) EC.[90]

Altogether, the distinction between services normally provided for remuneration and public services is less than crystal clear.[91] In *Grogan* the Court did not make any distinction between private and public abortion clinics.[92] In *Kohll* Advocate General Tesauro stated that the state involvement in financing of the medical benefit in question did not mean that there was no provision of services as the medical treatment was provided for consideration and the insured person bore a significant portion of the cost through health insurance contributions. The Court merely stated that the treatment in the case at hand was provided for remuneration outside any hospital infrastructure.[93] Finally, in the recent judgments in *Smits and Peerbooms*, and *Vanbraekel* the

---

[86] See Chalmers and Szyszczak (n 34 above) 356.   [87] See n 81 above.

[88] ibid, paras 18–20.

[89] Case C-109/92 *Stephan Max Wirth v Landeshauptstadt Hannover* [1993] ECR I-6447.

[90] ibid, para 17.

[91] It has sometimes been argued that an important factor may be whether the services are provided with the view to make a profit or not. See J. Handoll, *Free Movement of Persons* (Chichester 1995) 89, and S. O'Leary, 'The Free Movement of Persons and Services' in P. Craig and G. de Búrca (eds), *The Evolution of EU Law* (Oxford 1999) 399. This would be in line with Art 48(2) (ex 58(2)) EC which expressly excludes non-profit-making companies and firms from the scope of Chapters on right of establishment and, by virtue of Art 55 (ex 66) EC, on services. See also the Opinion of AG Slynn in *Humbel* (n 81 above) 5379–5380.

[92] Case C-159/90 *Society for the Protection of the Unborn Child v Grogan* [1991] ECR I-4685.

[93] Case C-158/96 *Raymond Kohll v Union des Caisses de Maladie* [1998] ECR I-1931, para 41 of the Opinion of AG Tesaro and para 29 of the judgment.

Court found that medical treatment in a hospital amounted to services.[94] These cases on medical services do not sit easily with the case law on education discussed above, and imply a more inclusive concept of remunerated services.

The principle behind the requirement of remuneration might also be useful in the field of goods. For example, if a Member State provides pregnant residents with free maternity kits, a foreign visitor denied such a kit should hardly be able to complain that this is an export ban in breach of Article 29 (ex 34) EC. The state is not seeking to engage in gainful activity but is fulfilling its duties towards its own population and the system is funded from the public purse. The free-rider argument applies just as it does in the case of public services.[95]

Articles 49 (ex 59) and 50 (ex 60) EC refer only to the freedom to *provide* services. However, Community legislation implementing the freedom also gives rights to the *recipients* of services.[96] It is also clear that restrictions imposed on recipients of services will indirectly hinder the provision of services. Thus, the Court decided in *Luisi and Carbone*[97] that the freedom to provide services includes the freedom, for the recipient, to go to another Member State in order to receive services there. Although the Treaty only mentions the freedom to provide services, the freedom to receive them is its necessary corollary, and serves to fulfil the objective of liberalising all gainful activity not covered by the other freedoms.[98]

Restrictions put on the capacity of non-Community nationals to receive services in a Member State may constitute an obstacle for a service provider from another Member State. This was established in the Court's judgment in *Svensson and Gustavsson*.[99] In the case two Swedes, prior to the Swedish

---

[94] Case C-157/99 *Geraets-Smits v Stichting Ziekenfonds VGZ and Peerbooms v Stichting CZ Groep Zorgverzekeringen*, judgment of 12 July 2001, paras 47–59, and Case C-368/98 *Abdon Vanbraekel and others v ANMC*, judgment of 12 July 2001, paras 38–43.

[95] See, however, Oliver (n 14 above) 26 who argues that, due to the completion of the internal market, to the fact that the Community is no longer exclusively concerned with economic matters, and to the actions of the Community institutions, the economic nature and, more widely, the whole purpose of the movement of goods is irrelevant to the application of Art 28 (ex 30) EC *et seq*. See also Oliver (n 46 above) 1383–1384.

[96] Council Directive 64/221/EEC of 25 February 1964 on the co-ordination of special measures concerning the movement and residence of foreign nationals which are justified on grounds of public policy, public security or public health OJ Spec Ed 1964 850/64, 117, Art 1, and Council Directive 73/148/EEC of 21 May 1973 on the abolition of restrictions on movement and residence within the Community for nationals of Member States with regard to establishment and the provision of services [1973] OJ L172/14, Art 1(1)(b).

[97] Joined Cases 286/82 and 26/83 *Luisi and Carbone v Ministero del Tesoro* [1984] ECR 377 paras 10 and 16.

[98] The right to receive services may have far reaching consequences as it brings Member State nationals travelling within the Community as tourists etc within the scope of the EC Treaty, and, thus, enables the application of the principle of non-discrimination. See Case 186/87 *Cowan v Le Trésor Public* [1989] ECR 195 and Case C-274/96 *Criminal Proceedings Against Horst Otto Bickel and Ulrich Franz* [1998] ECR I-7637.

[99] Case C-484/93 *Svensson and Gustavsson v Ministre du logement et de l'urbanisme* [1995] ECR I-3955.

accession to the Community, claimed that Luxembourg legislation, which only granted interest rate subsidies to those applicants whose loans had been raised with a credit institution authorised to operate in Luxembourg, violated Community law. The Luxembourg government argued that the plaintiffs did not have *locus standi* as they were not Community nationals.[100] Advocate General Elmer agreed with this argument. He was, however, of the opinion that the European Court of Justice should answer the question of the national court to aid the interpretation of domestic law.[101] The Court ruled for the plaintiffs without dealing with the issue of standing.[102]

3. The uniform interpretation of the freedoms

In this section, I will examine the economics of goods and services, and some general legal issues.[103] I will argue that there is a prima facie case for a parallel approach to the four freedoms, in particular to the free movement of goods and the freedom to provide services. Economically speaking goods are material and services non-material products. From the economic point of view there are no good reasons for treating them differently. From the legal point of view the basic notions of justice call us to treat two similar things in the same way. The building of a coherent and transparent European legal system demands a common approach that is based on generally accepted principles, not on dubious distinctions.

The international trade in services is not as great as the trade in goods. Transaction costs can prohibit such trade and in general economies of scale tend to be less important in the field of services than in the field of goods. Furthermore, a service provider must often perform activities in close proximity to the buyer, and this may make it necessary for the supplier to establish himself in the same country as the customer by using foreign direct investment.[104]

The importance of international trade in services is increasing, however. Inside the Community services are taking a growing share of the GDP[105] and in recent years intra-Community trade in services has increased particularly

---

[100] The Belgian credit institution from which the plaintiffs had obtained their loan was not represented in the proceedings.

[101] See paras 35–42 of his Opinion.

[102] See also V. Hatzopoulos, 'Recent Developments of the Case Law of the ECJ in the Field of Services' (2000) 37 CMLRev 43 at 44–62 for a recent analysis of the question what constitutes services within the meaning of the EC Treaty.

[103] It is important to note that some activities classified as services from the economic point of view fall under the right of establishment from the legal point of view.

[104] See Molle (n 2 above) 142, and M.E. Porter, *The Competitive Advantage of Nations* (London 1990) 248. Permanent establishment brings the situation outside the scope of the Treaty provisions on the freedom to provide services.

[105] In 1996 the service sector produced 67 per cent of gross value added in the European Union. See *Facts through Figures. Eurostat Yearbook at a Glance* (1998) 14.

quickly. When compared with trade in goods, however, the significance of trade in services is still rather limited.[106]

Several factors contribute to the internationalisation of services. Services are playing a growing role in domestic economic activity. Service needs are becoming more similar in many countries. Buyers are more mobile and better informed. Economies of scale are rising and service providers can differentiate themselves as European or global firms. Personnel are more mobile. New technologies are greatly increasing the capacity of service providers to supply services without the need for people to travel, enabling also competition in previously sheltered sectors. Furthermore, differences still persist as regards cost, quality and range of services available in different countries.[107]

At a general level, the economics of trade in goods and trade in services are similar. The classical theory of comparative advantage applies with equal force regardless of whether it is goods or services that are sold or bought.[108] The trade policy goals, principles, procedures and techniques that have been used to deal with goods can also be applied to services, especially when it comes to tools suitable for abolishing non-tariff barriers.[109]

In fact, markets in goods and services are generally characterised as product markets while labour, capital and entrepreneurship are considered to be parts of production factor markets.[110] Correspondingly, the former are dealt with under customs union theory and the latter under common market theory.

However, there are a number of points that have been raised to argue that goods and services are dissimilar and need to be treated differently. In my view, none of these arguments justifies a divergent approach. Before they are examined in detail, it is important to note that the mere fact that goods are different from services does not automatically mean that the two cannot be treated in the same way. Although alcohol is obviously not similar to advertising, it is also different from magazines, petrol or machines. Yet nobody is arguing that normal trade rules could not cover all of these goods.

First, the modes of supply of services can differ from those of goods and often involve the movement of factors of production. Services can move in four different ways:[111]

---

[106] See Molle (n 2 above) 146–147. For recent figures, see *The Economist*, 1 April 2000, 118.

[107] See Molle (n 2 above) 139–140, and Porter (n 104 above) 250–252. The Commission argues in Communication from the Commission to the Council and the European Parliament, *An Internal Market Strategy for Services* (COM (2000) 888 final) 4–5 that 'the information society has sparked a new dynamic in services' and has greatly increased the potential for cross-border provision of services.

[108] See G. Feketekuty, *International Trade in Services. An Overview and Blueprint for Negotiations* (Cambridge Massachusetts 1988) 123–124, and B. Hindley and A. Smith, 'Comparative Advantage and Trade in Services' (1984) 7 *The World Economy* 369 at 386 and 388–389.

[109] See Feketekuty (n 108 above) 160 and 174.   [110] See Molle (n 2 above) 10.

[111] See P. Eeckhout, *The European Internal Market and International Trade. A Legal Analysis* (Oxford 1994) 10. Slightly different classification can be found, eg, in G.P. Sampson and R.H. Snape, 'Identifying the Issues in Trade in Services' (1985) 8 *The World Economy* 171 at 172–175. Compare also the modes in GATS Art I:2, and see F. Weiss, 'The General Agreement on Trade

- the recipient moves towards the provider, for example a patient travels to another country to receive hospital treatment;
- the provider moves towards the recipient, for example a construction firm sends personnel to another state to build something;
- the provider and the recipient both move, for example in the course of providing a transport service;
- the service itself travels, for example via telecommunications.

Some services may only employ one mode of supply, but often different methods are substitutable.[112] For example, a doctor giving medical advice can do so in person by moving himself or through the movement of the patient. Alternatively, the advice can perhaps be given via telecommunications. The method chosen depends on the state of technology and on the market conditions.[113] The improvements in telecommunications have enabled the service itself to move in many cases where in the past the movement of persons was required.

The existence of the different modes of supply does not change the basic economic calculus. The rationale for trade is the same even if it involves the movement of production factors. The welfare effects are similar regardless of the mode of supply.[114] From the point of view of economic efficiency, liberalisation of all modes of supply is desirable in order to avoid distortions, but this does not mean that partial liberalisation cannot be beneficial.[115]

In the context of interpreting the Community rules on the free movement of services, the difference in the modes of supply is not very significant. First, the establishment of commercial presence, and often also the movement of labour, fall under the Treaty rules on the free movement of persons. Any differences caused by these considerations affect directly the interpretation of Articles 39 (ex 48) and 43 (ex 52) EC, not Article 49 (ex 59) EC.

Additionally, the movement of the factors of production is also a fundamental part of the Community system, which is not merely a simple customs union. The migration and investment issues that cause such problems in the global context do not create the same difficulties in the sphere of European integration.[116]

The second difference concerns regulation. Services tend to be much more heavily regulated than goods. Government intervention is significantly more prevalent in the services sector.[117]

in Services' (1995) 32 CMLRev 1177 at 1190–1193. Oliver (n 46 above) 1384–1386 contains an interesting comparison of the different modes of supply with import and export of goods.

[112] See J. Müller, 'An Economic Analysis of Different Regulatory Regimes of Transborder Services' in D. Friedmann and E.-J. Mestmäcker (eds), *Rules for Free International Trade in Services* (Baden-Baden 1990) 345–348, who examines the 'degree of separation' in locational, intermediate, and knowledge or skill-based services.

[113] See P. Nicolaides, 'Economic Aspects of Services: Implications for a GATT Agreement' (1989) 23 *JWT* 125 at 126–127, and Sampson and Snape (n 111 above) 173–174.

[114] See Feketekuty (n 108 above) 102–105, and Hindley and Smith (n 108 above) 375.

[115] See Feketekuty (n 108 above) 166–167, and Sampson and Snape (n 111 above) 177–178.

[116] See further below.

[117] See Bhagwati (n 33 above) 209, and Hindley and Smith (n 108 above) 377–378.

The form of regulation tends to differ as well. With goods, the regulation usually applies to the product. With services, the producer is most often the target. The content of the service itself is only seldom stipulated.[118] Instead, the legislation sets rules relating to the qualities of the service provider.[119] How a doctor should perform an operation is not determined, but the qualifications required of a doctor are regulated.

Legitimate concerns of consumer protection are partly behind the heavy regulation of many services. Consumers may be unable to assess the quality of a service. This may occur more often in the case of intangible services than tangible goods. Especially in the case of certain professional services, the consumers cannot determine the quality even *post facto*. As a result low-quality producers may be able to drive out high-quality providers, with detrimental consequences for the whole market. Hence, public regulation is needed to correct the information asymmetries.[120]

It has also been claimed that the service sector is more important for society than the goods sector and, therefore, needs to be regulated more intensively. This is too general.[121] Telecommunications and postal services are crucial for the functioning of a country but so are petrol and cars.

However, the existence of regulation does not make services fundamentally different from goods. Regulation is hardly unknown in the goods sector. A consumer has often less knowledge of the qualities of a good than the vendor, especially in the case of highly technical products.[122] In addition, much service trade, especially in business services, is conducted between professionals. They are better informed and able to protect their interests than private consumers.[123] The regulatory difference is one of degree, not one of kind.[124]

National regulation creates most barriers to trade in services. Unlike in the case of goods, it is very difficult to erect barriers to service trade at the

---

[118] In some sectors, such as insurance, the 'service product' may be subject to regulation as well.

[119] Bhagwati (n 33 above) 209, and Nicolaides (n 34 above) 44–45.

[120] See Nicolaides (n 113 above) 126–127, J.-M. Sun and J. Pelkmans, 'Regulatory Competition in the Single Market' (1995) 33 JCMS 67 at 85, and M. van Empel, 'The Visible Hand in Invisible Trade' (1990) 17 LIEI 23 at 30–31. A different question is whether the government should intervene merely by providing information on the quality, or should it go further and regulate the entry to the industry. See on this Hindley and Smith (n 108 above) 379.

[121] See G. Feketekuty, 'Trade in Professional Services: an Overview' reprinted in J.H. Jackson, W.J. Davey and A.O. Sykes, Jr., *Legal Problems of International Economic Relations. Cases, Materials and Text on the National and International Regulation of Transnational Economic Relations* (3rd edn St Paul Minn 1995) 894.

[122] V. Hatzopoulos, 'Exigences essentielles, impératives ou impérieuses: *une* théorie, *des* théories ou pas de théorie du tout?' (1998) 34 RTDE 191 at 223 has emphasised that consumers need more information about services and especially about service providers than about goods and producers. He accepts, however, that there is a similar need in case of some goods. In addition, it may be argued that the origin of goods is also often of paramount importance to the consumer, as evidenced by the increasing reliance on brands.

[123] van Empel (n 120 above) 28.

[124] See Chalmers and Szyszczak (n 34 above) 362, Feketekuty (n 108 above) 161–162, and van Empel (n 120 above) 31.

border.[125] Tariffs and quotas are therefore not significant in the service sector.

The danger with regulatory measures is that they may create protectionist obstacles to imports. In practice, this may even be the real reason for regulation. The aim is sometimes the protection of domestic firms from foreign competition.[126] For practical reasons, it may have been necessary to involve service providers in regulating the industry. This is the case, for example, when professional bodies, due to their superior knowledge, are involved in regulating and policing the entry into the profession. The industry's main concern may naturally enough be the protection of its own interests, which usually means limiting competition, especially from abroad.[127] Service sector undertakings may also wield political power which enables them to engage in rent-seeking by lobbying.[128]

There may also be a tendency to abstain from deregulation on equity grounds. Existing service providers in regulated industries have often paid some form of entry fee in compensation for being able to reap supra-competitive profits. For example, deregulation which would cut the resale value of a taxi-licence would seem inequitable to somebody who has previously purchased a licence expecting it to give a permanent right to operate in a protected market. There may be a systematic tendency to resist deregulation even when the reasons for the original regulation have vanished, for example as a result of technical change.[129]

In fact, the intensive regulation of services can provide arguments both against and for free trade in services. As far as regulation is necessary to protect legitimate interests, a *laissez-faire* approach could produce sub-optimal results. However, the heavy regulatory burden and the danger of protectionism, as a result of regulatory capture, mean that free trade may bring about great efficiency gains.[130]

The differences between goods and services in the intensity and methods of regulation are undoubtedly real. They do not seem to necessitate a fundamentally different approach, however. The differences can be contained within the harmonisation and justification mechanisms found in the EC Treaty and created by the case law. Some regulation of some services will be justified, just like some regulation of some goods. It may be that the Court will find more measures regulating services to be justified on the grounds of consumer protection than is the case with goods, and, thus, the harmonisation process becomes more important in the services sector. This does not mean that a whole new approach has to be created for services, however. As stated before, the differences are of degree, not of kind.

---

[125] See Eeckhout (n 111 above) 11, and Feketekuty (n 108 above) 135 and 162.
[126] See Molle (n 2 above) 145, and Porter (n 104 above) 250.
[127] See Hindley and Smith (n 108 above) 380.   [128] See Porter (n 104 above) 263.
[129] See Hindley and Smith (n 108 above) 380.   [130] See Feketekuty (n 108 above) 161.

Thirdly, a further difference between goods and services is the intangible, invisible character of many services. Services have been described as non-storable, requiring the simultaneity of provision and use, and as a process.[131] This factor is important in the global context.[132] Traditionally in GATT, concessions are granted on specified and defined goods. However, due to the process-nature of services, definitions of services themselves could amount to restrictions. If the steps in a certain process were defined as a particular service, which, and only which, could be traded freely, a foreign service provider could not adjust to changing market conditions. If the service provider wanted to benefit from the concession, he would have to provide the service exactly in the manner prescribed. Any changes in the process would remove the service from the scope of the concession. Thus, the definition itself could become a protectionist straitjacket.[133] In the Community this does not create the same problems as the system is not based on carefully defined concessions.[134]

The non-material character of services may also increase the importance of intellectual property rules. A non-material service may be particularly susceptible to unlawful copying and retransmission.[135] This problem is hardly unique to the services sector, however. The pirating of branded goods, videotapes, CD-disks and so on is all too common.[136]

Yet another important point is that some service sectors may be inherently imperfectly competitive. This may be due to information asymmetries about the characteristics of services.[137] In addition, in some services high costs of building and maintaining networks and large economies of scale may create (natural) monopolies or tight oligopolies. There may also be a universal service obligation which requires the (monopolist) provider to supply the same service at the same price for all recipients at all times, regardless of cost differences. Examples of such sectors are segments of transportation and telecommunications markets.[138]

---

[131] See Nicolaides (n 34 above) 6–12 for an excellent discussion. See also J. Bhagwati, 'Splintering and Disembodiment of Services and Developing Nations' (1984) 7 *The World Economy* 133 at 135–136.

[132] In the Community context this means that services are not able to enter into free circulation in the same manner as goods. See Eeckhout (n 111 above) 11.

[133] See Nicolaides (n 113 above) 127.

[134] See, however, Chalmers and Szyszczak (n 34 above) 423 according to whom the fact that a service is a form of transaction which does not crystallise until the moment of commercialisation means that the concept of double regulatory burden is inappropriate in the case of many services. In this context it is sufficient to say that most regulation of the service industry relates to the service provider rather than the service itself, and the issue of double burden is just as applicable as in the field of goods. See further Chapter 2 section 5civ below.

[135] See V. Hatzopoulos (n 122 above) 225.

[136] See also the discussion on intellectual property rights in Chapter 4 section 2biii below.

[137] See A. Sapir, 'The General Agreement on Trade in Services. From 1994 to the Year 2000' (1999) 33 JWT 51 at 52.

[138] See Feketekuty (n 108 above) 108–110 and 163–165.

This difference may increase the importance of the rules on public under-takings, and on competition in general, in the field of services, although it has to be recognised that new technologies and growth have in recent years opened up many segments in traditionally non-competitive markets.[139] The importance of competition rules in the service sector is demonstrated by Part II of GATS which includes rules on Monopolies and Exclusive Services Suppliers and on Business Practices.[140] A further discussion of the role of competition rules falls outside the scope of this study.[141]

Finally, it has been said that services constitute social, as well as economic, activities. Based on this it has been argued that the free movement of services could amount to economisation of the social sphere and have disruptive con-sequences. It has been claimed that this can take place in two different ways. First of all, the free movement of services may disrupt regimes based on social consensus and accommodation but lacking any clear external objective. Secondly, it may reward the haves but not the have-nots.[142]

In my view, the social aspects of services should not lead to a divergence with goods. First, the 'social consensus and accommodation' may well be the result of rent-seeking by powerful private interest groups aimed at limit-ing competition, especially from foreigners. The fact that a system is well entrenched (and even seemingly broadly supported) does not make it any less suspicious from trade point of view. Take as an example a situation where one form of gambling is prohibited but another form is allowed. This may well reflect the power of the local gambling industry which has concen-trated its efforts on the second market segment and does not want competi-tion from the first segment, especially if foreign firms are well placed to enter it. If the citizens really prefer the traditional domestic service providers and their methods, they can continue to purchase from them. Trade does not force consumers to change their habits, it just widens the choice available to them. Anyway, the problem is made less acute by the exclusion of many public services from the scope of the EC Treaty, as explained in section 2b above.

Secondly, it is somewhat difficult to complain that only rich consumers benefit from free trade in services. The trade does not worsen the position of poor consumers. A system where a service not available to everybody is not available to anybody would be detrimental to the general welfare—not to mention unreasonable. In a situation where two persons would need expensive

---

[139] See ibid, 108–109 and 164. An example of such a development is non-voice segments in telecommunications market.

[140] See generally Sapir (n 137 above) 54–55.

[141] See in general on developments in this field D. Geradin, 'L'overture à la concurrence des enterprises de réseau. Analyse des principaux enjeux du processus de libéralisation' (1999) 35 CDE 13 at 13–48, and L. Hancher, 'Community, State, and Market' in P. Craig and G. de Búrca (eds), *The Evolution of EU Law* (Oxford 1999) 721–742.

[142] Chalmers and Szyszczak (n 34 above) 363.

private medical treatment abroad, it is surely better to allow the one who is capable of paying to obtain it than to disallow it to both.[143]

It seems that the differences between goods and services have significant implications in the global context but not in the European one.[144] In an influential article in 1988 Professor Jackson listed reasons against incorporating services into GATT and argued for drafting a different agreement for them. His main arguments were the following: GATT was difficult to amend. It had inadequate institutional provisions. It would have been threatening and probably politically unacceptable to apply many GATT obligations, especially the national treatment requirement, in an indefinite and ambiguous way to all service industries; and finally, there were advantages in experimenting with rules for a few selected service industries.[145] None of these arguments seems to apply in the Community where the founding EC Treaty has made an unambiguous commitment to the general liberalisation of services.

Altogether, it may be said that all four freedoms found in the EC Treaty form part of what economists call a common market.[146] For the realisation of the full benefits of economic integration, both products and factors of production must be able to move freely so that economies of scale can be achieved and increased competition becomes possible. Free movement can also lead to competition between legal orders with all ensuing regulatory efficiencies. Thus, the different freedoms form a part of an economic unity. This is especially true in relation to goods and services as both form a part of the product market. Economically it makes little sense to have a different approach towards these two freedoms.

From the legal point of view, it is true that the four freedoms do appear in different provisions of the Treaty. The wordings of these provisions differ from each other. Some seem to place the emphasis purely on the discriminatory nature of national measures while others can more easily be interpreted as requiring the abolition of all obstacles. Therefore, from a legal point of view, it would seem that each freedom should be interpreted separately according to the principles valid in that field. I have called this the freedom-specific approach.

The are two main reasons for having four separate freedoms instead of just one freedom of trans-frontier economic activity. It was technically easier to write four sets of provisions instead of just one and, more importantly, the

[143] An additional difference mentioned in Hatzopoulos (n 122 above) 224–225 is that the moment of conclusion and execution of a contract may be more difficult to determine in the services sector. Also, according to him, the regulator may be able to intervene during the whole process of service provision while in the goods sector intervention is restricted to production or commercialisation stages. The importance of this from the point of view of free movement is unclear, however.

[144] See also van Empel (n 120 above) 38–42, who is much more optimistic about the prospects of free trade in services in the Community context than in the global context.

[145] J.H. Jackson, 'Constructing a Constitution for Trade in Services' (1988) 11 *The World Economy* 187 at 189–191.

[146] See Molle (n 2 above) 11.

Member States originally wanted to be able to control capital movements more strictly than the movement of goods, persons or services. This desire made a single set of rules impossible.[147]

However, it is clear that all four freedoms are based on the same general provisions of the Treaty. Article 3(1)(c) EC establishes as an activity of the Community 'an internal market characterised by the abolition, as between Member States, of obstacles to the free movement of goods, persons, services and capital'. Article 14 (ex 7a) EC, which defines the concept of the internal market, refers to all four freedoms as well. These provisions indicate that the general approach to all freedoms must be similar.

The unity of the four freedoms is also suggested by the provisions granting regulatory competences to the Community. For example, Article 94 (ex 100) EC does not distinguish between goods, persons, services and capital. Article 95 (ex 100a) EC grants the Community the regulatory competence inter alia to establish the internal market. Thus, the authority to remove obstacles is given by a single provision.[148]

Furthermore, Article 50 (ex 60) EC defines 'services' as a residual category. This means that the Chapter on the free movement of services applies only if no other freedoms are relevant. It would be peculiar if the interpretations of the free movement of goods, persons and capital diverged widely as they share a common residual category.[149]

Moreover, and most importantly, a common approach to different freedoms would help Community law to develop into a legal *system* where the law is not just a group of particular rules but rather a coherent whole. Such a system makes the rules easier to understand and use, and contributes to the respect for the law and for the European Court of Justice, as cases are decided on the basis of generally approved principles, not on obscure technicalities.[150] After all, one of the basic notions of justice is that similar things are treated in the same way.

The free movement of goods and services are especially closely related when services are provided, for example, by post or by telecommunications and the movement of persons is not involved. In both cases trans-frontier economic activity is at issue. The only difference is between the material and

---

[147] See P. Behrens, 'Die Konvergenz der wirtschaftlichen Freiheiten im europäischen Gemeinschaftsrecht' (1992) 27 EuR 145 at 146–147. On reasons for controlling capital movements see M. Andenas, 'The Interplay of the Commission and the Court of Justice in Giving Effect to the Right to Provide Financial Services' in P. Craig and C. Harlow (eds), *Law Making in the European Union* (London 1998) 333–334.

[148] Article 95 (ex 100a) EC does not apply to the free movement of persons, and there are also harmonisation provisions which only relate to certain freedom(s). However, it can be relevant if a specific legal basis is unavailable. For example, a regulation concerning services cannot be adopted under Arts 47 or 52 (ex 57 and 63) EC, which only provide for the use of directives.

[149] Opinion of AG Lenz in Case C-415/93 *Union Royale Belge des Sociétés de Football Association ASBL and others v Jean-Marc Bosman* [1995] ECR I-4921 para 200.

[150] See H.D. Jarass, 'Elemente einer Dogmatik der Grundfreiheiten' (1995) 30 EuR 202 on the importance of dogmatic clarity.

non-material nature of the product. In these situations the application of different rules to goods and services seems especially unjustified.[151] This has also been recognised in Opinion 1/94 (WTO)[152] of the European Court of Justice where it was held that the Common Commercial Policy covers the cross-frontier provision of services as well as trade in goods.

In purely practical terms, it is often difficult to distinguish between goods and services. For example, a service can be provided in the form of transmission of goods. An example given by Advocate General Jacobs in his Opinion in *Säger*[153] is illustrative in this respect. An educational service might be provided by sending a series of books or video-cassettes to a recipient in another Member State. This case might be dealt with either under Article 28 (ex 30) or Article 49 (ex 59) EC. It would be anomalous if the results were different depending on which provision was deemed to be applicable.[154]

The free movement of services clearly covers a wide range of circumstances. In many cases movement of persons is involved, and the closest connection is to the right of establishment. The distinguishing criterion is the temporary versus permanent nature of activities,[155] which is a matter of degree. Economic operators may in some instances even be able to select which set of rules applies to them by deciding whether to provide services across a border or to form an agency, a branch or a subsidiary. If the approaches to the free movement of services and the right of establishment varied greatly, the decisions on the form of economic activity would be affected by legal technicalities. They would not be made on purely commercial grounds as they should be. For these reasons the interpretation of Articles 43 (ex 52) and 49 (ex 59) EC should be roughly similar.[156]

However, the permanent nature of establishment makes it natural that all laws of the Member State in question are applied as long as they do not discriminate. The application of every rule cannot be easily justified in the case of temporary provision of services.[157] Therefore, Member States can justifiably

---

[151] Case C-76/90 *Manfred Säger v Dennemeyer & Co. Ltd* [1991] ECR I-4221 para 24 of the Opinion of AG Jacobs. See also Kapteyn and VerLoren van Themaat (n 1 above) 748.

[152] Opinion 1/94 [1994] ECR I-5276 para 44.

[153] See n 151 above, para 26 of the Opinion of AG Jacobs.

[154] In the USA both the free movement of goods and services are regulated by the same provision: the commerce clause of the US Constitution Art I, § 8, which gives Congress the power to 'regulate Commerce . . . among the several states'. Similarly in Australia, s 92 of the Constitution regulates both goods and services.

[155] See Case C-55/94 *Reinhard Gebhard v Consiglio dell'Ordine degli Avvocati e Procuratori di Milano* [1995] ECR I-4165.

[156] See S. Weatherill and P. Beaumont, *EU Law* (3rd edn London 1999) 671. The Court has declared that Arts 43 (ex 52) and 49 (ex 59) EC (and 39 (ex 48) EC) are based on the same principles and has sometimes even declined to decide which provision is applicable. See eg Case 48/75 *Royer* [1976] ECR 497, and Case 36/74 *Walrave and Koch v UCI* [1974] ECR 1405.

[157] See n 151 above, para 23 of the Opinion of AG Jacobs; L. Daniele, 'Non-Discriminatory Restrictions to the Free Movement of Persons' (1997) 22 ELRev 191 at 196–197, and Weatherill and Beaumont (n 156 above) 671.

impose stricter rules and the Court can afford to be more lenient over establishment than over services.[158]

It may be asked whether Member States should be allowed to control more strictly the instances where persons move than other situations. Both Articles 43(2) (ex 52(2)) and 50(3) (ex 60(3)) EC seem only to require that a person establishing himself or providing services is treated in the same way as the nationals of the host state. Moreover, free movement of persons is a sensitive area to the Member States, as illustrated by the decision-making rules in Articles 18(2) (ex 8a(2)) and 95(2) (ex 100a(2)) EC. These provisions require unanimity while most other measures affecting the internal market can be adopted with a qualified majority. It could also be argued that economically the movement of natural persons is not as critical for the internal market as the other freedoms. The purpose of the Community is not to create large-scale migration. Most of the benefits of economic integration are achieved when capital and undertakings are allowed to move to take advantage of abundant and correspondingly cheap human resources and when the products can then circulate freely. The movements of products and capital act as substitutes to the movement of persons.[159]

On the other hand, the wording of Articles 39 (ex 48), 43(1) (ex 52(1)) and 49 (ex 59) EC would seem to indicate that the provisions are not only concerned with (narrowly interpreted) discrimination.[160] In addition, the free movement of goods may also require that persons cross frontiers, for example to promote the products in question. Furthermore, the free movement of services applies also to situations where persons do not move. It would be somewhat difficult to have a split approach to a single freedom.

In a Community no longer restricted to economic issues it might be argued that the free movement of citizens is a fundamental human right which should never be restricted without a weighty justification.[161] The fact that decision-making rules, such as Article 18(2) (ex 8a(2)) EC, require unanimity may also be seen as a reason for the Court to interfere more actively. Without the

[158] Case C-58/98 *Josef Corsten*, judgment of 3 October 2000, paras 43–46. See further the Opinion of AG Slynn in Case 279/80 *Criminal Proceedings Against Alfred John Webb* [1981] ECR 3305 at 3332, Arnull (n 56 above) 332–333 and 353, Hatzopoulos (n 122 above) 225–226 and 233–234, and the Commission Interpretative Communication on freedom to provide services and the interest of the general good in the Second Banking Directive (SEC(97) 1193 final) 22.

[159] See Molle (n 2 above) 211. Treaty of Nice provides that the qualified majority rule will apply to Art 18(2) EC, subject to limitations listed in Art 18(3) EC.

[160] See the Opinion of AG Lenz in Case C-415/93 *Union Royale Belge des Sociétés de Football Association ASBL and others v Jean-Marc Bosman* [1995] ECR I-4921 paras 194–195 on the interpretation of Art 39 (ex 48) EC.

[161] See the Opinion of AG Lenz in ibid, para 203, and E. Johnson and D. O'Keeffe, 'From Discrimination to Obstacles to Free Movement: Recent Developments Concerning the Free Movement of Workers 1989–1994' (1994) 31 CMLRev 1313 at 1330. In the USA the persons' right to move freely has been interpreted as a fundamental right inherent in citizenship and given greater protection than a mere commerce clause can offer. See J.E. Nowak and R.D. Rotunda, *Constitutional Law* (5th edn St. Paul Minnesota 1995) 310. It is conceivable that a similar development will take place in the future also in the EU.

contribution of the Court, the more cumbersome nature of the decision-making process might leave the Community paralysed in this field.[162]

Another reason for defending the free movement of natural persons is that a narrow interpretation would endanger the movement of undertakings. After all, according to Article 48 (ex 58) EC companies and firms fulfilling certain criteria are treated in the same way as natural persons. The movement of undertakings is crucial for the achievement of the economic benefits of the internal market and for the creation of convergence between different regions of the Community.

Economic and monetary union would seem to require a greater mobility of natural persons inside the Community as exchange rate flexibility disappears. In the case of an asymmetric shock the declining area may have to 'export' persons. Take as an example a Member State whose economy depends on forestry, paper production etc. If there is a shock that hits this sector, but not the other sectors of the euro-zone economy, the unemployment in that Member State will rise relative to other Member States. As the Member State cannot use devaluation or lower interest rates to stimulate its economy,[163] it may be that some of its citizens will have to migrate to find work. Fiscal transfers from the small Community budget cannot deal with the situation. Free movement of natural persons becomes more important.

In general, it would seem that the approach of Community law to all four freedoms should be parallel. The free movement of goods and the free movement of services in particular should be dealt with in a uniform manner. There is a prima facie case for a uniform approach.

The Community institutions have recognised the need for uniform interpretation, at least in the level of language. In *Gebhard*[164] the Court stated:

national measures liable to hinder or make less attractive the exercise of fundamental freedoms guaranteed by the Treaty must fulfil four conditions: they must be applied in a non-discriminatory manner; they must be justified by imperative requirements in the general interest; they must be suitable for securing the attainment of the objective which they pursue; and they must not go beyond what is necessary in order to attain it.

4. Terminology

To avoid confusion, key concepts used in this study have to be defined. Some of these terms have also been used by the European Court of Justice. However, the usage here may in some respects differ from that of the Court.

---

[162] See Poiares Maduro (n 6 above) 101–102, and S. Weatherill, 'After *Keck*: Some Thoughts on How to Clarify the Clarification' (1996) 33 CMLRev 885 at 906. Art 18(2) EC will move from unanimity to qualified majority voting, with limitations provided for in Art 18(3) EC, when the Treaty of Nice enters into force.

[163] Expansive fiscal policy, within the limits set by the Growth and Stability Pact, and wage reductions remain available, however. It is also possible to build other domestic stabilisers.

[164] See n 155 above, para 37.

This is due to the fact that the Court, preoccupied with the need to settle a dispute rather than the need to achieve academic clarity, has sometimes been slightly unclear and erratic in its terminology.[165]

Direct or overt discrimination refers to a situation where differential treatment is afforded to domestic subjects and subjects originating from other Member States and the criteria used are openly based on nationality.[166]

Material discrimination is at hand when the effect of national rules is to put subjects originating from other Member States at a disadvantage when compared with domestic subjects. This is achieved by treating similar situations differently or different situations identically.

In a typical case of material discrimination national rules creating problems for foreign interests use criteria of differentiation that cannot be objectively justified. The rules themselves are inherently discriminatory. An example would be a restriction on the sale of spirits that are not grain-based. Presumably the national drinks industry would already be specialised in grain-based spirits, either because it had to adapt to the rules or because the rules were drafted with its interests in mind. Foreign competitors specialising in spirits produced according to other methods would be at a disadvantage. The criterion of differentiation, whether the spirits are grain-based or not, is not capable of objective justification as it cannot be rationally defended.

A special case of material discrimination occurs when a disparity between national rules creates problems for foreign interests. An example would be the prohibition of the sale of alcohol products whose alcohol content exceeds a certain level. A trader who lawfully produces and markets a drink in one Member State cannot enter the market of the Member State imposing the ban without modifying the drink and thus incurring additional costs.

The difference between these two types of material discrimination lies in the fact that in the latter case the criterion of differentiation is capable of being rationally defended, as strong alcohol may create health risks. The problem does not lie with the rule itself but with the application of the rule to a product coming from another Member State which has a different rule. In effect, different situations are being treated similarly. A national rule is applied to a product that has already complied with one set of regulations. The legislator has failed to consider the distinct situation of a foreign product.

---

[165] See eg the finding that the Wallonian measure was not discriminatory in Case C-2/90 *Commission v Belgium* [1992] ECR I-4431. See also C. Hilson, 'Discrimination in Community Free Movement Law' (1999) 24 ELRev 445 at 448.

[166] The concept, as used here, does not include 'obvious intentional protectionism' as suggested by Hilson (n 165 above) 450. It is submitted that this category is superfluous. A measure falling within this category will necessarily entail either direct or material discrimination, as a means of achieving the protectionist intent. Therefore, it will automatically constitute a prima facie restriction on the relevant freedom. Additionally, such a measure can never be justified. The whole idea behind justifications is to enable Member States to adopt rules to protect legitimate public interests, and protectionism obviously does not constitute such an interest. Cf however Hilson (n 165 above) 447.

In my view it is not necessary to draw a distinction between these differ-ent types of material discrimination. After an unequal burden has been found the question ultimately always boils down to the justifiability of the application of national rules to products coming from other Member States. It is irrelevant whether the lack of justification is due to the inherent nature of the criteria of differentiation or the non-acceptability of those criteria in a specific situation. Furthermore, the whole distinction is rather contrived and esoteric.[167]

This view seems to be accepted by the European Court of Justice in *De Agostini*.[168] In the case the Court stated that a Swedish rule on advertising was covered by the EC Treaty only if it did not affect in the same way, in law and in fact, the marketing of domestic and other Member States' products. If it did discriminate, it was for the national court to examine whether the meas-ure could be justified by overriding requirements or Article 30 (ex 36) EC. The Court clearly treated discrimination 'in fact' exactly the same way as it would have treated restrictions arising from disparity between national rules.[169]

5. The objective of the study

Based on the analysis presented in the previous sections, the study com-mences from the premise that the approach to both the free movement of goods and services ought to be fundamentally similar. This premise will be examined in three contexts. It will be asked: What amounts to a restriction on the free movement of goods or services? Which persons and bodies are bound by these freedoms? How can a prima facie restriction on the free movement of goods or services be justified? Each of these questions will be examined in turn, starting with the free movement of goods and then comparing and con-trasting the free movement of services with it. When the analysis reveals that a different approach has been adopted to the freedoms, the reasons and implications of the differences will be explored. It will also be examined whether a sensible unified approach could be found.

The study concentrates on three basic questions of the free movement law: restriction, persons bound, and justification. These will be examined in rela-tion to non-tariff barriers, which are relevant to both the free movement of goods and services. Customs duties, and other pecuniary barriers, are not investigated as customs duties are not relevant in the case of services.

---

[167] See, however, G. Marenco, 'Pour une interprétation traditionelle de la notion de measure d'effet équivalent à une restriction quantitative' (1984) 19 CDE 291 at 312–313, and Weatherill and Beaumont (n 156 above) 516–518.

[168] Joined Cases C-34/95, C-35/95 and C-36/95 *Konsumentombudsmannen v De Agostini (Svenska) Förlag AB and TV-Shop i Sverige AB* [1997] ECR I-3843.

[169] See in more detail J. Snell, 'De Agostini and the Regulation of Television Broadcasting' (1997) 8 EBLR 222 at 226.

Problems specific to public undertakings, subsidies or taxes are not analysed, as they give rise to special issues relating to the role of the state as a market participant, competition law, or tax law. The focus is on the internal aspects of trade in goods and services. The Common Commercial Policy will not be discussed. The study will examine both import and export restrictions, but the analysis of the latter will be incorporated into the discussion of the former. Import restrictions have traditionally been more prevalent, and export restrictions form only the flip side of the same coin.[170]

The study concentrates on the free movement of goods and services, although the free movement of persons will also feature in the discussion from time to time. The reason for excluding the latter from a full treatment is that goods and services, material and non-material products, are economically very similar, as argued in section 3 above. Therefore, it is interesting to examine whether they have been treated in the same way by the law. In contrast, the free movement of workers and the right of establishment concern factors of production, and it is more difficult to argue that they are also similar from the economic point of view. Therefore, any difference in treatment may be more easy to justify, and, hence, less interesting.

Due to the central role of the Court in the field of the free movement of goods and services, the study will concentrate on the case law. The judgments of the Court have often shown the general direction and acted as an inspiration to the Community legislature.

Traditional legal method will be used. However, economic aspects of legal rules will be examined more thoroughly than in a conventional, purely doctrinal study.

The aim of the study is to deepen the understanding of the nature and mechanisms of the freedoms. The legal developments in one field can be critically assessed in the light of the developments in the others. The study should help in the analysing and weighting of arguments when the progress made in one field is pleaded to support a new approach in another field. This is of particular importance in the aftermath of the ground-breaking decision of the European Court of Justice in the *Keck* case.[171] In *Alpine Investments*[172] the Court seems to have refused to apply the *Keck* doctrine to marketing of financial services despite the suggestions made by two Member States, but the issue is not resolved and will certainly resurface in the future.

---

[170] The issue of democratic legitimacy, while discussed, is not given the pride of place that some might wish to see. This study is not concerned with systems of taxes and benefits but with legal rules that should primarily be based on efficiency concerns. See eg A.M. Polinsky, *An Introduction to Law and Economics* (2nd edn Boston 1989) 119–127. Therefore, the questions of democratic legitimacy do not arise in the same manner and with the same force as with redistribution. See G. Majone, *Regulating Europe* (London 1996) 294–296.

[171] Joined Cases C-267/91 and C-268/91 *Criminal Proceedings Against Keck and Mithouard* [1993] ECR I-6097.

[172] Case C-384/93 *Alpine Investments BV v Minister van Financiën* [1995] ECR I-1141.

The developments in the field of the free movement of goods and services are inexorably linked to more general issues of Community law. The study also seeks to illustrate and analyse tensions between Member States and the Community on the one hand, and the legislature and the judiciary on the other.

2
Restriction

1. Vertical division of power in the Community and the scope given to the freedoms

a) Introduction

In this section I will examine the division of power between the Community and Member States in the areas touched by the provisions on the free movement of goods and services. The following argument will be advanced: the scope given to the freedoms partially determines the vertical division of power in the Community. A wide interpretation, corresponding to the economic freedom model, produces a centralised unitary system, while a narrower reading results in a decentralised federal one. The latter option is to be preferred, particularly as it enables competition between legal orders. Therefore, the European Court of Justice ought to adopt a relatively narrow interpretation of Articles 28 and 49 (ex 30 and 59) EC that is based on a broadly understood notion of discrimination.

b) From inter-governmentalism and supra-nationalism to decentralisation and centralisation

There are basic tensions that run through all the developments in the fields of the free movement of goods and services. The early conflict between inter-governmentalism and supra-nationalism and the more recent tension between decentralisation and centralisation have shaped both of these fields in a crucial manner.[1]

The main conflict in European integration has been between inter-governmentalism and supra-nationalism. From the first proposals on tighter co-operation between Western European states after the Second World War, to the Maastricht Treaty (Treaty on European Union) and beyond, these elements have fought to determine the shape of Europe.

---

[1] This is especially apparent in the case law of the European Court of Justice before, in and after the controversial decision in Joined Cases C-267/91 and C-268/91 *Criminal Proceedings Against Keck and Mithouard* [1993] ECR I-6097.

Typically, international organisations are based on institutionalised co-operation between governments. Decisions are made unanimously so that no participant will be bound without its consent. If majority voting is possible, it is only used to adopt declarations and other measures whose real effects are negligible.[2] The European Community, as opposed to the forms of inter-governmental co-operation in the second and third pillars of the European Union, has characteristics that separate it from traditional international organisations. Clearly the Community is both in law and in practice more than just a form of inter-governmental co-operation.[3]

The Community is not fully comparable to a federation, however. The Member States are still primary actors in the Community system, unlike the constituent parts of federations.[4] The Community has been called 'a constitutional order of States'.[5]

In internal market law, supra-national tendencies have become predominant. Article 95 (ex 100a) EC states that most approximation measures aimed at establishing and ensuring the functioning of the internal market are to be adopted using the co-decision procedure found in Article 251 (ex 189b) EC. This means qualified majority voting in the Council and a strong role for the European Parliament. An individual Member State faces a real possibility of being outvoted, and supra-national institutions have a real influence on the content of the legislation.

The most important Treaty provisions concerning free movement have been found to be directly effective by the Court.[6] Consequently, private parties are able to rely on these rules in national courts. In practice this has been of enormous significance for the process of integration, as frequent litigation

[2] T.C. Hartley, *The Foundations of European Community Law* (4th edn Oxford 1998) 9–10. See also J.-C. Piris, 'Does the European Union have a Constitution? Does it Need One?' (1999) 24 ELRev 557 at 559–561.

[3] Most of the decisions can be made with majority voting. Community institutions can act autonomously. Community law binds Member States and in many cases also individuals and is applied by national courts, which are thereby transformed into Community courts. There is a real possibility of sanctions being used both against Member States and against private parties if they breach Community law: Hartley (n 2 above) 10. See also Piris (n 2 above) 559–561.

[4] K. Lenaerts, 'Constitutionalism and the Many Faces of Federalism' (1990) 38 AJCL 205 at 262, and R. Dehousse, C. Joerges, G. Majone and F. Snyder, *Europe after 1992—New Regulatory Strategies* (EUI Working Paper LAW No. 92/31, 1992) at 3.

[5] A. Dashwood, 'The Limits of European Community Powers' (1996) 21 ELRev 113 at 114.

[6] See Art 25 (ex 12) EC in Case 26/62 *Van Gend en Loos v Nederlandse Administratie der Belastingen* [1963] ECR 1; Art 90 (ex 95) EC in Case 57/65 *Lütticke GmbH v Hauptzollamt Saarlouis* [1966] ECR 205 and in Case 27/67 *Fink Frucht GmbH v Hauptzollamt München-Landsbergerstrasse* [1968] ECR 223; Art 28 (ex 30) EC in Case 74/76 *Iannelli & Volpi S.p.A. v Ditta Paolo Meroni* [1977] ECR 557; Art 29 (ex 34) EC in Case 83/78 *Pigs Marketing Board v Raymond Redmond* [1978] ECR 2347; Art 39 (ex 48) EC in eg Case 15/69 *Württembergische Milchverwertung-Südmilch-AG v Salvatore Ugliola* [1969] ECR 363; Art 43 (ex 52) EC in Case 2/74 *Reyners v Belgium* [1974] ECR 631; Art 49 (ex 59) EC in Case 33/74 *Van Binsbergen v Bestuur van de Bedrijfsvereniging voor de Metaalnijverheid* [1974] ECR 1299, and Art 56 (ex 73b) EC in Cases C-163/94, C-165/94 and C-250/94 *Criminal Proceedings Against Lucas Emilio Sanz de Lera and others* [1995] ECR I-4821.

by companies and individuals[7] has resulted in many important national measures being struck down.

Moreover, even the Member States like the United Kingdom, which tend to be hostile towards further increases in supra-nationalism, accept strong European institutions in this field.[8]

In the field of internal market law, the basic tension is no longer between inter-governmentalism and supra-nationalism. The conflict has evolved into one between decentralisation and centralisation.

Decentralisation in this context means a system where most aspects of economic regulation are left to Member States. However, the competence of Member States is somewhat restricted by the Community rules on the free movement of goods, services, persons and capital.

Centralisation means a system where the Community regulates (or deregulates) most economic activity and the competence of Member States is largely pre-empted. Thus, the system of central government is replicated at Community level.

This conflict is by no means unique to the Community. In all states the vertical division of power between higher and lower levels of government has to be decided. The issue is especially relevant in federal states like Germany and the USA, where the correct allocation of competences has been debated for decades and centuries.

c) The scope of the freedoms

This 'constitutional' tension underlies the case law of the Court on the scope of the four freedoms.[9] When the Court decides that a Member State measure constitutes a prima facie restriction on the freedom, it allocates the competence to regulate to the Community and, thus, supports the centralisation argument.[10]

---

[7] This was one of the factors which prompted the Court to rethink its case law in Joined Cases C-267/91 and C-268/91 *Criminal Proceedings Against Keck and Mithouard* [1993] ECR I-6097.

[8] UK [Conservative] Government White Paper, *A Partnership of Nations* (1996) at 16 argued for the need for a 'strong, independent Court without which it would be impossible to ensure even application of Community law'.

[9] Similarly Poiares Maduro, *We The Court. The European Court of Justice and the European Constitution. A Critical Reading of Article 30 of the EC Treaty* (Oxford 1998) 1, 59 and 67–68.

[10] This is not to say that Community regulation is only possible if a restriction has been found. The existence of a restriction is a *sufficient* but not a *necessary* condition for harmonisation. See Case C-376/98 *Germany v European Parliament and Council of the European Union*, judgment of 5 October 2000, where the Court found that Art 95 (ex 100a) EC was available to remove obstacles and appreciable distortions of competition. See also N. Bernard, 'The Future of European Economic Law in the Light of the Principle of Subsidiarity' (1996) 33 CMLRev 633 at 647–650, and J.H.H. Weiler, 'The Constitution of the Common Market Place: Text and Context in the Evolution of the Free Movement of Goods' in P. Craig and G. de Búrca (eds), *The Evolution of EU Law* (Oxford 1999) 362.

The free movement provisions act as a driving force in the creation of the internal market. Article 3(1)(c) EC lists, among the activities of the Community, an internal market characterised by the abolition of obstacles to the free movement of goods and services between Member States. Article 95 (ex 100a) EC authorises the Community to adopt measures that have as their object the establishment and functioning of the internal market.[11] If a national measure is held to be within the scope of the free movement provisions, its abolition or harmonisation becomes necessary for the establishment of the internal market and the Community gains the competence to act.[12]

Furthermore, the measure is seen as a restriction and, thus, harmonisation becomes a natural, not merely a possible, policy option given the commitment of the Community to the internal market.[13] The logical reaction to a restriction is either to abolish or to harmonise it in order to remove the obstacles as required by Article 3(1)(c).[14] Thus, national regulation is seen only as a temporary stopgap solution pending Community action.[15]

If the Court, a central organ, goes further and finds a national measure unjustified or disproportionate, it dictates policy choices to Member States. Its activities are not politically neutral. It contributes, especially if the review of national rules is intense, to a centrally determined 'arch-liberal *laissez-faire* policy'.[16]

Thus, the wider the scope given to the free movement provisions, the more centralised the Community system becomes. However, if the Court decides that a measure does not fall within the scope of the freedoms, it sides with decentralisation, allocating the competence to the Member State.

There are different possible views of the scope of the free movement provisions, each reflecting a different vertical division of powers within the Community. First, if Article 28 (ex 30), or 49 (ex 59) EC, is thought to apply to all national regulations restricting the volume of trade and, thus, the volume of imports, almost any national measure can be caught by it as nearly all rules are capable of having an adverse effect on the demand for some goods or services.[17] This is a wide, centralising reading that is connected to the economic freedom model.

---

[11] See also Art 52 (ex 63) EC.

[12] See D. Chalmers, 'Repackaging the Internal Market—The Ramifications of the *Keck* Judgment' (1994) 19 ELRev 385 at 402, and K. Mortelmans, 'Article 30 of the EEC Treaty and Legislation Relating to Market Circumstances: Time to Consider a New Definition?' (1991) 28 CMLRev 115 at 129.

[13] See eg *Financial Times*, 9 March 2001, 19 on the efforts of the Commission to modify football transfer systems after the ruling in Case C-415/93 *Union Royale Belge des Sociétés de Football Association ASBL and others v Jean-Marc Bosman* [1995] ECR I-4921.

[14] This remains true regardless of whether overriding requirements are seen as justifying restrictions or as a part of the definition of Arts 28 and 49 (ex 30 and 59) EC themselves. Even in the latter case the effects of a national measure will bring it prima facie within the scope of the provisions, and the fact that the intentions of the Member State were legitimate will not remove those adverse effects.

[15] See N. Bernard, 'Discrimination and Free Movement in EC Law' (1996) 45 ICLQ 82 at 103.

[16] See Bernard (n 10 above) 637.

[17] See S. Weatherill and P. Beaumont, *EU law* (3rd edn London 1999) 608–609; E. White, 'In Search of the Limits to Article 30 of the EEC Treaty' (1989) 26 CMLRev 235 at 253–254 shows,

A second, narrower reading, which may be connected to the anti-protectionism model, is based on the absence of discrimination and leads to greater decentralisation. Member State regulations are respected as long as they do not place imported goods or services at a disadvantage. The exact definition of the concept of discrimination becomes important.

d) The economics of federalism

I will now turn to the economics of federalism, examining the advantages and disadvantages of a decentralised federal model, in particular the theory of regulatory competition.

Centralisation may sometimes be beneficial. A centralised system can be politically stable, which also brings benefits of economic stability and predictability. Centralisation reduces transaction costs of private operators, who only have to familiarise themselves with one set of regulations. A centrally run system can also cope with distortions caused by market failures, such as negative externalities.

However, the economics of federalism teaches us that it is better to have multiple legislators than just a single one. The best approach is to allocate regulatory competence to the lowest appropriate level, which of course corresponds to the principle of subsidiarity. Most importantly, the existence of different jurisdictions may allow competition between legal orders with all ensuing static and dynamic efficiencies.[18]

Different regulators can take into account differences in objective circumstances, namely endowments and technology, between jurisdictions.[19] In the field of environmental law, for example, one jurisdiction may have short fast-moving rivers and can therefore tolerate higher emissions into them than a

---

as an example of the wide reach of Art 28 (ex 30) EC so interpreted, how even national laws against violent crime could fall under the concept of a measure having equivalent effect to quantitative restriction, as they reduce the volume of sale of weapons.

[18] See F.H. Easterbrook, 'Federalism and European Business Law' (1994) 14 International Review of Law and Economics 125 at 125–132; D.W. Leebron, 'Lying Down with Procrustes: An Analysis of Harmonization Claims' in J. Bhagwati and R.E. Hudec (eds), *Fair Trade and Harmonization. Prerequisites for Free Trade? Vol I. Economic Analysis* (London 1996), especially at 88; W. Molle, *The Economics of European Integration. Theory, Practice, Policy* (3rd edn Aldershot 1997) 18–20, and R. van den Bergh, 'The Subsidiarity Principle and the EC Competition Rules: The Costs and Benefits of Decentralisation' in D. Schmidtchen and R. Cooter (eds), *Constitutional Law and Economics of the European Union* (Cheltenham 1997) 149. See generally on regulatory competition, eg, W. Bratton, J. McCahery, S. Picciotto and C. Scott (eds), *International Regulatory Competition and Coordination. Perspectives on Economic Regulation in Europe and the United States* (Oxford 1996), and N. Reich, 'Competition Between Legal Orders: a New Paradigm of EC Law' (1992) 29 CMLRev 861, and, classically, C.M. Tiebout, 'A Pure Theory of Local Expenditures' (1956) 64 Journal of Political Economy 416. See also G. Marks and L. Hooghe, 'Optimality and Authority: A Critique of Neoclassical Theory' (2000) 38 JCMS 795 at 796–803 on the neoclassical theory of authority.

[19] See Leebron (n 18 above) 67.

jurisdiction with long slow-moving ones. It would not be efficient to have a single rule stipulating emission levels that applied to both jurisdictions.

Thus, centralisation would produce problems in an enlarging, increasingly heterogeneous Community, especially as the industries in less developed Member States would not be able to cope with a growing regulatory burden. If, for example, social policy legislation was harmonised close to German or Nordic levels, companies in the Mediterranean countries would lose their competitive advantage and the result would be an increase in unemployment in those states.[20]

The citizens of different jurisdictions may also have different preferences, which makes uniform rules inefficient.[21] For example, the citizens of one jurisdiction may value a clean environment relatively more than the citizens of another jurisdiction. The different preferences would be best satisfied by two different rules, setting accepted emission levels higher in the latter jurisdiction than in the former.

Thus, centralisation can result in excessive uniformity in a heterogeneous Community where preferences differ. Indeed, centrally produced regulation can lead to 'euro-products' if traditional manufacturing methods are prohibited. The result is loss of diversity and diminished consumer choice.[22]

Federalism, as opposed to centralisation, does not only guarantee that the rules in force in a jurisdiction correspond to the preferences of the majority of its subjects, but it also enables the minority to seek a more suitable regulatory climate. Workers and more generally citizens[23] of the Community can seek to settle in an area where the regulatory system suits them.[24] Investors can benefit from a diverse Community by having a wider choice of investment opportunities.

Altogether, centralisation runs counter to the philosophy of international specialisation. The existence of different regulatory systems enables companies to establish their facilities in locations which are most favourable to the type of business carried out. The same regulatory environment does not suit

---

[20] See H. Siebert, 'The Harmonization Issue in Europe: Prior Agreement or a Competitive Process?' in H. Siebert (ed), *The Completion of the Internal Market* (Tübingen 1990) 60, and H. Siebert and M.J. Koop, 'Institutional Competition. A Concept for Europe?' (1990) 45 Aussenwirtschaft 439 at 443–444.

[21] See Leebron (n 18 above) 68–69 and Marks and Hooghe (n 18 above) 798.

[22] See Weatherill and Beaumont (n 17 above) 596.

[23] The EC Treaty does not recognise a universal right to free movement of persons. This is to be deplored as it deprives individuals of the possibility to choose a regulatory system that corresponds to their preferences and distorts competition between legal orders by increasing the influence of companies and capital. See M. Poiares Maduro, 'Striking the Elusive Balance Between Economic Freedom and Social Rights in the EU' in P. Alston (ed), *The EU and Human Rights* (Oxford 1999) 462 and 470. It has to be recognised, however, that there might be free-rider problems. For example, the unemployed would have an incentive to migrate to countries with high benefits, thus consuming public goods they have not paid for and taking a free ride on the efforts of the tax-payers.

[24] See R. van den Bergh, 'Subsidiarity as an Economic Demarcation Principle and the Emergence of European Private Law' (1998) 5 MJ 129 at 132.

every industry and every strategy. For example, some companies may thrive in a jurisdiction with an ultra-flexible labour market, which allows them to hire and fire as they see fit. Other companies may be better off in a regulatory environment that encourages long-term commitment of the workforce. A diverse Community can support more types of economic activities than a homogeneous one. In this respect, centralisation would reduce efficiency.[25]

In the absence of centrally drafted uniform rules, free movement enables regulatory competition between legal orders. This competition does not take place only between states but also between regional and local units. Free flow of goods, services and factors of production gives consumers and producers possibilities to engage in arbitrage.[26]

Consumers can show their preferences by purchasing products and services that have been produced under foreign regulatory systems if they correspond to their needs as regards price and quality. If domestic producers have to comply with inefficient regulations, their products will not be able to compete with those manufactured under a more favourable regulatory environment. Thus, consumers send signals to business by 'voting with their purses'.[27]

Firms can engage in arbitrage by relocating to another jurisdiction. Further investment, in particular, can be directed towards an area with a more favourable regulatory climate. This may be a response to signals received from consumers. The business demonstrates to public authorities that regulation is not optimal for the firms in question. The business 'votes with its feet'.[28]

Similarly, individual investors may invest their capital in a jurisdiction where the regulatory system produces a balance between risks and rewards that suits their preferences. Workers may relocate themselves to a jurisdiction with a system corresponding to their preferences.

Alternatively, private agents may react by using their 'voice' to vote or to lobby public authorities to make changes to the regulatory system. They react in the political market.[29]

Public authorities receive signals from private agents using the 'exit' or the 'voice' option. Flight of firms, capital and skilled workers can result in unemployment and lower productivity which threaten the welfare of the citizens.

---

[25] See Siebert and Koop (n 20 above) 445–446, and M.E. Porter, *The Competitive Advantage of Nations* (London 1990) 623–624.

[26] Mobility is a precondition to regulatory competition. See Easterbrook (n 18 above) 127, and H. Siebert and M.J. Koop, 'Institutional Competition Versus Centralization: Quo Vadis Europe?' (1993) 9 *Oxford Review of Economic Policy* 15 at 17. Alternatively, firms may be able to select the jurisdiction whose principles apply to a transaction or business if the private international law of their home jurisdiction allows it. See A. Ogus, 'Competition Between National Legal Systems: A Contribution of Economic Analysis to Comparative Law' (1999) 48 ICLQ 405 at 408.

[27] See Siebert (n 20 above) 56, and J.-M. Sun and J. Pelkmans, 'Regulatory Competition in the Single Market' (1995) 33 JCMS 76–77.

[28] See Siebert (n 20 above) 56, and Sun and Pelkmans (n 27 above) 76–77.

[29] Sun and Pelkmans (n 27 above) 77.

This gives an incentive to adapt the regulatory system in order to avoid the erosion of tax base and to ensure reelection. Due to low transaction costs, capital tends to be the factor reacting most quickly to unfavourable regulatory environment by relocating. High transaction costs limit the movement of natural persons.[30]

Thus, perhaps most importantly, competition between legal orders acts as a discovery mechanism. Individual jurisdictions receive signals from private agents engaged in arbitrage and are therefore able to determine more easily whether the regulatory system fits their preferences. This is especially important given the imperfect information possessed by public authorities.[31] Furthermore, voting is not always a very efficient way of revealing preferences due to the infrequency of elections and the bundling of issues. It is useful to have the exit option as an additional mechanism for signalling preferences.

The learning process is enhanced by competition between legal orders. Public authorities in different jurisdictions can observe a preference for a certain regulatory system among private agents and adapt the domestic system accordingly. Thus, jurisdictions can emulate efficient regulatory systems and benefit from experimentation. In a centralised system there is no comparable learning process.[32] A decentralised system can therefore lead to different jurisdictions adopting similar regulations. This is entirely desirable as it is a natural development arising out of the preferences of citizens of individual jurisdictions and the competitive process.

Public authorities may try to adopt efficient regulatory solutions as early as possible since this may give their firms decisive early mover advantages.[33] This increases the dynamism of the system.

Regulatory competition can also curb the expansionist tendencies of the public sector. The public authorities might not pursue the common good, but rather try to maximise their own utility if subject only to the weak constraints of reelection or reappointment. The possibility of the erosion of the tax base caused by private agents fleeing an oppressive system is an additional constraint and instils discipline on the public sector.[34]

In a centrally controlled system the legislature can be subjected to effective lobbying by rent-seeking groups. Protectionist producers will be able to set up

---

[30] See Siebert and Koop (n 20 above) 444–445, and S. Woolcock, *The Single European Market. Centralization or Competition among National Rules?* (London 1994) 28.

[31] See Sun and Pelkmans (n 27 above) 83.

[32] See H. Schmidt, 'Economic Analysis of the Allocation of Regulatory Competence in the European Communities' in R.M. Buxbaum, G. Hertig, A. Hirsch and K.J. Hopt (eds), *European Business Law. Legal and Economic Analyses on Integration and Harmonization* (Berlin 1991) 57, and Woolcock (n 30 above) 17–18.

[33] See Porter (n 25 above) 648, Schmidt (n 32 above) 55–57, and Siebert and Koop (n 20 above) 443.

[34] See H. Hauser and M. Hösli, 'Harmonization or Regulatory Competition in the EC (and the EEA)?' (1991) 46 Aussenwirtschaft 497 at 501–502, and Siebert and Koop, 'Institutional Competition versus Centralization: Quo Vadis Europe?' 18.

organisations at the European level and may influence centrally adopted regulation to the detriment of consumers. Regulation produced by the market mechanism cannot be influenced by interest group politics to the same extent.[35]

A further problem with centrally drafted legislation is the distance between the regulators and the regulated. This diminishes the opportunities of the citizens to participate meaningfully in the political process. It also exacerbates information problems facing the public authorities. A remote central organ may not be able to form a true picture of the situation.[36]

Harmonised legislation, once in place, can also be difficult to change. Central systems can suffer from gigantism, and the decision-makers may be reluctant to open and renegotiate compromises that have been achieved only with great difficulty.[37]

Finally, the procedural costs created by centralisation are reduced by competition between legal orders. A centralised harmonisation process may result in lengthy and costly negotiations, as shown by the experience of the Community in the 1970s. It seems to be extraordinarily difficult to engage in detailed harmonisation of rules that reflect different national circumstances and preferences. Decentralisation reduces the time and effort taken by the process.[38]

Altogether, regulatory competition has the potential for enhancing both static and dynamic efficiency in the economy. It is a particularly attractive concept in the context of the relatively heterogeneous Community. Some historians have concluded that the global dominance of Europe during the recent centuries was a result of the intense competition in the continent. Centralised empires stagnated while competing European states were pushed to ever greater advances.[39]

---

[35] See Hauser and Hösli (n 34 above) 503, and Siebert and Koop (n 26 above) 18. On the powers of different interest groups in the Community see A. McGee and S. Weatherill, 'The Evolution of the Single Market—Harmonisation or Liberalisation' (1990) 53 MLR 578 at 585 and 595.

[36] See R. van den Bergh, 'Economic Criteria for Applying the Subsidiariy Principle in the European Community: The Case of Competition Policy' (1996) 16 International Review of Law and Economics 363 at 365–366.

[37] See Schmidt (n 32 above) 57–58, and H. Willgerodt, 'Comment on Jaques Pelkmans, "Regulation and the Single Market: An Economic Perspective"' in H. Siebert (ed), *The Completion of the Internal Market* (Tübingen 1990) 122.

[38] See J. Pelkmans, 'Regulation and the Single Market: An Economic Perspective' in H. Siebert (ed), *The Completion of the Internal Market* (Tübingen 1990) 92, and Woolcock (n 30 above) 16.

[39] See B.S. Frey and R. Eichenberger, 'FOCJ: Creating a Single European Market for Governments' in D. Schmidtchen and R. Cooter (eds), *Constitutional Law and Economics of the European Union* (Cheltenham 1997) 209, and P. Kennedy, *The Rise and Fall of Great Powers. Economic Advantage and Military Conflict from 1500 to 2000* (London 1988) xvi–xvii and 20–28. However, the competition sometimes escalated to armed conflict, the costs of which became excessive with the development of modern weaponry and logistics. Thus, the competition had to be contained in peaceful structures like the European Union.

The advantages of a decentralised or federal system have been neatly encapsulated by Justice O'Connor of the US Supreme Court:

The federalist structure of joint sovereigns preserves to the people numerous advantages. It assures a decentralised government that will be more sensitive to the diverse needs of a heterogeneous society; it increases opportunity for citizen involvement in democratic processes; it allows for more innovation and experimentation in government, and it makes government more responsive by putting the States in competition for a mobile citizenry. . . Perhaps the principal benefit of a federalist system is a check on the abuses of government power.[40]

Sun and Pelkmans have expressed doubts as to whether regulatory competition will actually take place.[41] They argue that national regulations may not change. Imperfect mobility of factors of production or economic incentives to produce according to host country rules can lead to a lack of arbitrage. Even if arbitrage does take place, national regulations may remain intact due to the small impact of relocation and minuscule political strength of firms.[42]

This assessment may be too gloomy. Capital tends to be very mobile and capital flight can force public authorities to react.[43]

More fundamentally, unchanging regulations are not yet an argument for harmonisation, even if there are transaction costs which prevent arbitrage. It is not worthwhile to harmonise just for the sake of harmonisation. Diversity in the Community is not a weakness but a strength, as argued above.

An example of a situation where imperfect mobility prevents competition between legal orders, but harmonisation remains undesirable, would be different systems of vocational training. Some workers of state A might prefer the system of state B. They may, however, be deterred from moving to state B to acquire education by high transaction costs created by linguistic and cultural differences. This does not imply that training systems should be harmonised. It may well be that the vocational training system of state A suits the preferences of the majority of its citizens and fulfils the special needs of industries located in the country. The system is after all a product of historical development. The problem in this example is not the different education systems but the linguistic and cultural barriers.[44]

A firm may indeed have incentives to produce according to host country traditions. This may be caused by peculiar national preferences of the consumers; catering to these preferences is a normal part of economic competition and

[40] *Gregory v Ashcroft* 501 U.S. 452 (1991), at 458 (citations omitted).

[41] It is important to note that competition does not have to be perfect to be beneficial. Indeed, examples of perfect competition can usually only be found on the pages of economics textbooks.

[42] Sun and Pelkmans (n 27 above) 83–85.

[43] Molle (n 18 above) 239–240, and Siebert and Koop (n 20 above) 444. The changes in the EC Treaty that came into force in 1994 have probably enhanced this mobility even further, as has the adoption of the euro as a common currency.

[44] The elimination of barriers creating transaction costs is generally a legitimate role for harmonisation, although some barriers are likely to defy any harmonisation attempts. See below.

enhances consumer welfare. Only if the incentives are created by the need to accommodate a national regulator, is there a problem.[45]

In the case of a regulation not changing because of the lack of strength of firms engaged in arbitrage, it may well be that the regulation corresponds to preferences of most of the private agents in the jurisdiction, and accordingly should not be altered. If the majority of firms in one sector would be hindered by the regulation, they might well together wield sufficient power to make their voices heard.

Furthermore, experience from the USA suggests that competition between legal orders does take place. Especially in the field of company law the so-called Delaware effect[46] has been observed for a long time, and although its desirability is hotly disputed, its existence is generally not doubted.[47]

It has been feared that competition between regulators would lead to a 'race to the bottom'. Different Member States would lower the level of their regulation to attract companies from other countries. Companies might relocate to minimise the cost of complying with regulations and would then serve the whole Community from this new base. This would encourage other countries to lower their level of regulation even further. Thus, the level of regulation in the Community would become sub-optimal.[48]

There are checking factors, however. Firms can benefit from regulation as it can enhance inter alia their productivity; thus, they may not wish to relocate.[49] For example, strict environmental rules that create a cleaner environment may contribute to the health and accordingly the productivity of the employees. The state of the environment may also be important when attracting high quality labour. Clean water, quality of agricultural products, the rate of growth of forests etc can be important for the industry if they are inputs to production or if there is goodwill among consumers associated with products from a clean environment. Stringent requirements create opportunities for new industries as the demand for new clean technologies increase. Furthermore, if a jurisdiction is the first to adopt strict standards and others later follow, its industries will gain early mover advantages as they are the first

---

[45] As in the banking example given by Sun and Pelkmans (n 27 above) at 81.

[46] In the USA many companies have reincorporated themselves in Delaware to enjoy the benefits of its company law. See generally D. Charny, 'Competition Among Jurisdictions in Formulating Corporate Law Rules: An American Perspective on the "Race to the Bottom" in the European Communities' (1991) 32 Harvard Int LJ 423 at 427–434.

[47] J.P. Trachtman, 'International Regulatory Competition, Externalization, and Jurisdiction' (1993) 34 Harvard Int LJ 47 at 63. See also F.H. Easterbrook, 'Antitrust and the Economics of Federalism' (1983) 26 Journal of Law and Economics 23 at 43–45. The empirical evidence is weak, however. See also C. Barnard, 'Social Dumping and the Race to the Bottom: Some Lessons for the European Union from Delaware?' (2000) 25 ELRev 57 at 70–74 on the lack of social dumping in Europe.

[48] See Siebert and Koop (n 20 above) 446–447, and Weatherill and Beaumont (n 17 above) 700–701.

[49] See Siebert (n 20 above) 63–67, and Siebert and Koop (n 20 above) 447–449.

to adjust. Naturally, the effects vary from one industry to another so while some industries are better off some may experience difficulties.[50]

A sub-optimal level of regulation makes citizens worse off. The welfare gains caused by, for example, an inflow of capital do not necessarily offset welfare losses caused by, for example, environmental degradation, especially since marginal damage increases progressively as the level of pollution rises.[51] Citizens can respond by relocating to other countries. Although large-scale migration is unlikely to take place, the loss of highly skilled professionals may well result in a change of policy, as governments are likely to wish to stem the flow of these valuable factors of production. Industries that are dependent on a high level of regulation may either relocate or wither. A further response can be made in the political arena. Voters may not reelect a government engaged in excessive deregulation and industries may lobby for higher standards.[52]

It can be argued that instead of a race to the bottom, regulatory competition produces a race towards efficient regulation.[53] However, the area remains hotly disputed.[54]

Competition between legal orders does not remove transaction costs arising from different legal environments. For example, a company establishing a subsidiary in another Member State may need to get special legal advice, which would be unnecessary if the company laws of both countries were similar. These transaction costs can create a substantial obstacle, especially to the European expansion of smaller firms.[55]

The argument for harmonisation to avoid transaction costs is not unproblematic, however. Almost any Community measure could be defended on these grounds, widening the scope of Community competence and threatening the principle of enumerated powers established in Article 5 (ex 3b) EC. Furthermore, a harmonisation programme would be difficult to manage in practice if the agenda was this wide.[56] In fields where transaction costs pose

---

[50] See Porter (n 25 above) 651–652.

[51] See Siebert (n 20 above) 63–67 and 70, and Siebert and Koop (n 20 above) 447–449.

[52] From the game theory point of view the situation facing a state is generally similar to that of an oligopolist. The game is one of a large and unknown number of repetitions, and reactions of others affect the state's outcome matrix, as the state knows its competitive deregulation may be matched by others before it gains any benefits. In the same way an oligopolist is discouraged from lowering prices by the fact that competitors would match any price cuts, depriving him of market share gains.

[53] It has also been argued that competition between legal orders can lead to excessive regulation. See Sun and Pelkmans (n 27 above) 85.

[54] eg, Prosi states that '[t]he notion that institutional competition will lead to zero regulation and taxation is nonsense' (G. Prosi, 'Comments on Horst Siebert, "The Harmonization Issue in Europe: Prior Agreement or a Competitive Process?"' in H. Siebert (ed), *The Completion of the Internal Market* (Tübingen 1990) 77), while Meier-Schatz remarks that '[t]he only thing which is fairly well established is the fact that regulatory competition probably leads to a race to the bottom' (C. Meier-Schatz in R.M. Buxbaum, G. Hertig, A. Hirsch and K.J. Hopt (eds), *European Business Law. Legal and Economic Analyses on Integration and Harmonization* (Berlin 1991) 125). See also Barnard (n 47 above) 70–74, who argues that there is very little evidence of social dumping in Europe.

[55] See Bernard (n 10 above) 47, and Schmidt (n 32 above) 54.

[56] See Bernard (n 10 above) 647–648.

substantial obstacles to integration, harmonisation would be desirable. For example, voluntary product standards are capable of greatly facilitating free movement by reducing transaction costs without endangering innovation.[57]

The market in regulation is subject to market failures that can create a need for public intervention to remedy the problem. In the context of regulatory competition, externalities are the most common market failure and usually the strongest argument for centralisation.[58] Externalities occur when an activity regulated in one jurisdiction affects the well-being of people in other jurisdictions.[59] Externalities can result in a sub-optimal level of regulation. For example, if air pollution created in one country mainly causes damage in another country, the former does not have an incentive to curb emissions since it reaps the benefits but does not have to bear the costs. In the case of externalities central regulation may be desirable.[60] Appropriate regulatory level internalises all major effects of the activity regulated. This corresponds to one aspect of the principle of subsidiarity.[61]

Information asymmetries may create a need for regulation. In some situations consumers cannot properly assess the quality of a good or a service. An example is professional services. This may lead to a predominance of cheap poor quality products. To counter this trend, authorities have passed consumer protection rules which guarantee a certain minimum quality to the consumers. If goods and services from other jurisdictions with differing standards are now allowed a free access to the market, the consumers may not be able to identify the quality of these foreign products due to insufficient knowledge of foreign regulations.[62] Therefore, it may be necessary to draft common minimum standards when it comes to goods and services whose qualities consumers cannot assess.[63]

On the other hand, stringent regulation can become a guarantee of high quality. A jurisdiction may set high requirements for its products, and if producers have to comply with these rules whether the goods or services are for domestic or foreign consumption, the consumers in other countries have an assurance of quality.[64] Public regulation can fulfil a trademark-like function.

[57] See Bernard (n 10 above) 648, and Siebert and Koop (n 26 above) 27.

[58] See J. Kay and J. Vickers, 'Regulatory Reform: An Appraisal' in G. Majone (ed), *Deregulation or Re-regulation? Regulatory Reform in Europe and the United States* (London 1990) 244.

[59] See Hauser and Hösli (n 34 above) 507–508, and Siebert and Koop (n 20 above) 450–451.

[60] See van den Bergh (n 24 above) 140–145. Central regulation is not necessarily the only way to deal with externalities. In theory, proper allocation of property rights can serve to correct this failure. See Willgerodt (n 37 above) 123, and Woolcock (n 30 above) 18.

[61] See Easterbrook (n 18 above) 129, and W.P.J. Wils, 'Subsidiarity and the EC Environmental Policy: Taking Peoples' Concerns Seriously' (1994) 6 JEL 85 at 88.

[62] Thus, this problem is most prevalent in the case of private individuals.

[63] See generally Hauser and Hösli (n 34 above) 509, and P. Nicolaides, 'Competition Among Rules' (1992) 16 *World Competition* 113 at 119–120.

[64] In Case C-212/97 *Centros Ltd v Erhvervs of Selskabsstyrelsen* [1999] ECR I-1459 para 36 the Court emphasised that creditors knew that a UK company did not necessarily fulfil Danish requirements on share capital. The UK company law acted as a trademark indicating, in this instance, a potentially inferior quality.

Different jurisdictions may thus specialise in goods of different quality and consumer choice will increase.[65] Altogether, competition between legal orders may be beneficial despite asymmetric information.[66]

Furthermore, harmonisation may in some cases be necessary because of strategic behaviour,[67] natural monopolies,[68] systemic risks[69] or distributory considerations.[70] Moreover, regulatory competition may be unnecessary due to sufficient homogeneity or inefficient due to economies of scale since it may be cheaper to have just one central government machinery than separate institutions in each Member State.[71] A further problem with competition between legal orders is regulatory drift. Stability and predictability is important for business and changes in regulatory environment involve adjustment costs. Regulatory competition may lead to multiple changes as national rules are altered in response to competing 'better' rules. This is the downside of flexibility created by competition.[72] Generally, none of these considerations creates serious problems for the idea of competition between legal orders, however.

It may be seen from the previous discussion that neither regulatory competition nor centralisation is alone a feasible method for regulating the internal market.[73] Especially where there are major transaction costs or externalities, harmonisation remains necessary.[74] The peculiarities of each area of law have to be taken into account. In some fields, these factors have a strong impact, while in others they hardly feature at all.[75] Nevertheless, competition between

[65] Hauser and Hösli (n 34 above) 509–510. The Court has disallowed rules requiring mandatory origin-marking in Case 207/83 *Commission v United Kingdom* [1985] ECR 1202 but producers are able to state the origin of the products if they so choose.

[66] Kay and Vickers (n 58 above) 244.

[67] Siebert and Koop (n 20 above) 452–455, and G. Majone, 'Regulatory Federalism in the European Community' (1992) 10 Government and Policy, Environment and Planning C 299 at 308.

[68] Siebert and Koop (n 26 above) 21–22.

[69] This is a kind of externality. See P. Nicolaides, *Liberalizing Service Trade. Strategies for Success* (London 1989) 52–53 and 76.

[70] Hauser and Hösli (n 34 above) 509–510, and Woolcock (n 30 above) 20.

[71] See Marks and Hooghe (n 18 above) 797, 802, Pelkmans (n 38 above) 101, and van den Bergh (n 18 above) 161.

[72] E. Kitch, 'Business Organisation Law: State or Federal? An Inquiry into the Allocation of Political Competence in relation to Issues of Business Organisation Law in a Federal System' in R.M. Buxbaum, G. Hertig, A. Hirsch and K.J. Hopt (eds), *European Business Law. Legal and Economic Analyses on Integration and Harmonization* (Berlin 1991) 41, and Sun and Pelkmans (n 27 above) 86–87.

[73] See also R. Baldwin and M. Cave, *Understanding Regulation. Theory, Strategy, and Practice* (Oxford 1999) 185 according to whom 'regulatory competition and harmonizing measures should not be seen as direct alternatives but as modes of influence that can be used in harness so as to limit their individual weaknesses'.

[74] On other problems with regulatory competition see eg Sun and Pelkmans (n 27 above) 83–86, and Woolcock (n 30 above) 18–21.

[75] See, for example, Charny (n 46 above) 435–455 on company law, van den Bergh (n 24 above) 132–151 on private law, van den Bergh (n 18 above) 149–174 on competition law, and, critically, Barnard (n 47 above) 66–78 on social policy. See also an interesting distinction between 'facilitative' and 'interventionist' law made by Ogus, 'Competition beteen National Legal Systems: A Contribution of Economic Analysis to Comparative Law' (1999) 48 ICLQ 405, 410–418.

legal orders seems in many situations to be a superior instrument for managing the internal market.[76]

However, it has to be accepted that in actual practice optimal results may not be reached. Various political considerations may lead to a system that does not correspond to the prescriptions of economists. In particular, free movement may create hostility among business in countries where regulatory standards are high if firms feel that they are subject to unfair competition. This may cause governments to try to set up protectionist barriers to shelter domestic companies, removing the essential prerequisite of regulatory competition. Hence, harmonisation may in some instances be necessary to avoid a political backlash against the Community.[77]

On the other hand, extensive harmonisation by the Community may lead to fears concerning national sovereignty in the Member States. In recent years the expanding scope of Community law has created both political controversy and constitutional problems in various Member States.[78]

e) Implications for integration

The advantages of decentralisation have implications for both positive and negative integration, for both the Community legislature[79] and judicature. In the context of the scope of the free movement provisions, the Court should be careful not to extend their reach too far and should not embark on a project of wholesale negative harmonisation.[80] Instead, it should concentrate on national measures that prevent competition between legal orders by either sheltering the domestic industry from competitive pressures, thus removing the reason for arbitrage, or by preventing factors of production from relocating, thus removing the possibility of arbitrage. In the case of the free movement of goods and services, the Court should, therefore, guarantee that products from other Member States are able to compete on truly equal terms with domestic products and to maintain their competitive advantage. It

---

[76] This may be especially true when taking into account the risks of institutional malfunctions inherent in the Community political process. See Poiares Maduro (n 9 above) 113–126, who speaks of 'horizontal minoritarian bias' and 'vertical majoritarian bias', ie capture by supranational interest groups and over-representation of the majority or most powerful states. It has to be noted, however, that the Community political system is not static. The increasing power of the European Parliament will alter the picture, perhaps reducing the risk of malfunction by representing diverse interests and by being independent of Member States.

[77] Kitch (n 72 above) 40–41, and Weatherill and Beaumont (n 17 above) 700–701. See L. Siedentop, *Democracy in Europe* (London 2000) 25–27 on various 'political' advantages of federalism.

[78] See section 5aiii below.

[79] The Community legislator ought to concentrate on major trans-national externalities and transaction costs.

[80] It should also be noted that the Court should not change its approach to reverse discrimination. It is a crucial part of the decentralised system.

should go no further, as it may contribute to inefficient centralisation and diminish the possibilities of beneficial competition between regulators.[81]

It is clear that a test based on a narrow concept of discrimination is not sufficient. A mere national treatment does not always create truly equal terms for competition and allow the maintenance of competitive advantage. It is equally clear that a test bringing all Member State measures under the free movement provisions is too wide. National measures not compromising regulatory competition itself should be respected and left to compete with each other.

I will, therefore, advocate throughout this chapter a reading based on a very wide concept of discrimination. It encompasses situations where a Member State applies its rules to circumstances which have already been subject to the regulatory system of another Member State. Thus, a double regulatory burden is considered discriminatory. In my view, there is no significant difference between a national measure that treats similar situations differently, such as an imaginary French statute restricting advertising of whisky but not of cognac, and a national measure that treats different situations in a similar manner, such as the application of national composition requirements even though foreign products have already complied with the rules of the exporting Member State. In both situations there is discrimination. The national decision-making machinery has failed, in the second scenario by omitting to take into account the legal system of the other Member States and, therefore, the objectively different situations of domestic and imported goods and services. From the point of view of foreign interests both scenarios are similar: the disadvantage they suffer is no less in the second situation.[82]

The Court will also have to be aware that regulatory competition takes place in different ways for different rules. As regards *product requirements*, the competition[83] takes place through buying decisions of consumers. The competition between rules regulating *market circumstances* happens mainly through the movement of consumers. If they do not like the rules, they select another jurisdiction.[84] The competition in *production rules* (for example, labour law and environmental law) is effected mostly through the movement of producers. If the rules are inefficient, products will be expensive or of poor

---

[81] This consideration is of paramount importance in assessing the case law of the Court on the free movement of goods prior to Joined Cases C-267/91 and C-268/91 *Criminal Proceedings Against Keck and Mithouard* [1993] ECR I-6097 and the case law on services after it. See sections 4 and 5 below.

[82] On the reasons for this approach see further Snell, '*De Agostini* and the Regulation of Television Broadcasting' (1997) 8 EBLR 222, 226.

[83] Or rather, the competition in the economic market, since competition is also happening in the political market. In the interest of clarity, only the economic market is covered here. See further Poiares Maduro (n 9 above) 140.

[84] This competition usually takes place when a person is moving to an area and searches, according to his preferences, for a locality which is 'lively and exciting', 'family-friendly', or 'peaceful and idyllic'. The character of a locality is strongly influenced by decisions on zoning, licensing, opening hours etc.

quality and the consumers will not buy them. To survive, the producers will have to migrate by investing in facilities in other jurisdictions with more favourable regulation. For competition to take place, the freedom of these movements must be guaranteed *and* all national rules not genuinely endangering them must be respected.

In general, for regulatory competition to be maintained, the importing host country should not be required to mutually recognise the exporting home country's rules concerning market circumstances and the exporting home country should not be forced to mutually recognise the importing host country's production rules. Mutual recognition would lead to the destruction of beneficial diversity diminishing the number of choices available to citizens and undertakings, rules on market circumstances and production could not in many cases be applied only to domestic situations, and mere mutual recognition might not be enough to remove the 'barrier', especially if understood in the wide *Dassonville*[85] sense as anything potentially diminishing the volume of trade.

An example will clarify the situation. A consumer can select whether to buy a good conforming with domestic product rules, or a good conforming with the product rules of another Member State. He votes with his purse.

A consumer can select whether to be the target of roadside billboard advertising by selecting a jurisdiction whose rules correspond to his preferences.[86] He can vote with his feet. However, if rules concerning market circumstances were subject to mutual recognition, this would not be an option.[87] If local rules prohibiting certain sales methods could not be applied to products from other Member States, there would be no jurisdictions where, for example, roadside billboard advertising would be absolutely prohibited.[88] The competition would not take place.

Moreover, it would often be technically impossible to restrict rules regulating selling arrangements to domestic situations, and in some situations the 'obstacle' diminishing the volume of imports could only be removed by rendering national rules regulating market circumstances totally inapplicable. For example, allowing Sunday trading in products of other Member States would not be enough even if it was technically feasible. Shops could argue that their turnover from those products alone would not be sufficient to justify opening on Sundays and, therefore, the volume of imports would still be diminished. Thus, mutual recognition of home country rules concerning market circumstances by the host country would not lead to a proper competition between regulations.

[85] Case 8/74 *Procureur du Roi v Dassonville* [1974] ECR 837.
[86] Unfortunately, Community law does not (yet) guarantee the right of free movement to all citizens of the EU.
[87] Unless of course the Court has decided that the failure to mutually recognise is justified.
[88] Not only the Member States but also smaller units such as regions and municipalities would be unable to ban such activities. See eg Case C-67/97 *Criminal Proceedings Against Ditlev Bluhme* [1998] ECR I-8033 para 20.

Similarly, a consumer can select a jurisdiction which guarantees a clean environment through stringent production regulations.[89] The same is true for a producer who uses the clean environment as an input, as a method of attracting a high quality workforce, or as an element of a sales promotion strategy. If undertakings producing export goods were exempt from these production rules, there would be no jurisdiction where, for example, clean air could be guaranteed.

Furthermore, again it might be impossible in practice to apply domestic production rules only to export goods, and the producers would still be unable to achieve full economies of scale as they would have to divide their production lines. In most cases, mutual recognition of host country production rules by the home country would not lead to a proper competition between regulations.[90]

Based on this, the law of free movement ought to concentrate in allocating regulatory competences between different states. The host state should control rules concerning market circumstances and the home state the product and production rules. In each situation there should be one, and only one, jurisdiction with the power to regulate freely, as long as it is not discriminating.

f) Conclusion

The argument in this section has run as follows: Different interpretations of the free movement rules result in different vertical divisions of power between the Community and Member States. A wide economic freedom reading produces a centralised unitary system while a narrower one contributes to a decentralised federal system. For the Community, a fairly decentralised approach enabling regulatory competition is preferable. Therefore, the Court ought to adopt a relatively narrow reading of Articles 28 and 49 (ex 30 and 59) EC. The approach based on a wide concept of discrimination is best capable of dealing with obstacles while at the same time respecting Member State competences.

[89] For example, a consumer may move to a locality where planning permits are not easily granted for polluting activities or where good public transport and traffic arrangements ensure that emissions from motor vehicles are limited. Another way of selecting is eg by purchasing agricultural products coming from an area known for its clean environment. The model of course requires that the consumer has sufficient information.

[90] The analysis presented above corresponds to Professor Koenig's recent call for a new research agenda. He writes: 'Interjurisdictional competition between Member States must in future be incorporated in the formulation of European integration rules and principles . . . Even axiomatic rules and principles of the single market which have been never questioned must be fundamentally re-examined. The objective of research is to develop "model rules" which on the one hand create coherence between the dual-level competition between member States' jurisdictions and the competition between companies'. See C. Koenig, 'Some Brief Remarks on Interjurisdictional Competition between EU Member States' (1999) 10 EBLR 437 at 437.

In the following sections the case law of the Court on the scope of Articles 28 and 49 (ex 30 and 59) EC will be analysed in the light of this argument. It has to be stated from the very outset that it is not claimed that the Court's entire jurisprudence can be explained by a notion of discrimination. Rather, it can be employed to criticise the Court when it has over-extended the reach of the freedoms.

2. Early developments

a) Goods

Article 28 (ex 30) EC prohibits quantitative restrictions and measures having an equivalent effect. Quantitative restrictions have been interpreted by the Court to include 'measures which amount to a total or partial restraint of, according to the circumstances, imports, exports or goods in transit'.[91] A total ban is considered to be a quota of zero.[92]

Quantitative restrictions are at least as harmful to the general welfare as customs duties.[93] They have never created a major problem for the Community, however. Quotas were for the most part abolished already in the 1950s by virtue of international treaties.[94] Furthermore, they are usually relatively easy to detect and police.

A more difficult problem has been the definition and abolition of measures having an equivalent effect to quantitative restrictions. The Commission interpreted the notion in Directive 70/50.[95] In its view, Member States were required to abolish two types of measures. Article 2 of the Directive prohibits distinctly applicable measures hindering imports and gives a long, non-exhaustive list of examples of such measures. Article 3 forbids equally applicable measures governing the marketing of products if their restrictive effects on the free movement of goods exceed the effects intrinsic to trade rules. In particular, the provision bans product rules, that is rules dealing with shape, size, weight, composition, presentation, identification or putting up of products, whose restrictive effects are disproportionate to their purpose or whose objectives could be achieved by means less restrictive of trade.

---

[91] Case 2/73 *Geddo v Ente Nazionale Risi* [1973] ECR 865 para 7.

[92] Case 34/79 *R v Henn and Darby* [1979] ECR 3795.

[93] In some respects quotas are even more detrimental than customs duties. Quotas deliver windfall profits to some enterprises while customs duties benefit the public purse. In addition, quotas are not as transparent as tariffs. In the GATT, quotas have been totally prohibited while tariffs are allowed. See J.H. Jackson, W.J. Davey and A.O. Sykes Jr, *Legal Problems of International Economic Relations. Cases, Materials and Text on the National and International Regulation of Transnational Economic Relations* (3rd edn St.Paul Minn 1995) 377.

[94] Weatherill and Beaumont (n 17 above) 501.

[95] Commission Directive 70/50/EEC of 22 December 1969 based on the provisions of Art 33(7) (repealed), on the abolition of measures which have an effect equivalent to quantitative restrictions on imports and are not covered by other provisions adopted in pursuance of the EEC Treaty [1970] OJ Spec Ed I L13/29, 17.

The Directive has offered a useful guideline to the type of measures falling foul of Article 28 (ex 30) EC. In particular, the distinction between distinctly and equally applicable measures has been an important tool in developing the interpretation of Article 28 (ex 30) EC. Similarly, the principle that disproportionate product rules contravene Article 28 (ex 30) EC even when they are indistinctly applicable has been a significant aspect of the case law concerning measures having an equivalent effect. However, it is the Court, not the Commission, which has played the decisive role in developing Article 28 (ex 30) EC.

The seminal case where the Court defined the notion of a measure having an equivalent effect to a quantitative restriction was *Dassonville*.[96] The case concerned Scotch whisky imported from France to Belgium in 1970, prior to the British accession. Belgian law required a certificate of authenticity issued by British customs authorities. France did not demand such a certificate. Even though somebody importing whisky directly from Britain could easily get the necessary documentation, it was difficult to obtain the certificate for imports from a third country.

The Court ruled that the Belgian law constituted a prohibited measure having an equivalent effect to a quantitative restriction. Only direct importers were able to comply with the rules without significant problems. The measure created a serious impediment to the movement of whisky which had been placed in free circulation in the Community.

The result itself was not remarkable. The importance of the case lies in the language employed by the Court. In a far-reaching statement the Court held that '[a]ll trading rules enacted by Member States which are capable of hindering, directly or indirectly, actually or potentially, intra-Community trade are to be considered as measures having an effect equivalent to quantitative restrictions'. The Court did not seem to place any importance whatsoever on the discriminatory or non-discriminatory nature of the rules. The only thing it was concerned about was the effect of the measures on trade between Member States. The language was fully in line with the economic freedom model.

The *Dassonville* formula can be interpreted extremely widely. Any trading rule that is potentially capable of hindering inter-state trade even indirectly could be said to fall under Article 28 (ex 30) EC, although in fact the rule would not have any effect in the actual case.[97] Furthermore, it became clear in subsequent cases that Article 28 (ex 30) was not restricted to trading rules but covered all state measures.[98]

[96] Case 8/74 *Procureur du Roi v Dassonville* [1974] ECR 837.

[97] See eg Joined Cases C-321/94, C-322/94, C-323/94 and C-324/94 *Criminal Proceedings Against Jacques Pistre* [1997] ECR I-2434. However, the *Dassonville* formula does not quite catch each and every national rule. Some measures are too uncertain and indirect in their effect to constitute even potential obstacles. See eg Case C-69/88 *H. Krantz GmbH & Co v Ontvanger der Directe Belastingen et al* [1990] ECR I-583.

[98] See eg Case 4/75 *Rewe-Zentralfinanz GmbH v Landwirtschaftskammer* [1975] ECR 843.

The wording used by the Court is strongly reminiscent of judgments dealing with competition law. The requirement that agreements, decisions and practices covered by Article 81 (ex 85) EC must be able to affect trade between Member States has been interpreted very extensively by the Court.[99] It is submitted that in general inspiration should not be drawn from this jurisprudence, however. As the Court itself has recognised,[100] the requirement of an effect on trade in Article 81 (ex 85) is a jurisdictional criterion establishing the competence of the Community to deal with the issue. The crucial substantive test is whether competition is restricted. In the case of Article 28 (ex 30) EC the *Dassonville* formula constitutes an important part of the substantive test of the illegality of national measures. It establishes which Member State measures constitute prima facie infringements of Article 28 (ex 30) and have to be justified.

The Court itself did indicate, however, that some reasonable rules falling prima facie under the *Dassonville* formula might escape Article 28 (ex 30).[101] Furthermore, the formula still left some scope for interpretation. In particular, the requirement that the Member State measure had to be capable of *hindering* intra-Community trade could be read widely and be used to restrict the scope of Article 28 (ex 30) EC.[102]

During the early period the Court also took a decisive step away from intergovernmentalism in this field and found that Articles 28 (ex 30) and 29 (ex 34) EC were directly effective.[103] They created rights that private individuals could enforce in national courts.

b) Services

Unlike Article 28 (ex 30) on goods, EC Treaty provisions relating to the free movement of services make a special reference to the idea of non-discrimination. Article 50(3) (ex 60(3)) EC gives a person providing a service in a host country the right to 'temporarily pursue his activity. . . under the same conditions as are imposed by the State on its own nationals'.

It is clear, however, that the free movement of services extends beyond a simple prohibition of overt discrimination. Article 49 (ex 59) EC requires Member States to abolish all *restrictions* on the freedom to provide services. According to Article 54 (ex 65), even before that stage has been reached, 'each

---

[99] See eg Joined Cases 56/64 and 58/64 *Etablissements Consten SA and Grundig-Verkaufs-GmbH v Commission* [1966] ECR 299 para 28.
[100] ibid, para 27. See also D.G. Goyder, *EC Competition Law* (3rd edn Oxford 1998) 107–116.
[101] See n 96 above, para 6.
[102] See J. Steiner, 'Drawing the Line: Uses and Abuses of Article 30 EEC' (1992) 29 CMLRev 749 at 768–771.
[103] Case 74/76 *Iannelli & Volpi S.p.A. v Ditta Paolo Meroni* [1977] ECR 557 and Case 83/78 *Pigs Marketing Board v Raymond Redmond* [1978] ECR 2347. Already in 1968 it had held that the standstill provisions in Art 31 EC (repealed) and the first paragraph of Art 32 EC (repealed) were directly effective.

Member State shall apply such restrictions without distinction on grounds of nationality or residence'. This shows that restrictions that need to be abolished under Article 49 (ex 59) EC are something more than simple discrimination on grounds of nationality or residence.

One way of reconciling Article 50(3) (ex 60(3)) EC, which only requires national treatment, with Articles 49 (ex 59) and 54 (ex 65) EC would be by making a distinction between the different ways in which services may be provided. Thus, it could be argued that when the provision of services involves movement of persons, Member States are only required to observe the principle of national treatment. However, when services are provided through telecommunications, by post etc, without movement of persons, Member States would be under a further-reaching obligation not to hinder the movement of services.[104]

An early interpretation of the scope of Articles 49 (ex 59) and 50(3) (ex 60(3)) EC can be found in the General Programme on Services[105] dating from 1961. In that respect it can be compared with Directive 70/50 dealing with the free movement of goods. The General Programme was based on Article 63(1) EC (repealed), which required a proposal from the Commission and unanimity in the Council. Article 63(2) (now 52(1)) EC envisaged the adoption of directives to implement the General Programme. The General Programme could be used as a guidance in interpreting the provisions on the free movement of services but it did not bind the European Court of Justice.[106]

Title III of the General Programme deals with the removal of restrictions on the free movement of services. It sets out a list of distinctly applicable national measures that are considered to be restrictions and are to be eliminated. This corresponds to Article 2 of Directive 70/50.

In addition, and more importantly, the General Programme states that even equally applicable national requirements are to be 'regarded as restrictions, where . . . their effect is exclusively or principally to hinder the provision of services by foreign nationals'. This can be contrasted with Article 3 of Directive 70/50. The General Programme on Services condemns national measures whose main effect is to hinder foreigners. The Directive also condemns national measures whose effects on the free movement of goods exceed the normal, unavoidable effects of trade rules. From this it might be concluded that the reach of Article 49 (ex 59) EC is narrower than the reach of Article 28 (ex 30) EC as the former seems to be concerned only with discrimination against foreigners while the latter seems to be about excessive effects of national rules. It could be argued that the free movement of goods was concerned with economic freedom, while the provisions on services targeted only protectionism.

---

[104] See section 3b below.   [105] [1974] OJ Spec Ed 2nd series IX 3.
[106] See also F. Burrows, *Free Movement in European Community Law* (Oxford 1987) 221 and 188–189.

However, Article 3 of Directive 70/50 lists a number of national measures that 'in particular' may be caught by Article 28 (ex 30) EC in case their impact on the free movement of goods is excessive. These measures can be classified as product rules as they are intrinsically linked to the goods themselves. They prevent goods produced according to the home state specifications from entering the markets of another Member State without modifications. Therefore, they are inherently detrimental to foreigners. Thus, the difference between the General Programme and Directive 70/50 may be more perceived than real.

The European Court of Justice is the institution that has played the decisive role in developing the interpretation of the free movement of services, however. *Van Binsbergen*[107] was the first case in which the Court considered the scope of the freedom. The case was decided in 1974, a few months after *Dassonville*.

Mr van Binsbergen had authorised a Dutch legal adviser, Mr Kortmann, to represent him in a Dutch social security court. During the course of the proceedings Mr Kortmann changed his habitual residence from the Netherlands to Belgium. According to Dutch procedural law this made him ineligible to continue to act in the case. The question arose whether this was a restriction on his freedom to provide services.

The Court held that a Member State cannot lawfully 'by imposing a requirement as to habitual residence within that State, deny persons established in another Member State the right to provide services, where the provision of services is not subject to any special condition under the national law applicable'.[108]

The result itself was not remarkable. The requirement of habitual residence amounts at least to material discrimination, as nationals of other Member States tend not to be resident in the country imposing the restriction. Furthermore, a person residing in one Member State is often also professionally established there.[109] Therefore, the requirement of habitual residence in the Member State where the service is provided is likely to negate the whole free movement of services. A person would not be allowed to provide services from a different country of establishment. Cross-border movement of services would be impossible.

In contrast to its judgment in *Dassonville*, the Court adopted a rather more conservative stance to the directly effective scope of Articles 49 (ex 59) and 50 (ex 60) EC.[110] It merely stated that discrimination on grounds of nationality or place of establishment is to be abolished by virtue of Article 49 (ex 59) EC. In particular, the requirements imposed on the service provider because of his

---

[107] Case 33/74 *Van Binsbergen v Bestuur van de Bedrijfsvereniging voor de Metaalnijverheid* [1974] ECR 1299.
[108] ibid, para 17. [109] Burrows (n 106 above) 219.
[110] Admittedly, para 10 of the judgment does contain a hint of a wider reading.

nationality or habitual residence, which obstruct his activities, contravene the free movement of services.[111]

Despite the narrow view of the free movement of services adopted in the judgment, the Court held that some Member State measures, which prima facie fall under Article 49 (ex 59) and 50 (ex 60) EC, can nevertheless be justified. This would be the case as regards measures that apply to any person established in the Member State and have as their purpose the application of professional rules justified by the general good. Accordingly, the Court went on to examine whether the Dutch measure in question could be justified by the need to ensure observance of professional rules of conduct.[112] This balancing test introduced by the Court plays a similar role as the rule of reason introduced in *Dassonville*.[113]

The Court narrowed the scope of Articles 49 (ex 59) and 50 (ex 60) EC even further. It held that in situations where a person providing services is directing his activity principally towards one Member State in order to avoid the professional rules of conduct, the host state is allowed to control his activities as if he would be established in the host state.[114] *Dassonville* did not contain a similar statement.[115]

Altogether, it seems that the Court's approach to the free movement of goods and services was somewhat different in these cases. Although neither decision as such went very far, the language used by the Court in *Dassonville* could be interpreted expansively and could be seen as containing a purely effects-based economic freedom test, while *van Binsbergen* seemed to place the main emphasis on the existence of discrimination and can be connected to anti-protectionism.

Van Binsbergen was also the case where the Court decided that Article 49 (ex 59) EC had direct effect. Thus, it marked a step towards supranationalism in the field of the free movement of services. The obligations of Member States were also directed towards private parties, who could enforce their rights in national courts.

---

[111] See n 107 above, para 25.   [112] ibid, paras 10, 12 and 14–16.

[113] Case 8/74 *Procureur du Roi v Dassonville* [1974] ECR 837 para 6. See Chapter 4 section 3 below.

[114] See n 107 above, para 13.

[115] However in Case 120/78 *Rewe Zentrale AG v Bundesmonopolverwaltung für Branntwein* [1979] ECR 649 para 14 the Court held that goods lawfully produced and marketed in one of the Member States should in principle be granted access to the markets of the other Member States. Thus it is possible to argue, *e contrario*, that goods which have not been lawfully marketed in the home state do not have an automatic right to market access. This would be a sensible interpretation as it would ensure that goods do not escape all regulation and would bring the free movement of goods and services closer to each other. See also Case 229/83 *Leclerc and others v 'Au Blé Vert' and others* [1985] ECR 1 para 27.

3. Disparity between national rules

a) Goods

In *Cassis de Dijon*[116] the *Dassonville* formula was used to tackle a measure that applied equally to both domestic products and to goods originating from other Member States. The European Court of Justice showed that the statement in *Dassonville* establishing an effects-based test of compliance with Article 28 (ex 30) EC would actually be used to assess national measures.

Cassis de Dijon concerned a German rule setting a minimum alcohol content for fruit liqueurs. French 'Cassis de Dijon' liqueur did not meet this requirement and therefore its marketing was prohibited by the German authorities. The Court held that the German rule was a measure having an effect equivalent to quantitative restriction within the meaning of Article 28 (ex 30) EC.

Cassis was the Court's answer to the problem of disparity between national rules, which constituted a serious obstacle to the creation of the common market. A product manufactured and marketed in one Member State in accordance with its legal requirements was prevented from entering the market of another Member State because it did not correspond to the requirements of the latter. In these situations both national rules might be totally reasonable and non-discriminatory in themselves. However, the *application* of the rules of the importing state, because of the disparity between the rules of different Member States, forms an obstacle to trade. A product has to comply with two sets of rules. A double burden is created.[117]

The *use* of the rules of the importing state is materially discriminatory. Products from other Member States, which have to comply with two sets of rules, are put at a disadvantage when compared with domestic products, which only have to comply with a single set of rules. Two different situations are treated similarly.[118] The importing state applies its rules both to products that have already adhered to one set of regulations and to products that have not.

The Court solved the problem caused by the disparity between national rules by using the *Dassonville* formula to create a principle of mutual recognition. The Court stated that '[t]here is . . . no valid reason why, provided that they have been lawfully produced and marketed in one of the Member States, alcoholic beverages should not be introduced into any other Member State'.[119] The Court created a presumption that a product lawfully produced

---

[116] Case 120/78 *Rewe Zentrale AG v Bundesmonopolverwaltung für Branntwein* [1979] ECR 649.
[117] Weatherill and Beaumont (n 17 above) 565–567.
[118] This was prohibited in Case 13/63 *Commission v Italy* [1963] ECR 165. See also A.M. Arnull, A.A. Dashwood, M.G. Ross and D.A. Wyatt, *Wyatt and Dashwood's European Union Law* (4th edn London 2000) 329–330.
[119] See n 116 above, para 14.

and marketed[120] in a Member State has to be admitted to the markets of all other Member States.[121]

The Court qualified its approach, however. Building upon *Dassonville*,[122] it created a category of mandatory requirements that could be used to justify a national measure falling prima facie under Article 28 (ex 30) EC.[123]

Cassis de Dijon was followed by a long series of cases in which indistinctly applicable national measures creating a double burden on imports were challenged.[124] The decision also formed a basis for an important reevaluation of the harmonisation strategy of the Community.[125]

b) Services

In the field of services the development of the case law was slower than in the field of goods. The Court early on used similar principles as in *Cassis* but the language of the cases referred, until the early 1990s, to a narrowly-construed concept of discrimination.

Just four months before the ruling in *Cassis* the European Court of Justice had given the judgment in *Koestler*.[126] Mr Koestler, a German national residing in France, had instructed a French bank to carry out certain transactions based on price differences between transferable securities in the Paris stock exchange. The operations were not profitable but when the bank tried to recover from Mr Koestler, who meanwhile had moved his residence to Germany, the bank's claims were rejected by a German court, as the debts were considered to be non-actionable gambling losses. An appeal court referred a question to the Court asking whether the relevant German rules were in accordance with the EC Treaty provisions on the free movement of services.

The Court, following Advocate General Reischl, decided that the German law was not in conflict with Articles 49 (ex 59) and 50 (ex 60) EC. Referring to the General Programme for the abolition of restrictions on freedom to provide services, it held that the third paragraph of Article 50 (ex 60) EC only requires a Member State to give foreign service providers the same treatment as its own nationals.[127] It stated that:

[120] As Art 28 (ex 30) EC covers even potential restrictions, it is not necessary that the product in question has actually been marketed in the Member State as long as it could have been lawfully marketed there: J.P.H. Donner, 'Articles 30–36 EEC in General' (1982) 5 SEW 362 at 363.

[121] P. Craig and G. de Búrca, *EU Law. Text, Cases, and Materials* (2nd edn Oxford 1998) 607, and Weatherill and Beaumont (n 17 above) 569–570.

[122] Case 8/74 *Procureur du Roi v Dassonville* [1974] ECR 837 para 6.

[123] See n 116 above, para 8. See Chapter 4 section 3 below.

[124] See, eg, Case 788/79 *Italian State v Gilli and Andres* [1980] ECR 2071, Case 261/81 *Walter Rau Lebensmittelwerke v de Smedt Pvba* [1982] ECR 3961, and Case 178/84 *Commission v Germany* (Reinheitsgebot) [1987] ECR 1227.

[125] See eg European Commission White Paper, *Completing the Internal Market* (Milan, 28–29 June 1985, COM(85) 310 final, Brussels, 14 June 1985) para 77.

[126] Case 15/78 *Société Générale Alsacienne de Banque v Koestler* [1978] ECR 1971.

[127] ibid, para 4.

the Treaty, whilst it prohibits discrimination, does not impose any obligation to treat a foreigner providing services more favourably, with reference to his domestic law, than a person providing services established in the Member State where the services have been provided.[128]

The Court's ruling was based on a narrow concept of discrimination and was clearly very different from its approach in *Cassis*.[129] As the German law was not discriminatory in the narrow sense, it could be applied to the French undertaking. Service providers from other Member States were not to be treated more favourably than the domestic ones. In *Cassis*, on the other hand, the Court took into account the whole situation, which led to material discrimination, and held that certain indistinctly applicable national measures could not be applied to foreign goods.

Three months later, one month before the decision in *Cassis*, the Court changed its tack somewhat. *Van Wesemael*[130] concerned Belgian rules requiring fee-charging employment agencies for entertainers to hold licences issued by the minister responsible for employment. The defendants in the case were prosecuted for using or providing the services of employment agents without Belgian licences, although the agents held corresponding French licences.

The Court, following Advocate General Warner, found for the defendants. It held that Belgium was not allowed to require French employment agencies to obtain Belgian licences when they already held comparable French licences and were supervised by the French authorities.

The approach of the Court was fairly similar to the one later adopted in *Cassis*.[131] The application of Belgian rules to service providers who had already complied with French rules created a dual burden. Even though the Belgian Arrêté Royal was not discriminatory as such, its application to service providers licensed in France was, and could not be justified.[132]

It seems that the Court did not go as far as in *Cassis*, though. First of all, the licensing rules were quite similar in both countries, especially as both were based on ILO Convention No 96 concerning fee charging employment agencies. It was clear that the service providers had to fulfil the *same* requirements twice. In the *Cassis* jurisprudence the home and host country regulations did not have to be similar for the home country rule to be considered a prima facie restriction on the free movement of goods.[133] Therefore, it could be argued

---

[128] ibid, para 5.

[129] See E. Steindorff, 'Freedom of Services in the EEC' (1987–1988) 11 Fordham Int LJ 347 at 378 and 384.

[130] Joined Cases 110 and 111/78 *Ministère Public and Chambre Syndicale des Agents Artistiques et Impresarii de Belgique, A.S.B.L. v Willy van Wesemael and others* [1979] ECR 35.

[131] See P. Watson, 'Freedom of Establishment and Freedom to Provide Services: Some Recent Developments' (1983) 20 CMLRev 767 at 824.

[132] The Court also refined the justifications it had developed in Case 33/74 *Van Binsbergen v Bestuur van de Bedrijfsvereniging voor de Metaalnijverheid* [1974] ECR 1299. See Chapter 4 section 3 below.

[133] Donner (n 120 above) 362–364, and Gormley, *Prohibiting Restrictions on Trade within the EEC* (Amsterdam 1985) 47–48.

that *Van Wesemael* reflected only a relatively narrow anti-discrimination principle.

Secondly, the language employed by the Court in *Van Wesemael* was more conservative than the language used in *Cassis*. In the former judgment the Court stated that 'the essential requirements of Article 59 [now 49]', which are 'directly and unconditionally applicable', abolish *discrimination* against service providers for the reason of nationality or place of establishment.[134] Thus, it brought the notion of discrimination into play, a concept that has generally been narrowly interpreted by the Court as not including material discrimination resulting from the disparity between national rules.[135] In contrast, the *Cassis de Dijon* judgment did not refer to discrimination at all.

The decisions of the Court on the free movement of services adopted soon after *Cassis* did not change the general approach taken in *Van Wesemael*. This can best be seen in the judgment in *Webb*.[136] In that case, a British company had provided manpower to Dutch undertakings. The relevant Dutch legislation prohibited the provision of manpower without authorisation, and the manager of the company, Mr Webb, was prosecuted. The company held a UK licence for the activity, however. The question arose whether the Dutch Royal Decree was in accordance with Articles 49 (ex 59) and 50 (ex 60) EC.

The Court followed the approach taken by Advocate General Slynn. It stated that the provision of manpower amounted to services within the meaning of Article 50 (ex 60) EC.[137] It further held that a Member State was allowed to require the agencies providing manpower established in other Member States to obtain licences issued by the host state. However, the host state measures had to be indistinctly applicable and had to take into account the evidence and guarantees already produced by the applicant in the country of establishment.[138]

Webb was a confirmation and a refinement of *Van Wesemael*. It confirmed the basic approach, but refined it slightly by imposing an explicit obligation on national authorities to have regard to the evidence and guarantees furnished in the Member State of establishment.[139] Furthermore, it tackled an argument presented by the Danish and German governments that Article 50(3) (ex 60(3)) EC only requires the application of the same national measures to both domestic and foreign service providers. The Court dismissed this argument by stating that national legislation applicable to the permanent activities of undertakings cannot be applied in its entirety to, by definition,

---

[134] See n 130 above, paras 26–27.

[135] W.-H. Roth, 'Case C-76/90 *Manfred Säger v Dennemeyer & Co. Ltd.*, Judgment of 25 July 1991 (not yet reported)' (1993) 30 CMLRev 145 at 151–152. See also P.J.G. Kapteyn and P. VerLoren van Themaat, *Introduction to Law of the European Communities. From Maastricht to Amsterdam* (3rd edn by L.W. Gormley London 1998) 171, and G. Marenco, 'Pour une interprétation traditionelle de la notion de mesure d'effet équivalent à une restriction quantitative' (1984) 19 CDE 291, 320.

[136] Case 279/80 *Criminal Proceedings Against Alfred John Webb* [1981] ECR 3305.

[137] ibid, para 11.   [138] ibid, para 21.   [139] See ibid, para 20.

temporary activities of service providers established in other Member States.[140] These refinements did not imply that the case law on services had moved closer to the case law on goods, however.

A further example of the Court's approach is *Commission v Germany* (Insurance).[141] The case was one in a series of legal challenges initiated by the Commission to test the compatibility of national insurance rules with the Treaty. In issue was German legislation that required, among other things, undertakings providing certain types of direct insurance in Germany to be authorised and established there. The same requirements applied to leading insurers in Community co-insurance operations if the risks were situated in Germany. The Commission argued that the national rules were in breach of Articles 49 (ex 59) and 50 (ex 60) EC.

The Court held, partly disagreeing with Advocate General Slynn, that the authorisation requirement was legal in the case of direct insurance[142] but that the establishment requirement was not.[143] As regards leading insurers in connection with Community co-insurance, both the authorisation and the establishment requirements breached the provisions on the free movement of services.[144]

Once again the problems were created by the disparity between national rules. An insurance undertaking authorised and established in another Member State could not do business in Germany without complying with additional rules. A dual burden was created and, therefore, the application of national rules amounted to material discrimination. Once again the Court begun by examining whether the German authorisation and establishment requirements constituted prima facie restrictions on the free movement of services.[145] After deciding that this was the case, the Court went on to investigate the justification for the national measures and concluded that the authorisation requirement was justified in the case of direct insurance while the other requirements were not.

The language used by the Court in *Commission v Germany* was slightly different from the language used in the previous judgments on the free movement of services. The Court stated that:

[Articles 49 (ex 59) and 50 (ex 60)] require the removal not only of all discrimination against the provider of service on the grounds of his nationality but also all restrictions on his freedom to provide services imposed by reason of the fact that he is established in a Member State other than that in which the service is to be provided.[146]

It must be stated that the requirements in question in these proceedings, namely that an insurer who is established in another Member State, authorized by the supervisory authority of that State and subject to the supervision of that authority, must have permanent establishment within the territory of that State, constitute restrictions on the freedom to provide services inasmuch as they increase the cost of such services in the

---

[140] ibid, para 16. [141] Case 205/84 *Commission v Germany* [1986] ECR 3755.
[142] ibid, para 51. [143] ibid, para 57. [144] ibid, para 68. [145] ibid, para 28.
[146] ibid, para 25.

State in which they are provided, in particular where the insurer conducts business in that State only occasionally.[147]

This could not be read as a great widening of the ambit of the free movement of services, however. It did not yet open 'the door for inclusion into the restrictions within the meaning of Article 59 [now 49] of all State measures influencing the costs of the provider'.[148] It did not even bring the language used by the Court in the context of services fully into line with the language of *Cassis*.

The language of the Court still only targeted discrimination. Even though the Court used the word 'restrictions', it continued that they must be imposed by reason of the fact that the service provider is established in another Member State. Restrictions imposed for this reason are still connected to the idea of discrimination.

The Court did not target all measures raising costs either. It referred to insurers who are authorised and established in another Member State, and to occasional activities. Requirements of authorisation and establishment in the host state mean that the insurer has to pay the costs associated with them twice. The costs also hit the service provider disproportionately. The service providers are, by definition, only pursuing their activities temporarily. The establishment and authorisation costs will heavily burden their revenue, which comes only from temporary activities. These costs act as a real barrier to the expansion of their activities to other Member States. By contrast, domestic insurers are conducting permanent activities. Establishment and authorisation costs usually represent a much smaller proportion of their revenues, which do not arise only from occasional business.

Full equality with the *Cassis* jurisprudence was finally achieved in cases decided on 25 July 1991.[149] Both the language of the Court and the method of deciding the cases were brought into line with *Cassis*.

Säger[150] is the clearest example of the Court's new line. Dennemeyer & Co Ltd was a British company providing patent renewal services inter alia in Germany. Mr Säger, a German patent agent, applied for an injunction to restrain the activities of Dennemeyer in Germany. His action was based on German legislation reserving the maintenance of industrial property rights to lawyers and patent agents acting in their personal capacity. The question

[147] Case 205/84 *Commission v Germany* [1986] ECR 3755, para 28.
[148] cf Steindorff (n 129 above) 382.
[149] Case C-288/89 *Collectieve Antennevoorziening Gouda* [1991] ECR I-4007, Case C-353/89 *Commission v Netherlands* [1991] ECR I-4069, and Case C-76/90 *Manfred Säger v Dennemeyer & Co. Ltd* [1991] ECR I-4221. See on *Gouda*, J.-Y. Art, 'Legislative Lacunae, The Court of Justice and Freedom to Provide Services' in D. Curtin and D. O'Keeffe (eds), *Constitutional Adjudication in European Community and National Law. Essays for the Hon. Mr. Justice T.F. O'Higgins* (Dublin 1992) 121 and 132, and J. Feenstra, 'Case C-288/89, *Stichting Collectieve Antennevoorziening Gouda and Others v Commissariaat voor de Media*, Judgment of 25 July 1991, [1991] ECR I-4007; Case C-353/89 *Commission of the European Communities v Kingdom of the Netherlands*, Judgment of 25 July 1991, [1991] ECR I-4069' (1993) 30 CMLRev 424 at 427.
[150] See n 149 above.

arose whether the German rules were in accordance with Article 49 (ex 59) EC. The Court, following Advocate General Jacobs, decided that the German legislation created a restriction to the free movement of services[151] and was not justified.[152]

The Court's language differed from the language used in previous cases. It stated in a key paragraph that:

Article 59 [now 49] of the Treaty requires not only the elimination of all discrimination against a person providing services on grounds of his nationality but also the abolition of any restriction, even if it applies without any distinction to national providers of services and to those of other Member States, when it is liable to prohibit or otherwise impede the activities of the provider of services established in another Member State where he lawfully provides similar services.[153]

While the language in previous cases always referred to the idea of discrimination, the Court in *Säger* saw discrimination only as one special case of infringement of Article 49 (ex 59) EC. Other restrictions impeding the service provider were also caught.

The language adopted is similar to the language used in *Cassis*.[154] In that judgment the Court does not speak of discrimination either but refers to '[o]bstacles'.[155] Also, the requirement that activities must have been lawful in the home country comes up in both judgments.[156]

The judgment also goes slightly further in result than the previous cases dealing with services. The German system regulating the patent renewal services in question had no equivalent in the United Kingdom. Dennemeyer did not have to fulfil *similar* requirements twice.

Also in this respect the judgment in *Säger* resembles that in *Cassis*. The Court was simply not interested in the question whether the national measures resembled each other when determining the existence of a restriction. It was enough that the activities were lawful in the country of origin.

It should be noted that, on the facts of the case, the Court did not go so far as to establish a principle that also truly non-discriminatory national rules can fall within Article 49 (ex 59) EC. There still was material discrimination. The service provider had already complied with one set of regulations, namely UK law. Because the German rules differed from the British rules, a dual burden was created. Material discrimination was still present. Dennemeyer would have to create 'a second production line' to deal with patent renewals in Germany.

---

[151] ibid, para 14.   [152] ibid, para 20.   [153] ibid, para 12.

[154] Although the Court did not go so far as to refer to the measures being capable of hindering, directly or indirectly, actually or potentially, intra-Community trade. See V. Hatzopoulos, 'Case C-275/92, Her Majesty's Customs and Excise v. Gerhart and Jörg Schindler, [1994] ECR I-1039' (1995) 32 CMLRev 841, 845.

[155] Case 120/78 *Rewe Zentrale AG v Bundesmonopolverwaltung für Branntwein* [1979] ECR 649 para 8.

[156] ibid, para 14 and see n 149 above, para 12.

Furthermore, the rules had a protectionist effect. They protected German professionals from competition from service providers in other Member States who were producing similar services using other techniques.[157]

There were some references to the idea of discrimination in the language of the Court as well. First of all, the Court required that the services had to be lawfully provided in the home state. This is connected to the idea that the activities have to be regulated by one—and only one—set of rules.[158]

Secondly, the Court stated that it was not permissible to 'make the provision of services . . . subject to compliance with all the conditions required for establishment'.[159] This can be seen as referring to the principle of equality.[160] If the temporary activities of service providers are handled in the same way as permanent activities, two different situations are treated similarly, which is one form of discrimination.

An interesting question is whether the principles used in *Säger* apply equally to situations where the provider of services moves from one Member State to another. In *Säger* the service provider did not move between Member States but the service was transmitted by post or by telecommunications.

Article 50(3) (ex 60(3)) EC stipulates that a 'person providing a service may, in order to do so, temporarily pursue his activity in the State where the service is provided, under the same conditions as are imposed by the State on its own nationals'. This would seem to indicate that when movement of persons providing services is involved, the EC Treaty only requires national treatment.

In *Säger* Advocate General Jacobs suggested that *Cassis* should be applied by analogy, particularly in situations where the provision of service does not involve physical movement.[161] However, he thought it arguable that in situations where the provider of services is required to spend a longer period of time in the host state, the demands of the EC Treaty are more limited.[162] In its judgment the Court itself makes a similar, although fairly vague, suggestion,[163] and comparable propositions have been made by some commentators.[164]

In my view, for reasons stated above in Chapter 1 section 3, the four freedoms should be interpreted in a parallel manner. Movement of persons ought not to be treated fundamentally differently from other situations. The same reasons

---

[157] G. Marenco, 'The Notion of Restriction on the Freedom of Establishment and Provision of Services in the Case-law of the Court' (1991) 11 YEL 111 at 142, and Weatherill and Beaumont (n 17 above) 686. Cf the Opinion of AG Jacobs, paras 16–19, who argued that the 'case should be approached on the basis that no discrimination . . . has taken place'.

[158] See Roth (n 136 above) 152–153.   [159] See n 149 above para 13.

[160] Marenco (n 157 above) 142.

[161] See similarly the Opinion of AG Van Gerven in Case C-159/90 *Society for the Protection of the Unborn Child v Grogan* [1991] ECR I-4685 para 20.

[162] See n 149 above paras 24–26 of the Opinion of AG Jacobs.

[163] ibid, para 13 of the judgment.

[164] See eg P.R. Nielsen, *Services and Establishment in European Community Banking Law* (Copenhagen 1994) 122–127.

apply with even more force within one freedom than between two different freedoms. A person lawfully providing a service in one Member State should prima facie be allowed to do the same in any Member State. In principle, each service provider should have to comply with only one set of regulations.

It is true that the application of the principles developed in *Säger* creates a special problem in the context of the free movement of natural persons providing services. The Court would be faced with the need to evaluate different national requirements regarding professional qualifications as these present a barrier to the provision of professional services. This evaluation would be a difficult task for the Court.[165] However, the assessment of the justifiability of national qualifications is an issue the Court cannot avoid. The market-dividing impact of these rules is clear and has to be addressed at the Community level. Fortunately the Court's work is somewhat simplified by the existence of secondary legislation in this field.[166]

The recent judgments of the Court seem to support a unitary view of the free movement of services. First, in *Gebhard*[167] the Court brings all freedoms in line with each other, and the Court no longer requires national measures to be discriminatory in a narrow sense for the provisions on the free movement of persons to apply.[168]

Secondly, the recent rulings of the Court in the field of the free movement of services seem to indicate that the approach of the Court is not dependent on the absence of movement of the service provider. In *Vander Elst*[169] a Belgian service provider had been ordered to pay an administrative fine. He had not complied with French labour legislation that required undertakings to obtain work permits for their non-Community workers and reserved the monopoly on the recruitment of foreigners and on bringing them into France to the OMI, the French International Migration Office. The Vander Elst business had done demolition work in France by sending a team, which included four Moroccan workers, from Belgium to Reims. The Court, following Advocate General Tesauro, found that the French rules contravened Articles 49 (ex 59) and 50 (ex 60) EC.

That case did involve the movement of (natural) persons. Nevertheless, the Court quoted *Säger*, stating that not only discrimination but also all other

---

[165] Weatherill and Beaumont (n 17 above) 695–696. In Case 340/89 *Vlassopoulou v Ministerium für Justiz, Bundes- und Europaangelegenheiten Baden Württemberg* [1991] ECR 2357 the Court refused to compare qualifications itself but imposed a duty to do so on the host state authorities.

[166] See especially Council Directive 89/48/EEC of 21 December 1988 on a general system for the recognition of higher-education diplomas awarded on completion of professional education and training of at least three years' duration [1989] OJ L19/16.

[167] Case C-55/94 *Reinhard Gebhard v Consiglio dell'Ordine degli Avvocati e Procuratori di Milano* [1995] ECR I-4165 para 37. See Chapter 1 section 3 above.

[168] See eg Case C-415/93 *Union Royale Belge des Sociétés de Football Association ASBL and others v Jean-Marc Bosman* [1995] ECR I-4921.

[169] Case C-43/93 *Raymond Vander Elst v Office des Migrations Internationales* [1994] ECR I-3803. See also Case C-272/94 *Criminal Proceedings Against Michael Guiot* [1996] ECR I-1905.

restrictions have to be abolished.[170] This would imply that the same principles apply regardless of the mode of the movement of services.

However, the French legislation in question had a very clear, concrete, and measurable discriminatory impact on the Belgian service provider. He had already obtained work permits for the Moroccan employees in his home country and the French legislation imposed a second burden on him, which placed him at a clear competitive disadvantage against domestic service providers.[171] Therefore the judgment cannot be regarded as absolutely positive proof that the *Säger* principle applies to situations where persons move. In *Säger*, the discrimination did not take such a concrete form. The double burden was of a more abstract kind. The service provider was not so much placed at a competitive disadvantage rather than deprived of his competitive advantage.

In *Reisebüro Broede*[172] the Court dealt with a German law reserving professional representation in judicial debt collection proceedings to lawyers. This law was applied to a French debt collection undertaking which had given a power of attorney to its managing director in order to enforce a decision against a German debtor.[173]

Only material discrimination in a wide sense was present in the case.[174] Nevertheless, the Court followed Advocate General Fennelly and stated that the German law constituted a prima facie restriction on the freedom to provide services,[175] citing *Guiot* to support its statement that Article 49 (ex 59) EC requires the abolition of all restrictions.[176]

In the case itself, a person did not have to move across borders since the managing director of the French company was a German national residing in Germany. This did not play any part in the Court's reasoning on whether the law constituted a restriction, however. Therefore, it is submitted that the result would have been the same even if the managing director had been a French national residing in France. Thus, the case adds support to the theory of a uniform approach to all modes of movement of services.

Syndesmos ton en Elladi Touristikon kai Taxidiotikon Grafeion[177] was concerned with Greek legislation providing that licensed tourist guides who had entered into agreements with tourist or travel agencies in order to run programmes were bound by an employment relationship. Accordingly, tourist guides from other Member States who had acquired a Greek licence were

---

[170] See n 169 para 14.

[171] See the Opinion of AG Tesauro, para 17. The Court had already condemned the same French legislation on the grounds that it discriminated against foreign service providers in Case C-113/89 *Rush Portuguesa Lda v Office national d'immigration* [1990] ECR I-1417.

[172] Case C-3/95 *Reisebüro Broede v Gerd Sandker* [1996] ECR I-6511.

[173] The case is discussed in more detail in section 5cii below.

[174] See in more detail section 5cii below.   [175] See n 172 above, para 27.

[176] ibid, para 25.

[177] Case C-398/95 *Syndesmos ton en Elladi Touristikon kai Taxidiotikon Grafeion v Ypourgos Ergasias* [1997] ECR I-3091.

unable to make contracts for the provision of services with tourist and travel agencies, wherever those agencies were established.

The Court followed Advocate General Lenz and held that the Greek law, even though it clearly applied without distinction, was a restriction on the freedom to provide services.[178] It supported this finding by citing *Säger* and stating that Article 49 (ex 59) EC requires the abolition of all restrictions.[179]

It has been argued that the situation of tourist guides is different from the situation envisaged in Article 50(3) (ex 60(3)) EC since the service provider is of the same nationality as the recipient even though the service is actually provided in a different country.[180] In the case under consideration, however, the Court did not make any distinction between the situation where, for example, an Italian tourist guide is operating a programme for Italians and a situation where the same guide is providing services for Greeks. The Court's reasoning applies equally well in both circumstances. Therefore, the case offers support for the theory of a unified approach.

Even though none of the cases is quite to the point, their cumulative weight supports strongly the proposition that the absence of movement of persons is not decisive for the principles developed in *Säger* to apply. The case law has not taken Article 50(3) (ex 60(3)) EC at its face value but seems to have sensibly ignored it.[181]

Altogether, the Court has ended up dealing with the serious problems created by the disparity between national rules in the same way both in the field of the free movement of goods and in the field of the free movement of services. The principles behind *Cassis* and *Säger* are the same. Mutual recognition has been the Court's answer to the national rules whose differences partition the common market.

4. Obstacles created by truly non-discriminatory rules: early cases

a) Goods

As regard the free movement of goods, the European Court of Justice has gone even further than in *Cassis*.[182] Even measures which create a truly equal

---

[178] ibid, para 19.   [179] ibid, para 16.

[180] Nielsen (n 164 above) 126 referring to cases Case C-154/89 *Commission v France* [1991] ECR I-659, Case C-180/89 *Commission v Italy* [1991] ECR I-709, and Case C-198/89 *Commission v Greece* [1991] ECR I-735.

[181] If anything, the movement of EU citizens ought to be subject to a more liberal treatment. As AG Lenz argued in Case C-415/93 *Union Royale Belge des Sociétés de Football Association ASBL and others v Jean-Marc Bosman* [1995] ECR I-4921 para 203, free movement of citizens can be seen as a fundamental human right which should never be restricted without a weighty justification. Correspondingly, in the USA persons' right to move freely has been given greater protection than inter-state commerce. See J.E. Nowak and R.D. Rotunda, *Constitutional Law* (5th edn St Paul Minn 1995) 310.

[182] Case 120/78 *Rewe Zentrale AG v Bundesmonopolverwaltung für Branntwein* [1979] ECR 649.

burden have been held to fall within Article 28 (ex 30) EC. These are measures which are not directed at imports and do not discriminate against imports even indirectly. They do diminish the total volume of trade, but affect both imported and domestic goods equally. The obstacle to trade is not created by the disparity between national rules but by their very existence.[183] The hindrance caused by these rules cannot be removed by harmonisation but only by abolishing them altogether. They may be covered by the economic freedom reading but certainly not by the anti-protectionism model.

Cinéthèque[184] is interesting in this respect. At issue was a French law prohibiting the sale and rental of videos within a year from the release of the film.

Advocate General Slynn was of the opinion that:

where a national measure is not specifically directed at imports, does not discriminate against imports, does not make it any more difficult for an importer to sell his products than it is for a domestic producer, and gives no protection to domestic producers, then in my view, *prima facie*, the measure does not fall within Article 30 [now 28].[185]

Accordingly, on the facts of the case, the Advocate General found that the French measure fell outside the scope of Article 28 (ex 30) EC.

The Court did not agree with the Advocate General's approach. It proceeded to examine the justification for the French law, holding that the measure was prima facie within Article 28 (ex 30) EC although justified by the objective of encouraging the creation of cinematographic works.[186]

The approach of the Court in *Cinéthèque* might be explained with reference to the concept of quantitative restrictions. The French rules created a total ban on the distribution of imported videos, albeit for a limited time. The Court has equated total bans with a quota of zero, viewing them as quantitative restrictions rather than measures having an equivalent effect.[187] This might explain why the Court held that the French measure was potentially within Article 28 (ex 30) EC.[188]

Torfaen[189] is a clear example of the Court's wide-reaching approach. In issue was a truly equal-burden measure, and the national rule did not constitute a prohibition of imports.

In the case B&Q was prosecuted by Torfaen Borough Council for trading on Sunday in violation of the Shops Act 1950. The defendant argued that the law was a measure having equivalent effect to quantitative restrictions as defined in *Dassonville*[190] since it reduced the volume of imports by reducing the volume of sales.

---

[183] White (n 17 above) 246.
[184] Joined Cases 60 and 61/84 *Cinéthèque v Fédération Nationale de Cinemas Francaises* [1985] ECR 2605.
[185] ibid, 2611.　　　　　　[186] ibid, paras 22–23 of the judgment.
[187] Case 34/79 *R v Henn and Darby* [1979] ECR 3795.
[188] White (n 17 above) 244–245. See also paras 17–18 of the Opinion of Advocate General Van Gerven in Case 145/88 *Torfaen BC v B&Q* [1989] ECR 3851. See further section 5ci below.
[189] ibid.　　　　　　[183] White (n 17 above) 246.
[190] Case 8/74 *Procureur du Roi v Dassonville* [1974] ECR 837.

Advocate General Van Gerven was of the opinion that the measure fell outside Article 28 (ex 30) EC altogether as it did not affect imports any differently from domestic goods and did not screen off national markets.[191] The Court did not agree with his approach. Citing *Cinéthèque*, the Court held that the Sunday trading ban fell prima facie within Article 28 (ex 30) EC but might be justified.[192]

With *Torfaen* and other Sunday trading cases[193] the Court stretched the scope of Article 28 (ex 30) as far as possible. All measures diminishing the volume of imports, regardless of their equal-handed nature, were seen as potential obstacles to the free movement of goods that could be scrutinised by the Court for their justification. This was a true economic freedom reading of Article 28.

The approach was also very centralising. A large number of national measures fell to be inspected by the Court, a central institution applying central law, and were brought within the scope of approximation provisions. Regulatory competition was potentially stifled as national laws could be struck down or harmonised, instead of being left to compete against each other.

The Court was not entirely consistent in its approach, however, but seemed to have second thoughts. In a number of cases it held that national rules seeming to have an adverse effect on the volume of imports fell outside Article 28 (ex 30) EC altogether.[194] In these cases the impact of the measures on interstate trade was very remote. The judgments did not sit well with the Sunday trading cases but showed an alternative approach to the scope of Article 28.[195]

b) Services

The European Court of Justice did not go quite this far in the field of the free movement of services and soon changed its mind also as regards Article 28 (ex 30) EC.[196] In the cases concerning services some element of discrimination

---

[191] See n 188 above, Opinion of AG Van Gerven paras 16 and 25.

[192] ibid, paras 12–15 of the judgment.

[193] See C. Barnard, 'Sunday Trading: A Drama in Five Acts' (1994) 57 MLR 449 at 454–459.

[194] See eg Case 155/80 *Oebel* [1981] ECR 1993, Case 75/81 *Belgium v Blesgen* [1982] ECR 1211, Case 148/85 *Direction Générale des Impôts and Procureur de la République v Forest* [1986] ECR 3449, Case C-69/88 *H. Krantz GmbH & Co v Ontvanger der Directe Belastingen et al* [1990] ECR I-583, and Case C-23/89 *Quietlynn & Richards v Southend Borough Council* [1990] ECR I-3059.

[195] See on this line of case law Gormley (n 133 above) 55–56, 64–65, and 252–253, L. Gormley, '"Actually or Potentially, Directly or Indirectly"? Obstacles to the Free Movement of Goods' (1989) 9 YEL 197 at 198–200, and Steiner (n 102 above) 755–758.

[196] Joined Cases C-267/91 and C-268/91 *Criminal Proceedings Against Keck and Mithouard* [1993] ECR I-6097. See the next section on this. After *Keck* the Court has in Case C-384/93 *Alpine Investments BV v Minister van Financiën* [1995] ECR I-1141 extended the scope of Art 49 (ex 59) EC wider than the scope of Art 28 (ex 30) EC. See section 5civ below on this. The discussion in the current section concerns only developments which took place prior to the judgment in *Keck*.

was always evident. Measures creating a truly equal burden were not caught by Article 49 (ex 59) EC.

The basic formula used by the Court to define the scope of Article 49 (ex 59) EC was already narrower than the formula used in respect of Article 28 (ex 30) EC. In *Säger*[197] the Court stated that Article 49 requires:

the abolition of any restriction, even if it applies without distinction to national providers of services and to those of other Member States, when it is liable to prohibit or otherwise to impede the activities of a provider of services established in another Member State where he lawfully provides similar services.

This can be contrasted with *Dassonville*[198] where the Court stated that:

[a]ll trading rules enacted by Member States which are capable of hindering, directly or indirectly, actually or potentially, intra-Community trade are to be considered as measures having an effect equivalent to quantitative restrictions.

There are two main differences in the formulas.[199] First in *Säger* there is no reference to direct or indirect, actual or potential hindrance to intra-Community trade. The wording is narrower.

Secondly, the formula in *Säger* refers to the lawful provision of services in the home state. This makes sense in the context of measures creating an unequal impact: 'product rules'. The service provider has already complied with one set of regulations. To require that he also complies with the host state rules creates a dual burden. Disparity of national rules is an obstacle to free movement. Mutual recognition is required to deal with this form of material discrimination.[200]

By contrast, *Dassonville* does not refer to the idea of discrimination at all and is, therefore, easier to interpret as covering also genuinely non-discriminatory measures, which create an equal burden to imports and domestic goods.

Commission v Germany (Lawyers' services)[201] is a case that has sometimes been mentioned as providing support for the view that truly non-discriminatory obstacles to the free movement of services can also fall foul of Article 49 (ex 59) EC.[202] In issue was, among other things, a German rule of territorial exclusivity. German law required in a great majority of civil cases that the parties be represented by a lawyer admitted to practise before the judicial authority in question. A lawyer not so admitted was only entitled to present observations in the oral proceedings with the assistance of an admitted lawyer. The Commission challenged this rule insofar as it applied to service providers from other Member States. Germany argued that to place foreign service providers in the same position as lawyers admitted to practise before the particular court would put German lawyers at a disadvantage.

---

[197] Case C-76/90 *Manfred Säger v Dennemeyer & Co. Ltd* [1991] ECR I-4221 para 12.
[198] Case 8/74 *Procureur du Roi v Dassonville* [1974] ECR 837 para 5.
[199] See Hatzopoulos (n 154 above) 847.
[200] See section 3 above and Roth (n 135 above) 152–153.
[201] Case 427/85 *Commission v Germany* [1988] ECR 1123.
[202] Craig and de Búrca (n 121 above) 781–782.

Advocate General da Cruz Vilaça was not prepared to uphold the Commission's complaint in this respect. He compared the situation of foreign service providers to that of German lawyers not admitted to practise before the court in question. According to him, both groups were in the same position and therefore the law was indistinctly applicable and neither its purpose nor its effects were discriminatory.[203]

The European Court of Justice did not agree with the Advocate General. It cited *Webb*[204] and stated in a key paragraph that:

the rule of territorial exclusivity cannot be applied to activities of a temporary nature pursued by lawyers established in other Member States, since the conditions of law and fact which apply to those lawyers are not in that respect comparable to those applicable to lawyers established on German territory.[205]

The Court seems to have thought that service providers from other Member States were discriminated against. In effect, it said that lawyers established in Germany were not in the same situation as the lawyers established in other Member States. Thus, the German rules infringed Article 49 (ex 59) EC, as the treatment of different situations in the same way has always been considered to be a form of discrimination.[206]

In my view, the Court was correct in its decision. The comparison should not be made between the service providers from other Member States and German lawyers not admitted to practise before a particular court, but between the former and the best placed German lawyers providing legal services, ie, the admitted lawyers. A Member State cannot place *any* domestic economic operators in a better position than economic operators from other Member States. It cannot defend discriminatory measures by pleading that it also discriminates against some of its own nationals.[207]

This principle can also be observed in *Commission v Netherlands*.[208] Dutch law required national broadcasting organisations to purchase a large share of their programme production requirements from a state-owned company. The Court held that the law violated Article 49 (ex 59) EC as it prevented the Dutch broadcasting organisations from using service providers from other Member States and protected the domestic industry. The fact that other programme production companies established in the Netherlands were in an

---

[203] See n 201 above, Opinion of the Advocate General paras 121–122.
[204] Case 279/80 *Criminal Proceedings Against Alfred John Webb* [1981] ECR 3305.
[205] See n 201 above, para 42.   [206] Case 13/63 *Commission v Italy* [1963] ECR 165.
[207] Lawyers established in Germany were in all likelihood also German nationals. See also Case C-254/98 *Schutzverband gegen unlauteren Wettbewerb v TK-Heimdienst Sass GmbH*, judgment of 13 January 2000, dealing with goods, where the Court treated as material discrimination Austrian legislation prohibiting bakers, butchers and grocers from selling goods on rounds, unless they sold the same goods at a permanent establishment situated in the same administrative district or an adjacent municipality. The Court noted that a trader from another Member State wishing to sell goods on rounds in a given area, unless from a neighbouring municipality, was required to set up or purchase another permanent establishment, having to bear additional costs when compared to a domestic economic operator already established in the area.
[208] Case C-353/89 *Commission v Netherlands* [1991] ECR I-4069.

equally disadvantageous position did not remove the measure from the scope of Article 49 (ex 59) EC. Preferential treatment given to one domestic company was enough.

Thus, although the Court had extended the scope of Article 28 to truly non-discriminatory measures, it did not go so far in the field of the free movement of services, prior to changing its mind on Article 28 in a landmark case in 1993.

5. *Keck* and the free movement of services

a) Background to *Keck*

i) Excessive centralisation

A mechanical application of the *Dassonville* formula according to which '[a]ll trading rules enacted by Member States which are capable of hindering, actually or potentially, directly or indirectly, intra-Community trade are to be considered as measures having an effect equivalent to quantitative restrictions'[209] had led to a great widening in the scope of Article 28 (ex 30) EC, in line with the economic freedom approach. If Article 28 is thought to apply to all national regulations restricting the volume of trade and, thus, the volume of imports, almost any national measure can be caught by it, as nearly all rules are capable of having an adverse effect on the demand of some goods.[210]

This wide an interpretation of Article 28 means a very centralised vision of the Community. However, as has been argued in section 1d above, a more decentralised system may be beneficial for the Community. Most notably, centralisation prevents competition between legal orders and the discovery and learning processes associated with it. Varying national preferences cannot be taken into account and the possibilities for international specialisation are restricted. The range of choice available for consumers and producers is limited. A decentralised system avoids the dangers of inertia and gigantism inherent in centralisation and can help to control the expansionist tendencies of the public sector and harmful activities of private interest groups.

ii) The role of the Court

Wide reach of the free movement of goods can and did create problems relating to the role of the courts, in particular the European Court of Justice.[211]

---

[209] Case 8/74 *Procureur du Roi v Dassonville* [1974] ECR 837 para 5.
[210] Weatherill and Beaumont (n 17 above) 532–533, and White (n 17 above) 253–254.
[211] See Poiares Maduro (n 19 above) 59. He develops an interesting theory of Art 28 (ex 30) EC based on the institutional choice between an individual Member State and the European Court of Justice as the arbiter of the balance between the free movement and other values. I examine some of the issues in more detail in Chapter 4 section 4biii below.

A wide scope of Article 28 (ex 30) EC reduces the risk of protectionist national rules escaping judicial scrutiny. The Court can examine all measures reducing the volume of trade. It has been claimed that if a certain category of national rules were held to fall outside Article 28 altogether, the misuse of these rules could not be prevented.[212]

Article 28 can in this respect be compared with Article 81 (ex 85) EC. The wide scope of Article 81(1) (ex 85(1)) EC, especially as interpreted by the Commission, has been motivated by and defended with reference to the need to enable the Commission to control anti-competitive and anti-integrationist agreements effectively.[213] However, the system has also been forcefully criticised for subjecting *harmless* agreements to the Commission's scrutiny under Article 81(3) (ex 85(3)) EC.[214] The trend[215] in competition law seems to be towards a reduction in the area of Community supervision.[216]

It is possible to question the legitimacy of the role of the Court under a wide interpretation of the scope of Article 28 (ex 30) EC.[217] When deciding on the acceptability of the aims of a national measure and on the proportionality of the means, the Court is ruling on issues that are usually considered to be political. The aim pursued by the Member State may be controversial and opinions may vary greatly between different Member States. For example, views on how to balance the right to life of an unborn child and the right of self-determination of a woman diverge inside the Community (and inside Member States).[218] Even if the Court can decide on the legitimacy of the aim of the measure, it has to be balanced against any anti-integrationist effects. In these situations the

---

[212] See Gormley (n 133 above) 205–206.

[213] See R. Whish and B. Sufrin, 'Article 85 and the Rule of Reason' (1987) 7 YEL 1 at 14–20.

[214] See B.E. Hawk, 'System Failure: Vertical Restraints and EC Competition Law' (1995) 32 CMLRev 973 at 974–984, and V. Korah, *An Introductory Guide to EC Competition Law and Practice* (7th edn Oxford 2000) 349–352.

[215] Another interesting development is that goods and services are increasingly being treated in the same manner. See Commission Communication, *Application of the Community Competition Rules to Vertical Restraints*, follow-up to the Green Paper on Vertical Restraints [1998] OJ C365/03, and Art 2(1) of Commission Regulation 2790/1999/EC of 22 December 1999 on the application of Article 81(3) of the Treaty to categories of vertical agreements and concerted practices [1999] OJ L336/21.

[216] See R. Whish, *Competition Law* (3rd edn London 1993) 208–209 and the judgments of the Court cited therein; Commission Green Paper, *Vertical Restraints in EC Competition Policy* (COM(96)721 final) [1997] 4 CMLR 519, and Commission Communication (n 215 above). See also the extension of whitelisted clauses (Art 2) in the Technology Transfer Block Exemption 240/96 as compared with the whitelist (Art 2) in Patent Licensing Block Exemption 2349/84, and Commission Decision *Elopak/Metal Box-Odin* (EC Commission Decision 90/410) [1990] OJ L209/15, [1991] 4 CMLR 832. See also generally R. Wesseling, 'Subsidiarity in the Community Antitrust Law: Setting the Right Agenda' (1997) 22 ELRev 35. In the Commission White Paper, *Modernisation of the Rules Implementing Articles 85 [now 81] and 86 [now 82] of the EC Treaty* [1999] OJ C132/01, the emphasis is put on decentralised application of Community competition law.

[217] See also T.J. Friedbacher, 'Motive Unmasked: The European Court of Justice, the Free Movement of Goods and the Search for Legitimacy' (1996) 2 ELJ 226 at 238–240, and Wyatt and Dashwood (n 118 above) 328–329.

[218] See Case C-159/90 *Society for the Protection of the Unborn Child v Grogan* [1991] ECR I-4685. In practice the Court has shown deference towards national legislators in these circumstances.

non-representative nature of the Court becomes obvious and its considerable discretionary power a matter of concern. Democratically elected and accountable legislatures are generally assumed to be better suited to resolve such issues.

Furthermore, the Court's limited capacity to conduct an inquiry renders it difficult to investigate whether other equally effective means are available. This is an essential part of the proportionality test, however. The evidentiary and procedural limits inherent in any judicial review surface in these situations.[219]

The difficulties created by a wide test have been recognised by the judges themselves. Koen Lenaerts, Judge of the Court of First Instance, has written: 'Even the judge questions, at times, the legitimacy and the feasibility of making policy choices, of weighing the Community interest of having an internal market, and the Member States' interest in protecting what they see as fundamental local values'.[220] Similarly, President of the ECJ, Ole Due, has stated that: 'such cases often present the Court with an unnecessary and almost impossible task: to evaluate national policy choices in areas which have very little to do with intra-Community trade or with Community law in general'.[221] On the same topic, Judge René Joliet has said that: 'Können wir, die wir dreizehn sind, behaupten, über mehr Weisheit und Intelligenz als alle Regierungen und nationale Parlamente der Gemeinschaft zu verfügen?'[222]

The concerns over the legitimacy of the scrutiny by the Court and the difficulties inherent in the task might lead to problems in the application of the *Cassis* test. The Court might be forced to widen the list of mandatory requirements, as more and more questions relating to the justification of different national measures are submitted to it.[223] It would also be necessary to determine exactly which ground of justification was applicable in a specific case, as this might influence the outcome of the proportionality test. This could prove to be difficult as the ground of justification depends on the aims pursued by the national measure. These may not be clear or the measure may have many different purposes.[224]

---

[219] See G. de Búrca, 'The Principle of Proportionality and its Application in EC Law' (1993) 13 YEL 105 at 108 and 127, and Poiares Maduro (n 9 above) 59.

[220] K. Lenaerts, 'Some Thoughts About the Interaction Between Judges and Politicians in the European Community' (1992) 12 YEL 1 at 12 (footnotes omitted).

[221] O. Due, 'Dassonville Revisited or No Cause for Alarm?' in A.I.L. Cambell and M. Voyatzi (eds), *Legal Reasoning and Judicial Interpretation of European Law. Essays in Honour of Lord Mackenzie-Stuart* (Gosport 1996) 27.

[222] R. Joliet, 'Der freie Warenverkehr: Das Urteil Keck und Mithouard und die Neuorientierung der Rechtsprechung' (1994) GRUR Int 979 at 984. 'Can we, we who are thirteen, assert that we have more wisdom and intelligence at our disposal than all the governments and national parliaments of the Community?' See also G.C. Rodríguez Iglesias, 'Drinks in Luxembourg. Alcoholic Beverages and the Case Law of the European Court of Justice' in D. O'Keeffe and A. Bavasso (eds), *Liber Amicorum in Honour of Lord Slynn of Hadley. Vol I. Judicial Review in European Union Law* (The Hague 2000) 527.

[223] See the Opinion of AG van Gerven in Case 145/88 *Torfaen BC v B&Q* [1989] ECR 3851 para 26, and Barnard (n 193 above) 459.

[224] See Steiner (n 102 above) 759. In Sunday trading cases English judges came to different conclusions about the proportionality of the legislation as they perceived the purpose of the law differently. See Barnard (n 193 above) 454.

Furthermore, as a part of the examination of justification, the proportionality of the measures has to be established. This difficult task often falls to the national courts, as it involves questions of fact which the Court is not equipped to investigate and resolve. This inevitably leads to different results, especially as the answer to the question depends on the evidence presented to the national court.[225]

The Court's case law was not entirely coherent. It seems that the Court was feeling slightly uneasy about the reach of the mechanically applied *Dassonville* test. For example, in *Oebel*,[226] *Blesgen*,[227] *Krantz*,[228] and *Quietlynn*[229] the Court employed a method diverging from its normal approach and held the national measures to fall outside the scope of Article 28 (ex 30) EC altogether, without investigating their justification at all. In all of these cases the measures were capable of reducing the volume of trade and fulfilled the *Dassonville* criterion, as normally interpreted. The impact on inter-state trade was very remote, however. Unfortunately the poor reasoning of the judgments only created confusion.[230]

Traders, national courts and the Court itself can suffer detrimental consequences from a wide and uncertain scope of Article 28. Traders would be encouraged to bring cases that have an ever more tenuous connection with intra-Community trade.[231] This would result in fruitless and disappointing litigation, as in many cases national rules are saved by mandatory requirements or Article 30 (ex 36) EC.

National courts[232] would be faced with many more cases involving Article 28 (ex 30) EC. Because of the complexity of the tests, national courts would be obliged to make references to the European Court of Justice. This would increase the cost and the length of litigation, and cause problems for judges loyal to national legislatures. National courts would also need to apply the proportionality test in a great number of cases. This is a task they are not necessarily suited for or feel comfortable with.[233] The national courts might be tempted to resist the obligations imposed upon them by Community law.[234]

---

[225] See Steiner (n 102 above) 759–760. Hoffmann J expressed the doubts felt by a national judge faced with a task of deciding on proportionality of national legislation in *Stoke-on-Trent and Norwich City Councils v B&Q* [1990] 3 CMLR 31 paras 46–52.

[226] Case 155/80 *Oebel* [1981] ECR 1993.

[227] Case 75/81 *Belgium v Blesgen* [1982] ECR 1211.

[228] Case C-69/88 *H. Krantz GmbH & Co v Ontvanger der Directe Belastingen et al* [1990] ECR I-583.

[229] Case C-23/89 *Quietlynn & Richards v Southend Borough Council* [1990] ECR I-3059.

[230] See the critical analysis of this strand of the Court's case law in AG Tesauro's Opinion in the Case C-292/92 *Hünermund v Landesapothekerkammer Baden-Württemberg* [1993] ECR I-6787 paras 11–24, and in Gormley (n 195 above) 198–200.

[231] See White (n 17 above) 238.

[232] See M.A. Jarvis, *The Application of EC Law by National Courts. The Free Movement of Goods* (Oxford 1998) 129–132 on the problems the wide reading of Art 28 (ex 30) EC created for national courts.

[233] See generally on the proportionality test and national courts Jarvis (n 232 above) 204–230, especially 228–230, and 293–294.

[234] See Steiner (n 102 above) 750.

This would create a strain on the relationship between national courts and the Court, a relationship that has been crucially important for the development of Community law itself.[235]

An increase in the number of references would also be detrimental to the Court itself. One of the worst problems facing the Court is an ever-increasing caseload.[236] This leads to delays that are harmful, especially in the context of the Article 234 (ex 177) EC procedure, as they undermine the effective protection of individuals in practice.[237] Secondly, it may lead to a lower quality of judgments, as the Court is forced to deal with cases as quickly as possible. Such a development would be particularly worrying since the Court functions as the supreme court of the Community and its rulings should contribute towards the general development of Community law.[238] Thirdly, it may become difficult for citizens and the legal community to follow the development of the case law, which would diminish the value of the Court's decisions as precedents.[239]

It is worth noting that in other fields the Court's approach seems to have been influenced by the desire to limit its workload. In Article 230 (ex 173) EC cases, the Court has developed very restrictive tests of standing for private plaintiffs.[240] It has been argued that this has been done partly to avoid the

---

[235] See F. Mancini and D. Keeling, 'From *CILFIT* to *ERT*: The Constitutional Challenge Facing the European Court' (1991) 11 YEL 1 at 1–3, and J.H.H. Weiler, 'The Transformation of Europe' (1991) 100 Yale LJ 2403 at 2425.

[236] See European Court of Justice, *The EC Court of Justice and the Institutional reform of the European Union* of April 2000 (www.curia.eu.int/en/txts/intergov/index.htm); *Report of the Working Party on the Future of the European Communities' Court System* of January 2000 (www.europa.eu.int/comm/archives/igc2000/offdoc/discussiondocs/index_en.htm); *Additional Commission Contribution to the Intergovernmental Conference on Institutional Reform—Reform of the Community Courts* of 1 March 2000 (www.europa.eu.int/comm/archives/igc2000/offdoc/index_en.htm#contributions); L.N. Brown and T. Kennedy, *The Court of Justice of the European Communities* (5th edn London 2000) 385–397; J.P. Jacqué and J.H.H. Weiler, 'On the Road to European Union—a New Judicial Architecture: An Agenda for the Intergovernmental Conference' (1990) 27 CMLRev 185 at 187; P.J.G. Kapteyn, 'The Court of Justice of the European Communities after the Year 2000' in D. Curtin and T. Heukels (eds), *Institutional Dynamics of European Integration. Essays in Honour of Henry G. Schermers. Vol II* (Dordrecht 1994) 137, and T. Koopmans, 'The Future of the Court of Justice of the European Communities' (1991) 11 YEL 15 at 16. The Treaty of Nice includes changes to ease the pressure, such as the possible creation of judicial panels and increase in the jurisdiction of the Court of First Instance, and qualified majority voting on the Court's rules of procedure. From the mid-1980s to early 1990s the Court made approximately 20 decisions a year that were concerned with Arts 28–30 (ex 30–36) EC. This amounts to 8 per cent of all rulings: W.P.J. Wils, 'The Search for the Rule in Article 30 EEC: Much Ado About Nothing?' (1993) 18 ELRev 475.

[237] See Jacqué and Weiler (n 236 above) 188, Kapteyn (n 236 above) 137, and Koopmans (n 236 above) 17–18.

[238] See Jacqué and Weiler (n 236 above) 188, and Kapteyn (n 236 above) 137.

[239] See Jacqué and Weiler (n 236 above) 139.

[240] See especially Case 25/62 *Plaumann v Commission* [1963] ECR 95, Joined Cases 789/79 and 790/79 *Calpak v Commission* [1980] ECR 1949, and Case C-321/95P *Stichting Greenpeace Council (Greenpeace International) and others v Commission* [1998] ECR I-1651. The test may have been liberalised in Case C-309/89 *Codorniu SA v Council* [1994] ECR I-1853. Possible liberalisation would mainly serve to increase the workload of the Court of First Instance, as the European Court of Justice functions as an appeals court in these cases.

Court being swamped by challenges to Community action.[241] Similarly, it has been suggested that the Court's recent stricter investigation of its jurisdiction under Article 234 (ex 177) EC[242] has been influenced by the need to reduce its caseload.[243]

Ultimately all these problems might force the Court to adopt a more lenient approach to mandatory requirements and proportionality under Article 28 (ex 30) EC. This would endanger the effectiveness of the provision in dealing with national measures that create real problems for European integration.[244]

Clearly, a centralised scrutiny of nearly all Member State measures does not sit well with the decentralised structure of the Community judicature, where national courts take care of most Community law problems.[245] Centralised control would force national courts to deal with situations they are not equipped to handle and strain the resources of the Court. It would undermine the legitimacy of the whole system and impose a strain on the relations between national courts and the Court. It could also endanger the effectiveness of Article 28 (ex 30) EC. Against this background the advantages of a clear rule-like test[246] limiting the scope of Article 28 seem obvious.

In addition, a wide test based on, for example, a mechanical application of the *Dassonville* formula might act as a limitation on the discretion of the Community legislator. All Community organs are bound by the EC Treaty, including the rules on free movement.[247] If those rules are only breached by discriminatory measures, the discretion of the Community legislator is relatively unimpeded. The harmonisation of Member State rules creating obstacles to trade would be unhindered. Community measures which affect traders from all Member States uniformly could not be challenged. A wider approach, such as one based purely on *Dassonville*, however, would logically enable the Court to examine the justification of all Community measures reducing the number of imports when compared with an unregulated situation. It can be asked whether this would be a proper role for the Court.[248]

---

[241] See Craig and de Búrca (n 121 above) 484.

[242] Case C-83/91 *Meilicke v ADV/ORGA F.A. Meyer AG* [1992] ECR I-4871, and Case C-343/90 *Dias v Director da Alfandega do Porto* [1992] ECR I-4673.

[243] See T. Kennedy, 'First Steps Towards a European Certiorari?' (1993) 18 ELRev 121 at 129, and D. O'Keeffe, 'Is the Spirit of Article 177 under Attack? Preliminary References and Admissibility' (1998) 23 ELRev 509 at 528–529.

[244] See White (n 17 above) 239.

[245] On the role of the national courts in the Community judicial system see Jarvis (n 232 above) 1–2.

[246] On the difference between a rule-like and a standard-like test see Wils (n 236 above) 481. A test based on discrimination is rule-like. No weighing is needed to determine whether there is discrimination or not.

[247] See Chapter 3 section 3 below.

[248] In Australia the High Court ruled in the landmark case *Cole v Whitfield* (Crayfish) (1988) 165 CLR 360 that s 92 of the Constitution, which provides for freedom of trade and commerce among the states, only prevents discriminatory burdens of a protectionist kind. One of the reasons for this new narrow test was the desire to let the Commonwealth exercise its powers freely. See P.H. Lane, *A Manual of Australian Constitutional Law* (6th edn Sydney 1995) 333–349.

iii) General trends

The wide scope of Article 28 (ex 30) EC was not consistent with several general trends in the Community.

First of all, increased importance is being given to the principle of subsidiarity. The principle has arguably influenced the development of Community law for quite some time,[249] but it was not given general expression until the Maastricht Treaty on European Union,[250] in the Preamble and Articles A (now 1), B (now 2) and K.3.(2)(b), and in Article 3b(2) (now 5(2)) of the EC Treaty. In Amsterdam, Member States signalled the importance they give to subsidiarity by annexing a Protocol on the application of the principles of subsidiarity and proportionality to the EC Treaty.

One aspect of the principle implies that priority should generally be given to Member State action and that the Community should only get involved if Member States cannot deal with the problem adequately.[251] The principle lends weight to an argument for a restrictive construction of Article 28 (ex 30) EC in order to protect Member State competence against intervention by the Community.[252]

Secondly, in recent years the expanding scope of Community law has created both political controversy and constitutional problems in various Member States.[253] Increased attention is being paid to the competences of the Community, as evidenced by the careful drafting of the rules on public health and culture in Maastricht. This is logical, as under majority voting jurisdictional limits are much more important than under unanimous decision-making.[254]

[249] See J. Steiner, 'Subsidiarity under the Maastricht Treaty' in D. O'Keeffe and P.M. Twomey (eds), *Legal Issues of the Maastricht Treaty* (Chichester 1994) 50–51.

[250] The Single European Act incorporated the principle into Art 130r(4) EC, but the provision dealt only with action relating to the environment.

[251] See Bernard (n 10 above) 653–654, and N. Emiliou, 'Subsidiarity: An Effective Barrier Against "the Enterprises of Ambition"?' (1992) 17 ELRev 383 at 401.

[252] See Bernard (n 10 above) 638, C. Hilson 'Discrimination in Community Free Movement Law' (1999) 24 ELRev 445, 457, and Weatherill and Beaumont (n 17 above) 608.

[253] See Dashwood (1996) 21 ELRev 113; Poiares Maduro (n 9 above) 34; Weiler (n 235 above) 2450–2453, and J.H.H. Weiler, 'The Reformation of European Constitutionalism' (1997) 35 JCMS 97, 123–127. See also the decision of the German Constitutional Court concerning the ratification of the Maastricht Treaty, *Brunner v European Union Treaty* [1994] 1 CMLR 57, and the 'Danish Maastricht Judgment', Højesteret, *Carlsen and others v Prime Minister* [1999] 3 CMLR 854, annotated by K. Høegh, 'The Danish Maastricht Judgment' (1999) 24 ELRev 80.

[254] As shown by Case C-376/98 *Germany v European Parliament and Council of the European Union*, judgment of 5 October 2000, where the European Court of Justice took the principle of enumerated powers seriously and annulled the Tobacco Advertising Directive (Directive 98/43/EC of 6 July 1998, on the approximation of the laws, regulations and administrative provisions of the Member States relating to the advertising and sponsorship of tobacco products [1998] OJ L213/9). See also Weiler (n 10 above) 371–372, and Weiler (n 253 above) 122–127. In Nice the Member States agreed to hold an Intergovernmental Conference in 2004 inter alia to establish a more precise delimitation of competences between the EU and Member States. See Declaration on the Future of the Union adopted by the Nice Intergovernmental Conference. However, the practical impact on EC regulatory activity has been limited. See M.A. Pollock, 'The End of Creeping Competence? EU Policy-Making Since Maastricht' (2000) 38 JCMS 519 at 529–537.

Thirdly, the Court has not interpreted Article 81 (ex 85) EC, read together with Article 10 (ex 5) EC, as forming a basis for a Community economic constitution.[255] Instead it has sharply limited the reach of the provisions.[256] Also in this context the Court has proved unwilling to control local regulatory choices.[257]

Fourthly, the Court has recently seemed less inclined to engage in judicial activism than in the past. The Single European Act with its rules on majority voting revitalised the political process of the Community and, thus, enabled the Court to adopt a more conservative stance.[258] After the deadline for the achievement of the internal market, 31 December 1992, and even more so after the introduction of the euro, 1 January 1999, one might perhaps talk of a more mature market,[259] in need of market maintenance, not market building.[260]

Fifthly, the nature of Community legislative activity has changed. In the early years, there was an attempt to engage in total harmonisation. This proved to be impossible, as the Community legislative machinery could not cope with regulating large sectors of the economy in a detailed manner. The desirability of the approach was also questionable, as it reduced diversity and flexibility. As a response a new approach was instituted in 1980s, with much greater reliance on mutual recognition and minimum harmonisation. The Community legislator moved towards a more decentralised model. The limits of positive harmonisation were recognised.[261]

---

[255] Case C-2/91 *Meng* [1993] ECR I-5751. See in general K. Bacon, 'State Regulation of the Market and E.C. Competition Rules: Articles 85 and 86 Compared' (1997) 18 ECLR 283 at 283–291.

[256] See also section 5aii above on the more restrictive approach to the scope of Art 81 (ex 85) EC.

[257] See N. Reich, 'The "November Revolution" of the European Court of Justice: *Keck*, *Meng* and *Audi* Revisited' (1994) 31 CMLRev 459 at 479–482, and Weatherill and Beaumont (n 17 above) 619.

[258] See T.C. Hartley, 'The European Court, Judicial Objectivity and the Constitution of the European Union' (1996) 112 LQR 95 at 102, and Lenaerts (n 220 above) 34. For instance, Case C-91/92 *Faccini Dori v Recreb Srl* [1994] ECR I-3325, Case C-338/91 *Steenhorst-Neerings v Bestuur van de Bedrijfsvereiniging voor Detailhandel, Ambachten en Huisvrouwen* [1993] ECR I-5475 and Case C-249/96 *Lisa Jacqueline Grant v South-West Trains Ltd* [1998] ECR I-621, can be seen as examples of judicial restraint. On the other hand, there are judgments pointing the other way, such as Case C-312/93 *Peterbroeck v Belgium* [1995] ECR I-4599 and Joined Cases C-46 and C-48/93 *Brasserie du Pêcheur SA v Germany and R v Secretary of State for Transport, ex parte Factortame* [1996] ECR I-1029. The whole dichotomy between activism and self-restraint has been challenged by T. Tridimas, 'The Court of Justice and Judicial Activism' (1996) 21 ELRev 199.

[259] The Commission White Paper, *Modernisation of the Rules Implementing Articles 85 [now 81] and 86 [now 82] of the EC Treaty* [1999] OJ C132/01, suggests far-reaching decentralisation of the current 'centralised authorisation system' of competition law. One of the reasons given is that 'national markets are already extensively integrated'. See eg para 136. See also I. Maher, 'Competition Law and Intellectual Property Rights: Evolving Formalism' in P. Craig and G. de Búrca (eds), *The Evolution of EU Law* (Oxford 1999) 603, who argues that there is 'a recognition that market integration may no longer need to be the core of policy development in areas such as competition'.

[260] See Poiares Maduro (n 9 above) 88–99, who uses this terminology, and Weiler (n 10 above) 371.

[261] See generally eg Craig and de Búrca (n 121 above) 1124–1132. On the origins of the change see eg K.A. Armstrong and S.J. Bulmer, *The Governance of the Single European Market* (Manchester 1998) 13–22. On minimum harmonisation see eg M. Dougan, 'Minimum Harmonization and the Internal Market' (2000) 37 CMLRev 853 at 854–863.

Finally, it can be argued that the internal market is losing its premier position in the Community.[262] The Maastricht Treaty on European Union redefined the methods for achieving the tasks of the Community found in Article 2 EC. The methods now include the implementation of a wide variety of policies, not just the establishment of a common market and the harmonisation of the economic policies of the Member States.

Generally speaking, the Court has moved away from a wide, all encompassing view of the internal market. In *Titanium Dioxide*[263] it had established Article 95 (ex 100a) EC as the appropriate legal basis in a situation where a Community measure was designed both to eliminate distortions of competition and to protect the environment. However, in the *Waste Directive*[264] case, Article 175 (ex 130s) EC prevailed even though the measure had an ancillary effect on the internal market. Limited scope of the free movement provisions corresponds to these developments.

b) The *Keck* judgment

The Court's decision in *Keck*[265] should be understood against this background. In the case, the European Court of Justice, influenced by the views presented by Eric L. White[266] and following Advocate General Tesauro's Opinion in *Hünermund*,[267] 're-examined and clarified' its previous case law, overruling some of its earlier decisions[268] and taking a step away from the economic freedom approach.

The Court removed from the ambit of Article 28 (ex 30) EC national measures restricting or prohibiting certain selling arrangements even if they reduce the volume of sales. According to the Court, such rules by nature neither prevent other Member States' products from gaining access to the market nor impede their access more than the access of domestic products.[269]

---

[262] See Chalmers (n 12 above) 402–403, and D. Chalmers, 'The Single Market: From Prima Donna to Journeyman' in J. Shaw and G. More (eds), *New Legal Dynamics of European Union* (Oxford 1995) 68–71.

[263] Case C-300/89 *Commission v Council* [1991] ECR I-2867.

[264] Case C-155/91 *Commission v Council* (Waste Directive) [1993] ECR I-939, confirmed in Case C-187/93 *Parliament v Council* (Shipments of waste) [1994] ECR I-2857. See D. Geradin, 'Trade and Environmental Protection: Community Harmonization and National Environmental Standards' (1993) 13 YEL 151 at 170–171 who is of the opinion that the case is difficult or even impossible to reconcile with *Titanium Dioxide*.

[265] Cases C-267/91 and C-268/91 *Criminal Proceedings Against Keck and Mithouard* [1993] ECR I-6097.

[266] See White (n 17 above) 246–247. White was a member of the Commission's legal service and represented the Commission in Case 145/88 *Torfaen BC v B&Q* [1989] ECR 3851.

[267] Case C-292/92 *Hünermund v Landesapothekerkammer Baden-Württemberg* [1993] ECR I-6787.

[268] See n 265 above, paras 14 and 16.

[269] ibid, paras 13, 16 and 17. Also Due (n 221 above) 20, and P. Oliver, *Free Movement of Goods in the European Community* (3rd edn London 1996) 103 see para 17 as explaining the reasoning behind para 16.

Rules regulating selling arrangements must fulfil certain criteria to fall outside the scope of Article 28. First of all, they must 'apply to all affected traders operating within the national territory'.[270] The meaning of this requirement is not clear.[271] It has been interpreted by Advocate General Van Gerven as preventing national rules from impeding the market access of traders from another Member State more than the access of domestic traders, whilst leaving the Member States free to distinguish between categories of domestic economic operators.[272]

Secondly, and most crucially, national rules must 'affect in the same manner, in law and in fact, the marketing of domestic products and of those from other Member States'.[273] National measures discriminating on their face against imports are unequally applicable 'in law'. Provisions affording protection to similar or competing national products discriminate against other Member States' products 'in fact'.[274]

The Court has been criticised for unwillingness to analyse factual discrimination in a realistic fashion in the cases decided shortly after *Keck*.[275] However, more recently, in *De Agostini*[276] the Court followed Advocate General Jacobs and took a realistic view of the potentially discriminatory impact of Swedish advertising restrictions, although it was left for the national court to determine whether the measures actually did discriminate against imports. A ban on a form of advertising can in certain situations prevent new imported products from entering the market, thereby crystallising consumer habits that favour familiar domestic products. Similarly, in *TK-Heimdienst*[277] the Court treated as material discrimination Austrian legislation providing that bakers, butchers and grocers were not allowed to sell goods on rounds, unless they sold the same goods at a permanent establishment situated in the same administrative district or an adjacent municipality. The Court noted that a trader from another Member State wishing to sell goods on rounds in a given area, unless from a neighbouring

---

[270] See n 265 above para 16.

[271] See I. Higgins, 'The Free and Not so Free Movement of Goods since *Keck*' (1997) 6 IJEL 166 at 172–173. See also Kapteyn and VerLoren van Themaat (n 135 above) 635, who question the added value of the criterion.

[272] Opinion of AG van Gerven in Joined Cases C-401/92 and 402/92 *Criminal Proceedings Against Tankstation 't Heukske vof and J.B.E. Boermans* [1994] ECR I-2199 para 21.

[273] See n 265 above para 16.

[274] Oliver (n 269 above) 105–106, and Case C-391/92 *Commission v Greece* (Processed milk for infants) [1995] ECR I-1621 para 18.

[275] See Higgins (n 271 above) 173–176 and 179–180.

[276] Joined Cases C-34/95, C-35/95 and C-36/95 *Konsumentombudsmannen v De Agostini (Svenska) Förlag AB and TV-Shop i Sverige AB* [1997] ECR I-3843. See in more detail Snell (n 82 above) 224–226. This was in turn criticised by P. Oliver, 'Some Further Reflections on the Scope of Articles 28–30 (ex 30–36) EC' (1999) 36 CMLRev 783, 795–796. The approach adopted in *De Agostini* was confirmed in Case C-405/98 *Konsumentombudsmannen v Gourmet International Products Aktiebolag*, judgment of 8 March 2001, paras 18–25, again following AG Jacobs.

[277] Case C-254/98 *Schutzverband gegen unlauteren Wettbewerb v TK-Heimdienst Sass GmbH*, judgment of 13 January 2000. See C. Barnard, 'Fitting the Remaining Pieces into the Goods and Persons Jigsaw?' (2001) 26 ELRev 35 at 45–47 on this case in general.

municipality, was required to set up or purchase another permanent establishment, having to bear additional costs when compared to a domestic economic operator already established in the area. Again the Court, this time departing from the Opinion of Advocate General La Pergola, was prepared to examine closely the nature of a national measure to unearth any discrimination.[278]

Thirdly, the purpose of the national rules must not be the regulation of trade in goods between Member States. If this is their aim, Article 28 (ex 30) EC becomes applicable.[279]

Accordingly, the Court held in *Keck* that the French legislation imposing a general prohibition of resale at a loss fell outside Article 28 altogether.[280]

The *Keck* judgment can be seen as a general move towards a more decentralised system and away from the economic freedom model. Only national regulation partitioning the markets is open to scrutiny. The Court will not engage in general economic review. The competence of Member States is preserved, and the quest for regulatory uniformity is abandoned.[281]

The judgment establishes a multiple burden and an effects-based concept of discrimination as the determinant factors in drawing the limits of the concept of a measure having an equivalent effect to quantitative restrictions. A *product rule* has an unequal impact on imports as the imported products must comply with two regulatory systems. Goods legally produced in one country may have to be modified to correspond to the requirements of the other country. There is a multiple regulatory burden. Therefore, it can be presumed that rules relating to the products themselves fall within Article 28. However, a similar presumption is not valid as regards rules concerning *selling arrangements*, as they do not normally impose a heavier burden on imports. Therefore, it is only necessary to examine whether such rules apply equally 'in law and fact' to domestic and imported products to determine whether they fall inside the scope of Article 28. Thus, Article 28 applies

---

[278] It should be noted that, although the Court did not mention it, the discriminatory effect was strengthened because of the nature of the products. A local baker usually offers bread that is produced locally, not bread that has been imported from another Member State.

[279] See n 265 above, para 12. See Due (n 221 above) 28, and W.-H. Roth, 'Joined Cases C-267 and C-268/91, *Bernard Keck and Daniel Mithouard*, Judgment of 24 November 1993, [1993] ECR I-6097; Case C-292/92, *Ruth Hünermund et al. v Landesapothekerkammer Baden-Württemberg*, Judgment of 15 December 1993, [1993] ECR I-6787' (1994) 31 CMLRev 845 at 848. Gormley criticises the Court's reference to the purpose of the measure as incompatible with an effects doctrine in L. Gormley, 'Reasoning Renounced? The Remarkable Judgment in *Keck & Mithouard*' (1994) 5 EBLR 63 at 66. Cf Chief Justice Marshall's view of the American commerce clause. According to him the commerce clause prohibited the states from regulating commerce for its own sake, but allowed them to pursue other goals even if the rules did somewhat obstruct the trade among the states. See L.H. Tribe, *American Constitutional Law* (2nd edn Minneola, New York 1988) 404–405.

[280] See n 265 above, para 18.

[281] See Joliet (n 222 above) 987, Roth (n 279 above) 851, and Weatherill and Beaumont (n 17 above) 608 and 619.

only when the impact on imports is heavier than the impact on domestic goods.[282]

At the same time the Court took a step towards greater legal formalism. A rule-like test partially replaced the standard-based one. This approach has the capacity to provide legal certainty and, thus, reduce the administrative costs of applying Article 28.[283]

However, one aspect of the judgment is clearly open to criticism. The Court did not specify which judgments it was overruling,[284] nor did it define the elusive concept of 'certain selling arrangements'.[285] This has left traders and national courts in a state of uncertainty and has resulted in some new references to the Court.[286] Yet, by applying the criteria consistently and formalistically in its case law building on *Keck*, the Court has succeeded in achieving a degree of predictability in the application of Article 28 (ex 30) EC.[287]

In the light of the Court's recent case law, it seems that the categories 'product rules' and 'rules concerning selling arrangements' are mutually exclusive and that all measures regulating selling arrangements fall within the latter category unless they constitute product rules by relating to the product itself.[288] Rules concerning selling arrangements include, for example, measures that regulate when, how, by whom and where goods may be sold.[289]

Recently, the most interesting critical analysis of the Court's judgment in *Keck* has come from Miguel Poiares Maduro.[290] Poiares Maduro proposes an alternative test for applying Article 28. According to him, the Court should review, in addition to discrimination, measures suspected of a national bias due to representative malfunctioning of the national political process.[291] He

---

[282] See Joliet (n 222 above) 983–985, and Bernard (n 15 above) 91–93. See also Weatherill and Beaumont (n 17 above) 612–613, M.M. Dabbah, 'The Dilemma of *Keck*—The Nature of the Ruling and the Ramifications of the Judgment' (1999) 8 IJEL 84 at 89, and Hilson (n 252 above) 446. Marenco had advocated a similar approach already in 1984 in Marenco (n 135 above). The approach is fully in line with the Court's case law on Art 29 (ex 34) EC, which is also based on the absence of dual burden. See section 5civ below.

[283] See Craig and de Búrca (n 121 above) 627, Jarvis (n 232 above) 119–120 and 131, and Oliver (n 276 above) 793–799.

[284] For attempts to do this, see Joliet (n 222 above) 986–987, L.W. Gormley, 'Two Years after Keck' (1996) 19 Fordham Int LJ 866 at 877–880, and Higgins (n 271 above) 176–179.

[285] See Due (n 221 above) 21, Reich (n 257 above) 470–472, and Roth (n 279 above) 852. See Joliet (n 222 above) 985–987 for an answer to this critique.

[286] This was predicted by Chalmers (n 12 above) 386, and Reich (n 257 above) 471–472.

[287] See Oliver (n 276 above) 793–799, and T. Tridimas, *The General Principles of EC Law* (Oxford 1999) 129. This may be reflected in the number of new cases brought before the Court. In 1998, 32 new cases concerned goods, 34 services and 36 persons. In 1999, 23 concerned goods, 23 services and 69 persons. See www.curia.eu.int/en/stat/index.htm

[288] As in Case C-470/93 *Verein gegen Unwesen in Handel und Gewerbe Köln e. V. v Mars GmbH* [1995] ECR I-1923, and in Case C-368/95 *Vereinigte Familiapress Zeitungsverlags-und vertriebs GmbH v Heinrich Bauer Verlag* [1997] ECR I-3689. See Oliver (n 276 above) 794. It might be better to use a wider term such as 'market circumstances' instead of 'selling arrangements'.

[289] See Joliet (n 222 above) 985–986, and Higgins (n 271 above) 168–172. See also, generally, F. Picod, 'La nouvelle approche de la Cour de justice en matière d'entraves aux échanges' (1998) 34 RTDE 169 at 173–177.

[290] See Poiares Maduro (n 9 above) especially 83–87.   [291] See ibid, 173–174.

writes: 'Whenever there are no affected national interests equivalent to the interests of the nationals of other Member States affected by the legislation, the national political process will be suspected of institutional malfunction since the affected foreign interests were not represented'.[292]

I have misgivings about the usefulness of the test. Although representation is clearly an important issue, it seems very difficult to construct a test based on it. First of all, the foreign interests are almost always represented in one way or another.[293] Especially foreign producers' and domestic consumers' interests may coincide. Take an example, discussed by Poiares Maduro,[294] where the sale of a product is regulated, but there are no equivalent or competing national products. Even if there were no national producers, the national consumers' interests in wider choice would correspond to the foreign producers' interests in free trade. There would be some representation. Secondly, even if there is some representation, it is never given sufficient weight. Take the example given by Poiares Maduro[295] of a situation with no malfunction: a national regulation prohibiting the sale of sex articles in non-licensed establishments. In this situation the moral interests of citizens for regulation are pitted against the interests of the sex industry for commercial freedom and the interests of the consumers for cheaper prices. The second set of interests is not given enough weight, however, as only the domestic producers are taken into account by the national political process. To sum up: it always remains possible to argue that there is some but not sufficient representation.[296]

c) The case law on the free movement of services

i) Schindler

A different approach? Four months later the Court had a possibility to introduce the *Keck* doctrine into the field of the free movement of services in

---

[292] M. Poiares Maduro, 'The Saga of Article 30 EC Treaty: To Be Continued. A Comment on Familiapress v Bauer Verlag and Other Recent Episodes' (1998) 5 MJ 298 at 310. Ensuring the virtual representation of out-of-state interests has been one of the main themes in modern commerce clause analysis in the USA. See Tribe (n 279 above) 408–413. For criticism see D.H. Regan, 'The Supreme Court and State Protectionism: Making Sense of the Dormant Commerce Clause' (1985–1986) 84 Michigan LR 1091 at 1160–1167.

[293] See C.R. Sunstein, 'Protectionism, the American Supreme Court, and Integrated Markets' in R. Bieber, R. Dehousse, J. Pinder and J.H.H. Weiler (eds), *1992: One European Market? A Critical Analysis of the Commission's Internal Market Strategy* (Baden-Baden 1988) 142.

[294] Poiares Maduro (n 292 above) 309–310. He discussed this in the context of Case C-391/92 *Commission v Greece* (Processed milk for infants) [1995] ECR I-1621.

[295] Poiares Maduro (n 9 above) 174.

[296] For other criticism, see D. Chalmers, 'Book Review on We the Court' (1999) 115 LQR 148 at 150. See also U.B. Neergaard, 'Free Movement of Goods from a Contextual Perspective, A Review Essay' (1999) 6 MJ 151 at 162–167, who considers the proposal a still preliminary sketch.

its judgment in *Schindler*.[297] Although at first sight the decision might seem difficult to reconcile with *Keck*, in reality the ruling can be explained with reference to a wide concept of discrimination.

The case involved two Schindler brothers, who acted as independent agents for the Süddeutsche Klassenlotterie. They operated from the Netherlands and had sent some 20,000 invitations to participate in the lottery to residents of the United Kingdom. The letters were seized by Customs as the UK legislation at that time provided only for some local lotteries and disallowed the type in issue. In a subsequent action, the High Court asked the European Court of Justice inter alia whether Article 49 (ex 59) EC applied to the UK ban on such lotteries.

At first sight it might seem that the Court could have decided the case by directly applying the principles behind the *Keck* judgment. After all, if examined superficially, the legislation seemed to impose an equal burden on both domestic and foreign service providers, as neither were allowed to organise large-scale lotteries. The Court might therefore have been expected to rule that the UK measures were outside Article 49 altogether, in line with the ruling in *Keck*, which is based on the absence of an unequal burden.

Yet, the Court chose a different route. Following Advocate General Gulmann it held that the national legislation, although non-discriminatory, created an obstacle to the provision of services but was justified by concerns of social policy and the prevention of fraud.

The language used by the Court differs from that in *Keck*. The Court referred to its earlier decision in *Säger*[298] stating that 'national legislation may fall within the ambit of Article 59 [now 49] of the Treaty, even if it is applicable without distinction, when it is liable to prohibit or otherwise *impede* the activities of a provider of services established in another Member State, where he lawfully provides similar services'.[299]

Therefore, the judgment might be read as a confirmation that the free movement of services is not only concerned with discrimination and unequal burden but truly requires the abolition of all obstacles which cannot be justified, in accordance with the economic freedom model. The case law on services could be seen as diverging from the case law on goods. This view certainly finds support in the language used by the Court.[300]

The issue of discrimination   It is, however, possible to reconcile the case with the judgment in *Keck*. The UK legislation can be seen as a 'product rule' and

---

[297] Case C-275/92 *Her Majesty's Customs and Excise v Gerhart Schindler and Jörg Schindler* [1994] ECR I-1039. AG Tesauro, whose Opinion in Case C-292/92 *Hünermund v Landesapothekerkammer Baden-Württemberg* [1993] ECR I-6787 formed the foundation for the decision in *Keck*, is of the opinion that *Keck* should not be extended into the field of services at all. See G. Tesauro, 'The Community Internal Market in the Light of the Recent Case-law of the Court of Justice' (1995) 15 YEL 1 at 7.

[298] Case C-76/90 *Manfred Säger v Dennemeyer & Co. Ltd* [1991] ECR I-4221.

[299] See n 297 above, para 43 (emphasis added).

[300] See Hatzopoulos (n 154 above) 847–848.

thus automatically placing service providers from other Member States at a disadvantage. The rules did not ban all lotteries or games of chance but only large-scale lotteries. They imposed requirements that lotteries must meet as regards, for instance, their maximum price and turnover. It could be argued that the national regulation related to the characteristics of the service and created a dual burden on the provider. In order to gain access to the UK market, it would have been necessary to adapt the service to correspond to the national requirements. The language of the Court, which held the measure to be non-discriminatory, is not conclusive on this issue. In the past the Court has often stated that national measures have been equally applicable, even though they have actually imposed a heavier burden on out-of-state interests.[301]

The apparent non-discriminatory nature of the measure is also subject to doubt in a more concrete manner. The defendants and the Commission both argued that the legislation was discriminatory in fact.

The United Kingdom permitted one person to operate several small lotteries at the same time and allowed other games of chance comparable to large lotteries. Thus, it was argued that organisers of these domestic activities were protected from foreign competition by the ban on large-scale lotteries. Both the Advocate General and the Court disagreed with the argument. The Court held that differences in the objects, rules and methods of organisation between prohibited lotteries and legal games of chance meant that they were not in a comparable situation.[302] As the situations were different, they could be treated differently.

The different views illustrate the general difficulties inherent in the conceptually simple discrimination investigation.[303] The problems are common to all analyses of discriminatory effects made in the context of Community economic law. Thus the difficulties have also surfaced in the Court's decisions relating to Article 90 (ex 95) EC, which establishes the principle of non-discrimination as the basis for assessing national regimes of internal taxation. The case law has been slightly erratic.[304]

Imported goods or services are placed at a disadvantage if national measures protect *competing* national goods or services.[305] The decisive criterion is whether or not consumers perceive the products as inter-changeable. There has to be a degree of cross-elasticity of demand.

However, potential competition between the products is already sufficient to bring discrimination analysis into play. Otherwise, regulations would be

---

[301] See Marenco (n 157 above) 148.   [302] See n 297 above, para 51.

[303] See generally D. Chalmers and E. Szyszczak, *European Union Law. Vol II. Towards a European Polity?* (Aldershot 1998) 276–284.

[304] Craig and de Búrca (n 121 above) 578.

[305] Case C-391/92 *Commission v Greece* (Processed milk for infants) [1995] ECR I-1621 para 18. In the same case AG Lenz examined the substitutability of breast and bottle as methods for feeding babies. He came to the conclusion that they were not substitutes, as 'a mother's decision as to how to feed her child is determined by other factors [than price and difficulty of procurement], including the socio-economic ones'.

able to crystallise the existing situation. This could happen, for example, if different regulatory burdens create such large price differences between the products in question that consumers do not see them as inter-changeable.[306]

Substitutability is not an either/or but rather a more-or-less issue. There are different degrees of inter-changeability and, thus, different degrees of cross-elasticity.[307] For example, it is probable that the competitive relationship between different fruit juices is strong while the relationship between fruit juices and carbonated soft drinks is only weak.

This may lead to the problem of over-extension. Almost no regulation is completely economically neutral. The burden on some products is inevitably heavier than that placed on others.[308] If material discrimination were always found in situations where even a weak competitive relationship exists and one product is put at a disadvantage, discrimination would be established in the majority of cases.

The danger of over-extension means that the Court has to adopt a more sophisticated approach.[309] It has to take account of factors such as the degree of cross-elasticity and the weight of the burden. If both are very small, discrimination should not be found.

The relationship between prohibited dissimilar treatment and substitutability can be seen in the structure of Article 90 (ex 95) EC. Article 90(1) (ex 95(1)) EC prohibits all differences in treatment between similar products, while Article 90(2) (ex 95(2)) EC requires only that protection is not afforded to competing domestic products.[310] As inter-changeability decreases, the scope for differential treatment increases.

The demonstration of material discrimination can require sophisticated market analysis and the use of economic information. The importance of empirical evidence of market conditions increases. This may create difficulties for private plaintiffs who do not have the necessary resources and for national courts, which may not be familiar with these kinds of issues.[311]

It is difficult to say for sure whether the measures at issue in *Schindler* did place services originating from other Member States at a disadvantage in this way when compared to competing domestic services. The reasoning of the Court simply did not contain any scrutiny of substitutability.[312] However, it

[306] Case 170/78 *Commission v United Kingdom* (Wine/beer) [1983] ECR 2265 para 27. See Craig and de Búrca (n 121 above) 572–573, and Weatherill and Beaumont (n 17 above) 482.

[307] When deciding the issue of dominance under Art 82 (ex 86) EC, it is always necessary to take into account the competitive pressures flowing from outside the defined market. Markets are not isolated but overlapping. See Korah (n 214 above) 104, and Whish (n 216 above) 255–256.

[308] Chalmers (n 12 above) 399.

[309] ibid, 399–400, and Craig and de Búrca (n 121 above) 572–573.

[310] See Weatherill and Beaumont (n 17 above) 483–484.

[311] Chalmers (n 12 above) 400–401, and Weatherill and Beaumont (n 17 above) 618–619.

[312] The Court has been criticised for not examining thoroughly under Art 28 (ex 30) EC whether rules affecting selling arrangements discriminate 'in fact'. See Higgins (n 271 above) 179–180. However, more recently in Joined Cases C-34/95, C-35/95 and C-36/95 *Konsumentombudsmannen v De Agostini (Svenska) Förlag AB and TV-Shop i Sverige AB* [1997] ECR I-3843, following AG Jacobs, it took a realistic view of material discrimination, although

is submitted that there probably was a degree of inter-changeability between prohibited large-scale lotteries and permitted games of chance. As the difference in treatment was very significant, it may be argued that the national measures were materially discriminatory in a very concrete manner.[313]

The issue of total bans   Another way of reconciling the cases is to emphasise the distinction between quantitative restrictions and measures having an equivalent effect.[314] *Keck* determines only that certain measures fall outside the latter category while Article 28 (ex 30) EC also prohibits rules belonging to the former class.[315] In *Henn and Darby*[316] the Court held that an absolute ban on importation of pornography constituted a quantitative restriction as it limited the amount of imports to zero. The UK legislation at issue in *Schindler* imposed a total ban on large-scale lotteries and could be said to correspond to a quota of zero.

It has been argued that total prohibitions of importation can be assimilated with border measures, which are per se problematic and can be condemned even if there is no element of discrimination.[317] The argument is not wholly convincing. It is true that quotas can be called border measures, tend to be discriminatory, and are especially offensive to the aims of the Community. However, as White notes, the Court has not traditionally treated national measures differently solely on the ground that they take effect at the border.[318] Furthermore, prohibitions do not necessarily have to be related to the crossing of the border. Controls can be mainly or even wholly internal.

A better view relates to mutual recognition. A total ban runs counter to the philosophy of mutual recognition. A product lawfully marketed in one Member State is not granted access to the market of another Member State. This is a case of a multiple burden. A product corresponds to the regulations

it was for the national court to determine whether the national measures actually did discriminate against imports. The approach adopted in *De Agostini* was confirmed in Case C-405/98 *Konsumentombudsmannen v Gourmet International Products Aktiebolag*, judgment of 8 March 2001, paras 18–25, again following AG Jacobs. See also Case C-254/98 *Schutzverband gegen unlauteren Wettbewerb v TK-Heimdienst Sass GmbH*, judgment of 13 January 2000.

[313] It has to be noted that *Schindler* was decided shortly after *Keck* and the new principles were not yet argued before the Court.

[314] The decision of the Court in Case C-398/95 *Syndesmos ton en Elladi Touristikon kai Taxidiotikon Grafeion v Ypourgos Ergasias* [1997] ECR I-3091 can also be explained with reference to this distinction. The Court held that equally applicable Greek rules, which totally prevented the provision of services by licensed tourist guides, constituted a barrier for the purposes of Art 49 (ex 59) EC.

[315] The judgment explains the finding that non-discriminatory rules concerning selling arrangements fall outside the scope of the free movement of goods by stating, inter alia, that such measures do not prevent market access. See Joined Cases C-267/91 and C-268/91 *Criminal Proceedings Against Keck and Mithouard* [1993] ECR I-6097 para 17. A total ban naturally prevents market access completely.

[316] Case 34/79 *R v Henn and Darby* [1979] ECR 3795.

[317] Bernard (n 15 above) 98–99. In GATT a distinction is made between border measures and internal measures. See White (n 17 above) 239–241.

[318] White (n 17 above) 241.

of its home state. The requirement of an adherence to the host state rules creates a second burden. This, in my view, is the decisive point, the preferred way of reconciling the judgments in *Keck* and *Schindler* and the reason why the Court considers that total prohibitions fall automatically within the scope of the free movement provisions.[319]

In one sense, product rules and total bans are the same. In the case of product rules, a product has to be changed in order to gain access to the market. The same is true in the case of a ban. The change required is just more fundamental. Of course, in both cases it may be practically or commercially impossible to modify the product. Take as an example a Member State product rule requiring that kitchen knives be no more than 30 cm long. A 35 cm knife from another Member State has to be shortened to be allowed into the market. There is a clear double burden. The same Member State may have imposed a total ban on daggers. A dagger from another Member State has also to be modified, but so fundamentally that it no longer falls within the category of daggers. Again, there is a double burden. In both cases the national measures are discriminatory in the wide sense.

There is one further objection to total bans. If a product is subject to restrictive measures, it may be assumed that the producers in the regulating state will in many instances try to lobby to change the national rules.[320] This political pressure will also work for the benefit of imports. However, if the product is totally banned, such lobbying may not take place as the only interested parties, potential producers and potential consumers, tend not to be organised enough to mount such a campaign.[321]

Generally, the economic law of the Community ought to treat goods and services in the same manner.[322] Prohibitions of goods are considered to fall under Article 28 (ex 30) EC per se, and similarly prohibitions of services should automatically come within the scope of Article 49 (ex 59) EC. The fact that the wording of Article 49 does not make a distinction similar to the one between quantitative restrictions and measures having equivalent effect in Article 28 should not be decisive.[323]

If prohibitions fall automatically under Articles 28 and 49, what about quasi-prohibitions, which create such severe restrictions that access of the

---

[319] Daniele is also of the opinion that mutual recognition is the key to the Court's reasoning in *Schindler*. See L. Daniele, 'Non-Discriminatory Restrictions to the Free Movement of Persons' (1997) 22 ELRev 191, 195–196. On mutual recognition and rules concerning selling arrangements see section 1e above and section 5civ below.

[320] Unless the rules give protection to national producers against foreign competitors.

[321] Ensuring this virtual representation of out-of-state interests has been one of the dominant themes of modern commerce clause analysis in the USA. See Tribe (n 279 above) 408–413. For criticism see Regan (n 292 above) 1160–1167.

[322] See in more detail Chapter 1 section 3 above. See also Barnard (n 277 above) 48 who submits that the *Schindler* approach should also be applied to goods.

[323] See however Marenco (n 157 above) 149–150, and Wyatt and Dashwood (n 118 above) 477–478, where it is argued that total bans are in general genuinely non-discriminatory, with the implication that the Court should not challenge national rules prohibiting a certain service activity.

products to national markets is virtually impossible? Such measures can regulate either characteristics of the product or selling arrangements. An example of the latter would be legislation which allows trade in certain goods or services only in a couple of locations. White argues with respect to goods that such rules must be assimilated to quantitative restrictions.[324]

As regards services, the Court decided in *Koestler*[325] that a German refusal to allow a service provider to recover from a client, when recovery would be based on a stock-exchange contract treated like a wager, fell outside Article 49 since it entailed no discrimination.[326] The measure can be described as a quasi-prohibition. In practice, it made the provision of services relating to those contracts nearly impossible. Yet, the Court treated the measure in the same way as any other restriction.

The Court's post-*Keck* case law relating to goods does not offer much support to the theory that quasi-prohibitions amount to quantitative restrictions either. The Court has in general only analysed whether a measure is a product rule or regulates selling arrangements, and in the latter case whether it is discriminatory in law or in fact. In most cases it has not been concerned with the total impact of the measure.[327]

No matter which way the *Keck* and *Schindler* cases are reconciled, it is clear that the latter cannot be taken to mean that all truly equal-burden rules affecting the volume of trade in services are caught by Article 49, or that the principles behind free movement of goods and services are fundamentally different. This judgment neither amounts to the acceptance of the economic freedom model in the field of services nor repudiates the uniform approach to goods and services.

ii) Reisebüro Broede

Another case that may at first sight seem difficult to reconcile with *Keck* is *Reisebüro Broede*.[328] In issue was German legislation reserving the judicial

---

[324] White (n 17 above) 258–259.

[325] Case 15/78 *Société Générale Alsacienne de Banque v Koestler* [1978] ECR 1971.

[326] The Court did refer to the reason behind the measure. However, it did not enter into a proper examination of justification, but rather decided the issue on discrimination grounds. Case C-405/98 *Konsumentombudsmannen v Gourmet International Products Aktiebolag*, judgment of 8 March 2001, concerned a prohibition, with some limited exceptions, of alcohol advertising. The Court treated this as a restriction on export of services. Therefore, the issues that arose were different, as the ban was imposed by the home state. Also, the rule prevented the advertising of only one category of products. See further section 5cv below.

[327] See however section 5d below on cases which might give support to the theory in the field of goods. See also the Opinion of AG Jacobs in Case C-412/93 *Société d'Importation Édouard Leclerc-Siplec v TF1 Publicité SA and M6 Publicité SA* [1995] ECR 179 para 38 where he criticises *Keck* and argues that it would be wrong to allow measures creating serious obstacles merely because they happen to be regulating selling arrangements. The assimilation of quasi-prohibitions to quantitative restrictions is similar to the *de minimis* rule advocated by AG Jacobs in that both require analysis of the actual impact of the measure.

[328] Case C-3/95 *Reisebüro Broede v Gerd Sandker* [1996] ECR I-6511.

enforcement of debts to lawyers. This prevented INC Consulting SARL from collecting a debt for its client, Reisebüro Broede. As the debt-collecting undertaking had its seat in France, the question arose whether the legislation infringed EC Treaty provisions on the free movement of services.

The measure applied equally to domestic and foreign debt-collecting undertakings. All were required to retain the services of lawyers. Furthermore, it did not prevent lawyers from other Member States from being retained to act in the judicial proceedings and therefore did not afford direct protection to domestic interests.[329] Foreign lawyers were not prevented from competing with German ones. Nevertheless, the Court held, citing its previous case law and following Advocate General Fennelly, that the German legislation was prima facie in conflict with Article 49 (ex 59) EC.[330]

The Court's classification of the measure as a prima facie restriction on the free movement of services was undoubtedly correct. The French company was not able to provide the service in Germany it was providing in France. The legislation promoted the partitioning of the common market and had the effect of preventing the economies of scale. Therefore, it endangered another key objective of the internal market and free movement: the objective being to allow European undertakings to benefit from scale economies and to grow to optimal size. The intended result is to lower costs and to allow European enterprises to compete with American and Japanese firms benefiting from their own large home markets.

The measure also created a dual burden on the French service provider. Although it was complying with home country rules, it could not provide the service in Germany but was required to adhere to a second set of rules.

The German measure can be compared with product rules, not with rules concerning selling arrangements. It set out requirements that the service provider itself had to fulfil. This is comparable to a measure regulating the characteristics of the manufacturer of goods, not to a measure stipulating who may sell a product. It is intrinsically linked to the product itself.

The German legislation was at odds with the philosophy of mutual recognition. It did not allow the service provider to enter the market under home country control. Thus, it prevented full scale competition between legal orders. German customers were not allowed to vote with their purse for the more liberal French regime, which would have provided domestic undertakings and factors of production with an incentive to migrate or lobby and political actors with a signal that the regulation was too strict.

---

[329] The Commission had argued that German rules functioned for the monopolistic benefit of domestic lawyers. This argument was dismissed by AG Fennelly in his Opinion, ibid, para 34.

[330] ibid, paras 25–27. The parties had not contested the issue. The measures were, however, justified by reasons of protecting the recipients of the services and safeguarding the proper administration of justice.

Furthermore, the rules afforded some protection to German lawyers. Although competition from foreign lawyers remained possible, specialised debt-collecting undertakings were not able to challenge them.[331]

Thus, the Court's judgment in *Reisebüro Broede* is in line with the decision in the *Keck* case. The philosophy behind the rulings is similar.

iii) De Agostini

The approach of the Court to the free movement of services in *De Agostini*[332] is in line with *Keck* as well, although the answer given by the Court seems to widen the reach of Article 49 (ex 59) EC. In issue were Swedish rules prohibiting all advertising that was unfair to consumers or traders and television advertising designed to attract the attention of children under the age of 12. The Consumer Ombudsman sought to apply the rules to television advertisements broadcast from the United Kingdom by satellite.

The Court held, citing *Gouda*,[333] that the Swedish legislation did constitute a restriction on the freedom to provide services. It supported this view by stating that, in the absence of harmonisation, 'restrictions may result from application of national rules affecting any person established in the territory of another Member State who already have to satisfy the requirements of that State's legislation'.[334] It continued by ruling that it was for the national court to determine the potential justification of the law.

The Court then answered the national court's question by stating that:

on a proper construction of Article 59 [now 49] of the Treaty the Member State is not precluded from taking, on the basis of provisions of its domestic legislation, measures against an advertiser in relation to television advertising. However, it is for the national court to determine whether those provisions are necessary for meeting overriding requirements of general public importance or one of the aims mentioned in Article 56 [now 46] of the Treaty, whether they are proportionate for that purpose and whether those aims or overriding requirements could be met by measures less restrictive of intra-Community trade.[335]

This operative part of the judgment goes extremely far. The ruling proper, and paragraph 50, would seem to indicate that also truly non-discriminatory provisions of national law, which do not create an unequal burden, fall under Article 49.

Paragraph 51 shows, however, that the Court did not intend to widen the scope of the free movement of services. It justified the prima facie applicability of Article 49 (ex 59) EC by referring to the dual burden created by the

---

[331] See also Marenco (n 157 above) 142, who explains *Säger* in similar terms.

[332] Joined Cases C-34/95, C-35/95 and C-36/95 *Konsumentombudsmannen v De Agostini (Svenska) Förlag AB and TV-Shop i Sverige AB* [1997] ECR I-3843.

[333] Case C-288/89 *Collectieve Antennevoorziening Gouda* [1991] ECR I-4007.

[334] See n 332 above para 51.   [335] ibid, para 54.

application of two sets of regulations. Sweden was trying to apply its rules to an activity that was already regulated by the broadcasting state, the United Kingdom.

Although the operative part constitutes the 'ruling' in the strict sense, it must be construed in the light of the reasoning preceding it.[336] Therefore the answer, which seems to indicate that all measures taken against television advertisers fall within Article 4, does not have to be taken literally. The Court was not extending the reach of the free movement of services beyond *Keck*.[337]

iv) Alpine Investments

General The Court's ruling in *Alpine Investments*[338] could be reconciled with *Keck* and the principles behind it. This would create a sensible doctrine allocating regulatory competences between Member States. However, when read together with the judgment in *Bosman*,[339] the decision seems to create a new doctrine in the internal market law of the Community. The cases may imply that the Court's approach to the free movement of workers and services is diverging from its approach to the free movement of goods. Another possibility is that the Court will use the doctrine also in connection with Article 28 (ex 30) EC and refine *Keck*. The desirability of the entire development, which is a step towards the economic freedom model, is questionable.

The factual situation in *Alpine Investments* was unusual. A ministerial ban prevented Dutch undertakings providing financial services from cold-calling potential customers. The ban applied also to customers in the other Member States. Thus, the Netherlands created a restraint on the export of services and disadvantaged its own firms as compared with undertakings operating domestically in the host Member States.

The Dutch measure was a general one, it did not discriminate and neither its purpose nor its effect was to put the national market at an advantage over providers of services from the other Member States. Therefore, the Dutch and British governments, drawing an analogy from the Court's decision in *Keck*, argued that the measure fell outside Article 49 (ex 59) EC altogether.

The Court, following Advocate General Jacobs, held that the Dutch ban amounted to a prima facie restriction on the free movement of services but was justified on grounds of the general good. It distinguished the situation from *Keck* and rejected the arguments of the Dutch and British governments.[340] By distinguishing Keck on the facts without referring to any differences between Articles 28 (ex 30) EC and 49 (ex 59) EC, the Court seemed to

[336] See D.W.K. Anderson, *References to the European Court of Justice* (London 1995) 287.
[337] On other aspects of the case see Snell (n 82 above) 222–227.
[338] Case C-384/93 *Alpine Investments BV v Minister van Financiën* [1995] ECR I-1141.
[339] Case C-415/93 *Union Royale Belge des Sociétés de Football Association ASBL and others v Jean-Marc Bosman* [1995] ECR I-4921.
[340] See n 338 above, para 36.

implicitly accept that a similar approach could be used to deal with the free movement of both goods and services.

Dividing regulatory competences? *Alpine Investments* can indeed be distinguished from *Keck*. Both cases concerned marketing rules, but in the former the measure was imposed by the exporting home state, while in the latter the measure originated from the importing host state. In the former case there was a dual burden. The service provider had also to comply with rules regulating selling arrangements in the host country. In the latter only one set of rules applied. The home country rules affecting selling arrangements were of no relevance whatsoever. The situations were fundamentally different.

The dangers inherent in allowing the application of two sets of rules, whether they concern product requirements or selling arrangements,[341] were fully recognised by Advocate General Jacobs.[342] In the worst case scenario the rules could be contradictory, and thus negate the whole freedom. An example might be the following: if the home country rule requires the disclosure of the identity of the broker orders are placed with but the host country rule prohibits such disclosure in the interest of preventing customer confusion, the combined effect of these rules would be to prevent cross-border trade completely.

Alpine Investments can also be reconciled with the Court's case law on Article 29 (ex 34) EC. The Court has consistently refused to apply the *Cassis* test to export restrictions. It has held that Article 29 applies only to discriminatory measures.[343] As Advocate General Jacobs noted in his Opinion, the applicability of this case law to marketing rules was doubtful. *Product rules* are the exporting home country's responsibility. The importing country is not able to apply its regulations without subjecting them to scrutiny by the Court. A dual burden does not normally arise. Therefore, the Court does not need to be concerned unless the rules of the exporting home country are discriminatory.

Marketing rules, such as the one at issue in *Alpine Investments*, are different from product rules.[344] The importing host country is responsible for regulating selling arrangements and, according to *Keck*, does not infringe the EC Treaty unless it discriminates. If the exporting home country also tries to

---

[341] The situations where two sets of regulations apply to selling arrangements are rare. If a service provider moves to another Member State, the rules of his home state concerning market circumstances are seldom relevant. Similarly, the home state loses control of goods once they cross the border. In the case of services not requiring physical movement, the service provider may stay within the jurisdiction of the home state, however, while the host state imposes requirements as well. See V. Hatzopoulos, 'Case C-384/93, *Alpine Investments BV* v. *Minister van Financiën*, Judgment of 10 May 1995, nyr' (1995) 32 CMLRev 1427 at 1436–1437.

[342] See n 338 above, para 61 of his Opinion.

[343] Case 15/79 *Groenveld v Produktschap voor Vee en Vlees* [1979] ECR 3409, Case 155/80 *Oebel* [1981] ECR 1993, and Case C-339/89 *Alsthom Atlantique SA v Sulzer SA* [1991] ECR I-107.

[344] This was also recognised by AG Jacobs in his Opinion (n 338 above) para 55.

apply its rules to selling arrangements, a double burden is created. The justification for the measures has to be examined.

It could be argued that the Court's case law has divided the regulatory capacities between Member States in order to avoid a double burden. The home country controls the product rules while the host country deals with selling arrangements.[345] These measures do not fall under the EC Treaty provisions on free movement unless the rules discriminate against interests from other Member States. The exception to this scheme is the power of a state to impose justified restrictions if its legitimate non-economic policies would otherwise be frustrated. In these situations co-ordination between Member States is not enough; harmonisation by the centre becomes necessary.

The division of competences established by the case law is similar to the one prevailing in the financial services directives. Authorisation and prudential supervision are requirements relating to characteristics of the producer. They are the responsibility of the home country. Rules of conduct are a matter for the host Member State.[346]

This view of the free movement rules is fully in accordance with the philosophy of competition between legal orders. Products are allowed to enter markets freely and maintain all competitive advantages. At the same time Member States are given the greatest possible freedom to discover efficient rules suited to the preferences of their citizens.

The language of the Court emphasising that provisions on free movement apply also to non-discriminatory measures does not rule out this interpretation. The Court uses the term 'discrimination' in a strict, narrow sense: it only applies to situations where the unequal treatment can be *imputed* to a Member State.[347] However, it does not cover situations of a multiple burden. It might be argued that when, for example, a Member State of importation is applying its product rules to foreign goods, it is treating different situations similarly.[348] After all, it applies its rules equally to domestic and imported products even though the goods coming from another Member State have already conformed with one set of regulations. Be that as it may, the Court's insistence on a narrow definition of discrimination means that its statements on equally applicable rules being caught by the EC Treaty do not rule out the possibility that a multiple burden is required for the free movement provisions to enter into play.

[345] See N. Bernard, 'La libre circulation des marchandises, des personnes et des services dans le traité CE sous l'angle de la competence' (1998) 34 CDE 11 at 33–35, and Chalmers and Szyszczak (n 303 above) 304. The importing country may experience difficulties in enforcing its rules as regards services moving, eg, by telecommunications or by post. This is an argument for increased co-operation in the fields of justice and home affairs.

[346] See eg the Investment Services Directive 93/22/EEC [1993] OJ L141/27, Arts 3, 10 and 11. See also G. Hertig, 'Imperfect Mutual Recognition for EC Financial Services' (1994) 14 International Review of Law and Economics 177 at 179.

[347] See Kapteyn and VerLoren van Themaat (n 135 above) 171, and Marenco (n 135 above) 320.

[348] This was found to be a prohibited form of discrimination in Case 13/63 *Commission v Italy* [1963] ECR 165.

Viewed from this perspective, the Dutch measure at issue in *Alpine Invest-ments* was caught by Article 49 (ex 59) EC precisely because it was imposed by the exporting state, causing a double burden. If the measure had been imposed by the importing host state, it would have fallen outside Article 49 altogether (assuming no discrimination in law or in fact). The same would have been true even if products marketed by cold-calling had been goods, not services.

This view of *Alpine Investments* and the internal market law has its weak-nesses. The viability of a distinction between product rules and rules affecting selling arrangements can be questioned. Sometimes the marketing of prod-ucts combines presentation and appearance of the product with advertising; the product and its marketing cannot always be separated. The application of different rules to these interrelated aspects of distribution can create anom-alous results.[349]

To resolve this problem, it has been proposed that a distinction should be made between rules regulating static and dynamic selling arrangements. The former category would include measures regulating questions such as when products may be sold, while the latter category would contain rules not relat-ing to activities situated in a fixed location. According to this view, the rules concerning dynamic selling arrangements can have a strong link to the prod-uct itself, form a threat to the free circulation and should therefore be treated in the same way as measures regulating the characteristics of products.[350]

It may also be that the distinction between rules affecting selling arrange-ments and product rules cannot be applied 'as is' in the field of services. The distinction might be more difficult to use in practice. In addition, the Court would have to find another formula that clearly encompassed rules setting qualifications required of service providers. This is the most common form of regulating services. The application of these rules by the importing host state typically creates a double burden in the same manner as product rules do in the field of goods. However, in my view even if a new formulation could not easily be found, regulatory competences could still be divided in the field of services by applying the *principles* that underpin the judgment in *Keck*. The wide concept of discrimination is equally relevant in both fields.[351]

---

[349] See Higgins (n 271 above) 170, Roth (n 279 above) 852, and S. Weatherill, 'After *Keck*: Some Thoughts on How to Clarify the Clarification' (1996) 33 CMLRev 885, 896.

[350] See Mortelmans (n 12 above) 130. See also Craig and de Búrca (n 121 above) 620–621.

[351] J.L. da Cruz Vilaca, 'An Exercise on the Application of Keck and Mithouard in the Field of Free Provision of Services' in M. Dony and A. De Walsche (eds), *Mélanges en hommage à Michel Waelbroeck* (Bruxelles 1999) 815 suggests that *Keck* be transposed into the field of ser-vices, and that a distinction be made between '[r]ules concerning the *"intrinsic" characteristics* of the service . . . [and] . . . [r]ules relating to the *general* or *"extrinsic" conditions* in which . . . ser-vices can be provided'. Oliver, 'Goods and Services: Two Freedoms Compared' in M. Dony and A. De Walsche (eds), *Mélanges en hommage à Michel Waelbroeck* (Bruxelles 1999) 1395 argues that 'to distinguish between "product-bound" restrictions on services and those which concern "selling arrangements" will frequently be no easy matter . . . Nevertheless, in some cases such a distinction can usefully be made'. In Wyatt and Dashwood (n 118 above) 479 it is argued that 'principles analogous to those contained in the *Keck* judgment ought in principle be applicable'

The argument about the artificiality of the distinction is valid, but the problem may not be insurmountable. A sensible demarcation of selling arrangements and product presentation is possible in most cases. For example, in the *Clinique*,[352] *Mars*,[353] and *Familiapress*[354] judgments, the Court rightly found that the national measures fell under the category of product rules, not rules affecting selling arrangements. The concept of 'product rules' can often be construed in a wide manner so that rules genuinely threatening the internal market fall automatically under the relevant EC Treaty article.

Furthermore, even if such a measure is considered to affect only selling arrangements, it can quite often be found to discriminate in fact. This might be the case if the rules force the producer to adopt a different sales promotion strategy or to discontinue an especially effective scheme in one Member State.[355]

Most, if not all, Member State measures endangering the single market would be caught under this doctrine. Take the example of obstacles to direct television marketing.[356] A system where a distributor advertises goods on television, displaying a contact number for each country in which the channel is received, is becoming increasingly common. If a Member State prohibits this scheme, an obstacle to trade is without doubt created, as distributors are deprived of an international marketing strategy. This kind of restriction would fall foul of the EC Treaty even under the *Keck* doctrine. First of all, it

also in the context of the provision of services. Finally, A. Türk, 'Recent Case Law in Services and Establishment' (1998) EBLR 193 at 201 suggests that in the field of services 'the Court may instead apply a modified *Keck* test, which would exclude national measures from scrutiny when they apply indistinctly in law and in fact', but contrast this with Chalmers and Szysczcak (n 303 above) 406 and 423.

[352] Case C-315/92 *Verband Sozialer Wettbewerb v Estée Lauder* [1994] ECR I-317. The case concerned a German prohibition to use the name 'Clinique' for a cosmetic product as it might have misled consumers into believing that the product had medicinal properties. This forced the producer to relabel. The Court held that the German measure constituted a product rule and, therefore, a restriction, and was unjustified.

[353] Case C-470/93 *Verein gegen Unwesen in Handel und Gewerbe Köln e. V. v Mars GmbH* [1995] ECR I-1923. The case concerned German law on unfair competition and law on restraints of competition. The plaintiffs argued that marking of '+10%' in wrappers of ice-cream bars contravened German law as it was misleading to consumers and/or involved prohibited price fixing. The Court held that rules prohibiting certain publicity markings on the packaging of goods were product rules and, therefore, by their nature hindered intra-Community trade. The German measures were not justified.

[354] Case C-368/95 *Vereinigte Familiapress Zeitungsverlags-und vertriebs GmbH v Heinrich Bauer Verlag* [1997] ECR I-3689. In issue was an Austrian law containing a prohibition on offering consumers gifts linked to the sale of goods. This rule was used against a German magazine containing puzzles. The readers could send in their solutions and participate in a draw for prizes. The Court held, following AG Tesauro, that the legislation bore on the content of the products and was, therefore, not concerned with a selling arrangement. It was for the national court to determine whether the law was justified by the objective of maintaining press diversity.

[355] Case 286/81 *Oosthoek Uitgeversmaatschapij BV* [1982] ECR 4575. See Craig and de Búrca (n 121 above) 620.

[356] Example given by AG Jacobs in his Opinion in Case C-412/93 *Société d'Importation Édouard Leclerc-Siplec v TF1 Publicité SA and M6 Publicité SA* [1995] ECR I-179 para 54. Weatherill sees this situation as especially problematic. He is of the opinion that the issue could not be adequately dealt with under the *Keck* formula. Weatherill (n 349 above) 890–891 and 894.

could be challenged under Article 28 (ex 30) EC. Although the rule regulates selling arrangements, it has an unequal impact on importers as they are required to modify their marketing system, which creates additional costs.[357] Secondly, the rule could be seen as a restriction on the free movement of services. Advertising and broadcasting of television signals are services. Here the national rule affects the content of the advertisements. It is a product rule. It creates a dual burden as the commercial complying with the rules of the broadcasting state also has to comply with the rules of the receiving state. Thus, the national measure would be caught by Article 49 (ex 59) EC.[358]

A real example is provided by the *De Agostini* case.[359] Swedish rules prohibiting certain forms of advertising in television, which were used against advertisements broadcast from the United Kingdom, were examined under both Articles 28 (ex 30) and 49 (ex 59) EC. Following Advocate General Jacobs, the Court stated that the prohibition of one method of promotion, which affected selling arrangements, could have a greater impact on goods from other Member States, as a certain form of advertising may be the only way to penetrate the market. It was left to the national court to examine whether the rules were actually discriminatory 'in fact' in this manner. The rules also fell within the scope of Article 49 (ex 59) EC as they established a second set of controls creating a dual burden.[360]

It is true that the division between product rules and rules affecting selling arrangements is formalistic. This is not necessarily a bad thing. Formalism increases legal certainty, and this is a matter of great importance for national courts. It is only if formalism enables many national measures harmful to the internal market to escape scrutiny that there is a problem. This does not seem to be the case. And most importantly, even if the formalism can be criticised, this does not yet invalidate the principles behind *Keck* establishing a wide concept of discrimination as the basis of the free movement law.

It has, however, sometimes been claimed that the double burden theory is not appropriate for many services, as they only crystallise on commercialisation. This will often happen in the importing host state.[361] An example is a rock concert. If an English band goes to Sweden to perform, the service is provided in Sweden, even though the band may have held similar concerts in the United Kingdom.

---

[357] This is recognised by AG Jacobs in his Opinion (n 356 above) para 37.

[358] National procedural rules might create difficulties for a challenge based on Art 49 (ex 59) EC. However, Member States are under an obligation to grant access to the courts. See Case 222/84 *Johnston v Chief Constable of the Royal Ulster Constabulary* [1986] ECR 1651 paras 13–21, Case 222/86 *UNECTEF v Heylens* [1987] ECR 4097 para 14, M. Brealey and M. Hoskins, *Remedies in EC Law. Law and Practice in English and EC Courts* (2nd edn London 1998) 101–102, and J. Temple Lang, 'The Duties of National Courts Under Community Constitutional Law' (1997) 22 ELRev 3 at 7.

[359] Joined Cases C-34/95, C-35/95 and C-36/95 *Konsumentombudsmannen v De Agostini (Svenska) Förlag AB and TV-Shop i Sverige AB* [1997] ECR I-3843.

[360] See in more detail Snell (n 82 above) 222–227.

[361] Chalmers and Szyszczak (n 303 above) 405 and 423.

It is of course correct to say that the service is not subject to two rules at the same time. However, in my view the wide discrimination or double burden theory works in this context as well. The service has been shaped by the home country rules. The application of the host country rules would prevent the service provider from benefiting from his competitive advantage and would force him to make changes to the service product itself.

Take again the example of the rock band. Assume that the United Kingdom has liberal rules on noise levels in concerts while Sweden is more restrictive. The application of the Swedish rules would deprive the band from reaping the full benefits from its investments in loudspeakers etc. The band may have even advertised itself as 'the loudest band in the Universe'. If strict noise level rules were applied, this competitive advantage would be jeopardised. The band would have to alter the show. This might be as simple as turning the knobs down but might also bring some costs with extra sound checks etc. The application of the Swedish rules would certainly amount to a prima facie restriction, because of the double burden they create, although the rules might well be justified on health grounds.

Naturally there still remains the problem of enforcement. The home country authorities cannot go to the host country to ensure that their rules are respected. In my example, there will be no British noise inspectors in the concert in Sweden.

This problem is not unique to services. It may also occur in the goods sector, for example, if the exporting Member State's product rules are enforced at the retail level. An example might be found in the sex industry. A Member State may have no pre-publication control of printed material, for constitutional reasons. However, the police of the Member State might do random checks in sex shops to find indecent publications. This will create a problem for the importing Member State. If a product is lawfully produced and marketed in the exporting state, it has to be mutually recognised. However, the importing state cannot really be certain that the publications comply with the exporting state's product rules. The exporting state's authorities have not controlled them in any way.

In my view, the host state authorities are entitled to check that the imported goods and services comply with at least one set of rules.[362] Of course, similar checks would have to be carried out on domestic goods and services. This is implicit in the formulas 'lawfully produced and marketed in one of the Member States' and 'established in another Member State where he lawfully provides similar services' which form the precondition to mutual recognition.[363] The idea is not that no rules apply but that one set of rules applies.

---

[362] This does not give the host state a carte blanche to apply home state rules. For example, the host state could check that a service provider holds an appropriate licence but it could not second-guess the granting of the licence, as this would again constitute discrimination. See Commission Interpretative Communication, *Freedom to Provide Services and the General Good in the Insurance Sector* [2000] OJ C43/05, 12.

[363] Case 120/78 *Rewe Zentrale AG v Bundesmonopolverwaltung für Branntwein* [1979] ECR 649 para 14, and Case C-76/90 *Manfred Säger v Dennemeyer & Co. Ltd* [1991] ECR I-4221 para 12.

In my example this means that the Swedish authorities are automatically entitled to inspect that the performance of the British band complies with at least the UK noise level standards, assuming of course that they do similar checks at the concerts of domestic bands. In contrast, the authorities can check compliance with domestic rules only if they are justified.

The problem with this approach is that the host state authorities are forced to apply foreign rules. In my view this does not invalidate the theory. Foreign law is being applied all the time by national courts under private international law. The authorities in different Member States can, and should, co-operate. Article 10 (ex 5) EC imposes on the home state authorities a duty of sincere co-operation[364] so the host state authorities can seek help in determining the content of their rules.[365] If the application of the home state rules proves impossible in a particular situation, this can be easily taken into account when the justification of the host state rules is examined.

The whole problem may not be very significant in the end. The most common way to regulate services is to impose requirements on the service providers, not on the services themselves. These rules clearly create a double burden if they are applied by the host state to a service provider who has already complied with the home country requirements.

To sum up: when *Keck* and *Alpine Investments* are read together, it is possible to argue that the Court has divided regulatory competences so that the importing host state is responsible for regulating market circumstances while the exporting home state deals with product (and production) rules. The importing host state does not have to justify the application of its non-discriminatory rules concerning selling arrangements, only its product (and production) rules. Conversely, the exporting home state does not need to justify the application of its non-discriminatory product (and production) rules, only its rules concerning market circumstances. This co-ordination of national regulatory competences corresponds to a wide notion of discrimination, is very desirable form the point of view of vertical division of power in the Community and regulatory competition, as demonstrated in section 2 above, and also creates a rule-like test sitting well with the role of the Court, as argued in section 5a above. Unfortunately, recent developments in the case law indicate that the Court's approach cannot really be explained by allocation of regulatory competences but is based on a notion of market access.

The problem of Bosman   The judgment of the Court in *Bosman*[366] seems to invalidate the *Keck* doctrine based purely on multiple burden and discrimination. The ruling cannot be fully reconciled with *Keck* but must be seen as a

---

[364] See, eg, Case C-251/89 *Nikolaos Athanasopoulos and others v Bundesanstalt für Arbeit* [1991] ECR I-2797 para 57.

[365] The fact that non-co-operation would impede the export potential of 'their' companies might also be helpful.

[366] Case C-415/93 *Union Royale Belge des Sociétés de Football Association ASBL and others v Jean-Marc Bosman* [1995] ECR I-4921.

refinement, indicating that the Court's view of free movements may be based on market access and that *Alpine Investments* has to be read in that light as well,[367] in contradiction to the previous analysis.

Bosman is an Article 39 (ex 48) EC case. Mr Bosman was a Belgian football player who wanted to move from his Belgian club to a French club. Rules originating from international sporting associations required the receiving club to pay a transfer fee even though Mr Bosman's contract with the Belgian club had expired. A similar fee applied also to transfers within Belgium. The question arose whether the fee was a restriction on the free movement of workers.

The defendants argued that the ruling in *Keck* should be applied by analogy and that, therefore, the equally applicable transfer system should fall outside Article 39 (ex 48) EC altogether. The Court, following Advocate General Lenz, rejected that argument and held that the transfer system violated Article 39 (ex 48) EC and was not justified by reasons of public interest.

The judgment cannot be explained on the grounds of multiple burden or discrimination.[368] The transfer rules themselves may have indeed been discriminatory in practice, but the Court's ruling did not address the issue, instead it revolved around the concept of market access.[369]

---

[367] See Bernard (n 345 above) 23–25, and Poiares Maduro (n 9 above) 100–102. See also R. Greaves, 'Advertising Restrictions and the Free Movement of Goods and Services' (1998) 23 ELRev 305 at 314–315, and D. Martin, '"Discriminations", "entraves" et "raisons imperieuses" dans le traité CE. Trois concepts en quête d'identité' (1998) 34 CDE 261 at 624–625. For an attempt to connect discrimination and market access see H.D. Jarass, 'Elemente einer Dogmatik der Grundfreiheiten II' (2000) 35 EuR 705 at 710–712.

[368] A tempting way to explain *Bosman* away would be by concentrating on the fact that the case concerned the movement of natural persons. AG Lenz argued (n 366 above) para 203 that free movement of citizens is a fundamental human right which should never be restricted without a weighty justification, and in the USA persons' right to move freely has been given greater protection than inter-state commerce. See Nowak and Rotunda (n 181 above) 310. However, nothing in the reasoning indicates that this was a decisive factor, and in general citizenship has been of limited value in interpreting free movement rules. See J. Shaw, 'The Interpretation of European Union Citizenship' (1998) 61 MLR 293 at 309. See also S. Douglas-Scott, 'In Search of Union Citizenship' (1998) 18 YEL 29 at 37–39.

[369] AG Lenz examined the potentially discriminatory nature of the rules in his Opinion (n 366 above) paras 151–164. *Bosman* has been confirmed in Case C-190/98 *Volker Graf v Filzmoser Maschinenbau GmbH*, judgment of 27 January 2000, where the Court examined the effect of non-discriminatory national rules on market access. On the facts of the case the Court, however, held that the Austrian legislation granting compensation payment to a worker in the case of a contract of employment being terminated, except if the termination was attributable to the worker, was in accordance with Art 39 (ex 48) EC 'because the entitlement to compensation on termination of employment is not dependent on the worker's choosing whether or not to stay with his current employer but on a future and hypothetical event, namely the subsequent termination of his contract without such termination being at his own initiative or attributable to him . . . Such an event is too uncertain and indirect'. The reasoning attracts the question whether, *e contrario*, an entitlement that *is* dependent on the worker's choosing to stay, such as a loyalty bonus or even a pay rise based on the duration of service, falls within the scope of Art 39 (ex 48) EC. If so, the reach of the provision would be great indeed, especially as it is capable of covering private measures. It is also worth noting that it might not be easy to fit such a measure into the framework of *non-economic general* interests.

The wording used by the Court to distinguish *Keck* in *Alpine Investments* and *Bosman* is very similar. In both judgments it stated that the rules at issue directly affect the plaintiffs' access to the market in the other Member States.[370]

Market access played an important, though indirect, part also in the Court's reasoning in *Keck*. The Court used this concept to explain its decision that non-discriminatory rules affecting certain selling arrangements do not fall within the scope of Article 28 (ex 30) EC. It stated that the application of these rules 'is not by nature such as to prevent [other Member States' products] access to the market or impede that access any more than it impedes the access of domestic products'.[371]

In the light of this it seems that the currently used test of whether a measure falls within the free movement provisions is one concentrating on market access, at least in the field of workers and services. If the measure creates a direct impediment to market access, it has to be justified. This applies even if it does not create a multiple burden or discriminate otherwise against foreign interests.[372]

The requirement that an impediment to market access has to be *direct* can be interpreted in two ways. It could be argued that the impact of the national measure on market access has to be sufficiently great to trigger the application of the EC Treaty.[373] Alternatively, it may be argued that the cross-border nature of the restriction determines whether the impediment is direct.[374]

The first reading, based on the sufficient impact of the measure, accords with other parts of the Court's judgment in *Alpine Investments*. The Court found that the Dutch ban on cold-calling was a prima facie violation of Article 49 (ex 59) EC, arguing that the 'prohibition deprives the operators concerned of a rapid and direct technique for marketing and for contacting potential clients in other Member States'.[375] The Court examined the *impact* of the measure on market access.

This is an approach that Advocate General Jacobs argued for in his Opinions in *Leclerc-Siplec*[376] and in *Alpine Investments*. According to him, the guiding principle is that all undertakings should have an unimpeded access to the whole internal market. National measures creating substantial restrictions to that access must be open to scrutiny by the Court. The test is

---

[370] Case C-384/93 *Alpine Investments BV v Minister van Financiën* [1995] ECR I-1141 para 38 and n 366 above, para 103. This similar wording makes *Bosman* impossible to ignore, even though it was a case dealing with the free movement of workers.

[371] Joined Cases C-267/91 and C-268/91 *Criminal Proceedings Against Keck and Mithouard* [1993] ECR I-6097 para 17.

[372] See Weatherill (n 349 above) 896–897. See also V. Hatzopoulos, 'Exigences essentielles, impératives ou impérieuses: *une* théorie, *des* théories ou pas de théorie du tout?' (1998) 34 RTDE 191.

[373] This view of the scope of the free movements is advocated by Weatherill (n 349 above) 896–901.

[374] See M. Ross, 'Article 59 and the Marketing of Financial Services' (1995) 20 ELRev 507 at 513.

[375] See n 370 above, para 28.

[376] Case C-412/93 *Société d'Importation Édouard Leclerc-Siplec v TF1 Publicité SA and M6 Publicité SA* [1995] ECR I-179.

based on the impact of the measure on market access. It is a *de minimis* test. The test would not have to be applied to overtly discriminatory measures, which are per se prohibited by Article 28 (ex 30) EC, and rules creating a multiple burden could be presumed to have a substantial impact on market access. Thus, only rules regulating selling arrangements would have to be tested. The result of the test would depend on a number of factors such as the scope of application of the national measure, the availability of other selling arrangements, and the nature of the effect.[377]

However, a *de minimis* test suffers from a fundamental practical weakness. Although the test is conceptually clear, it is very difficult to use. The point where impact to market access becomes substantial cannot be easily determined.[378] It cannot depend on the nature of the national measures. From the point of view of the producer, there is no difference between rules prohibiting certain advertising methods and rules which limit shopping hours if the reduction in sales is the same. Sunday trading rules might become fair game again.[379]

Furthermore, similar measures may substantially impede market access in one Member State or in one sector but not in another.[380] For example, the importance of television advertising may vary depending on the availability and the penetration of other media and on the nature of the products. In addition, thresholds can fluctuate in time as circumstances change. For example, a ban on television advertising may become more problematic if the circulation of newspapers diminishes. Thus, the decisions of the Court would not have general applicability but each case would have to be decided individually on its merits. This would create legal uncertainty,[381] especially in national courts, and might give rise to similar problems as did the Court's pre-*Keck* case law.

In the field of competition law a *de minimis* test is not as problematic as in the field of trade law. In the former area the Commission is strongly involved[382] while in the latter national courts bear the primary responsibility

---

[377] ibid, paras 41–45 of the Opinion of AG Jacobs. A somewhat similar test was proposed by AG Van Gerven in Case 145/88 *Torfaen BC v B&Q* [1989] ECR 3851. The underlying principle would have been market access, and national measures screening off markets would have been caught. The partitioning effect would have been inspected in the light of the legal and economic context of the measure. The Court did not follow his suggestion. A *de minimis* test has also been supported, eg by A. Arnull, *The European Union and its Court of Justice* (Oxford 1999) 296, and Weatherill (n 349 above) 896–901. See also Barnard (n 277 above) 48–59.

[378] See Gormley (n 284 above) 882.   [379] See Craig and de Búrca (n 121 above) 624–626.

[380] Similarly Bernard (n 345 above) 18.

[381] See the Opinion of AG Tesauro in Case C-292/92 *Hünermund v Landesapothekerkammer Baden-Württemberg* [1993] ECR I-6787 para 21, Barnard (n 277 above) 55–56, Bernard (n 345 above) 19–20, Hilson (n 252 above) 456, L. Idot, 'Case C-412/93, *Société d'Importation Édouard Leclerc-Siplec* v. *TF1 Publicité SA and M6 Publicité SA*, Judgment of 9 February 1995, [1995] ECR 179' (1996) 33 CMLRev 113 at 120, Oliver (n 276 above) 792 and 797–798, and Weatherill (n 284 above) 898–901. On the other hand, it could be argued that the test is flexible and can respond to changing circumstances.

[382] Even if the matter is in the hands of a national court, it can consult the Commission. See Notice on Co-operation between National Courts and the Commission in applying Articles 85 [now 81] and 86 [now 82] of the Treaty [1993] OJ C39/5, in particular para 38.

for applying Community law. In addition, the former field lends itself better to the application of numerical criteria than the latter.[383]

If this reading of the judgments in *Alpine Investments* and *Bosman* is correct, the Court can be criticised for increasing legal uncertainty. If the Court wanted to introduce a *de minimis* test, it would have to define very carefully the circumstances and criteria relevant for its application.[384] Now the Court has merely talked about the directness of the impediment to market access, hardly a very helpful statement.[385]

It is submitted, however, that the Court's reasoning cannot be explained with reference to a *de minimis* doctrine.[386] The decisive element was not the impact of the measure but rather its cross-border nature.

In *Alpine Investments* the Court stated in a key paragraph:

A prohibition such as that at issue is imposed by the Member State in which the provider of service is established and affects not only offers made by him to addressees who are established in that State or move there in order to receive services but also offers made to potential recipients in another Member State. It therefore directly affects access to the market in services in the other Member States and is thus capable of hindering intra-Community trade in services.[387]

Similar reasoning can be found in *Bosman*.[388] Furthermore, in this case the Court did not examine how substantial the hindrance to free movement was. This examination would have been essential under a *de minimis* doctrine.

According to the Court, the decisive difference between these cases and *Keck* is that, in the latter case, the restriction directly affected only the relationship between economic operators in France. It took effect within one Member State. Its influence on products from other states was incidental. Thus, the measure had only an indirect effect on any decrease in the volume of imports through diminished demand in the country of importation. The rule did not directly affect the market access of imported products.

---

[383] See Bernard (n 345 above) 17–18, Craig and de Búrca (n 121 above) 626, and Idot (n 381 above) 120. Mortelmans (n 12 above) 127 criticised AG van Gerven's proposal for being exessively demanding for the national courts. He feared that the approach would lead to conflicting decisions.

[384] Opinion of AG Jacobs (n 376 above) para 42. The Opinion has been criticised for failing to set out clearly the criteria for applying the *de minimis* test, a very difficult task indeed. See Oliver (n 269 above) 109–110.

[385] Until the mid-1930s, the US Supreme Court's case law on the commerce clause focused on direct or indirect nature of the burden created by a state law. The approach caused difficulties in practice and the reasoning was criticised as 'conclusionary, mechanical, uncertain and removed from actualities'. See Nowak and Rotunda (n 181 above) 289–290, and Tribe (n 279 above) 408.

[386] The Court did not adopt the doctrine in Case C-67/97 *Criminal Proceedings Against Ditlev Bluhme* [1998] ECR I-8033 either. However, the case concerned national legislation regulating product characteristics—a type of rule not capable of benefiting from the *de minimis* exception as defined by AG Jacobs—and does not, therefore, offer any conclusive proof.

[387] Case C-384/93 *Alpine Investments BV v Minister van Financiën* [1995] ECR I-1141 para 38.

[388] Case C-415/93 *Union Royale Belge des Sociétés de Football Association ASBL and others v Jean-Marc Bosman* [1995] ECR I-4921 para 103.

By contrast, in *Alpine Investments* and *Bosman* the rules had an immediate effect on the relationships between economic operators in different countries. The measures were not confined within one Member State. The obstacles directly affected cross-border activities. The restrictions immediately hindered the provision of services and the movement of workers from one Member State to another. The effect on market access was direct.

Advocate General Tesauro understood *Alpine Investments* and *Bosman* in this way in his Opinion in *Familiapress*.[389] On the basis of these judgments and the jurisprudence of the Court on selling arrangements, he adopted a restrictive reading of *Keck*. He stated that:

the only measures excluded from the scope of Article 30 [now 28] are those which are absolutely general in nature, which apply—needless to say—without distinction, which do not impede imports and which might lead at most to a (hypothetical) reduction in the volume of imports only as a consequence of an equally hypothetical reduction in the overall volume of sales.[390]

He continued by emphasising that a general contraction in the volume of sales leading to a reduction in the volume of imports—the *Keck* scenario—is not enough to bring a measure under Article 28 (ex 30) EC.[391] He seems to make a distinction between general measures which affect trade only indirectly, through a reduction in the volume of sales, and measures which have a more direct impact on imports.[392]

The rules at issue in *Alpine Investments* and *Bosman* can in one sense be compared with border measures, such as charges having equivalent effect to customs duties. They also affect cross-border activities directly. Because of their close links to the crossing of borders, it has been claimed that they create problems per se. Thus, Community law has adopted a restrictive approach towards these measures.[393]

It may be that the Court has in *Bosman* adopted a distinction between rules restricting access to employment and rules regulating exercise of occupation advocated by Advocate General Lenz. Naturally, the former rules directly affect the hiring of workers from the other Member States and thus their access to the employment market, while the effect of the latter rules is more

---

[389] Case C-368/95 *Vereinigte Familiapress Zeitungsverlags-und vertriebs GmbH v Heinrich Bauer Verlag* [1997] ECR I-3689.

[390] ibid, para 10 of AG Tesauro's Opinion.   [391] ibid, paras 10–11 of his Opinion.

[392] For a somewhat similar, concrete, personal, rights-based interpretation of the fundamental freedoms see P. Eeckhout, 'Recent Case Law on Free Movement of Goods: refining Keck and Mithouard' (1998) 9 EBLR 267 at 270–271. He notes that from this perspective *Keck* will be difficult to transpose to services. See also N. Reich, 'Europe's Economic Constitution, or: A New Look at Keck' (1999) 19 OJLS 337 at 341–344, and A. Biondi, 'In and Out of the Internal Market: Recent Developments on the Principle of Free Movement' (1999–2000) 19 YEL 469 at 488.

[393] See generally Craig and de Búrca (n 121 above) 551–560, and Weatherill and Beaumont (n 17 above) 454–465.

indirect.[394] The Advocate General sees an analogy between this distinction and the case law on Article 28 (ex 30) EC.[395]

The approach adopted by the Court can be criticised. First of all, *Alpine Investments* and *Bosman* cannot be reconciled with *Keck*. As explained above, in *Keck* the decisive aspect was the absence of an unequal burden. This is also illustrated by the Court's language. The decisive factor according to the Court is that market access of other Member States' products is not prevented[396] or impeded *more* than the access of domestic products.[397] In *Alpine Investments* and *Bosman*, by contrast, the crucial factor was the *directness* of the effect to market access. Discrimination was not an issue.

By distinguishing *Keck* in *Alpine Investments* and *Bosman*, the Court did try to maintain the illusion of uniform interpretation of the freedoms. However, the principles behind the cases are truly different, and the distinction was highly dubious. In all these cases market access was subjected to certain conditions but not absolutely prevented. Furthermore, some post-*Keck* decisions, such as *Commission v Greece* (Processed milk for infants),[398] had a very strong cross-border element, and in that sense the national measures' impact on market access was direct, and yet the Court held that the domestic rules fell outside Article 28 (ex 30) EC altogether.[399] Thus, either the case laws on different freedoms are diverging, or the judgments in *Alpine Investments* and *Bosman* refine *Keck*.[400]

The reasons for the possible divergence can be only speculated upon. The non-application of *Keck* to services may be connected to the lack of tendency of traders to invoke Article 49 (ex 59) EC to challenge rules that limit their commercial freedom. As the provisions on the free movement of services apply only to cross-border situations,[401] Article 49 cannot be used as a basis

---

[394] A similar distinction is made in the EC Treaty, where Art 39(3)(a) (ex 48(3)(a)) EC gives a right to accept offers of employment, subject only to justified limitations, while Art 39(3)(c) (ex 48(3)(c)) EC gives only the right to stay in a Member State for the purposes of employment *in accordance with the provisions governing the nationals* of that state (emphasis added). See also Council Regulation 1612/68/EEC of 15 October 1968 on freedom of movement for workers within the Community as amended by Regulation 312/76/EEC [1968] OJ Spec Ed L275/2, 475, whose first title covers mainly access to employment, while the second title governs conditions of employment. The same distinction was made in relation to the free movement of services by AG Gulmann in his Opinion in Case C-275/92 *Her Majesty's Customs and Excise v Gerhart Schindler and Jörg Schindler* [1994] ECR I-1039 para 56.

[395] Opinion of AG Lenz (n 388 above) paras 205 and 210. The Court refers to para 210 of the Opinion in para 99 of the judgment. See also the discussion in Barnard (n 277 above) 58.

[396] A total ban on a foreign product would prevent market access and amount to a quantitative restriction.

[397] Joined Cases C-267/91 and C-268/91 *Criminal Proceedings Against Keck and Mithouard* [1993] ECR I-6097 para 17.

[398] Case C-391/92 *Commission v Greece* (Processed milk for infants) [1995] ECR I-1621.

[399] See Bernard (n 345 above) 22–25. See also Poiares Maduro (n 9 above) 101, Poiares Maduro (n 292 above) 315–316, and Hilson (n 252 above) 456.

[400] See Weatherill (n 292 above) 896–901, who supports the refinement theory.

[401] See Chapter 1 section 2b above.

for test cases or as a general euro-defence against the application of national rules as easily as Article 28 (ex 30) EC prior to *Keck*.

Secondly, one may wonder whether the *directness* of the effect on market access is really a fully relevant criterion. The existence of a multiple burden is obviously a danger to the single market as it prevents economies of scale and the maintenance of competitive advantage, and thus also an effective competition between legal orders. In addition, some views of the internal market logically lead to the conclusion that measures having a substantial impact on market access have to be open to scrutiny by the Court. However, directness of the effect on access to the market may not be important in itself. Why focus on the question whether the measure regulates formally internal relationships and thus has only an indirect effect on market access or directly controls cross-border situations? The former may well have a more significant impact than the latter.[402]

The fact that the rules may in some ways be comparable to border measures is not decisive. Duties and charges having an equivalent effect are repugnant to the internal market not only because they take place at the border but also, and more importantly, because they only apply to products which cross the border. Thus, they are inherently detrimental to products from other Member States. The same consideration does not apply to the rules under discussion.

Thirdly, the concept of 'a rule which directly affects market access' is not exactly a clear one. It has a conclusionary ring to it.[403] The employment of such a criterion is likely to lead to similar problems of legal uncertainty as did the pre-*Keck* case law under Article 28.[404] Admittedly, the tiger of *Cassis*[405] is unlikely to run free in the field of free movement of services and workers as a result of these judgments. After all, they correspond to a relatively narrow view of the internal market by stressing the cross-border nature of the activities.[406] However, the Court might be facing a long line of cases where it has to define the concept more clearly.[407] Due to the conclusionary nature of the concept and the variety of factual situations that may arise, this may prove to be a very difficult task indeed.

[402] See also D. O'Keeffe and A. Bavasso, 'Four Freedoms, One Market and National Competence: In Search of a Dividing Line' in D. O'Keeffe and A. Bavasso (eds), *Liber Amicorum in Honour of Lord Slynn of Hadley. Vol I. Judicial Review in European Union Law* (The Hague 2000) 555, who write: 'One could easily imagine a transnational case with little impact on the common market and internal matter with a major effect on the common market'.

[403] See n 385 above on American criticism of the directness test. [404] See section 5a above.

[405] A. Dashwood, 'The *Cassis de Dijon* Line of Authority' in St.J. Bates, W. Finnie, J.A. Usher and H. Wildberg (eds), *In Memoriam J.D.B. Mitchell* (London 1983) 158 used the expression of 'the Court riding a tiger' to describe the potential for over-extension in the *Cassis* line of cases.

[406] On *Alpine Investments* see Ross (n 374 above) 513.

[407] See J.M. Fernández Martín, 'Re-defining Obstacles to the Free Movement of Workers' (1996) 21 ELRev 313 at 323. The wider test may already be reflected in the number of new cases brought before the Court. In 1998, 32 new cases concerned goods, 34 services and 36 persons. In 1999, 23 concerned goods, 23 services and 69 persons. See www.curia.eu.int/en/stat/index.htm

Fourthly, the doctrine based on a direct impediment on market access is in conflict with the Court's well-established case law on Article 29 (ex 34) EC.[408] In *Groenveld*[409] and in subsequent cases such as *Spain v Council*[410] and *Alsthom Atlantique*,[411] the Court has held that Article 29 (ex 34) EC is only concerned with measures 'which have as their specific object or effect the restriction on patterns of exports and thereby the establishment of a difference in treatment between the domestic trade of the Member State and its export trade in such a way as to provide a particular advantage for national production or for the domestic market of the State in question at the expense of the production or of the trade of other Member States'.[412] Thus the EC Treaty catches measures affecting exports only if they are discriminatory. The *Cassis* doctrine does not apply.

The approach of the Court is easily explained by the fact that national rules affecting exports do not create a multiple burden for the exporter. He has to comply with only one set of rules. The same measures apply both to goods for domestic and export markets.[413]

It has been suggested that a more intensive control of the exporting home state's product rules would be desirable in special situations. This is the case in circumstances where the importing host state is exceptionally able to apply its product rules to imports, be they goods or services. If the application of host state rules is allowed, the application of home state regulations creates a double burden and thus discriminates factually against exports. This situation can materialise either when host state measures are justified by the general good or when the goods or services are not legally sold in the home state at all.[414] It has to be noted, however, that more intensive control would undermine the trademark function of national legislation. Consumers could no longer fully trust products from a country known for its high regulatory standards.[415]

---

[408] AG Lenz in Case C-415/93 *Union Royale Belge des Sociétés de Football Association ASBL and others v Jean-Marc Bosman* [1995] ECR I-4921 para 207, and Weatherill (n 349 above) 901–904. See also Daniele (n 319 above) 195 and 198–200, who criticises the judgments in *Alpine Investments* and *Bosman* for not applying an Art 29 (ex 34) type approach. See however AG Elmer in Case C-111/94 *Non-contentious Proceedings Brought by Job Centre Coop. arl* [1995] ECR I-3361 para 27 where he suggests an Art 29 (ex 34) type approach to restrictions on exports of services even after *Alpine Investments*.

[409] Case 15/79 *Groenveld v Produktschap voor Vee en Vlees* [1979] ECR 3409.

[410] Case C-9/89 *Kingdom of Spain v Council of the European Communities* [1990] ECR I-1383 para 21.

[411] Case C-339/89 *Alsthom Atlantique SA v Sulzer SA* [1991] ECR I-107.

[412] See n 409 above para 7. More modern formulation does not mention detriment to the production or trade of other Member States, or even the advantage to national production or markets. See Case C-388/95 *Belgium v Spain*, judgment of 16 May 2000, and E. Spaventa, 'Casenote on Belgium v. Spain' (2001) 38 CMLRev 211 at 214–216.

[413] See R. Barents, 'New Developments in MEEs' (1981) 18 CMLRev 271 at 302–303, and Weatherill and Beaumont (n 17 above) 605–606. If the exporting state tries to extend its rules affecting selling arrangements to another Member State's territory, it does create a multiple burden, however. See section 5civ above.

[414] See W.-H. Roth, 'Wettbewerb der Mitgliedstaaten oder Wettbewerb der Hersteller? Plädoyer für eine Neubestimmung des Art. 34 EGV' (1995) 159 ZHR 78 at 92–93.

[415] The Court has recently emphasised the importance of the 'trademark function' in *Belgium v Spain* (n 412 above). See also discussion in section 1d above. Producers complying with national

Alpine Investments and *Bosman* were concerned with obstacles making the 'export' of services and workers more difficult. The Court applied the test of impediment to direct market access, not a test based on multiple burdens and discrimination. The case laws on Article 49 (ex 59) and 39 (ex 48) EC and Article 29 (ex 34) EC are either diverging or *Groenveld* has to be reconsidered.[416] In its recent judgments in *Dusseldorp*[417] and in *ED Srl v Italo Fenocchio*[418] the Court stated that according to the settled case law, Article 29 applies to discriminatory national measures. Based on this, it seems that the case laws are diverging.

It is true that the free movement of services is only governed by one provision, Article 49 (ex 59) EC, and the free movement of workers by only Article 39 (ex 48) EC, while in the field of free movement of goods imports are regulated by Article 28 (ex 30) EC and exports by Article 29 (ex 34) EC. It might be argued that this division makes it easier for the Court to apply different standards to the import and export of goods. The one and only provision cannot be split in its application and therefore a similar distinction cannot be made with respect to services and workers. Therefore, it could be thought that while Articles 28, 49 and 39 are construed similarly, the interpretation of Article 29 may diverge. Thus, the *Groenveld* case law could survive despite *Alpine Investments* and *Bosman*.[419]

This formalistic structural argument is not convincing, however. The wording of Articles 28 and 29 is similar, so they would prima facie have to be applied in the same way. So far the interpretation of the two provisions has been based on the same principles of avoidance of a multiple burden and discrimination. Furthermore, the arguments for parallel construction of Articles 28, 49 and 39 also apply to Articles 29, 49 and 39.[420]

Moreover, the Court seems to have established the parallel interpretation of Articles 29 and 49 in *Peralta*.[421] In the judgment the Court based its finding that the Italian measures in issue did not infringe the freedom to export services on the fact that the rules applied equally to vessels providing services internally and to vessels transporting products to the other Member States. The policy behind the ruling seems to be the same as the one behind Article 29, and the language of the Court in these two fields was quite similar.

It is doubtful whether the direct market access doctrine makes good sense as regards export restrictions. Non-discriminatory obstacles to exports are

standards could of course indicate this in their advertisements etc. Many German beers, for example, already state in their labels that they have been produced in accordance with the German Beer Purity Law.

[416] See Tesauro (n 297 above) 16.
[417] Case C-203/96 *Chemische Afvalstoffen Dusseldorp BV and others v Minister van Volkshuisvesting, Ruimtelijke Ordening en Milieubeheer* [1998] ECR I-4075 para 40.
[418] Case C-412/97 *ED Srl v Italo Fenocchio* [1999] ECR I-3845 para 10.
[419] This possibility was brought up by Hatzopoulos (n 372 above) 1442.
[420] See Chapter 1 section 3 above.
[421] Case C-379/92 *Matteo Peralta* [1994] ECR I-3453. See Hatzopoulos (n 341 above) 1441. See also A. Torgersen, 'The Limitations of the Free Movement of Goods and the Freedom to Provide Services—in Search of a Common Approach' (1999) 10 EBLR 371 at 376–377 and 380–381.

generally not problematic from the viewpoint of competition between legal orders. Such rules, applying equally to products for domestic and foreign markets, may be perfectly legitimate expressions of national preferences. If such rules are burdensome on a business, it can relocate or start lobbying for a change in legislation. The plight of exporters should be taken seriously by politicians if only for balance of payments reasons. Normally the market should be allowed to find out the efficient rules and national preferences should be respected. Usually there is no need for the Court to get involved.

Control of export restrictions based on market access, not on discrimination, does not sit well with the philosophy of mutual recognition. The idea is that one set of rules apply and is then mutually recognised, not that no rules apply.

Paradoxically, the inapplicability of the rules of the exporting country makes the rules of the importing country applicable. Since *Cassis de Dijon* the Court has declared that products lawfully produced and marketed in one Member State have to be allowed into the market of the importing Member State.[422] If the rules of the exporting Member State are found to be contrary to the free movement provisions of the EC Treaty, the product can be exported out of that state but it does not gain the right to be marketed in the exporting state. The Treaty does not apply to fully internal situations.[423] Thus the product in question is not 'lawfully produced and marketed' in the sense of *Cassis*, and the importing state's rules may apply.[424]

Moreover, export restrictions are generally less prevalent than obstacles to imports. Member States have traditionally in a mercantilist spirit been eager to encourage exports, not to hinder them.[425] This does not mean that a discrimination analysis can be superficial, however. A Member State may very well want to limit the exports of valuable factors of production as this might reduce the productivity of the economy. Similarly, a Member State may try to require that raw materials be processed within its territory before exportation and, thus, force foreign producers to invest in the country and improve its employment situation.[426]

---

[422] Case 120/78 *Rewe Zentrale AG v Bundesmonopolverwaltung für Branntwein* [1979] ECR 649 para 14. See also eg Joined Cases C-267/91 and C-268/91 *Criminal Proceedings Against Keck and Mithouard* [1993] ECR I-6097 para 15 as regards product rules under Art 28 (ex 30) EC, and Case C-76/90 *Manfred Säger v Dennemeyer & Co. Ltd* [1991] ECR I-4221 para 12 as regards services.

[423] See, however, Joined Cases C-321/94, C-322/94, C-323/94 and C-324/94 *Criminal Proceedings Against Jacques Pistre* [1997] ECR I-2343.

[424] See Roth (n 135 above) 152–153. Similar philosophy is partly behind *van Binsbergen*. If the service is directed purely towards a Member State where the provider is not established, the host state is allowed to apply its own rules as the home state does not exercise control. See Case 33/74 *van Binsbergen v Bestuur van de Bedrijfsvereniging voor de Metaalnijverheid* [1974] ECR 1299 para 13. AG Jacobs interpreted *van Binsbergen* in a more narrow fashion in paras 40–54 of his Opinion in Joined Cases C-34/95, C-35/95 and C-36/95 *Konsumentombudsmannen v De Agostini (Svenska) Förlag AB and TV-Shop i Sverige AB* [1997] ECR I-3843, as did the Court in Case C-212/97 *Centros Ltd v Erhvervs og Selskabsstyrelsen* [1999] ECR I-1459 paras 24–30. See in general on this line of case law V. Hatzopoulos, 'Recent Developments of the Case Law of the ECJ in the Field of Services' (2000) 37 CMLRev 43, 62–64.

[425] See Marenco (n 135 above) 326–327.

[426] On the American experience see Tribe (n 279 above) 426–427.

The use of the doctrine based on an impediment to market access to export restrictions might also lead to over-extension.[427] A wide variety of national production rules ranging from environmental legislation to labour law can be said to impede the competitiveness of the undertakings of the exporting country and, therefore, affect the market access of their products. The control of these rules would extend the free movement provisions of the Treaty even further than the Court's pre-*Keck* case law did.

Here the directness criterion is actually helpful, for unless the Court consistently places the emphasis on the cross-border nature of the restrictions, this over-extension cannot be avoided. Yet, non-discriminatory national production rules do not create a dual burden, and accordingly their justification should not be examined.[428] A test focusing on the directness of the impediment to the market access could exempt them from the Court's control, as it can be argued that they hinder market access only indirectly by making the production of goods or services more costly in the home country. The directness criterion might be used in this way to keep the regulatory competence for production rules firmly with the exporting home state, where it belongs.

Finally, it has been recently argued that the Court should treat the export of goods differently from the export of services. It has been claimed that exported goods are a legitimate concern for the home state, unlike exported services, as the production of goods can cause pollution and exported goods can infiltrate the home market, and that, therefore, market access doctrine should be applied to the export of services but not to goods.[429] In my view this is misconceived. First, the production of services can give rise to equally legitimate concerns, such as worker protection. Secondly, according to *Säger*, services have to be present also in the home market to benefit fully from the free movement rules[430] and therefore the home state certainly has an interest in regulating them. Thirdly, if exported services are not a matter for the home state, they must be a matter for the host state, as otherwise a lacuna would form. The allocation of the regulatory competence to the host state would seriously compromise the achievement of the single market in services, however, as it contravenes the principle of mutual recognition upon which the market is built. Thus, the export of goods and services ought to be treated in a uniform manner.

---

[427] See D. O'Keeffe and P. Osborne, 'L'affaire Bosman: un arrêt important pour le bon fonctionnement du Marché unique européen' (1996) RMUE 17 at 36 who state, in reference to *Bosman*, that absolute freedom of access may be going just a little too far.

[428] See W.-H. Roth, 'Wettwerb der Mitgliedstaaten oder Wettbewerb der Hersteller?' (1995) 159 ZHR 78, 95.

[429] Hilson (n 252 above) 454 and 459.

[430] Case C-76/90 *Manfred Säger v Dennemeyer & Co. Ltd* [1991] ECR I-4221 para 12 and Roth (n 135 above) 152–153.

Altogether, the Court seems to have taken a step towards centralisation and economic freedom with its decisions in *Alpine Investments* and *Bosman*. This reverses the trend towards a more decentralised Community observable in *Keck*. It is a curious move as the general atmosphere in the Community seems to place more emphasis on subsidiarity and limitation of Community competences.[431] It is made even more remarkable by the fact that the Court was not required to develop a new doctrine to decide the cases in the way it did. In *Alpine Investments* it could just have argued that, in line with *Keck*, the competence for regulating selling arrangements rested with the host state and therefore the home state rule was in need of justification. It could have decided *Bosman* on competition law grounds. It is also surprising that the Court's case law on services and workers seems to have overtaken its case law on goods. In the past the decisions on Article 28 (ex 30) EC have led the way.[432]

---

[431] It can be hoped that the approach has not yet been set in stone. There is certainly still uncertainty about the scope of Art 49 (ex 59) EC. In Case C-266/96 *Corsica Ferries France SA v Gruppo Antichi Ormeggiatori del Porto di Genova Coop. arl and others* [1998] ECR I-3949 in issue was Italian legislation requiring shipping companies to use in Italian ports the services of local mooring groups. These groups held exclusive concessions and provided mooring services for a charge. The mooring groups argued that *Keck* should be applied to the freedom to provide services and that, therefore, the Italian law fell outside the scope of Art 49 (ex 59) EC and did not restrict the freedom to provide maritime transport services. The Commission was in general agreement with this view as the increased costs affected all undertakings equally. In contrast, AG Fennelly was of the opinion that the effects of the law were too remote and indirect to amount to a restriction. The Court did not decide the issue of restriction at all but simply stated that in any event the law was justified by reasons of public security. In Case C-405/98 *Konsumentombuds-mannen v Gourmet International Products Aktiebolag*, judgment of 8 March 2001, the Commission and the Norwegian government argued that a Swedish rule restricting alcohol advertisements would have to discriminate in order to fall foul of Art 49 (ex 59) EC. The Court disagreed, as did AG Jacobs who argued in para 71 that in the field of services 'there is no analogue to the exception laid down in *Keck and Mithouard*'.

[432] See also G. de Búrca, 'The Role of Equality in European Community Law' in A. Dashwood and S. O'Leary (eds), *The Principle of Equal Treatment in EC law. Papers Collected by the Centre for European Legal Studies, Cambridge* (London 1997) 20–23 who, however, sees the move away from discrimination-based approach as a positive development. Some recent Opinions of Advocates General provide further evidence of inconsistency between goods and services. AG Alber argued in Case C-263/99 *Commission v Italy*, Opinion of 8 March 2001, paras 43–50 that non-discriminatory Italian rules on maximum and minimum fees for the services of transport consultants violated Article 49 (ex 59) EC. In contrast, price controls only fall under Article 28 (ex 30) EC if they are discriminatory. See Case C-63/94 *Groupement National des Négociants en Pommes de Terre de Belgique v ITM Belgium SA and Vocarex SA* [1995] ECR I-2467 and Oliver (n 269 above) 161–171. AG Colomer argued in Case C-17/00 *François de Coster v Collège des Bourgmestres et Echevins de Watermael-Boitsfort*, Opinion of 28 June 2001, paras 132–135 that a Belgian tax on satellite dishes constituted a restriction on the free movement of services even in the absence of discrimination and without examining any possible protective effect, as required by Article 90 (ex 95) EC.

v) PRO Sieben Media *and* Gourmet International Products: Alpine Investments *confirmed*

The recent decisions of the Court in *PRO Sieben Media*[433] and *Gourmet International Products*[434] have confirmed that the case law on national measures restricting the export of goods and services is diverging.

PRO Sieben Media concerned German television advertising rules, which limited the number of advertisements that could be shown with certain broadcasts. The relevant provision stated that 'works such as feature films and television films . . . where they last longer than 45 minutes, may be interrupted once for each complete period of 45 minutes. A further interruption is allowed if those programmes last for at least 20 minutes longer than two or more complete periods of 45 minutes'. When calculating the duration of programmes, the length of advertisements was not taken into account, as Germany used the so-called 'net principle'. The referring national court asked, inter alia, whether the rules infringed the provisions on the free movement of goods or services.

The Court decided that the 'Television Without Frontiers' Directive[435] precluded Germany from using the net principle to broadcasters not under its jurisdiction.[436] It then turned to the application of the principle to broadcasters under German jurisdiction. Referring to *Keck*,[437] the Court held that the measure did not fall within the scope of Article 28 (ex 30) EC.[438] It then stated that 'since such rules limit the possibility for television broadcasters established in the State of transmission to broadcast advertisements for the benefit of advertisers established in other Member States, they involve a restriction on the freedom to provide services'.[439] It proceeded to find that the rules were justified and proportionate.[440]

Gourmet International Products concerned a Swedish law regulating the marketing of alcoholic beverages. The law prohibited, with a few limited exceptions, the advertising of alcoholic beverages. Gourmet International Products (GIP) had nonetheless placed advertisements for wine and whisky in a magazine it published. The Swedish Consumer Ombudsman applied for

---

[433] Case C-6/98 *Arbeitsgemeinschaft Deutscher Rundfunkanstalten (ARD) v PRO Sieben Media AG*, judgment of 28 October 1999.

[434] Case C-405/98 *Konsumentombudsmannen v Gourmet International Products Aktiebolag*, judgment of 8 March 2001.

[435] The case revolved mostly around Council Directive 89/552/EEC of 3 October 1989 on the co-ordination of certain provisions laid down by law, regulation or administrative action in Member States concerning the pursuit of television broadcasting activities [1989] OJ L298/23, as amended by Directive 97/36/EC of the European Parliament and of the Council of 30 June 1997 [1997] OJ L202/60.

[436] See n 433 above, para 33.

[437] Joined Cases C-267/91 and C-268/91 *Criminal Proceedings Against Keck and Mithouard* [1993] ECR I-6097.

[438] See n 433 above, paras 45–48. [439] ibid, para 49. [440] ibid, paras 50–52.

an injunction against GIP. The question arose whether the Swedish rules constituted a restriction on the freedom to provide services.

The Finnish and French governments argued that Article 49 (ex 59) EC was not applicable in the proceedings, while the Commission and the Norwegian government argued that discrimination was necessary for there to be a restriction on the free movement of services. The Court, however, following Advocate General Jacobs, did find a restriction. It argued that 'the legislation . . . restricts the right of press undertakings established in the territory of that Member State to offer advertising space in their publications to potential advertisers established in other Member States'.[441] It continued by holding that the prohibition on advertising alcoholic beverages, even if non-discriminatory, 'has a particular effect on the cross border supply of advertising space, given the international nature of the advertising market in the category of products to which the prohibition relates, and thereby constitutes a restriction on the freedom to provide services'.[442]

The cases confirmed that truly non-discriminatory export restrictions fall within Article 49 (ex 59) EC. The rules limited the possibilities of home state television broadcasters and press undertakings to provide services for advertisers from other Member States, and, therefore, restricted the volume of exports. The measures were truly non-discriminatory, as the reduction in the number of advertising slots and the prohibition of the advertising of alcoholic beverages affected domestic and cross-border services in the same manner. Thus, the rulings are in conflict with the *Groenveld*,[443] case law on Article 29 (ex 34) EC and are subject to the same criticism[444] as *Alpine Investments*.[445]

It is interesting to note that in neither judgment did the Court mention the concept of market access. It could well be argued that in *PRO Sieben Media* the impact of the measure on market access was neither substantial nor direct. It limited only one form of sales promotion, television advertising, and only with feature and television films. Even with these works, it did not impose a total prohibition but only restricted the number of interruptions for advertisements. Its impact was only felt through the reduction of desirable slots and, therefore, the increase in their price. It may be predicted that if the Court persists in finding that these kinds of rules fall within the scope of the free movement of services, it may soon be faced with an increasing tendency of traders to invoke Article 49 (ex 59) EC as a means of challenging any rules whose effect is to limit their commercial freedoms.[446] In this respect *Gourmet International Products* is easier to accept. The relevant rules prohibited advertising, with a very few limited exceptions, and the ban concerned products, as

---

[441] See n 434 above, para 38.   [442] ibid, para 39.
[443] Case 15/79 *Groenveld v Produktschap voor Vee en Vlees* [1979] ECR 3409.
[444] See section 5civ above.
[445] Case C-384/93 *Alpine Investments BV v Minister van Financiën* [1995] ECR I-1141.
[446] Services and persons have already overtaken goods in the number of new cases brought before the Court. In 1998, 32 new cases concerned goods, 34 services and 36 persons. In 1999, 23 concerned goods, 23 services and 69 persons. See www.curia.eu.int/en/stat/index.htm

the Court expressly stated, for which there undoubtedly is an international advertising market, although only one category of products was affected.

Another interesting omission was that in *PRO Sieben Media* the Court did not mention a possible import 'restriction' of services. As noted by Advocate General Jacobs, the measure affected the ability of foreign service providers to advertise in Germany.[447] For example, an insurance company from another Member State was faced with fewer and more expensive slots in which to advertise its products. In the case of goods this obviously amounted to a non-discriminatory rule concerning selling arrangements. However, in the case of services the Court has not shown itself willing to exclude these measures from the scope of Article 49 (ex 59) EC. Therefore, it might have been expected to find an import restriction as well. The fact that it did not even mention this effect of the German rule might suggest that it is willing to apply *Keck* in the field of services, at least in some circumstances.

Nevertheless, the judgments display a fundamental divergence from *Keck*.[448] There was no dual burden or any other form of discriminatory burden placed on the service providers, yet the measures were caught.[449] The state where the marketing activity was taking place could not apply its non-discriminatory rules without the Court scrutinising their justification and proportionality. In fact, the notion of restriction employed by the Court resembled the one used in relation to Article 28 (ex 30) EC in the 1980s.

The absurdity of maintaining two different approaches can be illustrated by the following thought experiment: What if retailers start to plead Article 49 (ex 59) instead of 28 (ex 30) EC? What if a supermarket prohibited from selling baby milk argues that it is prevented from providing retail services to potential suppliers established in other Member States?[450] What if a pharmacy banned from advertising quasi-pharmaceutical products outside its premises argues that its ability to provide advertising space for foreign manufacturers is limited, and that the advertising market for this category of products is international?[451] What if a shop wishing to be open on all days argues that a Sunday trading ban limits the number of attractive time slots it is able to offer?[452] What if a broadcaster argues that a rule prohibiting

---

[447] See n 433 above, para 75 of AG Jacobs' Opinion.

[448] AG Jacobs argued in his Opinion (n 434 above) para 71 that 'in assessing restrictions on the freedom to provide cross-border services there is no analogue to the exception laid down in *Keck and Mithouard*'.

[449] It could be argued that a ban on alcohol advertisements imposes a dual burden on an advertising agency from another Member State that has produced a promotional campaign complying with the rules of the home state but which cannot be exploited in Sweden. The Court did not discuss this possibility.

[450] cf Case C-391/92 *Commission v Greece* [1995] ECR I-1621.

[451] cf Case C-292/92 *Hünermund v Landesapothekerkammer Baden-Württemberg* [1993] ECR I-6787.

[452] cf Joined Cases C-69 and 258/93 *Punto Casa SpA v Sindaco del Commune di Capena* [1994] ECR I-2355, and Joined Cases C-418–421, 460–462 and 464/93, 9–11, 14–15, 23–24 and 332/94 *Semeraro Casa Uno Srl v Sindaco del Commune di Erbusco* [1996] ECR I-2975.

television advertising as regards the distribution sector restricts its ability to provide services for petrol stations established in a border region of another Member State?[453] Obviously the Court could and would deal with most of these challenges by holding that the national rules concern goods, as the service activity is purely ancillary, but this technical way of disposing of the issue does not dispel the questions concerning the rationality of the two different approaches. If a rule preventing a supermarket from selling baby milk falls outside the scope of the EC Treaty, why does a rule preventing a magazine from selling advertising space for alcoholic drinks fall within? If a rule limiting how often shops can be open falls outside the Treaty, why does a rule limiting how often advertisements can be broadcast fall within?

The judgments should perhaps not be given too much weight. Both were delivered by chambers, not the Full Court. In *PRO Sieben Media* the Court was mostly concerned with the Television Broadcasting Directive 89/552/EC, and Article 49 (ex 59) EC was merely a side issue. In *Gourmet International Products* the Court's attention was mostly focused on the free movement of goods. The analysis of the restrictions was very short in both judgments. The rulings confirm two things, however. They show that truly non-discriminatory measures restricting export of services do fall within Article 49, and they show that the approach of the Court is not nearly as coherent as it could be.

vi) Deliège

The recent judgment of the Court in *Deliège*[454] was concerned with an unusual factual situation and may best be limited to the area of sports. In issue were rules of sporting associations, according to which professional or semi-professional judokas could only participate in certain high level international competitions if they had been selected or authorised by their national judo federation. In general, only one male and one female judoka could be authorised for a given weight category. The nationality of the judoka was irrelevant, as long as he or she was a member of a club belonging to the federation. The Belgian federation had not selected Ms Deliège, a distinguished judoka in the under-52 kg category, for many important international competitions, including the Olympics, World Championships, European Championships and Category A International Tournaments. The referring national court asked whether the selection rules were in accordance, inter alia, with Article 49 (ex 59) EC.

The European Court of Justice begun its ruling by holding that the selection rules did not 'determine the conditions governing the access to the labour

---

[453] cf Case C-412/93 *Société d'Importation Édouard Leclerc-Siplec v TF1 Publicité SA and M6 Publicité SA* [1995] ECR I-179.

[454] Joined Cases C-51/96 and C-191/97 *Christelle Deliège v Asbl Ligue Francophone de judo et disciplines associées and others*, judgment of 11 April 2000.

market by professional sportsmen' and that Ms Deliège's exclusion from the competitions was not based on her nationality.[455] It continued by stating that:

although selection rules . . . inevitably have the effect of limiting the number of participants in a tournament, such a limitation is inherent in the conduct of an international high-level sports event, which necessarily involves certain selection rules or criteria being adopted. Such rules may not in themselves be regarded as constituting a restriction. . .

Moreover, the adoption, for the purposes of an international sports tournament, of one system for selecting participants rather than another must be based on a large number of considerations unconnected with the personal situation of an athlete, such as the nature, the organisation and the financing of the sport concerned.

Although a selection system may prove more favourable to one category of athletes than another, it cannot be inferred from that fact alone that the adoption of that system constitutes a restriction on the freedom to provide services.

Accordingly, it falls to the bodies concerned . . . to lay down appropriate rules. . .

. . . [T]he delegation of such a task to the national federations, which normally have the necessary knowledge and experience, is the arrangement adopted in most sporting disciplines . . . [T]he selection rules . . . apply both to competitions organised within the Community and to those taking place outside it and involve both nationals of Member States and those of non-member countries.[456]

Accordingly, the Court answered the national court's question by holding that the selection rules did not in themselves, as long as they derived from needs inherent in the organisation of competitions, constitute a restriction on the freedom to provide services.

The judgment gives rise to some questions. The first is whether the notion of market access forms the basis of a test capable of principled and coherent application or is merely a convenient label the Court uses to condemn measures it does not like. The selection rules themselves governed participation in high-level international sporting competitions. Their application had certainly affected Ms Deliège, *directly* limiting her opportunities to provide services to the organisers of competitions and probably *substantially* diminishing her ability to provide publicity for her existing sponsors and to attract new ones, as she could not participate in many of the most important international events. Advocate General Cosmas was of the opinion that the rules regulated directly the market access of high-ranking judokas, such as Ms Deliège.[457] Yet in the judgment the Court simply asserted that the rules did not determine the conditions governing market access, without giving any reasons for this statement. The lack of reasoning does not make it easy to predict what measures the Court will condemn on market access grounds.

---

[455] ibid, paras 61 and 62.   [456] ibid, paras 64–68.
[457] ibid, Opinion of AG Cosmas, para 66. See also S. Van den Bogaert, 'The Court of Justice on the Tatami: Ippon, Waza-Ari or Koka?' (2000) 25 ELRev 554 at 560–561.

Secondly, the Court's discussion of the need for the selection rules and their normalcy is slightly puzzling. This kind of analysis is common when the Court is examining the justification of a prima facie restriction, not when it is investigating whether a measure amounts to a restriction in the first place. In addition, the Court had already held that the rules did not govern market access and that Ms Deliège had not been a victim of discrimination. Was this insufficient to keep the measures outside the scope of Article 49 (ex 59) EC? The Court did refer to the fact that the rules limited the number of participants in a tournament, which brings to mind the criterion of 'limiting the volume of imports' from the mechanical application of the *Dassonville* formula, and in the ruling proper it did accept selection rules as long as they derived from the needs inherent in the organisation of competitions. Does this mean, *e contrario*, that a measure may constitute a restriction even if it neither discriminates nor governs market access but does contain limitations that the Court considers needless? This would be an extremely wide economic freedom reading of the EC Treaty.

It may be argued that the Court was not aiming to extend the reach of Article 49, however. First, it may have been motivated by the desire to emphasise that sporting bodies retain some of their independence. Secondly, and more importantly, the system of national federations selecting service providers is highly suspicious from the Community law point of view even if there is no nationality condition.[458] In effect, the system imposes a quota for service providers from each Member State, as judokas belonging to the clubs of a certain Member State are likely to be nationals of the same country. In most cases, the Court would surely condemn this kind of arrangement. For example, an attempt by national banking associations to select which of their members are entitled to provide banking services in other Member States would hardly be acceptable to the Court. Therefore, the discussion of the need for and the normalcy of the selection system must have been aimed at explaining why the Court accepted the rules despite the 'quantitative restriction' they created. In effect, the Court was saying that the measure did not fall within the scope of Article 49 because it was justified by needs inherent in the organisation of competitions.

It is submitted that *Deliège* is best seen as a case limited to the sports sector. The system under consideration is peculiar to sports, and the ruling of the Court seems to be of limited relevance for other economic activities.

d) The free movement of goods and a test based on market access

The recent case law of the European Court of Justice on the free movement of goods has only increased the lack of clarity surrounding the question of

---

[458] The fact that the same rules apply in every Member State is not decisive. For example, a rule providing that only nationals may engage in certain economic activities is not acceptable even if other Member States use similar rules.

what amounts to a restriction. In the *De Agostini*[459] judgment of 9 July 1997 the Court applied the *Keck*[460] test, finding that a measure only fell within Article 28 (ex 30) EC if it discriminated in fact. On the facts of the case, the market access test devised in *Alpine Investments*[461] could very well have resulted in a finding that the measure was prima facie within the scope of Article 28 (ex 30) EC, had that test been applied in the field of the free movement of goods. In *Franzén*[462] on 23 October 1997 the Court did not even mention *Keck* but seems to have based its judgment on the impediment to market access. The same happened in *Evora*[463] on 4 November 1997,[464] but after that the Court has continued to apply the *Keck* test. At the same time the Court has continued to find in a number of cases that the restrictive effects of some national rules are too uncertain and indirect for there to be an obstacle, which some commentators see as an introduction of a *de minimis* requirement. Finally, in *TK-Heimdienst*[465] and *Gourmet International Products*[466] the Court has hinted at a change in emphasis. The language employed by the Court in these two rulings suggests that market access is an increasingly important notion also in the application of *Keck*.

The interesting part of *De Agostini*[467] for these purposes is the Court's approach to the question whether Article 28 (ex 30) EC applied to the Swedish laws prohibiting misleading advertising and banning television advertisements designed to attract the attention of children under the age of 12. These rules were applied to advertisements of De Agostini, a Swedish company belonging to an Italian group. De Agostini had advertised a children's magazine *Allt om dinosaurier!* (*Everything about Dinosaurs!*), which was printed in Italy. The advertisements had been broadcast from the United Kingdom by satellite.

The Court held that the Swedish measures concerned selling arrangements and, thus, fell outside Article 28 (ex 30) EC unless it was shown that they discriminated, in fact or in law, against products from other Member States. This was for the national court to determine.[468] Advocate General Jacobs had argued in his Opinion that the prohibition of all television advertising directed at children might have a greater impact on other Member States'

---

[459] Joined Cases C-34/95, C-35/95 and C-36/95 *Konsumentombudsmannen v De Agostini (Svenska) Förlag AB and TV-Shop i Sverige AB* [1997] ECR I-3843.

[460] Joined Cases C-267/91 and C-268/91 *Criminal Proceedings Against Keck and Mithouard* [1993] ECR I-6097.

[461] Case C-384/93 *Alpine Investments BV v Minister van Financiën* [1995] ECR I-1141.

[462] Case C-189/95 *Criminal Proceedings Against Harry Franzén* [1997] ECR I-5909.

[463] Case C-337/95 *Parfums Christian Dior SA and Parfums Christian Dior BV v Evora BV* [1997] ECR I-6013.

[464] Similarly Eeckhout (n 392 above) 270.

[465] Case C-254/98 *Schutzverband gegen unlauteren Wettbewerb v TK-Heimdienst Sass GmbH*, judgment of 13 January 2000.

[466] Case C-405/98 *Konsumentombudsmannen v Gourmet International Products Aktiebolag*, judgment of 8 March 2001.

[467] See n 459 above.   [468] ibid, paras 39–44.

products.[469] If the national court decided that the Swedish legislation did not affect the marketing of foreign and domestic products in the same way, it would have to determine whether it could be justified.[470]

The Court could have easily selected another approach, however. It could have used the market access test it invented in *Alpine Investments*.[471] The rule at issue directly affected cross-border activities.[472] It was not confined to situations within one Member State. If the product was not able to gain entry into the market without television advertising, as De Agostini claimed, the measure had an immediate effect on market access of the magazine. Its impact was not only felt through a general decrease in the volume of sales.

Furthermore, as Advocate General Jacobs stated, in practice a total ban on television advertising directed at children 'will almost certainly have a perceptible effect on imports'.[473] The prohibition deprived operators of an effective way of marketing their products, thereby substantially restricting their access to the market.

Thus, whether one prefers the test based on the directness of the impediment to market access or the test based on the substantiality of the obstacle, the Swedish rule could well have been caught by either one of the tests. The fact that the Court, rightly in my view, stuck to the *Keck* orthodoxy seemed to indicate that it was not prepared to import a market access test into the field of the free movement of goods.

The Court muddied the waters three and a half months later in another case from Sweden, *Franzén*.[474] The case was concerned with Swedish rules dealing with production, importation and distribution of alcohol, and a national commercial monopoly. For current purposes, the most important part of the judgment was the Court's examination of the production and wholesale licensing system. The Swedish Law on Alcohol required that wholesalers and importers of strong beer, wine and spirits held either a production licence covering the relevant product or a wholesale licence. Licences were subject to payment of charges and annual supervision fees, and fulfilment of other conditions.

---

[469] See n 459 above, Opinion of AG Jacobs, para 99. See also the Opinion of AG Jacobs in Case C-405/98 *Konsumentombudsmannen v Gourmet International Products Aktiebolag*, judgment of 8 March 2001, paras 34–38.

[470] See n 459 above, para 45–46 of the judgment. The Court's answer in para 47 to the question referred by the national court was in conflict with the reasoning. The operative part indicates that the national rules must both affect in the same way the marketing of domestic and other Member States' products *and* be justified. The reasoning, and a comparison with the French version, make it clear that the conditions are not cumulative. See Snell (n 8 above) 226.

[471] See n 461 above.

[472] See J. Stuyck, 'Joined Cases C-34/95, C-35/95 and C-36/95 *Konsumentombudsmannen (KO)* v. *De Agostini (Svenska) Förlag AB* and *Konsummentombudsmannen (KO)* v. *TV-Shop i Sverige AB*, Judgment of 9 July 1997, nyr' (1997) 34 CMLRev 1445 at 1464–1465, who had earlier suggested that cross-border advertising was not within selling arrangements covered by *Keck*, and now had to review his opinion.

[473] See n 459 above.   [474] See n 462 above.

The Court began the examination of the licensing system by quoting the *Dassonville* formula.[475] It continued by listing all the conditions for obtaining a licence, and thus for importation, and by commenting on the high level of the charges and fees.[476] It then stated that:

The licensing system constitutes an obstacle to the importation of alcoholic beverages from other Member States in that it imposes additional costs on such beverages, such as intermediary costs, payment of charges and fees for the grant of a licence, and costs arising from the obligation to maintain storage capacity in Sweden.

According to the Swedish Government's own evidence, the number of licences issued is low (223 in October 1996) and almost all of these licences have been issued to traders established in Sweden.

Domestic legislation such as that in question in the main proceedings is therefore contrary to Article 30 [now 28] of the Treaty.[477]

The Court then went on to examine whether the system could be justified on grounds of the protection of human health. It found that the Swedish government had not shown that the measures were proportionate or that this aim could not have been attained by less restrictive means, and thus condemned this part of the Swedish legislation.[478]

The Court's reasoning was extremely terse. For that reason what the Court *did not* say is as interesting as what it did say. First, the Court did not refer to *Keck*[479] or to selling arrangements. Nevertheless, it might be argued that the system was concerned with the question who may sell certain alcoholic beverages in Sweden. Rules regulating this issue have always been considered to affect selling arrangements.[480] Furthermore, the Swedish, Finnish, French and Norwegian governments and the Commission had defended the rules applicable to the Swedish alcohol monopoly as only concerning selling arrangements.[481]

Secondly, the Court made just a fleeting reference to the possibility that the rules might be discriminatory. It only mentioned the fact that most of the licences were in Swedish hands.

Finally, the Court did not mention whether the system directly affected access to the Swedish market. Yet this consideration had been decisive in both *Alpine Investments*[482] and *Bosman*.[483]

In fact, it seems that the Court was looking at how substantially the Swedish rules impeded market access of goods from other Member States. It listed the conditions for obtaining a licence, commented on how high the

---

[475] ibid, para 69; Case 8/74 *Procureur du Roi v Dassonville* [1974] ECR 837.
[476] See n 462 above, para 70.   [477] ibid, paras 71–73.   [478] ibid, paras 74–77.
[479] Joined Cases C-267/91 and C-268/91 *Criminal Proceedings Against Keck and Mithouard* [1993] ECR I-6097.
[480] See Higgins (n 271 above) 168–169, and Oliver (n 269 above) 104.
[481] See n 462 above, para 33.
[482] Case C-384/93 *Alpine Investments BV v Minister van Financiën* [1995] ECR I-1141.
[483] Case C-415/93 *Union Royale Belge des Sociétés de Football Association ASBL and others v Jean-Marc Bosman* [1995] ECR I-4921.

charges and fees were and noted how few licences had been issued, especially to traders not established in Sweden. From all this it deduced that Swedish legislation was not in accordance with Article 28 (ex 30) EC. Thus, it would seem that the Court has adopted the doctrine suggested by Advocate General Jacobs in *Leclerc-Siplec*[484] prohibiting measures which are liable to restrict market access substantially.[485]

This judgment should not be given too much weight, however. The result achieved can be explained in other ways as well. First, it might be argued that one of the purposes of the Swedish licensing system was to regulate trade in goods between Member States. After all, a licence was required for importation. The judgment in *Keck* made it clear that the aim of regulating inter-state trade causes a measure to fall within Article 28.[486]

Secondly, the system was clearly discriminatory. It discriminated against goods coming from other parts of the Community by placing traders from other Member States at a disadvantage. An economic operator lawfully engaged in sales of alcoholic beverages in his home country was not allowed to pursue the same activity in Sweden without a licence. The trader had to fulfil the requirements of both home and host countries. Clearly a dual burden was placed on the trader. If the products had been services instead of goods, there would have been no difficulty in finding that the measures fell within the scope of Article 49 (ex 59) EC as defined in *Säger*[487] and even earlier cases. However, as the Court was dealing with material products, the provisions on the free movement of goods applied, since Article 50(1) (ex 60(1)) EC defines services as a residual category. Nevertheless, the result should not depend on the material or non-material nature of the products. It is also clear that discrimination against foreign traders in practice readily translates to factual discrimination against foreign goods. Advocate General Elmer was also of the opinion that the licensing system was discriminatory,[488] and the Court itself referred to the fact that almost all licences were issued to traders established in Sweden.[489]

Thirdly, the system most certainly affected access to the Swedish market directly. It did not simply restrict the volume of alcohol sales in Sweden thereby indirectly affecting also imports. It did not regulate solely internal relationships between Swedish parties but touched the very relationship between economic operators in different Member States, thus directly hindering cross-border activities.

---

[484] Opinion of AG Jacobs in Case C-412/93 *Société d'Importation Édouard Leclerc-Siplec v TF1 Publicité SA and M6 Publicité SA* [1995] ECR I-179 paras 38–49.

[485] Chalmers and Szyszczak (n 303 above) 309–310 come to this conclusion.

[486] See n 477 above, para 12.

[487] Case C-76/90 *Manfred Säger v Dennemeyer & Co. Ltd* [1991] ECR I-4221.

[488] Case C-189/95 *Criminal Proceedings Against Harry Franzén* [1997] ECR I-5909 paras 101–103 of his Opinion.

[489] ibid, para 72 of the judgment.

Very far-reaching conclusions should not be drawn from the judgment in *Franzén*. The factual situation was unusual due to the existence of a national commercial monopoly, and the case was primarily concerned with the application of Article 31 (ex 37) EC. The Court's terse reasoning seems to indicate that it is looking for substantial hindrance to market access[490] but the result can be explained in more traditional ways.

Another case where the Court's reasoning was based on the significant impact a national measure had on the market access of goods from other Member States was *Evora*.[491] In issue were trademark and copyright rules in force in the Netherlands. Evora had obtained Dior products by parallel imports and had advertised them for sale. Dior objected to this, claiming that Evora had infringed its trademark and copyright to the bottles and packaging. The referring court, the Hoge Raad, asked inter alia whether Articles 28 (ex 30) and 30 (ex 36) EC precluded Dior's claims. The question was based on the premise that national law permitted the trademark owner or the copyright holder to prohibit a reseller from advertising the commercialisation of the goods.[492]

Dior contested whether the rules in force in the Netherlands constituted a measure having an equivalent effect to quantitative restrictions. The Court answered this by stating that:

it is enough that . . . the main proceedings concern goods which the reseller has procured through parallel imports and that a prohibition of advertising such as that sought in the main proceedings would render commercialization, and consequently access to the market for those goods, appreciably more difficult.[493]

It continued by looking at the justification of the measures and, following Advocate General Jacobs, found them permissible only in certain circumstances.[494]

Once again the Court referred neither to *Keck*[495] nor to discrimination nor to direct impediment to market access. By basing its judgment on the fact that market access was made *appreciably* more difficult, the Court seems to have adopted the *de minimis* test suggested by Advocate General Jacobs in *Leclerc-Siplec*.[496]

It is true that the measures did significantly impede access to the market for the goods at issue. Parallel imports are hardly worthwhile if it is not possible

---

[490] cf however Hilson (n 252 above) 455 who sees this judgment as a confirmation that the Court is *not* willing to extend the market access doctrine into the field of goods.

[491] Case C-337/95 *Parfums Christian Dior SA and Parfums Christian Dior BV v Evora BV* [1997] ECR I-6013. See also S. O'Leary, 'The Free Movement of Persons and Services' in P. Craig and G. de Búrca (eds), *The Evolution of EU Law* (Oxford 1999), 405.

[492] See n 491 above, para 50. See also on the Uniform Benelux Law on Trade Marks the Opinion of AG Jacobs, para 9.

[493] ibid, para 51.   [494] ibid, para 59.

[495] Joined Cases C-267/91 and C-268/91 *Criminal Proceedings Against Keck and Mithouard* [1993] ECR I-6097.

[496] Case C-412/93 *Société d'Importation Édouard Leclerc-Siplec v TF1 Publicité SA and M6 Publicité SA* [1995] ECR I-179.

to advertise them. However some caution may still be necessary before the birth of a new doctrine is pronounced.

First of all, the Court's case law on intellectual property rights has formed 'an apparently separate and somewhat opaque chapter'[497] of its general case law on Article 28 (ex 30) EC. The approach of the Court in the judgments dealing with intellectual property has been rather different from its usual method.[498] Therefore, very far-reaching conclusions on the general scope of the free movement of goods should not be drawn from a trademark and copyright case.

Secondly, *Evora* is an extension of a long line of case law based on combating discrimination. The exhaustion of rights cases[499] dealt with situations where domestic intellectual property right laws stipulated that the first sale in national territory exhausted the copyright, patent or trademark holder's right to control the selling of the product, but allowed him to oppose imports when the product had been sold in another Member State with his consent. The Court dealt with these discriminatory rules by developing a system of Community exhaustion: the right was exhausted if the product had been distributed somewhere in the Community with the consent of the rightholder.[500] If Community law now allowed the prevention of advertising, the right to sell the products would not amount to much. Commercialisation would not be easy if the reseller could not tell his customers about the product in an efficient manner.[501] Similarly in the repackaging cases[502] the Court has curtailed the use of rights which could be used to circumvent the Community exhaustion doctrine.[503]

Finally, the rules in force in the Netherlands had in practice the greatest impact on parallel imports. They were not general measures affecting imports only indirectly. It is very unlikely that anybody would be able to resell commercially the products first distributed in the Netherlands. Within one country it may be fairly easy to ensure that the selective distributors do not sell to unauthorised retailers. Such control may become more difficult when the goods cross borders. In addition, the price differences within one country may be non-existent or so small that reselling would not be worthwhile. The

---

[497] G. Marenco and K. Banks, 'Intellectual Property and the Community Rules on Free Movement: Discrimination Unearthed' (1990) 15 ELRev 224 at 238.

[498] See on the Court's traditional approach to national laws on intellectual property Marenco and Banks (n 497 above) 224–238.

[499] Case 78/70 *Deutsche Grammophon GmbH v Metro-SB Grossmärkte GmbH & Co KG* [1971] ECR 487, Case 15/74 *Centrafarm BV v Sterling Drug Inc* [1974] ECR 1147, and Case 16/74 *Centrafarm BV v Winthrop BV* [1974] ECR 1183.

[500] See generally Craig and de Búrca (n 121 above) 1029–1041, and Weatherill and Beaumont (n 17 above) 977–993.

[501] See n 489 above, Opinion of AG Jacobs, para 31.

[502] See eg Case 102/77 *Hoffmann-La Roche & Co AG v Centrafarm Vertriebsgesellschaft Pharmazeutischer Erzeugnisse mbH* [1978] ECR 1139, and Case 1/81 *Pfizer Inc v Eurim-Pharm GmbH* [1981] ECR 2913. See also the discussion in Chapter 3 section 2aii below.

[503] Marenco and Banks (n 497 above) 245.

prices tend to vary much more between different Member States.[504] Thus, it might be said that the rules directly hindered the access of these goods to the Dutch market.

Taken together, *Franzén* and *Evora* may indicate that the Court has at least refined *Keck* and adopted the *de minimis* doctrine to limit the reach of the free movement of goods. If this is so, market access has become the key concept for both Articles 28 (ex 30) and 49 (ex 59) EC, and this time the case law on the free movement of services has shown the way. However, the emphasis has been on different aspects of the concept. In the field of services the Court has talked about the 'directness' of the impediment to market access while in the field of goods the appreciability of the obstacle to market access may have been decisive. Due to the frequent cross-fertilisation between the freedoms and the still small number of cases, too much weight should not be put on the differences, however.

Closely related to the issue of the *de minimis* doctrine is a line of cases where the Court has found that the restrictive effects of a national rule are too uncertain and indirect for it to constitute an obstacle. This line of cases dates from the 1980s and, somewhat puzzlingly, the Court has continued to use the test of remoteness even after *Keck*.[505] It has sometimes been argued that these cases, where no obstacle was found when the restrictive effect was uncertain and indirect, *e contrario* suggest that a non-discriminatory measure which does substantially hinder access to the market breaches the EC Treaty unless justified, and that this amounts to the introduction of a *de minimis* requirement.[506]

There are a number of objections to this view. First, it can be argued that the test of remoteness is conceptually different from a *de minimis* test.[507] There may be situations where a rule has a certain and direct impact on cross-border trade, even though the effect is very small. An example is provided by *Bluhme*.[508] The case concerned a Danish measure that only allowed the keeping of bees belonging to a certain sub-species, but which applied in a very limited geographical area. The Court found a restriction; the impact of the rule was slight in volume terms, but the restrictive effect was not remote.

Further, the Court has continuously rejected some challenges to national rules on the ground of remoteness, yet it has also consistently refused to apply a *de minimis* test. In *Blesgen*[509] in 1982 the Court found that a Belgian rule did

---

[504] See on price differences among the EU countries, Molle (n 18 above) 133–134.

[505] See eg Case 75/81 *Belgium v Blesgen* [1982] ECR 1211, Case C-69/88 *H. Krantz GmbH & Co v Ontvanger der Directe Belastingen et al* [1990] ECR I-583, Case C-379/92 *Matteo Peralta* [1994] ECR I-3453, Joined Cases C-140–142/94 *DIP SpA v Comune di Bassano del Grappa* [1995] ECR I-3257, and Case C-266/96 *Corsica Ferries France SA v Gruppo Antichi Ormeggiatori del Porto di Genova Coop. arl and others* [1998] ECR I-3949.

[506] Barnard (n 277 above) 51–52. See also J. Steiner and L. Woods, *Textbook on EC Law* (7th edn London 2000) 166–168.

[507] See Oliver (n 276 above) 789, and Hatzopoulos (n 424 above) 82.

[508] Case C-67/97 *Criminal Proceedings Against Ditlev Bluhme* [1998] ECR I-8033. Note that the rule in issue in the case would not benefit from the *de minimis* exception as defined by AG Jacobs.

[509] See n 505 above.

not infringe Article 28 (ex 30) EC, as it had in fact no connection with importation. In *van de Haar*[510] in 1984 it rejected the *de minimis* test, yet used
remoteness in *Krantz*[511] in 1990. In *Peralta*[512] in 1994 and *DIP SpA*[513] in 1995
the Court again cited remoteness, while implicitly declining to accept *de
minimis* in 1995 in *Leclerc-Siplec*.[514] In 1998 remoteness was again used in
Corsica Ferries[515] but *de minimis* did not feature in *Bluhme*.[516]

The Court has even explicitly distinguished the remoteness case law from a
de minimis rule. In 1993 in *Yves Rocher* Germany argued that a measure preventing the comparison of old and new prices in 'an eye-catching manner' did
not infringe Article 28 as it constituted only a marginal restriction. The Court
replied to this argument by stating that:

On this point, leaving aside rules having merely hypothetical effect on intra-
Community trade, it has been consistently held that Article 30 [now 28] of the Treaty
does not make a distinction between measures which can be described as measures
having equivalent effect to a quantitative restriction according to the magnitude of the
effects they have on trade within the Community.[517]

In the light of this it is very difficult to argue that the case law on uncertain and
indirect effect of national rules amounts to the adoption of a *de minimis* test.

Moreover, in 1993 the Court clearly did have the perfect opportunity to
give this line of case law a wider application.[518] Indeed, it used the test of
remoteness in *Motorradcenter*[519] on 13 October 1993. Yet, it did not apply it
in *Keck* on 24 November 1993 but rather felt compelled to reconsider and
clarify its previous case law. In 1993 the Court clearly did not see the test of
remoteness as an adequate definition of the outer limits of Article 28 (ex 30)
EC. It would be surprising if it changed its mind again so soon.

Finally, the test of remoteness seems a difficult one to apply, as tort lawyers
have found over the years.[520] Its use in the 1980s and early 1990s was subject
to fierce criticism,[521] and there is nothing to suggest that its utilisation has
become any easier since. Yet, the Court has not given any guidance on its

---

[510] Joined Cases 177 and 178/82 *Criminal Proceedings Against Jan vand de Haar and Kaveka
de Meern BV* [1984] ECR 1797.

[511] See n 505 above.　　　　　　　　　　[512] ibid.　　　　　　　　　　[513] ibid.

[514] Case C-412/93 *Société d'Importation Édouard Leclerc-Siplec v TF1 Publicité SA and M6
Publicité SA* [1995] ECR I-179.

[515] See n 505 above.　　　　　　　　[516] See n 508 above.

[517] Case C-126/91 *Schutzverband gegen Unwesen in der Wirtschaft e. V. v Yves Rocher GmbH*
[1993] ECR I-2361 para 21.

[518] In 1992, Steiner in 'Drawing the Line' (n 102 above) 767–772 advocated an approach based
on whether there is a *hindrance* to intra-Community trade arguing that in the *Blesgen* line of cases
the restrictive effects were not sufficient.

[519] Case C-93/92 *CMC Motorradcenter GmbH v Baskiciogullari* [1993] ECR I-5009.

[520] Barnard (n 277 above) 55. Cf however Hatzopoulos (n 424 above) 82.

[521] See Gormley (n 195 above) 198–200, who argued that the reasoning of the Court in at least
some of these cases 'pays scant attention to the demands of logic or careful attention'. See also
AG Tesauro in Case C-292/92 *Hünermund v Landesapothekerkammer Baden-Württemberg* [1993]
ECR I-6787 paras 11–24.

application.[522] If remoteness was the crucial test in determining the existence of a restriction, this lack of direction would be wholly unacceptable from the point of view of legal certainty.

Altogether, the finding that the restrictive effects of a national rule are too remote for it to amount to an obstacle is best seen as a simple application of the *Dassonville* formula. The Court is merely saying that the measure does not constitute even a potential or indirect hindrance to inter-state trade.[523]

Keck never displaced the *Dassonville* formula, which was indeed quoted in the judgment.[524] It merely imposed an additional and higher hurdle for those arguing that a rule concerning certain selling arrangements infringes Article 28 (ex 30) EC. It is quite logical that a rule regulating market circumstances, such as that in issue in *DIP SpA*,[525] making the opening of new shops subject to the grant of licence, never encounters the Keck test if it does not constitute a direct or indirect, actual or potential, hindrance to trade.

Finally, in some recent cases the Court has used the *Keck* test, but the language employed has hinted that the notion of market access is being given increasing importance in its application. *TK-Heimdienst*[526] concerned an Austrian rule which made the sale of foodstuffs on rounds subject to the trader having a permanent establishment in the area. The Court concluded that 'the national legislation . . . in fact impedes access to the market of the Member State of importation for products from other Member States more than it impedes access for domestic products' and cited *Alpine Investments*.[527] In its ruling in *Gourmet International Products*[528] on a Swedish ban on alcohol advertising the Court took as a starting point paragraph 17 of *Keck*, which deals with market access, rather than paragraph 16, which is concerned with discrimination in law or in fact.[529] This may indicate a subtle shift in emphasis hinting at a more pronounced role for market access.

Perhaps too much should not be read into these statements, however. In both judgments the Court conducted a thorough examination of the discriminatory impact of the national measures, in line with *Keck*, and on the facts both cases comply with the orthodoxy. Further, paragraph 17 of *Keck* does concern market access, but differs significantly from the notion of direct impediment to market access employed in *Alpine Investments* and *Bosman*. In *Keck* the Court stated that the application of non-discriminatory rules concerning selling arrangements 'to the sale of such products from another

---

[522] See Oliver (n 276 above) 789. [523] ibid. cf Biondi (n 392 above) 486–488.

[524] Joined Cases C-267 and 268/91 *Criminal Proceedings Against Keck and Mithouard* [1993] ECR I-6097 para 11.

[525] Joined Cases C-140–142/94 *DIP SpA v Comune di Bassano del Grappa* [1995] ECR I-3257.

[526] Case C-254/98 *Schutzverband gegen unlauteren Wettbewerb v TK-Heimdienst Sass GmbH*, judgment of 13 January 2000.

[527] ibid, para 29. The Court had referred to market access already earlier in para 26.

[528] Case C-405/98 *Konsumentombudsmannen v Gourmet International Products Aktiebolag*, judgment of 8 March 2001.

[529] ibid, para 18.

Member State is not by nature such as to prevent their access to the market or to impede access any more than it impeded the access of domestic products.'[530] This formula is concerned with market access being prevented, as in the case of a total ban, and with a differential impact on market access. Therefore, the reference to market access in *Keck* is still connected to the idea of discrimination.

Altogether, the Court's approach is open to criticism. First, it may be asked whether a centralising test based on market access is correct in principle[531] or workable in practice.[532] Secondly, the case law lacks coherence and clarity. The Court seems to be altering the test it uses at an alarming frequency. Furthermore, its reasoning is often minimal. This would be more acceptable if the Court was just applying familiar rules, but if the Court wants to develop a new test, surely it should clearly say so. It does not take long to lose the clarity achieved in *Keck* and the subsequent case law.

e) Conclusion

For the most part the Court's judgment in *Keck* and its subsequent decisions on Article 49 (ex 59) EC follow the philosophy of mutual recognition.[533] At the core of this doctrine is the principle that a product lawfully put on the market in one Member State must be allowed to enter the markets of the other Member States.

Prohibitions and product rules are inimical to the doctrine as they create a multiple burden. A product complying with the rules of the home state is not allowed to enter the market of the host state. Only one regulatory system, that of the home country, should apply.

The rules regulating selling arrangements fall under the competence of the host state. As long as the national measures do not discriminate against imports, the host country is free to legislate as it sees fit.

The doctrine allows the formation of economies of scale and provides for the preservation of the competitive edge, as an undertaking can take advantage of the most favourable business environment by producing goods and services according to the methods of one Member State and selling them inside the whole Community. This creates a framework for a European-wide competition between undertakings and also enables competition between legal orders, especially as factors of production can relocate. The free movement provisions of the EC Treaty create the best preconditions for regulatory competition when they guarantee free movement but leave as much room for

---

[530] See n 524 above, para 17.   [531] See the discussion in section 1 above.
[532] See the discussion in section 5civ above.
[533] Mutual recognition also still plays a crucial part in the Commission's internal market strategy, even in relation to services. See eg Communication from the Commission to the Council and the European Parliament, *An Internal Market Strategy for Services* (COM (2000) 888 final) 15.

regulation by Member States as possible. The doctrine based on mutual recognition achieves this aim well.

The doctrine contributes to a decentralised, federal Community, where Member States' regulatory competences are preserved. It allays fears of a centralised super-state insensitive to national preferences and traditions and the sheer diversity of the Community. Thus, it contributes to the campaign for the hearts and minds of the Community citizens, whose primary attachment is still to the nation state.

The market forces are given the principal responsibility for bringing about the integration of national markets. Regulation only creates a framework for the operation of the market. The multitude of private decisions by economic operators is given a decisive role. Public intervention by the centre is minimised. The desired result is not imposed but comes about through the operation of the invisible hand of the market.

Alpine Investments, when read alone, could be reconciled with this system. An equally applicable marketing rule can be considered a prima facie restriction when it is adopted by the exporting home state. The idea is that the importing host state regulates market circumstances and the exporting home state deals with products and production. Therefore, a non-discriminatory host state rule on selling arrangements does not constitute a restriction, but the application of a similar rule by the home state must be justified. Conversely, the application of host state product and production rules amounts to a restriction, while the home state is free to regulate in a non-discriminatory manner. Regulatory competence is divided between Member States to ensure that one, and only one, rule always applies. However, when *Alpine Investments* is read together with *Bosman*, it brings a new element into play. National rules creating a direct impediment to market access are scrutinised by the Court. Cross-border measures are attacked. A step is taken towards the economic freedom model and a more centralised Community where the Court determines the optimal regulation of the internal market. The desirability of this development can be questioned, and its extent is still uncertain.

3

Persons bound

1. Introduction

The next question is who is bound by the provisions on the free movement of goods and services. It is unequivocally clear that Member States are prohibited from adopting measures restricting trade in goods or services. That is the main purpose of these provisions and the great majority of cases and Community legislation has been aimed at dismantling barriers erected by national public authorities. What about measures adopted by private parties and by the Community itself? Are they bound by Articles 28 (ex 30) and 49 (ex 59) EC?

2. Private parties

a) The free movement of goods

i) General

The text of the EC Treaty indicates that Article 28 (ex 30) EC is aimed at state measures. Although the provision itself does not refer to the author of quantitative restrictions and measures having equivalent effect, prior to the Treaty of Amsterdam[1] other Articles of the same Chapter on Elimination of Quantitative Restrictions[2] specifically targeted measures adopted by Member States. Thus, Article 31(1) EC (repealed) stipulated that 'Member States shall refrain from introducing between themselves any new quantitative restrictions or measures having equivalent effect'. Similarly, Article 32(1) EC (repealed) stated that '[i]n their trade with one another Member States shall refrain from making more restrictive the quotas and measures having equivalent effect existing at the date of entry into force of this Treaty'. In addition, Articles 33–35 (partly repealed) all showed that Member State measures are the target of these provisions.[3]

---

[1] The deletions do not affect *acquis communautaire*. See Art 10 of the Amsterdam Treaty and Declaration 51 annexed to the Treaty.

[2] Now 'Prohibition of Quantitative Restrictions'.

[3] See P. Oliver, *Free Movement of Goods in the European Community* (3rd edn London 1996) 41, and the Opinion of AG Lenz in Case C-265/95 *Commission v French Republic* [1997] ECR I-6959 para 8. Note, however, Case 36/74 *Walrave and Koch v UCI* [1974] ECR 1405 para 20, which will be analysed in section 2b below.

The opinion of the Commission seems to be that Article 28 (ex 30) EC does not apply to measures adopted by private parties. In the recitals of Directive 70/50/EEC[4] it defined 'measures' for the purposes of Article 28 *et seq* as 'laws, regulations, administrative provisions, administrative practices, and all instruments issuing from a public authority, including recommendations'. In the next recital it made clear that 'administrative practices' referred to standards and procedures followed by public authorities.

A decade later, in reply to Written Question No 909/79[5] of Mr Moreland MEP which concerned industrial action preventing goods from crossing national borders, such as dock picketing, the Commission stated that:

The practices . . . do not in themselves constitute a quantitative restriction on trade within the meaning of Article 30 [now 28] of the EEC Treaty as interpreted by the Court of Justice.

However, the Commission agrees that, although the type of action . . . does not contravene Article 30 [now 28] of the Treaty, it could in certain circumstances disrupt trade within the Community. The Commission feels that this is a problem which warrants careful investigation. . .'

More recently, in Recital 7 of the proposal for a Regulation creating a mechanism whereby the Commission can intervene in order to remove certain obstacles to trade,[6] the Commission commented that a party injured by actions taken by private individuals which created obstacles to the free movement of goods has 'no appropriate instrument to rely on' in defending his rights.

These statements show clearly that, according to the Commission, Article 28 (ex 30) EC does not bind private parties but is only designed to catch measures adopted by public bodies.

The European Court of Justice has also declined to apply Article 28 to private measures.[7] In *Vlaamse Reisbureaus*[8] it had to consider contracts between travel agents and tour operators, contracts between the agents themselves, and a Belgian Royal Decree reinforcing the system. The agreements purported to oblige the travel agents to observe the prices and tariffs set by the tour operators. The agents were prohibited from sharing commissions with or granting rebates to their customers. The Court found that the Belgian system infringed Article 81(1) (ex 85(1)) EC, and Article 10 (ex 5) EC in conjunction with Articles 3(1)(g) and 81 (ex 85) EC.[9]

---

[4] Commission Directive 70/50/EEC of 22 December 1969 based on the provisions of Art 33(7) (repealed), on the abolition of measures which have an effect equivalent to quantitative restrictions on imports and are not covered by other provisions adopted in pursuance of the EEC Treaty [1970] OJ Spec Ed I L13/29, 17.

[5] [1980] OJ C156/10.   [6] [1998] OJ C10/14.

[7] Already in Case 8/74 *Procureur du Roi v Dassonville* [1974] ECR 837 para 5, the Court referred to 'trading rules enacted by the Member States'.

[8] Case 311/85 *VZW Vereniging van Vlaamse Reisbureaus v VZW Sociale Dienst van de Plaatselijke en Gewestlijke Overheidsdiensten* [1987] ECR 3801.

[9] ibid, paras 27 and 24.

The national court had, however, also asked whether the agreements and the Royal Decree were compatible with Articles 28 (ex 30) and 29 (ex 34) EC. The Court stated the following:

Since Articles 30 [currently 28] and 34 [currently 29] of the Treaty concern only public measures and not the conduct of undertakings, it is only the compatibility with those articles of national provisions of the kind at issue in the main proceedings that need be examined.[10]

The Court went on to decide that the sale of travel was provision of services so Articles 28 and 29 could not have been breached.[11]

This judgment shows clearly the view of the Court. Articles 28 and 29 are not concerned with private measures. Furthermore, the Court has been consistent in its approach. In *Commission v Italy*[12] the Court stated that the subject of the Chapter relating to the elimination of quantitative restrictions was state intervention in intra-Community trade.[13] In *Van de Haar*[14] the Court compared Articles 81 (ex 85) EC and 28 (ex 30) EC, stating that the former belongs to rules on competition addressed to undertakings and associations of undertakings while the latter belongs to rules which seek to eliminate measures taken by Member States which might impede the free movement of goods. In *Bayer v Süllhöfer*[15] the Court pronounced that Article 28 *et seq* form part of the rules intended to ensure the free movement of goods and to eliminate for that purpose any measures of Member States forming barriers to inter-state trade, while agreements between undertakings are governed by the rules on competition.

ii) Intellectual property rights

It has sometimes been argued that in its judgments dealing with intellectual property rights and unfair competition the Court has in fact prohibited private measures restricting the free movement of goods.[16] For example, in *Deutsche Grammophon*[17] the Court stated that:

the essential purpose of the Treaty, which is to unite national markets into a single market . . . could not be attained if, under the various legal systems of the Member States, *nationals of those States were able to partition the market* and bring about arbitrary discrimination or disguised restrictions on trade between Member States.

---

[10] ibid, para 30.   [11] ibid, paras 32–33.
[12] Case 7/68 *Commission v Italy* [1968] ECR 423.   [13] ibid, at 430.
[14] Joined Cases 177 and 178/82 *Criminal Proceedings Against Jan van de Haar and Kaveka de Meern BV* [1984] ECR 1797 paras 11–12.
[15] Case 65/86 *Bayer AG and Maschinenfabrik Hennecke GmbH v Heinz Süllhöfer* [1988] ECR 5249 para 11.
[16] See eg N. Green, T.C. Hartley, and J.A. Usher, *The Legal Foundations of the Single European Market* (Oxford 1991) 53–55, and P. Pescatore, 'Public and Private Aspects of European Community Competition Law' (1987) 10 Fordham Int LJ 373 at 380–383.
[17] Case 78/70 *Deutsche Grammophon GmbH v Metro-SB Grossmärkte GmbH & Co KG* [1971] ECR 487.

Consequently, it would be in conflict with the provisions prescribing the free movement of products within the common market for *a manufacturer of sound recordings to
exercise the exclusive right* to distribute the protected articles, conferred upon him by
the legislation of a Member State, in such a way as to prohibit the sale in that State of
products placed on the market by him or with his consent in another Member State
solely because such distribution did not occur within the territory of the first Member
State.[18]

Similarly, in *Dansk Supermarked*[19] the Court remarked that 'it is impossible in any circumstances for agreements between individuals to derogate from
the mandatory provisions of the Treaty on the free movement of goods'.[20] In
Merck v Stephar[21] the Court held that the rules concerning the free movement
of goods prevented in certain circumstances the patent owner 'from availing
himself of the right conferred by the legislation'.[22] Finally, in *Centrafarm v
American Home Products Corporation*[23] the Court applied the Treaty rules on
the free movement of goods to the subjective behaviour of a private undertaking in the context of artificial partitioning of the common market.[24]

Nevertheless, despite these and other judgments to the same effect,[25] it can
be argued that even in this field the conduct of private parties is not caught.

First, in these cases the Court was not motivated by the desire to widen its
interpretation of Article 28 (ex 30) EC. Its aim was not necessarily to bring
private acts within the scope of the provisions on the free movement of goods.
It was simply still influenced by a doctrine it had developed in the field of competition law in the 1960s.[26]

In *Consten and Grundig*[27] the plaintiffs had argued that the application of
Article 81 (ex 85) EC to a use of trademark violated Article 295 (ex 222) EC,
which stipulates that the 'Treaty shall in no way prejudice the rules in
Member States governing the system of property ownership'. The Court had
dealt with the argument by developing a distinction between the existence and
the exercise of intellectual property rights.[28] The former was not affected by

---

[18] Case 78/70 *Deutsche Grammophon GmbH v Metro-SB Grossmärkte GmbH & Co KG* [1971]
ECR 487, paras 12–13 (emphasis added).
[19] Case 58/80 *Dansk Supermarked A/S v A/S Imerco* [1981] ECR 181.
[20] ibid, para 17. See further J. Baquero Cruz, 'Free Movement and Private Autonomy' (1999)
24 ELRev 603 at 607–609.
[21] Case 187/80 *Merck & Co Inc. v Stephar BV and Petrus Stephanus Exler* [1981] ECR 2063.
[22] ibid, para 14.
[23] Case 3/78 *Centrafarm BV v American Home Products Corporation* [1978] ECR 1823.
[24] See G. Marenco and K. Banks, 'Intellectual Property and the Community Rules on Free
Movement: Discrimination Unearthed' (1990) 15 ELRev 224, 227 and 253–254.
[25] See ibid, 224–225.
[26] See E. White, 'In Search of the Limits to Article 30 of the EEC Treaty' (1989) 26 CMLRev
235, 269.
[27] Cases 56/64 and 58/64 *Etablissements Consten SA and Grundig-Verkaufs-GmbH v
Commission* [1966] ECR 299.
[28] The Court could presumably have dealt with the argument in another way too. Article 295
(ex 222) EC was namely intended to protect the right of Member States to determine the private
or public ownership of undertakings, not to protect property rights. See Marenco and Banks (n
24 above) 226, and T.C. Vinje, 'The Final Word on Magill' (1995) 14 EIPR 397, 398.

the Treaty while the latter could be limited to the necessary extent. This distinction, which has been severely criticised,[29] was then applied in the field of the free movement of goods to the exercise of intellectual property rights by private parties.

Secondly, the judgments dealing with intellectual property can be interpreted in another way as well. It can be said that the Court was attacking national legislation granting private parties the right to exercise their intellectual property in certain situations.[30] The real barriers were created by the national legislation. The only peculiarity was that the law was not enforced by public authorities but by the national courts[31] following an initiative of a private party.[32]

This interpretation is supported by the conflicting language in some of the Court's decisions. For example, in the classic cases *Centrafarm v Sterling*[33] and *Centrafarm v Winthrop*[34] the Court pronounced in the operative parts that the exercise of the intellectual property rights by their owners was incompatible with the rules concerning the free movement of goods. Yet, earlier in the judgments, the Court had stated that an obstacle to the free movement of goods arose from certain provisions of national legislation stipulating that the intellectual property right was not exhausted by the marketing of the protected product in another Member State.[35]

In addition, more recent judgments show clearly that even in the field of intellectual property rights Article 28 (ex 30) EC does not catch private measures. Starting from *Pharmon v Hoechst*[36] the Court has made it clear that it is only state action which is caught. The Court stated in a key paragraph that:

Articles 30 [now 28] and 36 [now 30] of the EEC Treaty *preclude the application of national provisions* which enable a patent proprietor to prevent the importation and marketing of a product which has been lawfully marketed in another Member State by the patent proprietor himself, with his consent, or by a person economically or legally dependent on him.[37]

The Court has been consistent in its approach over recent years. In *Basset*,[38] for example, the referring national court asked whether Articles 28

---

[29] See eg V. Korah, *An Introductory Guide to EC Competition Law and Practice* (7th edn Oxford 2000), 258–259.

[30] Marenco and Banks (n 24 above) 225–226, Oliver (n 3 above) 59, and White (n 26 above) 268 and 270.

[31] An alternative explanation could be that the measure in the sense of Art 28 (ex 30) EC is the application of legislation by a national court. This interpretation is not convincing as it is not the courts but the legislature that is the real source of the measure. White (n 26 above) 268–269. See also Baquero Cruz (n 20 above) 615.

[32] See also the Opinion of AG Jacobs in Case C-443/98 *Unilever Italia SpA v Central Food SpA*, judgment of 26 September 2000, para 98.

[33] Case 15/74 *Centrafarm BV v Sterling Drug Inc* [1974] ECR 1147.

[34] Case 16/74 *Centrafarm BV v Winthrop BV* [1974] ECR 1183.

[35] See n 33 above, para 10, and n 34 above, para 9.

[36] Case 19/84 *Pharmon BV v Hoechst AG* [1985] ECR 2281.

[37] ibid, para 22 (emphasis added).

[38] Case 402/85 *G. Basset v SACEM* [1987] ECR 1747.

(ex 30) and 30 (ex 36) EC prevented *a national copyright-management society from charging* users a royalty on public performances. The Court answered that the provisions did not preclude *the application of national legislation* that allowed the charging of a royalty. The language of the Court made it clear that the suspect measure originated from the Member State, not from the private party.[39]

The Court has also recently made it clear that subjective intention of an economic agent is not relevant to the application of Article 28 and thus tacitly overruled *Centrafarm v American Home Products*.[40] In *Bristol-Myers Squibb*[41] Paranova had imported drugs produced by the plaintiffs from various Member States to Denmark, repackaging them for the purposes of sale. The plaintiffs took action against Paranova for trademark infringements.

The Court held, inter alia, that repackaging could not be opposed if certain conditions were fulfilled. One of these conditions was that the reliance upon trademark rights would contribute to the artificial partitioning of the markets between Member States. However, contrary to the argument of the plaintiffs, the importer was not required to establish that the trademark owner deliberately sought to partition the markets.[42]

The case showed that 'artificial partitioning of the markets' was an objective, not a subjective condition. Thus, it offered further support for the proposition that Article 28 does not apply to measures adopted by private parties.

Bristol-Myers Squibb was not identical to *Centrafarm v American Home Products*, however. In the latter case the producer had used slightly different trademarks in different countries, so the importer changed the trademark. In the former case, the trademark was simply reaffixed.[43] As Advocate General Jacobs observed, the altering of a trademark creates more difficult problems than a simple act of repackaging.[44]

Furthermore, in *Bristol-Myers Squibb* the Court was interpreting Article 7(2) of the Trade Mark Directive,[45] not Articles 28 (ex 30) and 30 (ex 36) EC. This difference was not of significance, however. The Court observed that the Directive had to be applied in accordance with the EC Treaty rules on the free movement of goods, and interpreted it in the light of its previous case law.[46]

---

[39] For a recent example see Case C-316/95 *Generics BV v Smith, Kline & French Laboratories Ltd* [1997] ECR I-3929 para 17 and para 25 of the Opinion of AG Jacobs.

[40] Case 3/78 *Centrafarm BV v American Home Products Corporation* [1978] ECR 1823.

[41] Joined Cases C-427/93, 429/93 and 436/93 *Bristol-Myers Squibb and others v Paranova A/S* [1996] ECR I-3457.

[42] ibid, para 57.

[43] The facts were similar to Case 102/77 *Hoffmann-La Roche & Co AG v Centrafarm Vertriebsgesellschaft Pharmazeutischer Erzeugnisse mbH* [1978] ECR 1139, which was decided a few months prior to *Centrafarm v American Home Products*. In that case it remained unclear whether the test used by the Court was objective or subjective.

[44] See n 41 above, para 84 of his Opinion.

[45] First Council Directive 89/104/EEC of 21 December 1988 to approximate the laws of the Member States relating to trade marks [1989] OJ L40/1.

[46] See n 41 above, paras 27, 28, 31, 34, 36 and 41. See also the Opinion of AG Jacobs, paras 90, 91 and 98.

Obversely, in *Loendersloot v Ballantine*[47] the Court used its case law on the Trade Mark Directive to interpret Article 30 on the question of repackaging and the artificial partitioning of the market, arriving at the same conclusion as in *Bristol-Myers Squibb*.[48]

The subjective intention test of *Centrafarm v American Home Products* was finally put to sleep in *Pharmacia & Upjohn v Paranova*.[49] Upjohn Group had marketed an antibiotic, clindamycin, under different trademarks in different Member States. Paranova had purchased Upjohn's clindamycin capsules and injection phials in France and Greece and sold them in Denmark after replacing the trademarks with the one used there, Dalacin. Upjohn challenged Paranova's actions. It referred to *Centrafarm v American Home Products* and argued that it had the right to oppose the replacement of the trademarks unless it could be shown that it had used the different trademarks with the subjective intention to partition the markets.[50]

The Court did not accept Upjohn's argument. It held that the condition of artificial partitioning had to be applied similarly in repackaging and replacing cases, as the effect on intra-Community trade was the same and the parallel importer was in both cases using a trademark not belonging to him. According to the Court, the decisive question is whether the replacement of the trademark is objectively necessary in order for the product to be marketed by the parallel importer, and the intention of the trademark owner is immaterial.[51]

These recent judgments are to be welcomed. Doctrinal clarity requires that the subjective behaviour of an undertaking is not given weight.[52] It is now certain that even in the field of intellectual property rights it is Member State measures, not private actions, that are caught by Article 28 (ex 30) EC.

iii) The concept of Member State

The conclusion that Article 28 (ex 30) EC applies only to state measures does not end the inquiry, however. It has to be determined what meaning is given to the concept of 'Member State' in this context. In general, the concept does not have a fixed content in Community law. It must be interpreted in the light

---

[47] Case C-349/95 *Frits Loendersloot, trading as F. Loendersloot Internationale Expeditie v George Ballantine & Son Ltd and others* [1997] ECR I-6227, especially para 36.

[48] See especially ibid para 36 and paras 22–23 and 42 of the Opinion of Advocate General Jacobs.

[49] Case C-379/97 *Pharmacia & Upjohn SA v Paranova A/S*, judgment of 12 October 1999.

[50] The use of different marks was explained by an agreement between Upjohn and American Home Products Corporation in 1968.

[51] See n 49 above, paras 37–46.

[52] See Marenco and Banks (n 24 above) 253–254. In addition a test based on subjective factors is 'illogical and impracticable'. See the Opinion of AG Jacobs in *Bristol-Myers Squibb* (n 41 above) para 83. The Court admitted that intention is difficult to prove in *Pharmacia & Upjohn v Paranova* (n 49 above) para 41.

of the purpose and the context of the provision in which it appears. The concept is given the meaning which best enables the provision to achieve its aim.

Thus, in Article 230 (ex 173) EC the words 'Member State' refer only to the governmental authorities of the country. Regional governments or autonomous municipalities are not covered. This follows from the general system of the EC Treaty. The institutional balance has to be preserved. Therefore, the number of Member States in this context cannot be higher than the number of parties to the Treaty.[53] Similarly, Article 226 (ex 169) EC actions are rightly taken against the central government even though the fault for a breach of Community obligations may lie with, for example, regional authorities.[54]

In contrast, the duty to implement directives flows from Article 249 (ex 189) EC (and Article 10 (ex 5)) EC, which stipulates that '[a] directive shall be binding . . . upon each Member State to which it is addressed'. In this context the concept of 'Member State' has been interpreted broadly for the purpose of preventing the state from taking advantage of its own failure.[55] Thus, the concept encompasses, unlike in Article 230 (ex 173) EC, local and regional authorities.[56]

In other fields the concept of 'Member State' has been given yet other meanings.[57] Thus, Advocate General Van Gerven has stated that 'an interpretation is sought of each measure which is most in keeping with the purpose of the concept of public authority which is used'[58] and that '[there is] a desire to ensure that the concept of "The State" is given full and proper effect, that is to say a meaning which achieves the goals of the measure in question'.[59]

The Court has interpreted the concept of Member State widely when determining which measures fall under Article 28 (ex 30) EC. It is clear, first of all, that the provision applies both to central and regional or local authorities,[60] and not only to the executive, but also to the legislature or the judiciary.[61]

Secondly, the involvement of private parties does not make Article 28 (ex 30) EC inapplicable if the state can be seen as the source of the measure. This is the case if the state uses a controlled private body as a medium through which the measure is brought into effect.[62]

---

[53] Case C-95/97 *Region of Wallonia v Commission* [1997] ECR I-1789 para 6.

[54] See eg Case C-211/91 *Commission v Belgium* [1992] ECR I-6757.

[55] Case 152/84 *Marshall v Southampton and South-West Hampshire Area Health Authority (Teaching)* [1986] ECR 723 para 49. See also the Opinion of AG Van Gerven in Case C-188/89 *A. Foster and others v British Gas plc* [1990] ECR I-3313 paras 10 and 21.

[56] Case 103/88 *Fratelli Constanzo SpA v Commune di Milano* [1989] ECR 1839.

[57] See the analysis of AG Van Gerven in Case C-188/89 *A. Foster and others v British Gas plc* [1990] ECR I-3313 paras 11–16.

[58] ibid, para 11.   [59] ibid, para 16.

[60] See Case 45/87 *Commission v Ireland* [1988] ECR 4929, and Joined Cases C-1/90 and C-176/90 *Aragonesa de Publicidad Exterior SA and Publivía SAE v Departamento de Sanidad y Seguridad Social de la Generalitat de Cataluña* [1991] ECR I-4151. See also Oliver (n 3 above) 41–42, and S. Weatherill and P. Beaumont, *EU Law* (3rd edn London 1999) 523–524.

[61] See Oliver (n 3 above) 42–43, and Weatherill and Beaumont (n 60 above) 523–524.

[62] It should additionally be noted that Art 86 (ex 90) EC may serve to bring public undertakings and undertakings to which Member States have granted special or exclusive rights under the

Commission v Ireland (Buy Irish)[63] concerned a programme promoting Irish products, which was mainly run by the Irish Goods Council, a company limited by guarantee. The Irish government argued that the activities of the Irish Goods Council could not be attributed to the state. The Court disagreed. Since the government appointed the members of the Council's Management Committee, granted it subsidies covering the majority of its expenses and defined the aims and the outline of the campaign, the fact that the campaign was conducted by a private company did not remove it from the scope of Article 28.[64]

Similarly, in *Apple and Pear Development Council*[65] the functions of the Council, which was established by a ministerial order, were defined by the state and its members were appointed by the relevant minister. However, the Council's activities were financed by a charge, which the Order enabled it to impose on growers, not by direct subsidies from the government as in *Commission v Ireland* (Buy Irish). This final fact was not considered significant, and the Court stated that:

a body . . . which is set up by the government of a Member State and is financed by a charge imposed on growers, cannot under Community law enjoy the same freedom as regards the methods of advertising used as that enjoyed by producers themselves or producer's associations of a voluntary character.[66]

Thus, if a policy is executed through a body established by a state and financed by it, either directly or indirectly, by means of coercive power, it can be caught by Article 28 (ex 30) EC. By contrast, actions of individuals or voluntary associations do not fall within the scope of the provision.

Article 28 also catches measures adopted by bodies which have been granted special powers by a state. The *Royal Pharmaceutical Society*[67] case concerned a code of ethics adopted by the Society. The first question examined by the Court was whether the code could constitute a 'measure' within the meaning of Article 28.

The Court noted that the Society was incorporated by a Royal Charter and was recognised by UK legislation. The Society maintained a register in which every pharmacist had to enrol, and adopted rules of ethics applicable to them. It also, most importantly, had a disciplinary committee established by law which could impose sanctions, including removal from the register, for professional misconduct. An appeal could be made to the High Court against a decision of the Committee. The Court, following Advocate General Darmon,

rules on the free movement of goods (and services). On these issues generally see F. Blum and A. Logue, *State Monopolies under EC Law* (Chichester 1998) 99–152.

[63] Case 249/81 *Commission v Ireland* [1982] ECR 4005.   [64] ibid, para 15.

[65] Case 222/82 *Apple and Pear Development Council v K.J. Lewis Ltd and others* [1983] ECR 4083.

[66] ibid, para 17.

[67] Joined Cases 266 and 267/87 *R v Royal Pharmaceutical Society of Great Britain, ex parte Association of Pharmaceutical Importers and others* [1989] ECR 1295.

stated that 'measures adopted by a professional body on which national legislation has conferred powers of that nature may . . . constitute "measures" within the meaning of Article 28 (formerly 30)'.[68]

The Court reached the same conclusion in *Hünermund*[69] where the relevant measure was again adopted by a pharmacists' professional association. The fact that in this case the association could not revoke a pharmacist's authorisation to practise did not change the result, as other disciplinary measures such as fines could be imposed.[70]

In these situations power was delegated by the state proper to a semi-private body. Instead of regulating a profession itself, the state gave the necessary powers to a professional organisation.[71]

It is submitted that the concept of Member State encompasses all bodies through which the state is able to achieve a protectionist effect. The objectives of Article 28 (ex 30) EC, namely the achievement of the internal market as stipulated in Articles 3(1)(c) and 14 (ex 7a) EC through the abolition of quantitative restrictions and measures having an equivalent effect, and the uniform scope of Community law, regardless of the different regulatory structures in different Member States, require a wide, flexible concept of Member State, not a formalistic one.

It is interesting to note that the Court in *Dubois*[72] seems to have adopted a widely similar approach[73] for Articles 23 (ex 9) and 25 (ex 12) EC, which prohibit customs duties and charges having equivalent effect. The case concerned a contractual charge between Garonor, a private company operating an international road station, and its customers, Dubois and Général Cargo. The charge was to compensate for various services provided by Garonor, including the costs of customs and veterinary services.

The Court found that Articles 23 and 25 applied to the charge even though it was not imposed by the state but arose from an agreement concluded by a private undertaking with its customers.[74] A Member State breaches Community law if it charges economic agents the cost of inspections and administrative formalities carried out by customs offices.[75] The nature of the measure requiring the economic agents to bear these costs is

---

[68] Joined Cases 266 and 267/87 *R v Royal Pharmaceutical Society of Great Britain, ex parte Association of Pharmaceutical Importers and others* [1989] ECR 1295, para 15.

[69] Case C-292/92 *Hünermund v Landesapothekerkammer Baden-Württemberg* [1993] ECR I-6787.

[70] ibid, paras 14–16.

[71] It may be noted that the existence of special powers has assumed some significance in the jurisprudence concerning the extent of direct effect of directives. See Case C-188/89 *A. Foster and others v British Gas plc* [1990] ECR I-3313 paras 18 and 20, and the decision of the English Court of Appeal in *Doughty v Rolls Royce* [1992] 1 CMLR 1045.

[72] Case C-16/94 *Édouard Dubois et Fils SA and Général Cargo Services SA v Garonor Exploitation SA* [1995] ECR I-2421.

[73] See G. Tesauro, 'The Community Internal Market in the Light of the Recent Case-law of the Court of Justice' (1995) 15 YEL 1, 13.

[74] See n 72 above, para 21.   [75] ibid, para 19.

immaterial. Even if the charge is imposed as a result of a private contract, it stems from the failure of the Member State to fulfil its financial obligation.[76]

Once again the decisive factor was that the measure (charges) originated from the Member State[77] even though it was implemented through a private undertaking. Payments for truly private services do not fall under Articles 23 and 25[78] but the concept of Member State is interpreted widely and flexibly.

b) The free movement of services

The wording of the EC Treaty would seem to indicate that Article 49 (ex 59) EC does not cover 'restrictions' created by private parties. Although the Article itself, like Article 28 (ex 30) EC, is silent about the author of prohibited measures, other provisions in the same Chapter on Services show that it is Member States that are targeted by the rules on the free movement of services. Article 50(3) (ex 60(3)) EC states that 'the person providing the service may . . . temporarily pursue his activity in the State where the service is provided, under the same conditions as are imposed by the State on its own nationals'. Prior to the Treaty of Amsterdam, Article 62 EC (repealed) contained a standstill clause prohibiting Member States from introducing any new restrictions. In Article 53 (ex 64) EC Member States declare their readiness to undertake further liberalisation of services. Article 54 (ex 65) EC requires Member States to apply restrictions that have not yet been abolished without distinction on grounds of nationality or residence of the service provider. Finally, Article 46 (ex 56) EC, applicable by virtue of Article 55 (ex 66) EC, allows for the application of 'provisions laid down by law, regulation or administrative action providing for special treatment for foreign nationals on grounds of public policy, public security or public health'. Both the reference to law, regulation and administrative action, and the public nature of the exceptions indicate that the provision is targeted at Member States.[79]

The text does not necessarily rule out the possibility that Article 49 (ex 59) EC could catch restrictions created by private bodies, however. Article 49 itself does not refer to Member States as authors of the prohibited restrictions.

Moreover, as organs of Member States, national courts might be called upon to ensure that private measures breaching the EC Treaty are not upheld.

---

[76] ibid, para 20.

[77] In fact, as pointed out by AG La Pergola, the charges were created by the omission of France to bear the cost.

[78] See the Opinion of AG La Pergola (n 72 above) para 5.

[79] Council Directive 64/221/EEC of 25 February 1964 on the co-ordination of special measures concerning the movement and residence of foreign nationals which are justified on grounds of public policy, public security or public health, [1964] OJ Spec Ed 850/64, 117, specifies the scope of the exceptions. According to Art 2 of Directive 64/221, the Directive relates only to measures taken by Member States.

In the case of *Defrenne v Sabena*[80] the European Court of Justice decided on the scope of Article 141 (ex 119) EC on equal pay between men and women. At that time the provision stipulated that '[e]ach Member State shall during the first stage ensure and subsequently maintain the application of the principle that men and women should receive equal pay for equal work'. The Court found that the Article could be applied directly in national courts and, despite the reference to Member States, covered equally the actions of public authorities, collective agreements and contracts between individuals, because of its mandatory nature.[81]

The General Programme on Services,[82] adopted unanimously by the Council on the Commission's proposal in 1961, defines as restrictions to be eliminated:

Any measure which, pursuant to any provision laid down by law, regulation or administrative action in a Member State, or as a result of application of such provision, or of administrative practices, prohibits or hinders. . . .[83]

This clearly indicates that the Council was only concerned with Member State measures, not with the actions of private parties. However, as noted by Advocate General Warner in *Walrave and Koch*,[84] the General Programme was not complete. It did not even deal with all restrictions imposed by Member States.

The Commission was originally of the view that Article 49 (ex 59) EC did not apply to private measures. In its submission in the seminal case *Walrave and Koch*[85] the Commission argued that the freedom to provide services, as well as the freedom of establishment, demanded only the abolition of 'discrimination arising from provision laid down by law, regulation or administrative action of *the Member States* or those "administrative procedures and practices, whether resulting from *national legislation* or from *agreements previously concluded between Member States*"'.[86]

The Court expressed its view in the same case. In issue were the rules of the Union Cycliste Internationale (International Cycling Association) requiring that a pacemaker riding a motorcycle had to be of the same nationality as the stayer cycling in the lee of the motorcycle. The Union Cycliste Internationale was an association of national bodies concerned with cycling as a sport. It was constituted of the International Amateur Cycling Federation comprising over 100 national federations and the International Professional Cycling Federation comprising 18 national federations. The private nature of the Union Cycliste Internationale was not called into question during the proceedings.

---

[80] Case 43/75 *Gabrielle Defrenne v Société Anonyme Belge de Navigation Aérienne Sabena* [1976] ECR 455.

[81] ibid, paras 37, 39 and 40.　　　　　　　　　　[82] [1974] OJ Spec Ed 2nd Series IX 3.

[83] ibid, Title III A.　　　　[84] Case 36/74 *Walrave and Koch v UCI* [1974] ECR 1405, at 1425.

[85] ibid.　　　　　　　　　　　　　　　[86] ibid, 1410 (emphasis added).

Advocate General Warner was of the opinion that Article 49 (ex 59) EC was not only binding on Member States but was also 'apt to relate to restrictions imposed by anyone'. This was due to the general terms and the residual nature of Article 49. As his view was that Article 39 (ex 48) EC, a more specific provision, binds everyone, he thought it would be odd if the residuary provision applied to a narrower category of persons.[87]

The Court followed its Advocate General. It decided that the prohibition of discrimination on the basis of nationality contained in Articles 12 (ex 6), 39 (ex 48) and 49 (ex 59) did not only apply to the actions of public authorities but extended 'likewise to rules of any other nature aimed at collectively regulating gainful employment and services'.[88] The Court stated that otherwise organisations not under public law could compromise the achievement of the freedom of movement for persons and services, and there could be unequal application of the Treaty freedoms. Moreover, the prohibition contained in Article 49 was expressed in general terms. Furthermore, it had been established that Article 39 (ex 48) EC extended to rules which did not emanate from public authorities and Article 49 had to be interpreted similarly.[89]

It is interesting to note that the Court did not go quite so far as to make Article 49 binding on all private measures, although it did not rule this out either. In *Walrave and Koch* only rules aimed at *collectively regulating services* were caught. The scope of Article 49 remained open.

The Court confirmed its approach in the case of *Donà v Mantero*,[90] which concerned the rules of the Italian Football Federation. The Court, following Advocate General Trabucchi, cited *Walrave and Koch* and stated that 'rules or a national practice, even adopted by a sporting organisation' could infringe Article 49, as well as Articles 12 (ex 6) and 39 (ex 48) EC, if they limited the participation in professional or semi-professional football to nationals of the state in question.[91] Again, the private nature of the rules was not questioned and again the Court did not extend the prohibition to all private measures but did not exclude it either.

The judgment of the Court in *Van Ameyde*[92] started from the assumption that private parties can infringe Article 49. The defendant, UCI, was a national insurance bureau, recognised in domestic legislation. All or most national insurers against civil liability in respect of motor vehicles were affiliated with it. Under the so-called green card system based on a network of bilateral agreements between national bureaux and on the domestic law, it was responsible for compensation for accidents caused by motor vehicles

---

[87] ibid, 1424–1425. It is interesting to contrast this with the Opinion of AG Warner in Cases 55 and 57/80 *Musik-Vertrieb Membran v Gema* [1981] ECR 147 where he stated that 'when Art 30 [now 28] refers to a "measure," it means a measure taken by a Member State; it does not mean a measure taken by a private person.'

[88] See n 84 above, para 17.   [89] ibid, paras 18–24.

[90] Case 13/76 *Gaetano Donà v Mario Mantero* [1976] ECR 1333.   [91] ibid, paras 17 and 19.

[92] Case 90/76 *Srl Ufficio Henry van Ameyde v Srl Ufficio Centrale Italiano di Assistenza Assicurativa Automobilisti in Circulazione Internazionale (UCI)* [1977] ECR 1091.

insured abroad. The foreign insurer, against which UCI had a right of regress, had to correspond in this situation with a local insurance company nominated by UCI. The nominated company was then the only entity capable of investigating the case. Van Ameyde, a loss adjuster not capable of being nominated, was thus deprived of the possibility to investigate and settle accidents on behalf of foreign insurance companies.

The Court decided, following Advocate General Reischl, that there was no restriction within the meaning of Article 49 as there was no discrimination. However, the Court was of the opinion that in principle the rules or conduct were capable of infringing Article 49. Discrimination resulting from rules of whatever kind seeking collectively to regulate the business could have been condemned. In the Court's view it was irrelevant whether the restriction 'originated in measures of public authority or, on the contrary, in measures attributable to national insurers' bureaux'.[93]

Once again, therefore, the Court confirmed that some private parties could infringe Article 49 (ex 59) EC but again it stressed the collective nature of the rules.

Haug-Adrion[94] was another case involving motor vehicle insurance. Mr Haug-Adrion, a German national, had purchased a car from Germany and registered it under customs plates as he was planning to export it to Belgium where he resided. The third-party liability insurance required was issued by the Frankfurter Versicherungs-AG. The insurance company did not grant him a no-claims bonus despite the fact that Mr Haug-Adrion had driven several years without causing an accident. The tariff conditions of the company did not take into account the insured person's driving records when insuring vehicles with customs plates. The conditions had been officially approved by the relevant public authorities. Mr Haug-Adrion claimed, inter alia, that there was a restriction on the freedom to provide services.

The Court stated that Article 49 was intended to eliminate *all measures* which treat nationals of other Member States more severely or place them at a disadvantage when compared with the Member State's own nationals.[95] It then examined the tariff conditions,[96] and found, mostly following Advocate General Lenz, that there was no infringement of Community law in so far as the refusal of a no-claims bonus was based on objective actuarial criteria and applied without discrimination.[97] Thus, the Court implicitly accepted that the tariff conditions could, in principle, have fallen foul of Article 49. Yet the conditions were adopted by a single firm, not an association, and they were simply permitted, not mandated, by the public authorities.[98]

---

[93] Case 90/76 *Srl Ufficio Henry van Ameyde v Srl Ufficio Centrale Italiano di Assistenza Assicurativa Automobilisti in Circulazione Internazionale (UCI)* [1977] ECR 1091, paras 28–30.

[94] Case 251/83 *Eberhard Haug-Adrion v Frankfurter Versicherungs-AG* [1984] ECR 4277.

[95] ibid, para 14 (emphasis added).   [96] ibid, paras 15–17.   [97] ibid, para 23.

[98] As pointed out by AG Lenz, who expressed doubts as to whether the approval by public authorities could be regarded as equivalent to a governmental measure and thus bring the situation within the scope of Art 29 (ex 34) EC. See ibid, para 6 of his Opinion.

It is submitted, however, that this judgment does not represent a shift in doctrine.[99] First of all, there was a certain element of collectivity, as observed by the Commission.[100] In issue was not a single decision by an independently acting firm but a tariff condition based on governmental regulation and authorisation and, thus, also presumably commonly used by other insurance companies.

Secondly, and in my view more importantly, this was a tersely reasoned judgment by a three-judge Chamber. Attention was not focused on the private character of the rules as they clearly did not infringe Article 49 anyway. If the Court really had wanted to change its doctrine, surely it would have done so in the composition of the Full Court and would have expressed itself more clearly.

Recently, in *Deliège* the Court was once again confronted with rules of sporting organisations. In accordance with settled case law it held that Article 49 (ex 59) EC applies to rules of any nature aimed at regulating the provision of services in a collective manner.[101]

Thus, the Court has not so far applied Article 49 to all private measures but has not ruled it out either. The judgments have gone further than in the field of the free movement of goods. Truly private measures have been caught. Crucially, the Court has not even considered it necessary to examine the potential affiliation between the author of the restriction and the state, as it always does in cases concerning the free movement of goods. It has resorted to a freedom-specific approach.

It is true that the Court has used the words 'rules' and 'regulating', which have a quasi-statal ring. It is submitted that this is a red herring and should not be given weight, however. The Court will surely condemn a private collective action restricting the free movement of services whether it takes the form of rules regulating services or not, for example actual conduct or practice.[102] The whole system of the free movement law is based on the effect a measure has, not on its form.

Despite the doctrinal disparity, the practical effect of the difference between the free movement of goods and services has not been great. The wide interpretation given to the concept of 'Member State' in the context of goods means that the involvement of private parties does not rule out the possibility of Article 28 (ex 30) EC applying.

As regards the free movement of workers, the interpretation is even wider. Article 39 (ex 48) EC applies to all private measures, at least as long as they discriminate.

---

[99] Doubts were also expressed by W.-H. Roth, 'Drittwirkung der Grundfreiheiten?' in O. Due, M. Lutter and J. Schwarze (eds), *Festschrift für Ulrich Everling* (Baden-Baden 1995) 1239.

[100] See n 94 above, 4283–4284.

[101] Joined Cases C-51/96 and C-191/97 *Christelle Deliège v Asbl Ligue Francophone de judo et disciplines associées and others*, judgment of 11 April 2000, para 47.

[102] See also Baquero Cruz (n 20 above) 618.

Most parts of Article 39 and the Chapter on Workers are expressed in general terms capable of applying to private measures restricting the free movement of workers. Also, the Community legislator seems to have opted for such a solution in Article 7(4) of Regulation 1612/68/EEC,[103] which provides that '[a]ny clause of a collective or *individual* agreement or of any other collective regulation concerning eligibility for employment, employment, remuneration and other conditions of work or dismissal shall be null and void in so far as it lays down or authorises discriminatory conditions'.[104] The Regulation was adopted to implement Article 39 (ex 48) EC, and the Court has held that the provision 'merely clarifies and gives effect to rights already conferred by Article 48 [currently 39] of the Treaty'.[105] Moreover, academic literature seems generally, though by no means universally, to support the view that Article 39 (ex 48) EC applies to all private measures.[106]

The Court has now ruled explicitly in *Angonese*[107] that Article 39 (ex 48) EC applies to an individual as well as to a collective[108] private restriction on the free movement of workers, at least if the measure is discriminatory. In the case, a private banking undertaking required that prospective employees provide a certificate of bilingualism issued by the public authorities of the province of Bolzano. The Court held that Article 39 'precludes an employer from requiring persons applying to take part in a recruitment competition to provide evidence of their linguistic knowledge exclusively by means of one particular diploma issued only in one particular province of a Member State'.[109]

c) Criticism

The Court's approach to the free movement of goods and services has been doctrinally fundamentally different, for no obvious reason. It seems that no effort has been made to co-ordinate the jurisprudence. It is submitted that the Court should adopt a similar interpretation in both fields. It is further submitted that the Court's current approach to Article 49 (ex 59) EC is too wide,

---

[103] Council Regulation 1612/68/EEC of 15 October 1968 on freedom of movement for workers within the Community as amended by Regulation 312/76 [1968] OJ Spec Ed 1968 L257/2, 475.

[104] Emphasis added.

[105] Case C-15/96 *Kalliope Schöning-Kougebetopoulou v Frei und Hansestadt Hamburg* [1998] ECR I-47 para 12.

[106] See J.M. Fernández Martín, 'Re-defining Obstacles to the Free Movement of Workers' (1996) 21 ELRev 313, 323, and S. Weatherill, 'Discrimination on Grounds of Nationality in Sport' (1989) 9 YEL 55 at 65 and 90, and the footnotes contained therein.

[107] Case C-281/98 *Roman Angonese v Cassa di Risparmio di Bolzano SpA*, judgment of 6 June 2000.

[108] For a recent discussion on the status of collective agreements, see the Opinion of AG Fennelly in Case C-234/97 *Maria Teresa Fernández de Bobadilla v Museo Nacional del Prado and others*, judgment of 8 July 1999, paras 23–24.

[109] See n 107 above, para 46.

as it creates a conflict with competition rules, and that the approach to Article 28 (ex 30) EC is too narrow, as it does not cover obstacles created by private non-undertakings.

The Court should view the issue of private parties from the perspective of the system of the EC Treaty as a whole. Neither Article 28 (ex 30) EC nor Article 49 (ex 59) EC should apply if the measures under investigation are created by one or more private undertakings. Measures adopted by private undertakings or associations of undertakings fall under the competition rules, Articles 81 (ex 85) and 82 (ex 86) EC, which should be regarded as *lex specialis*.[110]

Agreements between undertakings, decisions by associations of undertakings and concerted practices as well as actions by one or more undertakings in a dominant position are caught by Articles 81 (ex 85) and 82 (ex 86) EC if they affect trade and constitute prevention, restriction or distortion of competition, or an abuse. According to the Commission practice and the Court's case law, import and export restrictions do constitute a restriction of competition[111] or an abuse of a dominant position.[112]

Vertical agreements can be used by undertakings to partition the internal market. A supplier can, for example, prohibit a distributor from exporting his products. Both the Commission[113] and the Court[114] have found that these agreements restrict competition.[115] An agreement restricting exports can even be said to have as its object the restriction of competition, in which case it is not necessary to analyse its actual restrictive effects.[116]

Horizontal agreements can restrict trade between Member States.[117] They can be used to share markets, which is mentioned as an example of an anti-competitive practice in Article 81(1)(c) (ex 85(1)(c)) EC, or a national cartel can act to keep foreign competitors out of the domestic market. Again, these

---

[110] See however the Opinion of AG Cosmas in Joined Cases C-51/96 and C-191/97 *Christelle Deliège v Asbl Ligue Francophone de judo et disciplines associées and others*, judgment of 11 April 2000. According to the Advocate General the same restriction could infringe both the provisions on the free movement of services and competition law. The Court found the national court's question concerning competition rules inadmissible as the reference did not contain sufficient information, and decided the case on the grounds of Art 49 (ex 59) EC.

[111] See generally D.G. Goyder, *EC Competition Law* (3rd edn Oxford 1998) 121–123, Korah (n 29 above) 229–233, and R. Whish, *Competition Law* (3rd edn London 1993) 203–205.

[112] See generally Goyder (n 111 above) 336–337, Korah (n 29 above) 137–138, and Whish (n 111 above) 276–277.

[113] See eg Commission Decision in *Distillers* [1978] OJ L50/16.

[114] See eg the classic case Joined Cases 56/64 and 58/64 *Etablissements Consten SA and Grundig-Verkaufs-GmbH v Commission* [1966] ECR 299.

[115] See generally Whish (n 111 above) 560–563.

[116] See n 114 above, Case 19/77 *Miller International Schallplatten GmbH v Commission* [1978] ECR 131, Case T-66/92 *Herlitz AG v Commission* [1994] ECR II-531, Case T-77/92 *Parker Pen v Commission* [1994] ECR II-549, and Case T-175/95 *BASF Coatings AG v Commission* [1999] ECR II-1581. See also Case T-62/98 *Volkswagen AG v Commission*, judgment of 6 July 2000, para 336.

[117] See generally Whish (n 111 above) 402–403.

agreements are clearly caught by Article 81 (ex 85) EC[118] and often the main problem is not establishing restriction of competition but the detection and the proving of the agreement or the concerted practice.

A firm can abuse its dominant position by restricting imports or exports.[119] The Commission and the Court have condemned such actions in many cases[120] and imposed significant fines on the undertakings in question.[121]

Actions by a single non-dominant firm or agreements between firms having only an insignificant effect on the market do not fall under competition rules.[122] This does not mean that the free movement rules ought to apply. These undertakings do not constitute a threat to market integration as they lack the power to create a protectionist effect.[123] If a supermarket, for example, decides to offer inferior or expensive domestic products instead of superior or cheap foreign ones, its customers will simply shop elsewhere.

Application of the free movement rules to acts of private undertakings with no market power would in fact amount to inefficient and unnecessary public intervention, contrary to the principle of free enterprise.[124] The Court, with imperfect information, could end up striking down private measures which in fact are based on sound business judgement. If the actions were based on other considerations, market forces would punish the undertaking anyway. It would lose market share to competitors offering better value foreign products.

Additionally, it is clear that the use of free movement provisions would be unfeasible. It would be impossible, not to mention ridiculous, to demand a justification for every decision not to buy imported goods or services.[125]

Moreover, the application of Article 28 (ex 30) or 49 (ex 59) EC would be unnecessary as private undertakings with no market power do not normally have any motivation to engage in protectionist activities, and if they do, they do not stay in business for long. For a politician protectionist policies may

[118] See eg Case 41/69 *ACF Chemiefarma NV v Commission* [1970] ECR 661 upholding a Commission Decision, and Case 246/86 *S. C. Belasco and others v Commission* [1989] ECR 2117. Market-sharing has been classified as an 'obvious restriction of competition', ie having as its object the restriction of competition, in Joined Cases T-374/94, T-375/94, T-384/94 and T-388/94 *European Night Services Ltd (ENS) and others v Commission* [1998] ECR II-3141 para 136.

[119] See generally Whish (n 111 above) 276–277.

[120] See eg Joined Cases 40–48, 50, 54–56, 111 and 113–114/73 *Cooperatiëve Vereniging 'Suiker Unie' UA v Commission* [1975] ECR 1663, and the green banana clause in Case 27/76 *United Brands Co. and United Brands Continental BV v Commission* [1978] ECR 207.

[121] See eg Case T-30/89 *Hilti AG v Commission* [1991] ECR II-1439, upheld on appeal in Case C-53/92P *Hilti AG v Commission* [1994] ECR I-667.

[122] Case 5/69 *Völk v Vervaecke* [1969] ECR 295 para 7. See also Commission Notice on Agreements of Minor Importance which do not Fall within the Meaning of Art 85(1) [now 81(1)] of the Treaty Establishing the European Community [1997] OJ C372/04.

[123] See G. Marenco, 'Competition between National Economies and Competition between Businesses—a Response to Judge Pescatore' (1987) 10 Fordham Int LJ 424 at 425.

[124] ibid and Case T-41/96 *Bayer AG v Commission*, judgment of the CFI, 26 October 2000, in particular paras 176 and 180.

[125] See L. Gormley, *Prohibiting Restrictions on Trade within the EEC* (Amsterdam 1985) 261, and Oliver (n 3 above) 59.

bring votes and campaign contributions. For an undertaking such policies bring only diminished profits and decreasing market share.[126]

The system of the Treaty indicates that Articles 81 (ex 85) and 82 (ex 86) EC should be given the status of *lex specialis* when it comes to actions of undertakings. Articles 28 (ex 30) and 49 (ex 59) EC are primarily directed against Member State measures, while the competition rules clearly target the behaviour of private firms. The latter rules were in fact adopted in order to prevent undertakings from recreating barriers after Member State restrictions have been abolished.[127] They would be deprived of much of their utility if the free movement rules applied.[128]

The fact that Articles 81 (ex 85) and 82 (ex 86) EC, in conjunction with Article 10 (ex 5) EC, have been applied to state measures,[129] does not mean that Articles 28 (ex 30) and 49 (ex 59) EC should apply equally to actions of private undertakings. There is nothing in the EC Treaty that imposes on private parties an obligation corresponding to the duty of sincere co-operation contained in Article 10.[130]

The system of the Treaty would also be endangered if actions exempted individually or in a group exemption by the Commission under Article 81(3) (ex 85(3)) EC could be challenged under the free movement rules. The power devolved to the Commission would be made illusory and the compromises worked out by it rendered meaningless, as they could be opened by litigants using free movement rules to circumvent obstacles to action under Article 81.[131]

Furthermore, the grounds of exemption listed in Article 81(3) (ex 85(3)) EC are clearly designed with private agreements, decisions and concerted practices in mind. Such actions can be exempted if they improve the production or distribution of goods or promote technical or economic progress, allow consumers a fair share of the benefit, the restrictions imposed are indispensable, and competition is not eliminated.

In contrast, exceptions given in Articles 30 (ex 36) EC and, even more explicitly, in Article 46 (ex 56) EC are just as clearly meant to justify Member State measures.[132] The latter Article spells out that it exempts 'provisions laid

---

[126] See Marenco (n 123 above) 425.

[127] Roth (n 99 above) 1242, and D. O'Keeffe and A. Bavasso, 'Four Freedoms, One Market and National Competence: In Search of a Dividing Line' in D. O'Keeffe and A. Bavasso (eds), *Liber Amicorum in Honour of Lord Slynn of Hadley. Vol I. Judicial Review in European Union Law* (The Hague 2000) 543.

[128] See M. Quinn and N. MacGowan, 'Could Article 30 Impose Obligations on Individuals?' (1987) 12 ELRev 163 at 168.

[129] See in general K. Bacon, 'State Regulation of the Market and EC Competition Rules: Articles 85 and 86 Compared' (1997) 18 ECLR 283, 283–284.

[130] See Quinn and MacGowan (n 128 above) 170–171.

[131] See Quinn and MacGowan (n 128 above) 168–169, and S. Weatherill, 'Discrimination on Grounds of Nationality in Sport' (1989) 9 YEL 55, 87.

[132] See Quinn and MacGowan (n 128 above) 175–176, and Roth (n 99 above) 1241–1242. See also G. Orlandini, 'The Free Movement of Goods as a Possible "Community" Limitation on Industrial Conflict' (2000) 6 ELJ 341 at 347–348. For a similar interpretation of Art 39(3) (ex 48(3)) EC see Weatherill (n 131 above) 66–67.

down by law, regulation or administrative action'. Private measures are not mentioned. Public policy and public security, which are found in both provisions, as well as public morality and public health are *public* concerns. This is confirmed by Directive 64/221/EEC,[133] which co-ordinates special measures protecting these interests, and applies by virtue of Article 2 of the Directive only to measures taken by Member States. A truly private party is seldom interested in or suitable for protecting these concerns.

In *Bosman*[134] the Court did rule that individuals could, in principle, justify restrictions to the free movement of workers on grounds of public policy, public security or public health.[135] However, as pointed out by Fernández Martín, this aspect of the judgment is problematic, and can sensibly only be applied when private organisations are entitled 'to regulate conditions of employment in a collective manner . . . and perform therefore a semi-public function'.[136]

Other heads of justification found in Article 30 (ex 36) EC, the protection of health and life of humans, animals or plants, the protection of national artistic, historic or archaeological treasures, and the protection of industrial or commercial property, could in principle be used by private parties, but more naturally by public authorities. Even the last interests, industrial or commercial property, are protected by Member States through their laws, to which private parties then have recourse.

Public interest exceptions,[137] developed in the Court's case law,[138] are also public in their nature.[139] Even though a private party could conceivably justify its actions on the ground of, for example, consumer protection, a state can have recourse to all of the exceptions, and some of them, such as maintaining the cohesion of the national tax system,[140] are clearly available only to public bodies.

It should also be noted that the Commission has been given great powers of enforcement against private undertakings under the competition rules, while under the free movement rules its only enforcement powers are directed against Member States. Regulation 17[141] grants the Commission inter alia the power to require that undertakings stop infringing Article 81 (ex 85) or 82 (ex

---

[133] Council Directive 64/221/EEC of 25 February 1964 on the co-ordination of special measures concerning the movement and residence of foreign nationals which are justified on the grounds of public policy, public security or public health [1964] OJ Spec Ed 850/64, 117.

[134] Case C-415/93 *Union Royale Belge des Sociétés de Football Association ASBL and others v Jean-Marc Bosman* [1995] ECR I-4921 para 86.

[135] See also Case C-350/96 *Clean Car Autoservice GmbH v Landeshauptmann von Wien* [1998] ECR I-2521 para 24.

[136] Fernández Martín (n 106 above) 324.   [137] Or 'mandatory requirements'.

[138] Case 33/74 *Van Binsbergen v Bestuur van de Bedrijfsvereniging voor de Metaalnijverheid* [1974] ECR 1299, and Case 120/78 *Rewe Zentrale AG v Bundesmonopolverwaltung für Branntwein* [1979] ECR 649. See further Chapter 4 section 3 below.

[139] See Quinn and MacGowan (n 128 above) 176, and Roth (n 99 above) 1241–1242.

[140] Case C-204/90 *Hans-Martin Bachmann v Belgian State* [1992] ECR I-249.

[141] Regulation No 17, First Regulation implementing Articles 85 [currently 81] and 86 [currently 82] of the Treaty [1962] OJ Spec Ed 204/62, 87.

86) EC and to reinforce this decision by imposing periodic penalty payments. It even has the power to fine the undertakings concerned. In contrast, to protect the free movement of goods or services the Commission can take Article 226 (ex 169) actions, but only against the Member States, and Article 228 (ex 171) EC allows the Commission to request that the Court impose a lump sum or penalty payment if the *Member State* fails to comply with the judgment. Council Regulation 2679/98/EC of 7 December 1998 on the functioning of the internal market in relation to the free movement of goods among the Member States[142] does give the Commission some additional options in the field of the free movement of goods but again the powers can only be used against Member States. This discrepancy in the Commission's powers is another indication that the free movement rules are primarily directed against Member States, not against private parties.

All of this makes it abundantly clear that competition rules are much more suitable for dealing with private parties than the free movement provisions. Thus, this aspect of the system of the Treaty strongly supports the argument that Articles 28 (ex 30) and 49 (ex 59) EC should not apply if Articles 81 (ex 85) and 82 (ex 86) are available.[143]

In fact, it may be speculated that the relationship between the competition rules and the different free movement rules might have been at least one reason for the dissimilar scope given to Articles 28 and 49 by the Court. For a long time the competition rules were not used aggressively in the services sector. Very few cases reached the Court and as recently as 1981 in *Züchner*[144] the Counsel for the Bayerische Vereinsbank AG asserted, without much success, that banks were to a large degree exempt from the competition rules. Therefore, it was natural for the Court to use Article 28 solely against Member States as restrictions on the free movement of goods imposed by

---

[142] [1998] OJ L337/8.   [143] cf however Baquero Cruz (n 20 above) 619.

[144] Case 172/80 *Gerhard Züchner v Bayerische Vereinsbank AG* [1981] ECR 2021. Similarly, the limited impact of competition law on workers, as shown by the recent decisions in Case C-22/98 *Criminal Proceedings Against Jean Claude Becu and others*, judgment of 16 September 1999 and Case C-67/96 *Albany International BV v Stichting Bedrijfspensioenfonds Textielindustrie*, judgment of 21 September 1999, may partly explain the finding in Case C-281/98 *Roman Angonese v Cassa di Risparmio di Bolzano SpA*, judgment of 6 June 2000, that Art 39 (ex 48) EC binds even individual private employers. See for critical comments on these developments P. Nihoul, 'Do Workers Constitute Undertakings for the Purpose of the Competition Rules?' (2000) 25 ELRev 408 at 410–414 and R.J. van den Bergh and P.D. Camesasca, 'Irreconcilable Principles? The Court of Justice Exempts Collective Labour Agreements from the Wrath of Antitrust' (2000) 25 ELRev 492 at 499–501. *Albany* can be contrasted with another decision concerning pension funds, Joined Cases C-180/98 to 184/98 *Pavel Pavlov and others v Stichting Pensioenfonds Medische Specialisten*, judgment of 12 September 2000. In the former decision Art 81 (ex 85) EC was found not to apply due to collective bargaining, while in the latter the same provision was found to be in principle applicable, as the system was established by medical specialists. The development of EU citizenship might in the future grow to explain and justify a stricter approach to private measures directed against natural persons holding the nationality of another Member State, but so far the Court has not used this argument. However, the prohibition of discrimination in Art 12 (ex 6) EC might constitute a more natural and easily controlled means of dealing with the issue.

private parties were in practice dealt with under competition rules, and correspondingly to extend the scope of Article 49 to cover some private parties.

However, if the private party creating obstacles to the free movement of goods or services is not an undertaking, or an association of undertakings, Articles 28 and 49 should be applicable in certain circumstances. Otherwise, a lacuna is formed.

The concept of an undertaking within the meaning of Articles 81 (ex 85) and 82 (ex 86) EC is a wide one. It encompasses any person or entity carrying on a commercial or economic activity, in the meaning of economic trade, regardless of its legal form, even if it does not have a profit motive or an economic purpose.[145] Thus, the Commission or the Court have found that, for example, an opera singer,[146] an inventor exploiting his invention,[147] an agricultural co-operative,[148] a trade association,[149] and a customs agent[150] are undertakings for the purposes of competition rules.

However, there are some purely private entities that do not fall under the competition rules but can seriously threaten market integration. If an entity does not carry out any commercial or economic activity, it is not an undertaking and its actions are not regulated by Articles 81 and 82. Examples of such bodies are an environmental pressure group or a trade union.[151] Yet, such a private non-undertaking may have both the means and the motive to recreate the barriers the EC Treaty seeks to abolish.

A private non-undertaking can create obstacles to the free movement of goods and services. For example, industrial action disrupting air traffic or blocking roads, direct action by an environmental pressure group paralysing

---

[145] See generally Goyder (n 111 above) 86–87, Korah (n 29 above) 36–37, and Whish (n 111 above) 187–188.

[146] *RAI v Unitel* [1978] OJ L157/39.   [147] *Reuter/BASF* [1976] OJ L254/40.

[148] Case 61/80 *Coöperative Stremsel-en Kleurselfabriek v Commission* [1981] ECR 851.

[149] Case 71/74 *FRUBO v Commission* [1975] ECR 563.

[150] Case C-35/96 *Commission v Italy* [1998] ECR I-3851 paras 33–38 and the Opinion of AG Cosmas paras 45–55. See also Case T-513/93 *Consiglio Nazionale degli Spedizionieri Doganali v Commission*, judgment of 30 March 2000. Other examples abound. See eg Joined Cases C-180/98 to 184/98 *Pavel Pavlov and others v Stichting Pensioenfonds Medische Specialisten*, judgment of 12 September 2000, paras 73–82 for a finding that medical specialists and their pension funds are undertakings.

[151] D.W. Bellamy and G. Child, *Common Market Law of Competition* (4th edn by V. Rose London 1993) 40–41, and Whish (n 111 above) 189. For an opposite view see K.S. Desai, 'E.C. Competition Law and Trade Unions' (1999) 20 ECLR 175 at 175–176. In Case C-67/96 *Albany International BV v Stichting Bedrijfspensioenfonds Textielindustrie*, judgment of 21 September 1999, AG Jacobs pointed out in paras 218–227 of his Opinion that a trade union may run a business, in which case competition rules would apply, but that in many situations a trade union is not engaged in economic activities and may in any event only be acting as an agent of its members. The Court did not concentrate on this point but decided that collective agreements on conditions of work and employment fall outside the scope of Art 81 (ex 85) EC by virtue of their nature and purpose. See paras 59–60 of the judgment. In Case C-22/98 *Criminal Proceedings Against Jean Claude Becu and others*, judgment of 16 September 1999, paras 25–31, the Court decided that dockers performing dock work in the Port of Ghent were not undertakings, but did not rule out the possibility that an organisation of dockers could constitute an undertaking.

port facilities, or a general strike aimed to pressure firms or the state to prefer domestic products can severely restrict the movement of products across frontiers.

Obstacles created by these kinds of action can be just as harmful to the internal market as state-imposed restrictions. Well-directed industrial or direct action, or a general strike can have devastating consequences on the movement of products between Member States.

This is not to say that such actions always constitute restrictions or should be condemned. Rather, it is argued that the Court ought to have the possibility of examining these actions and they should not automatically fall outside the Treaty.

Furthermore, a private non-undertaking may well have a motivation to restrict the free movement of goods or services, unlike private undertakings, which are usually motivated by profit. Members of a trade union may well calculate that protectionism would help them to achieve higher wages or to avoid lay-offs. A pressure group might place a much higher value on its particular objective than on free trade.

The application of the free movement rules to private non-undertakings would also safeguard the uniform application of Community law, which is an important principle in the Community legal system. The application of the EC Treaty should not be dependent on whether an individual Member State has placed certain issues into the private or the public sphere. A Member State which leaves many aspects of its socio-economic life for private groups to manage should not be placed in a more favourable position than a state which regulates these issues itself.[152]

Furthermore, in the case of trade unions, pressure groups etc, the exceptions found in Articles 30 (ex 36) and 46 (ex 56) EC as well as the public interest exceptions developed in the Court's case law are easier to apply than in the case of private profit-orientated undertakings. It is more conceivable that such an entity is in reality pursuing a goal in the general interest than that a private firm is.

Private individuals acting as ultimate consumers of goods or services should not be caught by the free movement rules, however. First, the idea of the internal market is to allow consumers to choose between products from any Member State and thus allow the free market to work, not to force consumers to buy foreign products. Secondly, it would be ridiculous and impossible in practice to question the justification of an individual consumer's purchasing decisions even if they discriminated in favour of domestic goods and services. Finally, it can be argued that an individual consumer's decisions will usually lack the protective effect needed for the application of the free

---

[152] See Case 36/74 *Walrave and Koch v UCI* [1974] ECR 1405 para 19, and Roth (n 99 above) 1246–1247. Additionally, the public/private dichotomy is being blurred inter alia through privatisation. See Baquero Cruz (n 20 above) 617.

movement rules.[153] They are not capable of hindering trade actually or potentially, directly or indirectly.[154]

The last point is relevant also as regards other private non-undertakings. Some of their actions may fall outside the scope of the free movement rules as they do not have the necessary protective effect. It is important not to stretch this concept too far, however. Even though, for example, a locally arranged campaign against foreign products may have next to no effect on trade in itself, when taken together with similar actions elsewhere the cumulative effect may be substantial.

The fact that the actions of a private non-undertaking may be legal under domestic law is not of importance. National law cannot authorise the private party to infringe the EC Treaty. A more complicated situation arises if the action amounts to an exercise of fundamental rights. In these cases the court dealing with the case would usually find the action justified.[155]

In fact, it may be noted that in practice the result would not be too dissimilar from the current state of law in the field of the free movement of services. It would not amount to a retrograde step.[156] It would just fill the gaps in the present system, make it more coherent, and unify the approach to goods and services. Restrictions on the free movement of goods created by private non-undertakings would no longer escape the Court's scrutiny. Restrictions on the free movement of services created by private undertakings would no longer fall under both Article 49 and the competition provisions.

It must be admitted that the proposed system would not be reconcilable with the Court's interpretation of Article 39 (ex 48) EC, however. In *Bosman*[157] Advocate General Lenz discussed the relationship between Article 39 on the one hand and Articles 81 (ex 85) and 82 (ex 86) EC on the other. He came to the conclusion that nothing prevented the application of both rules to the same situation[158] and proceeded to find that both Articles 39 and 81 prohibited the actions of football clubs and sports associations.[159] The Court did not find it necessary to give a ruling on the competition issues as the challenged rules were already contrary to Article 39.[160]

---

[153] See Case C-379/92 *Matteo Peralta* [1994] ECR I-3453, and Case C-266/96 *Corsica Ferries France SA v Gruppo Antichi Ormeggiatori del Porto di Genova Coop. arl and others* [1998] ECR I-3949, especially para 29 of the Opinion of AG Fennelly.

[154] Case 8/74 *Procureur du Roi v Dassonville* [1974] ECR 837.

[155] See on these issues also section 2d below.

[156] See also Weatherill (n 131 above) 90 who considers an interpretation of Art 39 (ex 48) EC depriving it of horizontal direct effect an 'unacceptable retrograde step for Community law'.

[157] Case C-415/93 *Union Royale Belge des Sociétés de Football Association ASBL and others v Jean-Marc Bosman* [1995] ECR I-4921.

[158] ibid, para 253 of the Opinion.

[159] ibid, para 287 of the Opinion. See also the Opinion of AG Alber in Case C-176/96 *Jyri Lehtonen and Asbl Castors Canada Dry Namur-Braine v Asbl Fédération royale belge des sociétés de basket-ball und Asbl Basket Liga-Ligue Basket Belgium*, judgment of 22 June 1999.

[160] See n 157 above, para 138 of the judgment.

Thus *Bosman*,[161] together with the mention of individual agreements in Article 7(4) of Regulation 1612/68/EEC,[162] seems to lead to the conclusion that both the provisions on the free movement of workers and the competition rules can apply to the same situation.[163] Here the interpretation of different freedoms may simply have to diverge.[164]

d) Member State responsibility for private restrictions

An alternative method of dealing with the problem of obstacles to the free movement of goods and services created by private individuals is to hold a Member State responsible for private conduct in its territory. In the recent case *Commission v France*[165] the Court, following Advocate General Lenz, opted for this solution in the field of the free movement of goods.

In issue in the case were violent acts committed by French farmers, which were directed against agricultural products of other Member States. The actions had been going on for more than a decade and the French authorities had displayed astonishing passivity towards these breaches of law and order.

The Court ruled that Article 28 (ex 30) EC, when read together with Article 10 (ex 5) EC, requires a Member State to take all appropriate measures to ensure that the free movement of goods is respected in its territory.[166] Although Member States have the exclusive competence as regards the maintenance of public order and the safeguarding of internal security and have a wide discretion in determining the measures needed, it was for the Court to verify whether the appropriate measures had been taken.[167] The acts of violence and threats constituted obstacles, France had failed to take adequate and appropriate measures to deal with these obstacles, and the lack of action by the French authorities was not justified.[168] Thus, France had infringed Community law by failing 'manifestly and persistently' to adopt 'necessary and proportionate' measures to prevent actions by private individuals obstructing the free movement of goods.[169]

One year after the judgment was given, Council Regulation 2679/98/EC of 7 December 1998 on the functioning of the internal market in relation to the

---

[161] The Opinion of AG Lenz in *Bosman* demonstrates that even in this field competition rules are a formidable weapon against market partitioning actions of undertakings. I am of the opinion that *Bosman* should have been decided on competition law grounds. See Chapter 2 section 5civ above.

[162] Council Regulation 1612/68/EEC of 15 October 1968 on freedom of movement for workers within the Community as amended by Regulation 312/76 [1968] OJ Spec Ed 1968 L257/2, 475.

[163] On the problems of using both sets of rules, see Weatherill (n 106 above) 87–89.

[164] See, however, the Opinion of AG Cosmas in Joined Cases C-51/96 and C-191/97 *Christelle Deliège v Asbl Ligue Francophone de judo et disciplines associées and others*, judgment of 11 April 2000. The Advocate General uses a similar approach to services, examining the alleged restriction against both free movement and competition rules.

[165] Case C-265/95 *Commission v French Republic* [1997] ECR I-6959.   [166] ibid, para 30.
[167] ibid, paras 33–35.   [168] ibid, paras 38–64.   [169] ibid, paras 65–66.

free movement of goods among the Member States, was adopted.[170] The Regulation allows the Commission to initiate a special speedy process inter alia where Member State passivity in the face of actions taken by private individuals results in an obstacle to the free movement of goods.

It is submitted that the reasoning of *Commission v France* applies equally if a Member State fails to take appropriate measures against private individuals creating obstacles to the free movement of services. There is simply no reason to treat the failure of a Member State to take measures against, for example, demonstrators preventing foreign doctors from operating in an abortion clinic, any differently from a similar failure affecting the free movement of goods. The fact that private parties may in some instances be infringing Article 49 (ex 59) EC themselves does not alter the conclusion. If a Member State is under an obligation to take measures to prevent actions committed by private parties which do not violate the EC Treaty, surely it must also have the duty to take measures to prevent private infringements of the Treaty.

The principle of Member State responsibility for private conduct does not remove the need for the interpretation of the free movement of goods and services that acknowledges their binding force towards private non-undertakings. The principle is useful especially in respect to actions by private unorganised groups with no legal personality, but there are still many uncertainties and problems surrounding the principle, and it may not prove to be an adequate remedy in practice.

First, it is logically a rather curious move to place a Member State under obligation to adopt appropriate measures to ensure that private individuals do not create obstacles to the free movement of goods, when those private individuals do not have any obligation not to create those obstacles in the first place. In effect, the Court is creating an indirect obligation to private parties after failing to create the direct obligation in its earlier case law.[171]

Furthermore, it is uncertain what actions of private individuals a Member State should prevent or punish. Advocate General Lenz seems to depart from the very far-reaching assumption that a Member State has to adopt measures to prevent the same acts by private parties that it itself is prohibited from committing.[172] Thus, if the action fell *ratio materiae* under the *Dassonville*[173] and *Keck*[174] formulas and was not justified, a Member State would have to take preventative or punitive measures.

It has, however, been argued that for a Member State to have a duty to take measures, the actions of private individuals would have to have an effect on

---

[170] [1998] OJ L337/8. The Regulation was based on a more robust Commission Proposal [1998] OJ C10/14.

[171] See section 2a above.

[172] See the Opinion of AG Lenz (n 165 above) para 12. For criticism, see Orlandini (n 132 above) 346–347.

[173] Case 8/74 *Procureur du Roi v Dassonville* [1974] ECR 837.

[174] Joined Cases C-267/91 and C-268/91 *Criminal Proceedings Against Keck and Mithouard* [1993] ECR I-6097.

trade that is not purely local or totally insignificant. The effect and nature of the actions would have to be comparable to the effects and nature of a restriction adopted by a Member State.[175] It may be noted that Article 1 of Regulation 2679/98 states that it only applies to:

obstacle . . . which:
— leads to serious disruption of the free movement of goods,
— causes serious loss to the individuals affected,
— requires immediate action in order to prevent any continuation, increase or intensification of the disruption or loss in question.

The conditions given in Regulation 2679/98 should not be used to limit the general duty of Member States, however. The Regulation authorises the Commission to start a speedy process to deal with obstacles to the free movement of goods. It is natural that the scope of application of this special system is limited to the most flagrant violations.

It has also to be noted that a test based on comparability with the effects and nature of a Member State measure appears somewhat empty of meaning. A public measure may have a minimal effect on free movement and still infringe the EC Treaty.[176] It may take many different forms, fall under public or private law, be legally binding or non-binding, and still fall foul of the free movement rules. There is no agreement within or between states on the spheres of life that properly fall outside state intervention. Therefore, almost any private measure could be said to be comparable to a state measure as to its effects or nature.[177]

Furthermore, in effect the *Dassonville* formula already requires that the actions must have some protective effect to fall within the scope of the free movement rules. This can be used to weed out absolutely insignificant acts of private individuals. Great care has to be exercised, however, as the individual actions may have a strong cumulative impact.

Moreover, it is important to notice that the factual situation in *Commission v France* was special. First, the acts of the private parties were clearly illegal under French law. It has been argued that the principle of Member State responsibility does not sit well in situations where the actions are perfectly legal under domestic law.[178] In my view, however, the legality under national law is irrelevant. If a Member State is condemned for not applying its criminal law to a certain conduct, surely it has to be equally condemned for failing to criminalise the behaviour in the first place. Quite rightly, the Court did not limit its judgment in this respect.

A more problematic situation emerges if the private individuals are exercising their fundamental rights. This would have been the case, for example,

[175] A. Maunu, 'Jäsenvaltion vastuu yksityisen oikeussubjektin aiheuttamasta sisämarkkinakaupan esteestä' (1998) DL 358 at 364.
[176] See eg the arguments and the reply of the Court in Case 249/81 *Commission v Ireland* (Buy Irish) [1982] ECR 4005.
[177] cf however Baquero Cruz (n 20 above) 618.   [178] Maunu (n 175 above) 363–364.

if the farmers had used their right to free speech by distributing leaflets advertising domestic products by appealing to the patriotism of consumers or attacking the quality of foreign goods. This kind of advertising campaign would infringe Article 28 (ex 30) EC if adopted by a Member State.[179] It is uncertain whether a Member State has the responsibility to take measures to stop such a campaign conducted by private parties, however. At issue would be the balancing of two rights, the right to free trade and the fundamental right to free speech. Article 2 of Regulation 2679/98 expressly states that the Regulation does not affect in any way the exercise of fundamental rights as recognised in Member States.

More importantly, the remedy created by the principle may not be very useful in practice. An individual who has suffered due to Member State inaction may not be able to gain effective protection.

The situation will always be complicated by the fact that the Member State, against which the legal action will be taken, is not the real source of the problem. Additionally, the Member State may try to justify its inaction by referring to a lack of resources, which may be a difficult argument for a court to deal with.[180] A judicial authority cannot, for example, easily determine that funds should have been transferred from one area of policing to another, or from health services to policing, to deal with obstacles to the free movement of goods created by private individuals.[181] Furthermore, it may be difficult for an aggrieved private party to determine in advance whether a Member State has infringed Article 28 (ex 30) EC, in conjunction with Article 10 (ex 5) EC, as the Member State has a wide discretion in determining exactly what measures to adopt.[182] This may act as a deterrent for starting proceedings.

Moreover, there may not even be any remedy available as a Member State may have adopted all necessary and appropriate measures. The fact that a private party may have created an obstacle to free trade does not automatically indicate a violation by the Member State. It is after all not under an obligation to guarantee a specific result, only to adopt suitable measures.[183]

---

[179] Case 249/81 *Commission v Ireland* (Buy Irish) [1982] ECR 4005.

[180] See in this respect the judgment of the House of Lords in *R v Chief Constable of Sussex, ex parte International Trader's Ferry Limited* [1999] 1 CMLR 1320.

[181] A court would face an even more difficult problem in a case where it was alleged that a Member State's failure to deal with structural difficulties, such as insufficient port facilities or bad roads, amounted to a violation of Art 28 (ex 30) EC, read together with Art 10 (ex 5) EC.

[182] See n 165 above, paras 33–35 of the judgment and para 49 of the Opinion of AG Lenz. See also K. Muylle, 'Angry Farmers and Passive Policemen: Private Conduct and the Free Movement of Goods' (1998) 23 ELRev 467 at 471–474, who compares the approach of the European Court of Justice to the approach of the English Court of Appeal in *R v Chief Constable of Sussex, ex parte International Traders' Ferry Ltd* [1997] 2 CMLR 164 and comes to the conclusion that the scrutiny of the European Court is not as marginal as one might think. Similarly Orlandini (n 132 above) 349.

[183] AG Lenz was careful to make a distinction between 'obligation de moyens' and 'obligation de résultat'. See n 165 above, para 45 of his Opinion.

An individual affected by private acts creating obstacles to free trade may attack Member State inaction either by complaining to the Commission or by starting proceedings against the Member State in a national court.[184] Both of these options have their weaknesses.

The Commission can start proceedings in the European Court of Justice against a Member State which has failed to take measures against private conduct under Article 226 (ex 169) EC. The Article 226 procedure may be time-consuming. It usually involves informal negotiations, a formal notification, a reasoned opinion, and the Member State's replies, after which the Commission may refer the case to the Court.[185] In 1999, direct action proceedings in the Court alone took on average 23 months.[186] In addition, all Commission activities are constrained by the lack of resources as well as political considerations. Moreover, the judgment of the Court may not have the desired effect. It is just a declaration that a Member State has not fulfilled its EC Treaty obligations and carries no sanction. It will only have a real 'bite' if the Commission institutes further proceedings under Article 228 (ex 171) EC.[187]

An aggrieved individual can also take legal action in a national court[188] against the Member State which has failed to fulfil its obligations.[189] This action can be based either on the alleged direct effect of Article 28 (ex 30) EC, in conjunction with Article 10 (ex 5) EC, or regardless of the finding on direct effect the individual can claim damages from the state.[190]

It may well be that the obligation of a Member State to take necessary and proportionate measures to prevent free trade from being obstructed by private conduct lacks direct effect.[191] A Member State is not under a duty to achieve free trade but only under a duty to adopt appropriate measures. It has

---

[184] In theory another Member State may also challenge the inaction under Art 227 (ex 170) EC.

[185] Note, however, the Commission's intention to impose tight deadlines for these procedures in this context. See Resolution of the Council and of the representatives of the Governments of the Member States meeting within the Council of 7 December 1998 on the free movement of goods [1998] OJ L337/10 paras 5–6.

[186] http://curia.eu.int/en/stat/index.htm. The Council has invited the Court to consider whether cases within the scope of Regulation 2679/98 can be expedited. See ibid, para 7.

[187] See P. Craig, 'Once Upon a Time in the West: Direct Effect and the Federalization of EEC Law' (1992) 12 OJLS 453 at 454–457 generally on problems relating to public enforcement by the Commission.

[188] Member States have agreed to ensure that rapid and effective review procedures are available for any person who has been harmed as a result of a breach of the EC Treaty caused by an obstacle within the meaning of Regulation 2679/98. See n 185 above, para 3.

[189] Weatherill points out that with its judgment the Court supplies the Commission with private allies in policing the internal market. See S. Weatherill, 'Free Movement of Goods' (1999) 48 ICLQ 217 at 222–223.

[190] Joined Cases C-6/90 and C-9/90 *Francovich and Bonifaci* [1991] ECR I-5357, where Member State liability for a breach of Community law was first established, was a case in which the infringed provision did not have a direct effect.

[191] See also the opinion of Lord Hoffmann in *R v Chief Constable of Sussex, ex parte International Trader's Ferry Limited* [1999] 1 CMLR 1320.

a wide discretion as to the exact measures it takes, and the Court stated in *Commission v France* that it is:

not for the Community institutions to act in place of the Member States and to prescribe for them measures which they must adopt and effectively apply in order to safeguard the free movement of goods in their territory.[192]

It seems that the obligation imposed by Article 28, in conjunction with Article 10, cannot easily be characterised as clear and precise, unconditional and not contingent on any discretionary implementing measures, which are the requirements for a provision of Community law to have direct effect.[193]

An individual who has suffered damage as a result of Member State inaction can claim damages from the state under the principle of Member State liability established in *Francovich*[194] and further specified in *Brasserie du Pêcheur* and *Factortame*.[195] However, certain conditions have to be fulfilled. In many cases where it is alleged that a Member State has infringed Article 28, in conjunction with Article 10, these conditions make it difficult for the action to succeed.[196]

It may not be easy to show that the breach is sufficiently serious.[197] According to *Brasserie du Pêcheur* and *Factortame*[198] the margin of discretion left to national authorities is a (major) factor that a court has to take into account when deciding on the seriousness of the infringement. Article 28, when read in conjunction with Article 10, leaves the Member State a wide discretion to decide what measures to adopt. A specific act may be more easily found to be a sufficiently serious breach than general inaction.

In addition, it may be difficult to establish a direct causal link between the breach and the damage.[199] The individual will have to show that if the Member State had adopted necessary and proportionate measures, the damage would not have occurred. For example, in the situation of *Commission v France*[200] the plaintiff would have to prove that if the French police had been more active and the French criminal law had been applied more vigorously, the damage caused by the violent farmers would have been prevented, or alternatively the climate of insecurity would have been avoided and trade

---

[192] See n 165 above, para 34.

[193] See in general P. Craig and G. de Búrca, *EU Law. Text, Cases and Materials* (2nd edn Oxford 1998) 168–175 and T.C. Hartley, *The Foundations of European Community Law* (4th edn Oxford 1998) 191–196.

[194] See n 190 above.

[195] Joined Cases C-46 and C-48/93 *Brasserie du Pêcheur SA v Germany and R v Secretary of State for Transport, ex parte Factortame* [1996] ECR I-1029.

[196] For a perhaps more optimistic view see Weatherill (n 189 above) 221–223.

[197] The second condition established in n 195 above, paras 51 and 55–64.

[198] ibid, para 56.

[199] ibid, paras 51 and 65. See also M.A. Jarvis, 'Case C-265/95, *Commission v French Republic*, Judgment of the Court of Justice of 9 December 1997, [1997] ECR I-6959' (1998) 35 CMLRev 1371 at 1382.

[200] See n 165 above.

been conducted bringing more profits than were otherwise achieved. This is not a simple task.[201]

Altogether, the principle of Member State responsibility for conduct of private parties in their territory is a useful addition to Community law but does not remove the need to interpret the free movement rules in such a way that they catch the actions of private non-undertakings in certain circumstances.[202]

e) Conclusion

It has been demonstrated that the scope of application of Articles 28 (ex 30) and 49 (ex 59) EC to the actions of private parties is not the same. The provisions on the free movement of goods only apply to Member State measures while at least some restrictions created by private parties are caught by Article 49. There does not seem to be any sensible grounds for this difference of interpretation. It is submitted that the European Court of Justice ought to adopt a unified approach to both freedoms. This approach should recognise the *lex specialis* status of competition rules, but apply Articles 28 and 49 to obstacles created by private non-undertakings. The decision of the Court in *Commission v France*[203] helps to alleviate the problem but does not remove the need for this reinterpretation.

The analysis has also demonstrated the inadequacy of the vertical/horizontal direct effect dichotomy in interpreting EC Treaty provisions. It is simply not an appropriate tool.[204] The crucial starting point is that the Treaty provisions are *capable* of having both forms of direct effect, unlike for example directives. After this has been established, the relevant provisions are best construed by using normal interpretative principles, such as *lex specialis*, found also in domestic legal systems.

3. The Community

a) The binding nature of the free movement of goods and services

Analysis of the EC Treaty and the case law of the European Court of Justice shows that the Community, as well as Member States and some private parties, is bound by the free movement of goods and services.

---

[201] It has also been argued that it may be not be easy to establish that Art 28 (ex 30) EC, in conjunction with Art 10 (ex 5) EC, is a rule of law intended to confer rights on individuals. See Jarvis (n 199 above) 1382. This condition was established in *Brasserie du Pêcheur* n 195 above, paras 51 and 54. According to para 54 of the judgment, Art 28 (ex 30) EC in itself does fulfil the condition.
[202] See also Baquero Cruz (n 20 above) 611.
[203] Case C-265/95 *Commission v French Republic* [1997] ECR I-6959.
[204] See Baquero Cruz (n 20 above) 604–606.

It is not clear whether the Treaty provisions on free movement in Part Three of the EC Treaty, Community policies, are addressed to the Community. Even though the main provisions in Articles 28, 29 and 49 (ex 30, 34(1) and 59) EC can be interpreted as applicable also to the Community, the standstill clauses in former Articles 31 EC (repealed) and 62 EC (repealed) would seem to indicate that only Member States are targeted by these rules.

However, provisions in Part One of the EC Treaty, Principles, make it clear that the Community cannot escape the four freedoms. According to Article 2, the Community pursues its objectives by establishing a common market. Article 3 stipulates that the activities of the Community include an 'internal market characterised by the abolition, as between Member States, of obstacles to the free movement of goods, persons, services, and capital'. The freedoms constitute the very heart of the common/internal market to which the Community is committed. The Community cannot infringe them.

It has been debated, especially in German literature,[205] whether the Community is bound by the free movement provisions themselves or merely by the principle of free movement. The Court has not answered this question directly but recently some Advocates General have stated that the free movement Articles themselves apply to the Community.[206] The significance of this distinction is unclear.[207]

In addition, there is another, very direct, way in which the Community legislature is bound by the freedoms. Many provisions of the EC Treaty capable of constituting a legal basis stipulate that the legislative power can only be used in order to achieve the internal market (eg, Article 95 (ex 100a) EC) or the common market (eg, Article 94 (ex 100) EC) or to achieve liberalisation (eg, Article 52 (ex 63) EC). If a Community measure infringes the free movement of goods or services, it could not be adopted on the basis of these provisions. [208]

The Court has recognised in its case law that the freedoms bind the Community. The leading case in the field of the free movement of goods is *Ramel*,[209] which was decided under the Chapter on the Customs Union. In issue was Council Regulation 816/70/EEC of 28 April 1970 laying down

---

[205] See eg U. Scheffer, *Die Marktfreiheiten des EG-Vertrags als Ermessensgrenze des Gemeinschaftsgesatzgebers* (Frankfurt 1997) 32–48, and R.-O. Schwemer, *Die Bindung des Gemeinschaftsgesetzgebers an die Grundfreiheiten* (Frankfurt 1995) 41–45.

[206] See the Opinion of AG Gulmann, para 14 in Case C-51/93 *Meyhui NV v Schott Zwiesel Glaswerke AG* [1994] ECR I-3879, and the Opinion of AG Elmer, para 21 in Case C-114/96 *Criminal Proceedings Against René Kieffer and Romain Thill* [1997] ECR I-3629.

[207] Similarly P. Oliver, 'La législation communautaire et sa conformité avec la libre circulation des marchandises' (1979) 15 CDE 245 at 255.

[208] See the extensive discussion by AG Fennelly in Cases C-376/98 *Germany v European Parliament and Council of the European Union*, judgment of 5 October 2000, paras 58–119 and 146–150. The Court followed its Advocate General and annulled the Tobacco Advertising Directive 98/43/EC, as it could not be legally adopted on the basis of Arts 95, 47(2) and 55 (ex 100a, 57(2) and 66) EC.

[209] Joined Cases 80 and 81/77 *Société Les Commissionnaires Réunis Sàrl v Receveur des Douanes; Sàrl Les Fils de Henri Ramel v Receveur des Douanes* [1978] ECR 927.

additional provisions for the common organisation of the market in wine.[210] Article 31(2) of the Regulation authorised a wine-producing Member State to take measures limiting imports from another Member State in order to avoid disturbances in its markets. France had imposed a duty on Italian wines to limit their influx into the French market. The plaintiffs argued that the duty was unlawful and sought refund and compensation. The French authorities relied on the authorisation given in the Regulation.

The Court ruled that Article 31(2) of Regulation 816/70 was incompatible with numerous EC Treaty provisions, in particular Article 13(2) EC (repealed). In an important paragraph it stated that:

the extensive powers, in particular of a sectorial and regional nature, granted to the Community institutions in the conduct of the Common Agricultural Policy must, in any event as from the end of the transitional period, be exercised from the perspective of the unity of the market to the *exclusion of any measure compromising the abolition between Member States of customs duties and quantitative restrictions or charges or measures having equivalent effect.*[211]

Subsequent case law has confirmed *Ramel* and extended it also to quantitative restrictions and measures having equivalent effect.[212] For example, recently in *Bettati*[213] the Court restated that:

It is settled law that the prohibition of quantitative restrictions and of all measures having equivalent effect applies not only to national measures but also to measures adopted by the Community institutions.[214]

The case *Commission v France* (Tourist guides)[215] demonstrates that the free movement of services binds the Community as well.[216] In issue was French legislation requiring that guides accompanying tourists from other Member States held a licence. The licence was proof of a specific qualification, which was generally obtained by success in an examination. The French government argued, inter alia, that the action under Article 226 (ex 169) EC was in conflict with the Commission proposal[217] for a Council Directive on a second general system for the recognition of professional education and training which complements Directive 89/48. Under that proposal, Member States were allowed to determine the minimum level of necessary qualifications if the Community had not done that.

The Court stated tersely that 'provisions of secondary legislation can only concern national measures which are compatible with the requirements of Article 59 [now Article 49] of the Treaty, as defined in the case law of the

---

[210] [1970] OJ Spec Ed I 234.   [211] See n 209 above, para 35 (emphasis added).
[212] For analysis see Oliver (n 3 above) 45–56.
[213] Case C-341/95 *Gianni Bettati v Safety Hi-Tech Srl* [1998] ECR I-4355.
[214] ibid, para 61.   [215] Case C-154/89 *Commission v France* [1991] ECR I-659.
[216] See also the Opinion of AG Tesauro in Case C-120/95 *Nicolas Decker v Caisse de Maladie des Employés Privés* [1998] ECR I-1831 and Case C-158/96 *Raymond Kohll v Union des Caisses de Maladie* [1998] ECR I-1931 paras 11 and 43.
[217] [1989] OJ C263/1.

Court'.[218] It went on to declare that the French legislation infringed Article 49 (ex 59). The statement shows that the free movement of services also binds the Community.[219]

An earlier case concerning the free movement of services, *Commission v Germany* (Insurance),[220] illustrates the important point that instead of invalidating a Community measure for its non-compliance with one of the four freedoms the Court can simply interpret the measure in conformity with the relevant freedom. This approach is used if the wording of the measure can be construed appropriately.

The German government claimed that Council Directive 78/473/EEC of 30 May 1978 on Community co-insurance[221] allowed Germany to require that the leading insurer was established and authorised in Germany if the risks were situated there. The Court replied that 'when the wording of secondary Community law is open to more than one interpretation, preference should be given to the interpretation which renders the provision consistent with the Treaty'.[222] It continued by ruling that in the circumstances of the case both the establishment and the authorisation criteria were contrary to Articles 49 and 50 (ex 59 and 60) EC and *therefore also to the Directive.*[223]

b) Restrictions imposed by the Community

The concept of restriction must have the same meaning both for the Community and Member States.[224] It would be intolerable if the Community was able to authorise in its secondary legislation a restriction that a Member State itself could not maintain. This would amount to a change of the EC Treaty by secondary legislation, without following the procedure set out in Article 48 (ex N) of the Treaty on European Union. This cannot be allowed in a Community bound by the rule of law.

The same applies to a Community measure which lays down a certain restriction rather than merely authorises Member States to adopt it. It is very difficult to see why a directive requiring a Member State to impose a restriction, or a regulation imposing it, ought to be treated any differently from a directive allowing a Member State to prescribe the same restriction.[225]

Therefore, it has to be examined what amounts to a restriction in relation to the different freedoms. Unless specifically authorised by the EC Treaty, the Community cannot create these barriers any more than a Member State can.

---

[218] See n 215 above, para 24. See also para 40 of the Opinion of AG Lenz.

[219] For a similar opinion predating the case see W.-H. Roth, 'The European Economic Community's Law on Services: Harmonisation' (1988) 25 CMLRev 35 at 72–74.

[220] Case 205/84 *Commission v Germany* [1986] ECR 3755.   [221] [1978] OJ L151/25.

[222] See n 220 above, para 62.   [223] ibid, paras 63–68.

[224] Similarly AG Tesauro (n 216 above) paras 12–13, 35, 39 and 43.

[225] For an attempt to distinguish between 'material Community legislation' and 'authorisation' of Member States see Scheffer (n 205 above) 121–131.

In the field of the free movement of goods the Court has recognised in *Keck*[226] that Article 28 (ex 30) EC is a measure aimed at preventing discrimination.[227] In the case the Court held that national product requirements fall automatically within Article 28 while rules concerning selling arrangements infringe Article 28 if they discriminate in law or in fact. The main problem caused by national product requirements is that they tend to discriminate materially against economic operators from other Member States. This discriminatory effect can be caused even by equally applicable product rules since they create a double burden. In contrast, national regulation of selling arrangements does not usually discriminate against goods from other Member States. The burden is felt equally by domestic and imported goods. In its case law on exports the Court has held that only discriminatory national measures infringe Article 29 (ex 34) EC. This can easily be explained by the absence of a double burden. A product and a producer only have to comply with the product requirements and production rules of the exporting state. Thus, there is normally no material discrimination.[228]

The post-*Keck* case law on impediments to the free movement of goods created by Community measures does not contradict the proposition that the concept of restriction is the same for a Member State and the Community.[229] In *Clinique*[230] the Court expressly stated that it was interpreting Article 6(2) of Council Directive 76/768/EEC of 27 July 1976 on the approximation of the laws of the Member States relating to cosmetic products[231] in the light of its judgment in *Keck*.

In *Meyhui*[232] the Court examined the validity of Council Directive 69/493/EEC of 15 September 1969 on the approximation of laws relating to crystal glass.[233] The Directive stipulated that certain products could only be labelled in the languages of the country where they were marketed. The Court held that this 'constitutes a barrier to intra-Community trade in so far as products coming from other Member States have to be given different labelling causing additional packaging costs'.[234] This shows clearly that the

---

[226] Joined Cases C-267/91 and C-268/91 *Criminal Proceedings Against Keck and Mithouard* [1993] ECR I-6097.

[227] The concept of discrimination is understood very widely and includes material discrimination resulting from rules which create a double burden.

[228] See Chapter 2 section 5 above.

[229] See also Joined Cases C-427/93, 429/93 and 436/93 *Bristol-Myers Squibb and others v Paranova A/S* [1996] ECR I-3457 para 36 concerning intellectual property, Case C-180/96 *United Kingdom v Commission* [1998] ECR I-2265 para 63, Case C-284/95 *Safety Hi-Tech Srl v S. & T. Srl* [1998] ECR I-4301, and Case C-341/95 *Gianni Bettati v Safety Hi-Tech Srl* [1998] ECR I-4355 paras 61–65. In the last two cases total bans were considered prima facie restrictions. The same would be true for a total ban imposed by a Member State. See Case 34/79 *R v Henn and Darby* [1979] ECR 3795.

[230] Case C-315/92 *Verband Sozialer Wettbewerb v Estée Lauder* [1994] ECR I-317 paras 12–13.

[231] [1976] OJ L262/169.

[232] Case C-51/93 *Meyhui NV v Schott Zwiesel Glaswerke AG* [1994] ECR I-3879.

[233] [1969] OJ Spec Ed II 599.

[234] See n 232 above, para 13. However, it found that the restriction was justified.

restriction, as interpreted by the Court, was the result of the extra burden imposed on imported goods. The discriminatory aspect necessitated an investigation of the justification of the measure.

In *Kieffer and Thill*[235] in issue was Council Regulation 3330/91/EEC of 7 November 1991 on statistics relating to the trading of goods between Member States.[236] The Regulation required undertakings engaged in intra-Community trade to supply statistical information to the Intrastat system. The Court held:

It is common ground that the detailed nature of the declarations required and the fact that it is obligatory to make a declaration in both the Member State of consignment and that of the destination of the goods have restrictive effects with regard to the free movement of goods.[237]

It is clear that the measure imposed an additional burden on intra-Community trade when compared with trade in domestic markets as the information requirements only applied to cross-border transactions. In addition, the information had to be supplied twice. The measure was undoubtedly discriminatory. The statement by the Court relating to the detailed nature of the information might be explained with reference to the argument put forward by the Luxembourg government, the Council and the Commission. They claimed that the restrictive effect of the declaration requirement was too indirect and uncertain to form a barrier to intra-Community trade. The fact that the information required was described as 'detailed' may have been intended to answer this argument.[238]

In general, a Community measure very seldom falls foul of the free movement of goods. First, uniform Community rules create an equal burden for all economic operators and do not therefore impede the free movement of goods. The adoption of a Community-wide standard, for example, does not create an obstacle, no matter how rigorous the standard is. Secondly, if a Member State could have used a national measure by virtue of Article 30 (ex 36) EC or mandatory requirements developed in *Cassis*[239] jurisprudence, the Community is not imposing any new restrictions. It is simply replacing national rules with a Community one. Thirdly, the Community, unlike an individual Member State, usually has no incentive to adopt discriminatory

---

[235] Case C-114/96 *Criminal Proceedings Against René Kieffer and Romain Thill* [1997] ECR I-3629.

[236] [1991] OJ L316/1.

[237] See n 235 above, para 28. The Court held that the measure was justified, however.

[238] It is curious though that the Court said this to be 'common ground'. Furthermore, as AG Elmer noted, there is no minimum threshold to the application of the free movement of goods provisions. See the Opinion of AG Elmer, paras 22–23. It is unlikely that a Chamber would make a major change to the established case law, however. The same is true for Case C-127/95 *Norbrook Laboratories Limited v Ministry of Agriculture, Fisheries and Food* [1998] ECR I-1531 para 97 where the Community Directives created a dual burden but the Court referred, in my view carelessly, to the stringent requirements imposed by the measures.

[239] Case 120/78 *Rewe Zentrale AG v Bundesmonopolverwaltung für Branntwein* [1979] ECR 649.

measures. The interests of other Member States are not represented in a national political process. In the Community every Member State is heard.

The Court is able to exercise some control over unnecessarily strict Community rules, however. Although the heaviness of the burden created by a uniform Community standard cannot cause it to contravene the free movement of goods, disproportionately strict rules can infringe fundamental rights, the respect of which forms a part of the general principles of Community law.[240] These principles are autonomous but inspired by constitutional traditions common to the Member States and by international agreements to which they are party, especially the European Convention on Human Rights.[241] Fundamental rights protected by the Community include the right to property and the freedom to pursue trade or business.[242] If the substance of these rights is impaired by a Community measure, it must either be interpreted in conformity with the right in question or struck down.[243]

The approach adopted in the field of the free movement of goods is consistent with the economically agnostic nature of the EC Treaty. It does not impose a certain economic model on the Community but contains elements of different models. It allows the Community to develop in many directions.[244]

The EC Treaty does include many neo-liberal elements. Activities of the Community include an internal market characterised by the abolition of obstacles to the free movement of goods, persons, services and capital, where competition is undistorted. The economic policy of the Community is based inter alia on the internal market and is conducted in accordance with the principle of an open market economy with free competition.

Non-market elements exist side by side with the neo-liberal ones, however. The tasks of the Community listed in Article 2 EC include many statements indicative of a mixed economy. The Community has a common agricultural and transport policy, social policy, industrial policy, regional policy and research and technological development policy. These grant it far-reaching interventionist powers. Moreover, already the original EEC Treaty contained

---

[240] Case 29/69 *Stauder v City of Ulm* [1969] ECR 419 para 7.

[241] See eg Case 44/79 *Hauer v Land Rheinland-Pfalz* [1979] ECR 3727 para 15.

[242] See eg Case C-200/96 *Metronome Musik GmbH v Musik Point Hokamp GmbH* [1998] ECR I-1953 para 21.

[243] See Schwemer (n 205 above) 204–208 who also emphasises the importance of fundamental rights in this area.

[244] For a more extensive discussion, coming essentially to a similar open-ended conclusion, see C. Joerges, 'European Economic Law, the Nation-State and the Maastricht Treaty' in R. Dehousse (ed), *Europe after Maastricht. An Ever Closer Union?* (Munchen 1994) 29, M. Poiares Maduro, *We The Court. The European Court of Justice and the European Economic Constitution. A Critical Reading of Article 30 of the EC Treaty* (Oxford 1998) especially 159–161, and M.E. Streit and W. Mussler, 'The Economic Constitution of the European Community: From Rome to Maastricht' (1995) 1 ELJ 5. Recently in Case C-9/99 *Échirolles Distribution SA v Association du Dauphiné and others*, judgment of 3 October 2000, the Court rejected a challenge to the French system of book pricing. The challenge was based on the alleged failure of the system to respect the concept of a market.

Article 295 (ex 222) EC, which protects national systems of property owner-ship and thereby allows for state-owned enterprises.

The discrimination-based interpretation of the free movement of goods sits well with this system. It leaves a considerable area of discretion to the Community (and the Member States) and does not compel it to follow a *laissez-faire* policy. As argued by Advocate General Tesauro in his Opinion in *Hünermund*,[245] which was later followed by the Court in *Keck*, the free movement of goods is about liberalisation of intra-Community trade, not about unhindered pursuit of commerce.[246]

In the field of the free movement of services the Court seems to have adopted a different approach[247] from the free movement of goods in *Alpine Investments*,[248] read together with *Bosman*.[249] In the former case it was decided that national rules having a direct impact on market access of services prima facie infringed the free movement of services. In the latter the same principle was applied to the free movement of workers. It is likely that the Court will use the same approach to the right of establishment due to its close connections to the free movement of services and workers.[250]

This approach seems to enable the Court to strike down even uniform Community measures if they create direct impediments to market access. Rules imposing an equal burden can be challenged on this ground if they apply to cross-border situations.[251]

When applied to Community measures, this approach endangers the dis-cretion of the other Community institutions, and therefore the institutional balance of the Community.[252] In addition, as an institution the Court is not well placed to second-guess the cost/benefit analysis of the Community legis-lature. It may lack expertise, its possibilities for obtaining evidence are limited and all relevant interests may not be represented in the judicial process.[253]

---

[245] Case C-292/92 *Hünermund v Landesapothekerkammer Baden-Württemberg* [1993] ECR I-6787.

[246] The whole system also makes sense from the efficiency point of view. It allows regulatory competition between national rules with all the ensuing benefits. See Chapter 2 section 1 above.

[247] The Court did try to reconcile the cases with *Keck* but it is submitted that this is not feasi-ble. See Chapter 2 section 5civ above.

[248] Case C-384/93 *Alpine Investments BV v Minister van Financiën* [1995] ECR I-1141.

[249] Case C-415/93 *Union Royale Belge des Sociétés de Football Association ASBL and others v Jean-Marc Bosman* [1995] ECR I-4921.

[250] For an indication of just such an approach see Case C-55/94 *Reinhard Gebhard v Consiglio dell'Ordine degli Avvocati e Procuratori di Milano* [1995] ECR I-4165.

[251] For a more thorough analysis of measures having a direct impact on market access see Chapter 2 section 5 above.

[252] On the institutional balance and its importance in the Community system see G. de Búrca, 'The Institutional Development of the EU: A Constitutional Analysis' in P. Craig and G. de Búrca (eds), *The Evolution of EU Law* (Oxford 1999) 55–80, and P. Craig, 'The Nature of the Community: Integration, Democracy, and Legitimacy' in P. Craig and G. de Búrca (eds), *The Evolution of EU Law* (Oxford 1999) 37–40.

[253] A similar view of the weaknesses of a court is presented in Poiares Maduro (n 244 above) 59. See also G. de Búrca , 'The Principle of Proportionality and its Application in EC Law' (1993) 13 YEL 105, 108, and Chapter 4 section 4 below.

The approach also entails serious legitimacy problems. It is one thing for the Court to examine the justification of Community measures which create discriminatory barriers between Member States. There is a real risk of protectionism, the very first thing the Community set out to abolish. However, the examination of neutral, non-discriminatory measures is quite another matter. Here the Court is potentially replacing the cost/benefit assessment conducted by other Community institutions by its own evaluation. It sets the Court, an unelected organ, as the ultimate arbitrator of these strongly political questions.[254] What point is there in increasing the democratic elements in Community decision-making if in the end it is the judges who have the say?[255]

---

[254] In Australia the High Court held in the landmark case *Cole v Whitfield* (Crayfish) (1988) 165 CLR 360 that s 92 of the Constitution, which provides for freedom of trade and commerce among the states, only prohibits discriminatory burdens of a protectionist kind. One of the resons for this narrow test was the desire not to interfere with the exercise of power by the Commonwealth. See P.H. Lane, *A Manual of Australian Constitutional Law* (6th edn Sydney 1995) 333–349.

[255] The Court would be able to use fundamental human rights review in these fields as well. See, eg, a cogent challenge to the legality of the procedural guarantees in Council Directive 64/221/EEC of 25 February 1964 on the co-ordination of special measures concerning the movement and residence of foreign nationals which are justified on grounds of public policy, public security, or public health [1964] OJ Spec Ed 117, by S. O'Leary, 'The Free Movement of Persons and Services' in P. Craig and G. de Búrca (eds), *The Evolution of EU Law* (Oxford 1999) 407–412. The challenge is based on the free movement of workers and on the right to judicial protection, which is a fundamental human right common to the constitutional traditions of the Member States and enshrined in Arts 6 and 13 of the European Convention for the Protection of Human Rights and Fundamental Freedoms.

4

Justification

1. Introduction

Free markets do not always produce results that are in the public interest, but need to be regulated. Private law rules in fields such as property and tort law are necessary for the markets to function at all. They constitute the framework for the operation of the markets.[1] In addition, more specific rules are needed, in particular to deal with market failures and market absences such as monopolies,[2] externalities, and information problems.[3]

Externalities arise when the costs and benefits of an action fall to different economic agents. An example is a producer who discharges pollution into a river that is used for fishing and swimming. The producer receives the revenue for his activities without having to pay the full cost, as part of it is borne by fishers and swimmers. The result is socially excessive production as the price of the product does not reflect the true costs. The remedy may be to regulate in a manner that internalises the costs, for example, by forcing the producer to clean up the pollution.[4]

Information problems are another common market failure.[5] In particular, there may be asymmetric information[6] about product quality in the sense that the seller knows more about the quality than the buyer. If the customer is unable to inform himself of the quality of a good or a service prior to the purchase, he will rationally buy the cheapest available product. This may drive high quality goods and services out of the market. Take the example of a professional service. Let us say it costs 2,000 euros to produce a high quality professional service and 1,000 euros to produce a low quality one. A rational

---

[1] See generally A. Ogus, *Regulation. Legal Form and Economic Theory* (Oxford 1994) 15–28.

[2] Monopolies and other competition law concerns fall outside the scope of this study.

[3] See in general on reasons for regulation R. Baldwin and M. Cave, *Understanding Regulation. Theory, Strategy and Practice* (Oxford 1999) 9–17, J. Kay and J. Vickers, 'Regulatory Reform: An Appraisal' in G. Majone (ed), *Deregulation or Re-regulation? Regulatory Reform in Europe and the United States* (London 1990) 225–230, Ogus (n 1 above) 29–54, and C.R. Sunstein, *After the Rights Revolution. Reconceiving the Regulatory State* (Cambridge, Massachusetts 1990) 47–73.

[4] See in general on externalities Baldwin and Cave (n 3 above) 11–12, Kay and Vickers (n 3 above) 226, Ogus (n 1 above) 33–38, and Sunstein (n 3 above) 54–55.

[5] See on information problems generally Baldwin and Cave (n 3 above) 12, Kay and Vickers (n 3 above) 228–230, Ogus (n 1 above) 38–41, and Sunstein (n 3 above) 52–53.

[6] This market failure was analysed in a seminal article by G.A. Akerlof, 'The Market for "Lemons": Quality Uncertainty and the Market Mechanism' (1970) 84 *QJ Econ* 488.

customer who cannot assess the quality of the service prior to the purchase will go for the cheaper one. This may force the high quality professional to lower standards in order to compete in the market.[7]

The problem of asymmetric information arises with so-called 'experience' and 'credence' products. A buyer can only tell the quality of the former after the purchase. An example might be a highly technical product where the quality is only revealed after installation and use. In the case of credence products the customer cannot tell the quality even after the purchase. Some professional services fall into this category. It may be impossible for a layman to tell whether an illness was cured by the medications prescribed or by the natural healing process, or whether a lawsuit was won because of good quality advocacy.[8]

In general, services are more seriously affected by asymmetric information problems than goods. Some goods fall into the category of 'search products' where the buyer is able to determine the quality by inspecting the good, while with services this is not the case. In addition, in the case of many services the customer will not be able to tell the quality of the product even *ex post*.[9]

There are many ways to remedy information asymmetries. The producers themselves may build reputation or offer warranties as an indication of high quality. Especially with experience products that are purchased repeatedly or where the customers communicate quality-information to each other, these market mechanisms may be enough to deal with the problem. Few consumers will buy a product if one of the same brand has proved to be a 'lemon'[10] or if friends or relatives have had bad experiences with the brand. However, in some instances it is necessary for public authorities to intervene, for example by certifying service producers who meet certain criteria, such as having passed professional exams.[11]

As seen from the previous discussion, some regulation of the market may be necessary in the public interest. However, in many circumstances public intervention is not an optimal solution. Even if there is a public interest at stake, it may be that measures will suffer from regulatory failures that are more serious than the original problem. For example, in the case of minor externalities transaction costs created by a regulation may well outweigh its benefits.[12]

A regulation may also fail to pursue the public interest in the first place. Different interest groups may have had undue influence in the legislative

---

[7] See in general Kay and Vickers (n 3 above) 229, Ogus (n 1 above) 132, and Sunstein (n 3 above) 52. The description above is highly simplified.

[8] See Kay and Vickers (n 3 above) 230, and Ogus (n 1 above) 132–133.

[9] See Ogus (n 1 above) 132–133 and 216–217, and M. van Empel, 'The Visible Hand in Invisible Trade' (1990) 17 LIEI 23, 30–31.

[10] An American term for a bad product, eg a dud second-hand car.

[11] See B. Hindley and A. Smith, 'Comparative Advantage and Trade in Services' (1984) 7 *The World Economy* 369, 379–380, Kay and Vickers (n 3 above) 230 and 236–242, and Ogus (n 1 above) 133–135 and 217.

[12] See in general Sunstein (n 3 above) 74–110.

process and the resulting measure may be calculated to protect their interests at the expense of the public at large. In addition, representatives or officials may design or administer the regulation to benefit their own private interests rather than the public interest.[13]

In conclusion, some regulations may be vital for the public interest while others do not advance it or cause more harm than good. This is true for both goods and services.

In the context of the European Community, national regulations create an additional problem. They may act as non-tariff barriers hindering inter-state trade. Even regulations that seem to apply equally to goods or services regardless of their origin can have a protectionist effect if they treat similar situations differently or different situations similarly. An example of the former is a national measure which restricts the marketing of whisky but not of cognac. An example of the latter is the application of a national law to a product or a service coming from another Member State that has already complied with the home state requirements.[14]

However, the interests of free trade cannot automatically override the interests protected by the national measure. In the Community the common market is simply a means to an end, a method used to achieve the public interest goals set out in Article 2 of the EC Treaty.[15] Naturally, in most cases free movement contributes to the attainment of these objectives, but in some circumstances it can be counterproductive. For example, free trade can be in conflict with the aim of a 'high level of protection and improvement in the quality of the environment' if it requires the non-application of national environmental regulations.[16]

Once again, there is a tension between the anti-protectionist and economic freedom readings of the EC Treaty.[17] The former allows a Member State to regulate as long as it is not pursuing a protectionist purpose, while the latter requires the Court to balance the interest of trade against other interests. In the former reading the Member State sets the level of public intervention, in the latter the Court, a central organ, makes the decision applying central rules. Therefore, the former reading is decentralised and empowers Member State legislatures, while the latter is centralised and empowers the Court.

In this section I will examine how the Court has dealt with this issue, comparing its approach to goods and services. I will begin with an investigation of express Treaty exceptions. I will then proceed to analyse judicially created justifications. This will be followed by an examination into the application of the principle of proportionality. Finally, I will conduct a brief empirical study

---

13 See generally Baldwin and Cave (n 3 above) 21–25, and Ogus (n 1 above) 57–75.
14 See discussion in Chapter 2 above.   15 See Chapter 1 section 1 above.
16 See on the conflict between trade and the environment eg D. Geradin, *Trade and the Environment. A Comparative Study of EC and US Law* (Cambridge 1997) 1–3, and A.R. Ziegler, *Trade and Environmental Law in the European Community* (Oxford 1996) 2–3.
17 See Chapter 1 section 1 above.

on the intensity of the Court's review of national measures in both goods and services sectors.

2. EC Treaty exceptions

a) General

The EC Treaty itself contains provisions that allow Member States to interfere with free trade in order to achieve certain legitimate aims.[18] In the field of goods Article 30 (ex 36) EC stipulates:

The provisions of Articles 28 and 29 shall not preclude prohibitions or restrictions on imports, exports or goods in transit justified on grounds of public morality, public policy or public security; the protection of health and life of humans, animals or plants; the protection of national treasures possessing artistic, historic or archaeological value; or the protection of industrial and commercial property. Such prohibitions or restrictions shall not, however, constitute a means of arbitrary discrimination or a disguised restriction on trade between Member States.

The corresponding provision of the Treaty dealing with services is Article 46 (ex 56) EC, applicable by virtue of Article 55 (ex 66):

The provisions of this Chapter and measures taken in pursuance thereof shall not prejudice the applicability of provisions laid down by law, regulation or administrative action providing for special treatment for foreign nationals on grounds of public policy, public security or public health.

Despite the different wordings of these provisions, their basic aim is the same. They allow Member States to derogate from free movement rules to protect certain interests and, thus, to balance free trade against other interests.

The wording of Article 30 (ex 36) EC seems to set stricter limits to Member State actions. It requires that the national measures must be *justified*. This is, inter alia, connected to the idea of pre-emption. If the Community has taken action to protect a certain interest, Member State action is no longer justified and is, therefore, excluded.[19] Thus, the provision does not reserve certain matters to exclusive Member State jurisdiction.[20]

---

[18] The same may apply to private parties. In Case C-415/93 *Union Royale Belge des Sociétés de Football Association ASBL and others v Jean-Marc Bosman* [1995] ECR I-4921 para 86 the Court stated that '[t]here is nothing to preclude individuals from relying on justifications on grounds of public policy, public security or public health. Neither the scope nor the content of those grounds of justification is in any way affected by the public or private nature of the rules in question'.

[19] See Case 35/76 *Simmenthal SpA v Italian Minister for Finance* [1976] ECR 1871 para 19.

[20] Case 5/77 *Carlo Tedeschi v Denkavit Commerciale srl* [1977] ECR 1555 para 34, and Case 153/78 *Commission v Germany* (Meat preparations) [1979] ECR 2555 para 5. See generally P.J.G. Kapteyn and P. Verloren van Themaat, *Introduction to the Law of the European Communities. From Maastricht to Amsterdam* (3rd edn by L.W. Gormley London 1998) 652–654, and S. Weatherill and P. Beaumont, *EU Law* (3rd edn London 1999) 544–546. See also H.D. Jarass, 'Elemente einer Dogmatik der Grundfreiheiten II' (2000) 35 EuR 705, 720.

Article 46 (ex 56) EC is open to a different interpretation. The word *justified* does not appear,[21] and the provision expressly states that Community measures shall not exclude Member State reliance on the listed grounds.[22] It might be argued that these matters are therefore actually reserved to Member States in the field of services.

There do not seem to be any good policy reasons for this difference. It does not sit well with the system of the EC Treaty either. In the literature it has been suggested that this issue be dealt with in the same manner as in the field of goods,[23] and in practice the Court has not paid attention to these textual variations.[24] Recently in *Kohll*,[25] following Advocate General Tesauro, the Court made it clear that the existence of Community legislation can prevent Member States from relying on public health justification. Luxembourg could not justify its rules requiring prior authorisation for medical treatment abroad on grounds of the need to ensure the quality of medical services. The relevant harmonising directives guaranteed the adequate protection of patients in all Member States.[26] In *Commission v Spain*[27] the Court made it clear that Member States cannot exclude economic sectors from the freedom of movement on grounds of public policy, public security and public health. They are only entitled to 'refuse access to their territory or residence there to persons whose access or residence would in itself constitute a danger' to these interests. Therefore, it seems to be clear that this difference in the wording of the provisions is of no significance.

Another textual difference is that Article 46 (ex 56) EC refers only to a possibility to justify 'provisions laid down by law, regulation or administrative action', while Article 30 (ex 36) EC contains no such limitation.[28] The significance of this difference is uncertain,[29] especially after *Bosman*,[30] a case in which the Court held that private restrictions on the free movement of workers can be justified on grounds of public policy, security and health. It would be most surprising if private parties could not do the same in the field of services (and establishment). It may well be that in practice the Court will also ignore this difference in wording.

[21] The word 'justified' appears also in Art 39(3) (ex 48(3)) EC dealing with derogations to the free movement of workers.

[22] Exceptions have been expressly given in Community legislation. See eg Art 6 of Directive 90/388/EEC on competition in the market for telecommunication services [1990] OJ L192/10.

[23] See Kapteyn and VerLoren van Themaat (n 20 above) 758. See also F. Burrows, *Free Movement in European Community Law* (Oxford 1987) 209, and J. Handoll, *Free Movement of Persons* (Chichester 1995) 225.

[24] See eg Joined Cases 115 and 116/81 *Rezguia Adoui v Belgium and City of Liège; Dominique Cornuaille v Belgium* [1982] ECR 1665 where the Court made no distinction between Arts 39(3) and 46 (ex 48(3) and 56) EC.

[25] Case C-158/96 *Raymond Kohll v Union des Caisses de Maladie* [1998] ECR I-1931.

[26] ibid, paras 43–49.   [27] Case C-114/97 *Commission v Spain* [1998] ECR I-6717 para 42.

[28] Art 39 (ex 48) EC does not contain this limitation either.

[29] See H.D. Jarass, 'Elemente einer Dogmatik der Grundfreiheiten' (1995) 30 EuR 202, 222.

[30] Case C-415/93 *Union Royale Belge des Sociétés de Football Association ASBL and others v Jean-Marc Bosman* [1995] ECR I-4921.

Articles 30 and 46 provide exceptions to 'fundamental freedoms'. As exceptions, they are interpreted narrowly, and the list of the grounds of justification is exhaustive.[31] The burden of proof lies with the party invoking the exceptions.[32]

Purely economic justifications have not been accepted in either field.[33] Economic difficulties brought about by increased competition cannot serve to justify national measures. Otherwise the whole purpose of the free movement provisions could be frustrated by Member States. Competition leading to economic efficiencies always has losers as well as winners. Economically speaking, the losers represent resources freed for other activities. If Member States were allowed to protect these losers by imposing restrictions, free trade could be stopped the moment its impact was felt.[34]

However, the Court has sometimes accepted justifications which do have an economic aspect. In the field of goods in *Campus Oil*[35] it held that Irish rules demanding petrol importers to purchase a proportion of their requirements from a state-owned refinery at a price fixed by the relevant minister were justified by public security. The measure aimed to protect the refinery and, therefore, certainly was economic in nature. However, the survival of the only refinery in Ireland was deemed to be essential for ensuring the continuous supply of petroleum. Thus, the economic aim was not an end in itself, but only the means to achieve a legitimate public security objective.[36]

The same approach has been adopted in the field of services. In *Kohll*[37] the Court examined the Luxembourg rules relating to medical services obtained

---

[31] On goods, see eg Case 46/76 *Bauhuis v Netherlands* [1977] ECR 5, Case 113/80 *Commission v Ireland* [1981] ECR 1625, and Kapteyn and VerLoren van Themaat (n 20 above) 653. On services, see eg Case 352/85 *Bond van Adverteerders v Netherlands* [1988] ECR 2085, Case C-360/89 *Commission v Italy* [1992] ECR I-3401, Handoll (n 23 above) 225, and Kapteyn and VerLoren van Themaat (n 20 above) 757.

[32] On goods, see eg Case 251/78 *Firma Denkavit Futtermittel GmbH v Minister für Ernährung, Landwirtschaft und Forsten des Landes Nordrhein-Westfalen* [1979] ECR 3369 para 24, and Kapteyn and VerLoren van Themaat (n 20 above) 657. Cf however Case C-55/99 *Commission v France*, judgment of 14 December 2000. On services, see Case C-158/96 *Raymond Kohll v Union des Caisses de Maladie* [1998] ECR I-1931 para 52.

[33] On goods, see eg Case 7/61 *Commission v Italy* [1961] ECR 317, Case 238/82 *Duphar and others v Netherlands* [1984] ECR 523, and Kapteyn and VerLoren van Themaat (n 20 above) 654–655. On services, see eg Case 352/85 *Bond van Adverteerders v Netherlands* [1988] ECR 2085, Art 2(2) of Council Directive 64/221/EEC of 25 February 1964 on the co-ordination of special measures concerning the movement and residence of foreign nationals which are justified on grounds of public policy, public security or public health [1964] OJ Spec Ed 850/64, 117, and Kapteyn and VerLoren van Themaat (n 20 above) 757.

[34] It could perhaps be argued that the Community is entitled to resort to economic justifications. See Case C-233/94 *Federal Republic of Germany v European Parliament and Council of the European Union* [1997] ECR I-2405. In the Community political process both winners and losers are represented. It might be useful to have an option to mitigate the short-term costs of increased competition, such as unemployment, as in the real world freed resources do not flow costlessly to other uses.

[35] Case 72/83 *Campus Oil v Minister for Industry and Energy* [1984] ECR 2727.

[36] See also Case C-324/93 *R v Secretaty of State for the Home Department, ex parte Evans Medical Ltd and Macfarlan Smith Ltd* [1995] ECR I-563 paras 34–39 and paras 65–70 of the Opinion of AG Lenz.

[37] See n 32 above.

abroad also in the light of the objective of maintaining a balanced medical and hospital service open to all. It held that this aim may fall within the public health derogation despite being intrinsically linked to the method of financing the social security system. As Advocate General Tesauro argued in his Opinion, domestic hospital wards would be under-utilised but would have full staff and equipment overheads if a large number of insured persons used hospital facilities of other Member States.[38] In the case at hand, the rules were not necessary to achieve the public health objective, however. Again the Court showed its willingness to accept economic protection (of local health facilities) if it was essential for the achievement of a legitimate (public health) aim. The approach was the same as in the goods sector.

The approach of the Court to economic aims in *Campus Oil* and *Kohll* could be criticised from a doctrinal point of view. When it comes to the necessity of the measures, it seems that there is often an alternative means available to the state that is less restrictive of trade but more expensive. In theory, the refinery could have been financed from the public purse, and hospital infrastructure can certainly be maintained by pouring sufficient amounts of money into the system.[39] The Court has not been overly dogmatic, rather, its approach has been a pragmatic and mostly balanced response to the competing interests.

b) Grounds of justification

The clearest difference between Articles 30 (ex 36) EC and 46 (ex 56) EC is that the former provides for many more grounds of justification than the latter. On the one hand, this might indicate that the fundamental objective of the two provisions is not the same. The derogations to the free movement of services seem to be more directly connected to the exercise of state sovereignty, as they touch upon core areas of state competence, while the exceptions to the free movement of goods cover a much wider area and are connected to the regulation of commercial relations.[40] On the other hand, the differences may not have been deliberate. In general, it is easier to imagine situations where the interests mentioned in Article 30, but not in 46, are relevant in the goods sector than in the services sector.[41] Be that as it may, in practice the differences have been of limited significance.

---

[38] ibid, para 59 of AG Tesauro's Opinion. [39] Subject to state aid rules.

[40] See V. Hatzopoulos, 'Exigences essentielles, impératives ou impérieuses: *une* théorie, *des* théories ou pas de théorie du tout?' (1998) 34 RTDE 191, 218.

[41] AG Warner stated in his Opinion in Case 62/79 *SA Compagnie Générale pour la Diffusion de la Télévision, Coditel, and others v SA Ciné Vog Films and others* [1980] ECR 881 at 878 that 'the omission from Articles 59 to 66 [now 49 to 55] of the Treaty of any provision for the protection of industrial and commercial property is much more likely to have been due to an oversight than to deliberate intention'.

i) Public policy and public security

In general, these heads of derogation have been characterised in both fields by a limited number of cases where they have been invoked and an even smaller number of successful attempts at justification. It has been generally accepted that the Court has in the main dealt with these exceptions in the same manner.[42]

One difference can be found, however. In the field of services, according to Article 3(1) of Directive 64/221/EEC,[43] '[m]easures taken on grounds of public policy or of public security shall be based exclusively on the personal conduct of the individual concerned'.[44] In contrast, in the field of goods the conduct of persons having no connection to the products themselves can serve as a justification. In *Cullet v Centre Leclerc*[45] the Court was faced with French rules setting minimum prices for fuel. The French government argued that the rules were justified on grounds of public order and security. It was claimed that if the French retailers were affected by competition from low-price fuel sales, they would react violently, endangering the social order. The Court did not accept the argument but stated that 'the French government has not shown that it would be unable, using the means at its disposal, to deal with the consequences . . . upon public order and security'.[46] This indicates that in certain, very extreme, circumstances social unrest could serve as a justification to measures restricting the free movement of goods, even though it is not the product itself that endangers public policy but the reaction of third parties. The Court came to the same conclusion in *Commission v France*[47] but added that although serious disruption to public order may in certain circumstances justify non-intervention by the police, it may not justify a general pattern of passivity.

It is difficult to find any good reasons for this difference. It does not seem to make sense that riots against the import of foreign vegetables can serve to justify a restriction but riots against the use of foreign service providers cannot. In fact, doctrinally the approach adopted by Advocate General VerLoren van Themaat in *Cullet v Centre Leclerc* is preferable to the approach of the Court.[48] The Advocate General rejected totally the

---

[42] See generally Burrows (n 23 above) 209, Kapteyn and VerLoren van Themaat (n 20 above) 660, P. Oliver, *Free Movement of Goods in the European Community* (3rd edn London 1996) 191, and T. Tridimas, *The General Principles of EC Law* (Oxford 1999) 134. In relation to public policy see L. Gormley, *Prohibiting Restrictions on Trade within the EEC* (Amsterdam 1985) 128–129 and 132–133 but cf D. Chalmers and E. Szyszczak, *European Union Law. Vol II. Towards a European Polity?* (Aldershot 1998) 343 who state that the term has been interpreted far more narrowly in the field of goods than in the field of workers.

[43] See n 33 above.

[44] See also Case 41/74 *Van Duyn v Home Office* [1974] ECR 1337 para 17, and Case C-348/96 *Donatella Calfa* [1999] ECR I-11 para 24. The Directive applies only to natural persons, not to companies.

[45] Case 231/83 *Henri Cullet v Centre Leclerc* [1985] ECR 305.   [46] ibid para 33.

[47] Case C-265/95 *Commission v French Republic* [1997] ECR I-6959 paras 56–58.

[48] Similarly M.A. Jarvis, 'Case C-265/95 *Commission v French Republic*, Judgment of the Court of Justice of 9 December 1997, [1997] ECR I-6959' (1998) 35 CMLRev 1371, 1381. See also Weatherill and Beaumont (n 20 above) 532–534.

possibility of civil disturbances justifying infringement of the free movement of goods. He expressed concern that this might have drastic consequences as it would enable private interest groups to determine the scope of the freedom.[49] These groups would actually be encouraged to take violent action, as this would enable their government to impose restrictions on imports. In any event, Article 297 (ex 224) EC dealing with serious internal disturbances, war, or threat of war applies equally to both freedoms.

ii) Public health

The recent judgments in *Decker*[50] and *Kohll*[51] illustrate well the essentially similar approach of the Court to this ground of justification in relation to both goods and services.[52] Both cases concerned Luxembourg law providing that medically insured persons could only be treated abroad if the competent social security institution had given prior authorisation. Mr Decker had purchased spectacles from Belgium but was not reimbursed because of the lack of prior authorisation. Mr Kohll had applied for such authorisation for his daughter to receive treatment from an orthodontist in Germany, but the request was rejected.

In both cases the Court found a restriction on free movement, and the governments involved attempted to justify the rules on grounds of public health and the related overriding requirement of the risk of seriously undermining the financial balance of the social security system.[53] In both cases the Court rejected the public health argument based on the need to ensure the quality of products and treatment. The Court referred to the harmonisation of the taking up and pursuing of the regulated professions which, according to the Court, affords equivalent guarantees of quality.

In *Kohll* the Court dealt with an additional public health argument based on the need to maintain a balanced medical and hospital service open to all in the national territory, holding that the necessity of the rules had not been shown. This argument was not discussed in *Decker*. The Opinion of Advocate

[49] See n 45 above at 312. See also the Opinion of AG Léger in Case C-1/96 *R v Ministry of Agriculture, Fisheries and Foods, ex parte Compassion in World Farming* [1998] ECR I-1251 para 111.

[50] Case C-120/95 *Nicolas Decker v Caisse de Maladie des Employés Privés* [1998] ECR I-1831.

[51] Case C-158/96 *Raymond Kohll v Union des Caisses de Maladie* [1998] ECR I-1931.

[52] See also Case C-405/98 *Konsumentombudsmannen v Gourmet International Products Aktiebolag*, judgment of 8 March 2001, paras 26, 33 and 40–41, and the Opinion of AG Jacobs, para 80. The importance of public health has been clearly recognised in the case law, recently eg by the Court of First Instance in Joined Cases T-125/96 and T-152/96 *Boehringer Ingelheim Vetmedica GmbH v Council*, judgment of 1 December 1999.

[53] This was treated as an overriding reason in the general interest, but it has been argued by R. Giesen, 'Case C-120/95 *Nicolas Decker v Caisse de Maladie des Employés Privés*, Judgment of 28 April, [1998] ECR I-1831; Case C-158/96 *Raymond Kohll v Union des Caisses de Maladie*, Judgment of 28 April 1998, [1998] ECR I-1931' (1999) 36 CMLRev 841 at 846 that it could have been subsumed under health protection.

General Tesauro explains this difference. He demonstrated that this argument may only be valid in the hospital sector,[54] which certainly was not endangered on the facts of Decker, that is by the purchase of spectacles from abroad.

Finally, the Court dealt with the overriding requirement of financial balance of the social security system. In both cases it noted that this interest was not at risk, as the spectacles and dental treatment were reimbursed in accordance with the Luxembourg tariff.

The similar structure and reasoning of the judgments clearly demonstrates the unified approach of the Court in this context. Indeed, Advocate General Tesauro gave a single Opinion covering both cases, so closely parallel were the issues.

iii) Other grounds of justification

At first sight a comparison between Articles 30 and 46 (ex 36 and 56) EC would seem to indicate that Member States have more room to interfere in the field of goods than in the field of services. The former provision lists many more grounds of derogation than the latter, and these heads can justify even overtly discriminatory national measures as long as they do not discriminate arbitrarily.

The development of the doctrine of overriding requirements in general interest by the Court[55] has narrowed this discrepancy. The Court has found that, for example, the protection of intellectual property rights[56] and the conservation of the national historical and archaeological heritage[57] can also serve to exempt indistinctly applicable restrictions on the free movement of services.

The Court has interpreted these exceptions to the free movement of services in the same way as Article 30 (ex 36) EC. In *Coditel*[58] the Court was dealing with the freedom to provide services and the copyright to the film 'Le Boucher'. The copyright-holder had assigned the exclusive right to distribute the film in Belgium to Ciné Vog, while granting the right to exploit the film in Germany to another company. The film was then broadcast on German television. The broadcast was picked up by a Belgian cable television company, which relayed it to its subscribers in Belgium. Ciné Vog brought an action for

---

[54] See para 59–60 of AG Tesauro's Opinion and Case C-157/99 *Geraets-Smits v Stichting Ziekenfonds VGZ and Peerbooms v Stichting CZ Groep Zorgverzekeringen*, judgment of 12 July 2001, para 76. See also P. Cabral, 'Cross-border Medical Care in the European Union—Bringing Down the First Wall' (1999) 24 ELRev 387 at 394–395, and A.P. van der Mei, 'Cross-Border Access to Medical Care within the European Union—Some Reflections on the Judgments in *Decker* and *Kohll*' (1998) 5 MJ 277 at 295–296, but cf Giesen (n 53 above) 849.

[55] See section 3 below.

[56] See eg Case 62/79 *SA Compagnie Générale pour la Diffusion de la Télévision, Coditel, and others v SA Ciné Vog Films and others* [1980] ECR 881.

[57] Case C-180/89 *Commission v Italy* [1991] ECR I-709.   [58] See n 56 above.

infringement of its intellectual property rights. The Court examined, using the same language as in Article 30 cases, what the essential function of copyright was and whether the application of national intellectual property legislation constituted a means of arbitrary discrimination or a disguised restriction on trade. It concluded that Ciné Vog could rely on its right, as performance rights were not exhausted in the same manner as the right to the reproduction of a work through manufacture and sale.[59]

Later cases dealing with performance rights and the free movement of goods confirmed that not only the language but also the results were the same in both fields. *Ministère public v Tournier*[60] concerned criminal proceedings against Mr Tournier, who was the director of the French copyright management society. It was claimed that the society demanded undue payments from discos playing imported music. The Court held that the EC Treaty precluded the charging of a levy on the marketing of goods put into free circulation in another Member State with the consent of the copyright owner. However, the Court then referred to *Coditel* and ruled that royalty payments could be charged for public performances, as the copyright owner had a legitimate interest in calculating his fees based on the number of performances.[61] The Court applied the same principle to video-cassette lending rights in *Warner Brothers v Christiansen*,[62] again referring to *Coditel* and coming to the same result in a case concerning the free movement of goods.

It is true that the overriding reasons in general interest cannot exempt distinctly applicable national measures, unlike Article 30.[63] The significance of this difference should not be exaggerated, however. The Court does not often accept overtly discriminatory measures purporting to protect one of the interests mentioned in Article 30.[64]

In addition, the Court has been studiously vague on the exact definition of distinctly applicable measures[65] and has proved to be very creative in finding legitimate national rules indistinctly applicable if that is the only way to save them. In *Commission v Belgium* (Wallonian waste)[66] the Court was faced with a decree of the regional government of Wallonia which prohibited the storage, tipping or dumping of waste not originating from Wallonia. The measure was defended on grounds of environmental protection, as it was designed to stop the inflow of waste into Wallonia. The Commission argued that environmental protection could not serve to justify the decree as it discriminated

---

[59] See on exhaustion of rights Case 78/70 *Deutsche Grammophon GmbH v Metro-SB Grossmärkte GmbH & Co KG* [1971] ECR 487, and P. Watson, 'Freedom of Establishment and Freedom to Provide Services: Some Recent Developments' (1983) 20 CMLRev 767, 805–807.

[60] Case 395/87 *Ministère public v Jean-Louis Tournier* [1989] ECR 2521.

[61] ibid, paras 11–15.

[62] Case 158/86 *Warner Brothers Inc. and Metronome Video ApS v Erik Viuff Christiansen* [1988] ECR 2605. Recent case law has confirmed this. See N. Travers, 'Rental Rights and the Specific Subject-matter of Copyright in Community Law' (1999) ELRev 171 at 171–177.

[63] See section 3b below.

[64] See eg Case 152/78 *Commission v France* [1980] ECR 2299 para 18.

[65] See section 3b below.   [66] Case C-2/90 *Commission v Belgium* [1992] ECR I-4431.

against waste originating in other Member States. The Court accepted that environmental protection could only save indistinctly applicable measures. However, it then referred to the 'particular nature' of waste and to the principle that environmental damage should be remedied at source, and held that 'having regard to the differences between waste produced in different places and to the connection of the waste with its place of production, the contested measure cannot be regarded as discriminatory'. It was, therefore, not contrary to the free movement of goods.[67] The crucial point here is that the Court held that the decree was indistinctly applicable. It did so even though the decree expressly differentiated between waste originating in Wallonia and waste coming from other Member States. The Court was clearly prepared to engage in rather creative reasoning[68] to save national measures which it saw as legitimate.

The same creativity can be seen in *PreussenElektra*.[69] The case concerned German legislation requiring electricity supply undertakings to purchase a proportion of their electricity from domestic renewable sources. The measure discriminated openly against electricity coming from other Member States, and its main aim was clearly the protection of the environment, a ground of justification not found in Article 30. The Court, however, stated that the rule was also designed to protect the health and life of humans, animals and plants and was thus able to save the measure.[70] Yet the reduction in greenhouse gases, which the German law sought to achieve, is only remotely and in the long term connected to health objectives, and such a wide concept of health seems capable of covering almost any environmental measures. The Court clearly did not wish to find the measure incompatible with Community law and therefore stretched the concept of health.

Finally, the concept of public policy could easily be extended to cover a great variety of situations. In general, the Court has adopted a strict interpretation of this heading. The Court has held that it may only 'be relied upon in the event of a genuine and sufficiently serious threat to the requirements of public policy affecting one of the fundamental interests of society'.[71] However, if the Court was faced with a clearly legitimate but overtly discriminatory national measure restricting the free movement of services, it might well be tempted to try to fit it into this framework.

To sum up: the differing grounds of derogation in the EC Treaty provisions constitute a clear difference in the field of goods and services. In practice, the significance of this difference is limited and there are very few national measures

---

[67] Case C-2/90 *Commission v Belgium* [1992] ECR I-4431, paras 28–37.

[68] The reasoning was not shared by AG Jacobs and has been strongly criticised eg in D. Geradin, 'The Belgian Waste Case' (1993) 18 ELRev 144 at 148.

[69] Case C-379/98 *PreussenElektra AG v Schleswag AG*, judgment of 13 March 2001.

[70] ibid, para 75. AG Jacobs analysed the environmental justification but did not even mention the possibility of the health ground applying.

[71] See Case C-348/96 *Donatella Calfa* [1999] ECR I-11 para 21, and Case C-114/97 *Commission v Spain* [1998] ECR I-6717 para 46.

that could conceivably be justified in the field of goods under Article 30 (ex 36) EC but not in the field of services.

c) Arbitrary discrimination and disguised restrictions

Article 46 (ex 56) EC does not contain a statement equivalent to the second sentence of Article 30 (ex 36) EC which prohibits measures constituting 'a means of arbitrary discrimination or a disguised restriction on trade between Member States'. It may be asked whether this means that the Member States are more free to act in the field of services?

The second sentence of Article 30 is of doubtful significance. Many see it only as an expression of the principle of proportionality,[72] which certainly applies to Article 46 (ex 56) EC as well. Others give it some independent weight as a 'notwithstanding provision' or an 'emergency break',[73] but even then it seems that there will be few, if any, measures that pass the proportionality test but still constitute arbitrary discrimination or a disguised restriction on trade.[74]

Be that as it may, the Court has in any case applied the test also to services. In *Coditel*[75] it examined whether the application of national copyright legislation constituted arbitrary discrimination or disguised restriction on trade in services.

Thus, the second sentence of Article 30 does not create any significant differences between the free movement of goods and services. It may lack independent value and may in any event also be applied in the services sector. This reflects the general trend. Even though the wording of Article 30 looks at first sight very different from the wording of Article 46, the Court has in actual practice interpreted the provisions in a similar manner. There will not be many national measures that can be justified in one field but not in the other.

3. Judicially created exceptions

a) Origin

In addition to the derogations expressly mentioned in the EC Treaty, the Court has in its case law developed exceptions with no obvious basis either in

[72] See eg Weatherill and Beaumont (n 20 above) 527, and M.A. Jarvis, *The Application of EC Law by National Courts. The Free Movement of Goods* (Oxford 1998) 232.

[73] See eg Gormley (n 42 above) 210–211, Kapteyn and VerLoren van Themaat (n 20 above) 673, and N. Emiliou, *The Principle of Proportionality in European Law. A Comparative Study* (London 1996) 258–260.

[74] See P.-C. Müller-Graff in H. von der Groeben, J. Thiesing and C.-D. Ehlermann (eds), *Kommentar zum EU-/EG-Vertrag* (5th revised edn Baden-Baden 1997) 839–840.

[75] Case 62/79 *SA Compagnie Générale pour la Diffusion de la Télévision, Coditel, and others v SA Ciné Vog Films and others* [1980] ECR 881 para 15.

the text of the EC Treaty or in Community legislation.[76] This process has taken place both in the goods and services sectors.

The development began in 1974. In *Dassonville*[77] the Court both gave a wide formulation to the scope of Article 28 (ex 30) EC and hinted at an exception for 'reasonable' rules. The facts of the case took place before the British accession. In issue was a Belgian prohibition of the import of Scotch whisky without a certificate of origin from the British customs authorities, even though it was in free circulation in France. The aim of the rules was to guarantee that products bearing a designation of origin, such as 'Scotch', in fact were of that origin. The Court began by defining measures having an effect equivalent to quantitative restriction as '[a]ll trading rules enacted by Member States which are capable of hindering, directly or indirectly, actually or potentially, intra-Community trade'.[78] However, it stated in the next paragraph:

In the absence of Community system guaranteeing for consumers the authenticity of a product's designation of origin, if a Member State takes measures to prevent unfair practices in this connexion, it is however subject to the condition that these measures should be *reasonable*.[79]

It continued by stating that the measures must not in any event constitute arbitrary discrimination or a disguised restriction on trade, and came to the conclusion that this was in fact the case, as only direct importers would be able to satisfy the requirement. Therefore, the measure was prohibited by the EC Treaty.[80] The Court had left a door open for national measures fulfilling the criterion of reasonableness.

A few months later, the Court adopted a similar judge-made exception in the field of services. *Van Binsbergen*[81] concerned a Dutch rule preventing a lawyer whose habitual residence was in Belgium from acting as a legal representative. The Court held that Articles 49 and 50 (ex 59 and 60) EC caught not only discrimination on grounds of nationality but also discrimination on grounds of establishment in another Member State.[82] However, it then stated that:

taking into account the particular nature of the services to be provided, specific requirements imposed on the person providing the service cannot be considered

---

[76] Commission Directive 70/50/EEC of 22 December 1970 based on the provisions of Art 33(7) (repealed), on the abolition of measures which have an effect equivalent to quantitative restrictions on imports and are not covered by other provisions adopted in pursuance of the EEC Treaty [1970] OJ Spec Ed I L13/29, 17, did contain some seeds for development. See A. Arnull, *The European Union and its Court of Justice* (Oxford 1999) 229–230. The case law has later heavily influenced Community legislation. See eg Commission White Paper, *Completing the Internal Market*, 14 June 1985 (COM (85) 310 final) paras 77 and 102.

[77] Case 8/74 *Procureur du Roi v Dassonville* [1974] ECR 837.   [78] ibid, para 5.
[79] ibid, para 6 (emphasis added).   [80] ibid, paras 7–9.
[81] Case 33/74 *Van Binsbergen v Bestuur van de Bedrijfsvereniging voor de Metaalnijverheid* [1974] ECR 1299.
[82] ibid, paras 10 and 25.

incompatible with the Treaty where they have as their purpose the application of *professional rules justified by the general good*—in particular rules relating to organization, qualifications, professional ethics, supervision, and liability—which are binding upon any person established in the State. . .

. . . the requirement that persons whose functions are to assist the administration of justice must be permanently established for professional purposes within the jurisdiction of certain courts or tribunals cannot be considered incompatible . . . where such requirement is *objectively justified* by the need to ensure observance of professional rules of conduct.[83]

It concluded that this was not the case here, as the exercise of the professional activity was unrestricted within the territory of the Netherlands, and the administration of justice could be ensured by less restrictive means. Therefore, the national law was not in accordance with the provisions on the freedom to provide services.[84] Again, the Court held out the possibility that certain national rules falling within the scope of a free movement provision could be justified on grounds that were not explicitly expressed in the EC Treaty.

The language the Court used in *Dassonville* was very different from that used in *Van Binsbergen*. Nevertheless, the function of the statements was the same: to ensure that legitimate national measures could be saved even if Articles 30 and 46 were unavailable.

The next important development took place in 1979. In *Van Wesemael*[85] the Court refined and slightly developed the justifications in the field of services. In relation to the service of placing entertainers in employment, it stated that specific requirements imposed on the service provider were not incompatible with the EC Treaty 'where they have as their purpose the application of professional rules, justified by the general good or by the need to ensure the protection of the entertainer', as long as they were applied to all persons established in the state and did not duplicate the home state requirements.[86] On the one hand, the Court extended the scope of justifications by referring to the protection of the entertainer. On the other hand, it imposed a condition of non-duplication and narrowed the exception.[87]

A month later the Court gave its most important judgment on the issue of justification. *Cassis de Dijon*[88] concerned German rules prohibiting the sale of liqueur having an alcohol content below a certain level. This measure was applied to French cassis liqueur, and was challenged by an importer. The Court held that in the absence of common rules it was for Member States to regulate the production and marketing of alcohol on their own territory. However, it then stated:

---

[83] ibid, paras 12 and 14 (emphasis added).   [84] ibid, paras 15–17.

[85] Joined Cases 110 and 111/78 *Ministère Public and Chambre Syndicale des Agents Artistiques et Impresarii de Belgique, ASBL v Willy van Wesemael and others* [1979] ECR 35.

[86] ibid, para 28.

[87] See Burrows (n 23 above) 234. The condition of non-duplication will be discussed in section 4bii below.

[88] Case 120/78 *Rewe Zentrale AG v Bundesmonopolverwaltung für Branntwein* [1979] ECR 649.

Obstacles to movement within the Community resulting from disparities between the national laws relating to the marketing of the products in question must be accepted in so far as those provisions may be recognized as being *necessary in order to satisfy mandatory requirements* relating in particular to the effectiveness of fiscal supervision, the protection of public health, the fairness of commercial transactions and the defence of the consumer.[89]

The Court continued by examining the public health and consumer protection justifications advanced by Germany, finding them inadequate. It therefore concluded that the German rules were not in accordance with Article 28 (ex 30) EC.

In its judgment in *Cassis* the Court confirmed that Article 28 extended beyond a narrow concept of discrimination and caught restrictions created by disparities between national rules. However, it also confirmed that justified national measures would not contravene the provisions on the free movement of goods even if they did not fall under any of the grounds listed in Article 30 (ex 36) EC.

The free movement of services reached a full parity with goods in this respect only in 1991. In a series of cases the Court found that disparities between national rules could amount to a restriction on the free movement of services but might be justified on grounds of imperative requirements in the public interest. For example, in *Gouda*[90] the Court was faced with Dutch rules concerning advertising in cable television. In the case of advertising specifically intended for the Dutch public, the advertisements had to be produced by a separate legal person, they had to be clearly identifiable as advertisements, separated from other parts of the programmes, not broadcast on Sundays, and their duration could not exceed 5 per cent of the total air time. In addition, the broadcasting body could not be used to enable a third party to make a profit, and the entire revenue had to be used for the production of programmes. The Court held that these conditions were a restriction on the freedom to provide services. However, it then stated that:

restrictions come within the scope of Article 59 [now 49] if the application of the national legislation to foreign persons providing services is not justified by overriding reasons relating to the public interest.[91]

It continued by listing some overriding reasons[92] and went on to analyse the conditions imposed by the Dutch law, coming to the conclusion that the measures could not be justified.[93]

[89] Case 120/78 *Rewe Zentrale AG v Bundesmonopolverwaltung für Branntwein* [1979] ECR 649, para 13 (emphasis added). The requirement of non-duplication was inherent in the term 'necessary'. See section 4bii below.
[90] Case C-288/89 *Collectieve Antennevoorziening Gouda* [1991] ECR I-4007. See also Case C-76/90 *Manfred Säger v Dennemeyer & Co. Ltd* [1991] ECR I-4221, and Case C-353/89 *Commission v Netherlands* [1991] ECR I-4069.
[91] See n 90 above, para 13.   [92] ibid, para 14.   [93] ibid, paras 19–30.

With these judgments the Court achieved full parity with the *Cassis de Dijon* line of case law. Differences between national rules could amount to a restriction but would be saved if justified.

Parity has recently been achieved also at the level of language. In its earlier jurisprudence the Court used different terminology for exceptions in different fields. In the goods sector it referred mainly to 'mandatory requirements', while in relation to services it used terms such as 'overriding reasons relating to the public interest'. In its more recent case law the Court has started to use similar terminology in both fields. In *Gebhard*[94] it referred to 'imperative requirements in the general interest' in relation to all four freedoms, while in *De Agostini*[95] the Court spoke of 'overriding requirements of general public importance' in relation to both Articles 28 and 49 (ex 30 and 59) EC.

It is interesting to note that the widening of the scope of the free movement rules has gone hand in hand with the development of justifications. In fact, justifications only become necessary when a Member State is deprived of the possibility of applying all of its legislation to foreign goods or services. As long as a Member State's legislation can be applied in its entirety, the public interest can be protected. Therefore, if Articles 28 and 49 contained only a national treatment requirement, the whole doctrine would be superfluous.[96] The development can be seen as a compromise: the wider the scope of the freedom, the better developed the doctrine of justification needs to be.[97]

In theory, it might have been argued that the Community legislative process could have stepped in and removed the legislative disparities filling the regulatory gaps created by the application of the widely defined free movement rules. In practice, the Community legislative process, especially in the 1970s and early 1980s, was not capable of taking on this task.[98]

The developments also reflect the changing societal attitudes and values. The narrow list of acceptable grounds of justification devised in the 1950s was not capable of answering the rapidly changing societal concerns. The protection of the environment and consumers are nowadays considered to be at least as worthy goals as the safeguarding of public morality.[99]

---

[94] Case C-55/94 *Reinhard Gebhard v Consiglio dell'Ordine degli Avvocati e Procuratori di Milano* [1995] ECR I-4165 para 37.

[95] Joined Cases C-34/95, 35/95 and 36/95 *Konsumentombudsmannen v De Agostini (Svenska) Förlag AB and TV-Shop i Sverige AB* [1997] ECR I-3843 paras 45 and 52. See also Case C-120/95 *Nicolas Decker v Caisse de Maladie des Employés Privés* [1998] ECR I-1831 para 39.

[96] See Burrows (n 23 above) 233, and Hatzopoulos (n 40 above) 230–231.

[97] See Kapteyn and VerLoren van Themaat (n 20 above) 675, and Weatherill and Beaumont (n 20 above) 578–580.

[98] See K.A. Armstrong, 'Regulating the Free Movement of Goods: Institutions and Institutional Change' in J. Shaw and G. More (eds), *New Legal Dynamics of European Union* (Oxford 1995) 175–176.

[99] See generally the Opinion of AG Jacobs in Case C-379/98 *PreussenElektra AG v Schleswag AG*, judgment of 13 March 2001, para 232, Chalmers and Szyszczak (n 42 above) 314, and J.H.H. Weiler, 'The Constitution of the Common Market Place: Text and Context in the Evolution of the Free Movement of Goods' in P. Craig and G. de Búrca (eds), *The Evolution of EU Law* (Oxford 1999) 374.

b) Application

In some respects the application of the judge-made justifications is governed by the same principles as the use of Articles 30 and 46 (ex 36 and 56) EC. If the field is fully occupied by Community measures, Member States are not able to rely on overriding requirements.[100] The burden of proof rests with the party that invokes the exception.[101] Purely economic reasons do not constitute overriding requirements.[102]

The most significant difference between the exceptions found in Articles 30 and 46 and the overriding requirements lies in their scope of application.[103] The judge-made exceptions may only justify equally applicable measures, while the grounds of derogation listed in the EC Treaty can also save distinctly applicable rules.[104]

The distinction between distinctly and equally applicable rules is not a clear one. The Court has sometimes held that even measures that do not discriminate in law but only in fact are distinctly applicable, while more recently it seems to have (mostly) adopted a view that a discriminatory effect is not sufficient to render a measure distinctly applicable.

In the field of goods, the discriminatory impact of a national measure has caused overriding requirements to become unavailable for example in *Commission v United Kingdom* (Origin marking).[105] The case was concerned

---

[100] In relation to goods, see eg Case 8/74 *Procureur du Roi v Dassonville* [1974] ECR 837, and Case C-39/90 *Denkavit Futtermittel GmbH v Land Baden-Württemberg* [1991] ECR I-3069. In relation to services, see eg Case 205/84 *Commission v Germany* [1986] ECR 3755, and Case C-353/89 *Commission v Netherlands* [1991] ECR I-4069.

[101] In the field of goods see A. Dashwood, 'The *Cassis de Dijon* Line of Authority' in St. J. Bates, W. Finnie, J.A. Usher and H. Wildberg (eds), *In Memoriam J.D.B. Mitchell* (London 1983) 149, and Kapteyn and VerLoren van Themaat (n 20 above) 657. In the field of services see P. Troberg in H. von der Groeben, J. Thiesing and C.-D. Ehlermann (eds), *Kommentar zum EU-EG-Vertag* (5th revised edn Baden-Baden 1997) 1463, and M. Tison, 'What is "General Good" in EU Services Law?' (1997) 24 LIEI 1 at 15–16.

[102] In the goods sector, see Case 216/84 *Commission v France* [1988] ECR 793 para 12 and Case C-220/98 *Estée Lauder Cosmetics GmbH & Co. OHG v Lancaster Group GmbH*, judgment of 13 January 2000, para 33. In the services sector, see Case C-398/95 *Syndesmos ton en Elladi Touristikon kai Taxidiotikon Grafeion v Ypourgos Ergasias* [1997] ECR I-3091 para 23. However, in eg Case C-204/90 *Hans-Martin Bachmann v Belgian State* [1992] ECR I-249, Case C-120/95 *Nicolas Decker v Caisse de Maladie des Employés Privés* [1998] ECR I-1831 and Case C-158/96 *Raymond Kohll v Union des Caisses de Maladie* [1998] ECR I-1931 the Court has shown its willingness to accept justifications even if they do contain an economic aspect. See comments in section 2a above and also the Opinion of AG Tesauro in *Decker* and *Kohll* above, para 53.

[103] This partly explains why the Court did not simply extend the concept of public policy found in both Arts 30 and 46 (ex 36 and 56) EC. See P. Craig and G. de Búrca, *EU Law. Text, Cases and Materials* (2nd edn Oxford 1998) 629–630, and Weatherill and Beaumont (n 20 above) 578.

[104] In the field of goods, see eg Case 113/80 *Commission v Ireland* [1981] ECR 1625. In the field of services, see eg Case 352/85 *Bond van Adverteerders v Netherlands* [1988] ECR 2085, and Case C-288/89 *Collectieve Antennevoorziening Gouda* [1991] ECR I-4007. If the measure is intentionally discriminatory in the sense that its aim is protectionst, it can never be saved, as it pursues neither an objective mentioned in the EC Treaty derogation clauses nor an overriding requirement in the general interest.

[105] Case 207/83 *Commission v United Kingdom* [1985] ECR 1202.

with British rules requiring that certain goods be marked with an indication of origin. As the measure applied both to British and foreign goods, it was argued that it could be saved by the imperative requirement of consumer protection. The Court rejected this argument. It held that the measure 'was applicable without distinction to domestic and imported products only in form'.[106] It continued by stating that the rules were intended to enable the consumers to favour national products, and that the measure was unnecessary, as it was in the manufacturers' interest to indicate voluntarily the origin of goods if the consumers associated it with high quality.[107] Based on this and other judgments, such as *Kohl v Ringelhan & Rennett*,[108] many authors have concluded that a discriminatory effect suffices to render a national measure distinctly applicable.[109]

In the field of services the Court has sometimes stated that national rules having discriminatory effects can only be justified on grounds found in Article 46 (ex 56) EC.[110] It has also deemed national measures to be distinctly applicable if they discriminate on grounds of establishment. Yet, these measures do not necessarily discriminate on grounds of nationality, as they treat foreigners and nationals established abroad alike. An example of this approach is *Svensson and Gustavsson*[111] where the Court stated that 'discrimination based on the place of establishment . . . can only be justified on general interest grounds referred to in Article 56(1) [now 46(1)] of the Treaty, to which Article 66 [now 55] refers'.[112] Statements to the same effect can be found in other judgments as well.[113] Many authors have concluded that discriminatory effect is sufficient to make a measure distinctly applicable also in the field of services.[114]

However, in many instances a clear discriminatory effect has not been enough to render a measure distinctly applicable.[115] Even the very cases where the doctrine of overriding requirements has been developed can be seen in the light of discrimination. A disparity between national rules creates

---

[106] ibid, para 20.   [107] ibid, paras 20–21.

[108] Case 177/83 *Theodor Kohl KG v Ringelhan & Rennett SA and Ringelhan Einrichtungs GmbH* [1984] ECR 3651.

[109] See eg Weatherill and Beaumont (n 20 above) 577.

[110] Case C-260/89 *Elliniki Radiophonia Tileorassi AE v Dimiotiki Etairia Pliroforissis and Sotirios Kouvelas* [1991] ECR I-2925 para 24.

[111] Case C-484/93 *Svensson, Gustavsson v Ministre du logement et de l'urbanisme* [1995] ECR I-3955.

[112] ibid, para 15.

[113] See eg Case 352/85 *Bond van Adverteerders v Netherlands* [1988] ECR 2085 para 32, and more recently Case C-224/97 *Erich Ciola v Land Vorarlberg* [1999] ECR I-2517 para 16. See also the Opinion of AG Van Gerven in Case C-159/90 *Society for the Protection of the Unborn Child v Grogan* [1991] ECR I-4685 para 22 where he stated that '[n]ational rules which are *per se* (overtly or covertly) discriminatory as regards providers of services from other Member States may . . . be justified "on grounds of public policy, public security or public health"'.

[114] See eg D. Martin and E. Guild, *Free Movement of Persons in the European Union* (London 1996) 78.

[115] See also in the context of Art 12 (ex 6) EC Case C-274/96 *Criminal Proceedings Against Horst Otto Bickel and Ulrich Franz* [1998] ECR I-7637 paras 27–30.

a double burden if imported products have to comply with two regulatory systems.[116]

In the goods sector a clear example of a national measure having a discriminatory effect but still considered indistinctly applicable is provided by the *De Agostini*[117] case. Swedish rules prohibited misleading advertising and all television advertising directed at children under 12 years of age. Applying the *Keck*[118] formula the Court accepted that an outright ban of a type of sales promotion might have a greater impact on products from other Member States, and therefore discriminate in fact. However, if the national court found this was so, it had to examine whether the measure was necessary to satisfy overriding requirements.[119] Thus, the measure only fell within the scope of Article 28 (ex 30) EC if it was discriminatory, and yet it could be justified without resorting to Article 30 (ex 36) EC.

Another recent example[120] is provided by *Decker*.[121] Luxembourg rules required prior authorisation for the reimbursement of the costs of medical products purchased abroad. There was no similar rule concerning goods bought in Luxembourg. Again the measure had a clear discriminatory impact but the Court went on to examine possible justification on grounds of overriding reasons in the general interest.[122]

In the services sector, the Court has always treated measures imposing an establishment requirement as indistinctly applicable.[123] For example, in *Commission v Germany* (Insurance)[124] the Court examined whether an establishment condition was justified by imperative reasons relating to the public

---

[116] See Chapter 2 section 3 above. See also Arnull (n 76 above) 274–275.

[117] Joined Cases C-34/95, 35/95 and 36/95 *Konsumentombudsmannen v De Agostini (Svenska) Förlag AB and TV-Shop i Sverige AB* [1997] ECR I-3843.

[118] Joined Cases C-267/91 and C-268/91 *Criminal Proceedings Against Keck and Mithouard* [1993] ECR I-6097.

[119] See n 117 above, paras 42–47.

[120] See also Case C-389/96 *Firma Aher-Waggon GmbH v Germany* [1998] ECR I-4473 where the contested German measure exempted from noise level regulations the aircraft that were registered in Germany prior to a certain date, but not those registered in other Member States. The Court examined, inter alia, whether the measure could be justified by considerations of environmental protection. See also Case C-203/96 *Chemische Avfalstoffen Dusseldorp BV and others v Minister van Volkshuisvesting, Ruimtelijke Ordening en Milieubeheer* [1998] ECR I-4075 para 44.

[121] Case C-120/95 *Nicolas Decker v Caisse de Maladie des Employés Privés* [1998] ECR I-1831.

[122] ibid, paras 34–40. See also M. Poiares Maduro, 'The Saga of Article 30 EC Treaty: To Be Continued. A Comment on Familiapress v Bauer Verlag and Other Recent Episodes' (1998) 5 MJ 298, 311.

[123] The same is true concerning residence, see Case 39/75 *Robert Gerardus Coenen and others v Sociaal-Economische Raad* [1975] ECR 1547. Yet it could be argued on the grounds of the wording of Art 49 (ex 59) EC that discrimination by reason of establishment amounts to direct discrimination and discrimination on the grounds of nationality is in fact only material discrimination. See Case C-283/99 *Commission v Italy*, Opinion of Advocate General Jacobs of 15 February 2001 para 19, and G. Marenco, 'The Notion of Restriction on the Freedom of Establishment and Provision of Services in the Case-law of the Court' (1991) 11 YEL 111, 128.

[124] Case 205/84 *Commission v Germany* [1986] ECR 3755 paras 52–57.

interest, namely the protection of insured persons and policyholders.[125] Yet the establishment requirement discriminates directly on grounds of establishment and indirectly on grounds of nationality, as a domestic economic operator fulfils the condition automatically, while a service provider established in another Member State, who is likely to be a national of that country, has to comply with an additional requirement before beginning his activities. A domestic entrepreneur can just start to operate, while a foreign one needs to, for example, set up an agency.

Some other measures discriminating on grounds of establishment have been treated as equally applicable as well. This is logical: if a Member State can, on grounds of an overriding requirement, prohibit the activities of a service provider established in another part of the Community, surely the state must also be allowed to impose other, less restrictive conditions.[126] *Bachmann*[127] concerned a Belgian law providing that payments of insurance contributions were tax deductible. Tax deductions could, however, only be made for payments to insurers established in Belgium. Service providers established in other Member States were clearly placed at a disadvantage when compared to domestic insurers but the Court still found that the measure could be justified on grounds of the cohesion of the tax system.[128] In the same manner, in *Kohll*[129] the Court examined whether the Luxembourg system requiring prior authorisation for the reimbursement of medical expenses incurred abroad could be justified by the overriding reason of safeguarding the financial balance of the social security system. Again, services originating from other Member States were put at a clear disadvantage but the Court did not restrict itself to Article 46 (ex 56) EC grounds of justification.[130] In *Safir*[131] the Court was faced with Swedish legislation setting different tax regimes for capital life assurance policies depending on whether they were taken with companies established in Sweden or not. The regime was in certain circumstances disadvantageous to insurers established in other Member States. The Court avoided the question of whether the measure was distinctly or equally applicable. However, it did examine the Swedish arguments about the impossibility of applying the same tax regime and the need to fill the fiscal vacuum.[132] The

---

[125] The condition was not justified as it was not indispensable. See also Case C-106/91 *Ramrath v Ministère de la Justice* [1992] ECR I-3351, and Case C-101/94 *Commission v Italy* [1996] ECR I-2691.

[126] See the Opinion of AG Tesauro in Case C-158/96 *Raymond Kohll v Union des Caisses de Maladie* [1998] ECR I-1931 para 49.

[127] Case C-204/90 *Hans-Martin Bachmann v Belgian State* [1992] ECR I-249.

[128] ibid, paras 31–33. See also Case C-55/98 *Skatteministeriet v Bent Vestergaard* [1999] ECR I-7641 where the cohesion of tax system was examined but rejected on the facts.

[129] See n 126 above.

[130] See also S. van Raepenbusch, 'La libre choix par les citoyens Européens des produits médicaux et des prestaires de soins, conséquence sociale du marché intérieur' (1998) 34 CDE 683 at 697.

[131] Case C-118/96 *Jessica Safir v Skattemyndigheten in Dalarnas Län* [1998] ECR I-1897.

[132] ibid, paras 24–34. P. Cabral and P. Cunha, 'The Internal Market and Discriminatory Taxation: Just How (Un)steady is the Ground?' (1994) 24 ELRev 396, 401 criticise the 'laconic manner in which the Court deals with the issue of justification . . . [avoiding] an in-depth analysis'.

Swedish system certainly appeared to be discriminatory on grounds of establishment and yet again the Court was prepared to entertain arguments that do not seem to have any basis in Article 46. Finally, in *Svensson and Gustavsson*,[133] where the Court stated that discrimination on grounds of establishment can only be justified by express EC Treaty derogations, it nevertheless went on to examine the need to maintain the integrity of the fiscal regime, which is an overriding requirement.

In addition, the Court has examined overriding requirements in cases where a national measure grants a monopoly. In *France v Commission* (Terminal equipment)[134] and in *Commission v Netherlands* (Mediawet)[135] the Court made it clear that the existence of a monopoly may constitute a restriction to the free movement of goods and services but that such a monopoly may be justified by overriding requirements.[136] Yet in these situations a Member State has usually granted the exclusive right to operate in a certain economic sector to a *national* undertaking. The fact that the measure not only discriminates against undertakings from other Member States but also against other domestic undertakings does not render it non-discriminatory, as the measure still exclusively benefits domestic ones. This would be different only if the monopoly was granted after a tendering process open to undertakings from all Member States.

The recent case law permitting recourse to overriding requirements except in cases of overt discrimination[137] serves to answer, at least partly, the criticism expressed by Oliver. In his view mandatory requirements ought to be treated as additions to Article 30 (ex 36) EC to avoid 'undue harshness. . . with respect to "distinctly applicable" measures necessary on, for instance, consumer protection grounds'.[138] If the category of distinctly applicable rules is restricted to measures containing direct discrimination on grounds of a product being imported or the nationality of a service provider, the number

---

[133] Case C-484/93 *Svensson, Gustavsson v Ministre du logement et de l'urbanisme* [1995] ECR I-3955 paras 15–19.

[134] Case C-202/88 *France v Commission* [1991] ECR I-1223 dealing with the free movement of goods.

[135] Case C-353/89 *Commission v Netherlands* [1991] ECR I-4069 dealing with the free movement of services.

[136] See in general F. Blum and A. Logue, *State Monopolies Under EC Law* (Chichester 1998) 106–118 and 140–152.

[137] See also D. Martin, '"Discriminations", "entraves" et "raisons imperieuses" dans le traité CE. Trois concepts enquête d'identité' (1998) 34 CDE 261, 300, 582–583 and 630–631 who criticises the development. A similar trend can be observed in the field of establishment. See V. Hatzopoulos, 'Case C-250/95, *Futura Participations SA & Singer v Administration des Contributions (Luxembourg)*, Judgment of 15 May 1997, [1997] ECR I-2471' (1998) 35 CMLRev 493 at 508.

[138] Oliver (n 42 above) 112. See also Oliver, 'Some Further Reflections on the Scope of Articles 28–30 (ex 30–36) EC' (1999) 36 CMLRev 783, 804–805, and N. Notaro, 'The New Generation Case Law on Trade and Environment' (2000) 25 ELRev 467 at 489–491. AG Jacobs has argued in his Opinion in Case C-379/98 *PreussenElektra AG v Schleswag AG*, judgment of 13 March 2001, paras 230–234 that there are reasons for a more flexible approach in particular in respect of the overriding requirement of environmental protection.

of national rules capable of benefiting from overriding requirements increases. In addition, measures that discriminate in law are inherently less justifiable than measures containing only factual discrimination. For example, the requirement that service providers in a certain sector be nationals is much less likely to be acceptable than the requirement that they be established in the Member State in question.

c) Grounds of justification

Overriding requirements are not a closed class but the Court may accept new grounds of justification. This is clear from the language of the Court in the cases where the doctrine was developed. In *Cassis de Dijon*[139] the Court gave a short list of possible mandatory requirements but used the words 'in particular' to indicate that the list was not exhaustive. In *Gouda*[140] the Court listed 'overriding reasons relating to public interest which [it had] already recognized' and then went on to accept cultural policy as an additional overriding requirement. In subsequent cases it has continued to accept new requirements.

The Court seems to have used other Community policies and the European Convention on Human Rights as a source of inspiration when ruling on the acceptability of a new head of justification.[141] Yet it may be doubted whether the Court in actual fact exercises any review at this level. It has never refused to accept the possibility that a certain non-economic ground of justification that is not purely administrative in nature could save an indistinctly applicable measure. The real scrutiny comes at a later stage when the Court considers the proportionality of the measure. In the main, it does not question the aim, only the means.[142]

The list of the heads of justification that have been accepted so far is a long one. As the function of the exceptions and the terminology used with them is the same for both freedoms, a ground accepted in relation to goods must also be available in the field of services.[143] It is hard to imagine two distinct lists of 'overriding requirements', and in practice the same grounds have appeared in relation to both freedoms. Thus, the grounds accepted so

---

[139] Case 120/78 *Rewe Zentrale AG v Bundesmonopolverwaltung für Branntwein* [1979] ECR 649 para 8.

[140] Case C-288/89 *Collectieve Antennevoorziening Gouda* [1991] ECR I-4007 paras 14 and 23.

[141] See S. Weatherill, 'Recent Case Law Concerning the Free Movement of Goods: Mapping the Frontiers of Market Deregulation' (1999) 36 CMLRev 51 at 82–84.

[142] See Hatzopoulos (n 40 above) 202, and G. Marenco, 'Pour une interprétation traditionelle de la notion de mesure d'effet équivalant à une restriction quantitative' (1984) 19 CDE 291, 323. See also Notaro (n 138 above) 475.

[143] See also Kapteyn and VerLoren van Themaat (n 20 above) 676, and Commission Interpretative Communication, *Freedom to Provide Services and the Interest of the General Good in the Second Banking Directive* (SEC(97) 1193 final) 17. Cf apparently C. Barnard, 'Fitting the Remaining Pieces into the Goods and Persons Jigsaw?' (2001) 26 ELRev 35, 56.

far include: prevention of tax evasion[144] and cohesion of the tax system,[145] prevention of unfair competition,[146] consumer protection[147] and protection of the recipients of services,[148] improvement of working conditions[149] and protection of workers[150] including social protection,[151] protection of the environment,[152] freedom of the press,[153] preservation of the financial balance of the social security system,[154] preservation of the good reputation of the national financial sector,[155] prevention of fraud,[156] social order,[157] protection of intellectual property,[158] cultural policy,[159] preservation of national historical and artistic heritage,[160] road safety,[161] protection of creditors,[162] protection of the proper administration of justice,[163] and avoidance of deterioration in the conditions under which goods are supplied at short distance in relatively isolated areas.[164]

---

[144] Case 120/78 *Rewe Zentrale AG v Bundesmonopolverwaltung für Branntwein* [1979] ECR 649 dealing with goods.

[145] Case C-204/90 *Hans-Martin Bachmann v Belgian State* [1992] ECR I-249 dealing with services.

[146] See n 144 above. See also Joined Cases C-34/95, 35/95 and 36/95 *Konsumentombudsmannen v De Agostini (Svenska) Förlag AB and TV-Shop i Sverige AB* [1997] ECR I-3843 in relation to services.

[147] See n 144 above, and Case 205/84 *Commission v Germany* [1986] ECR 3755 in relation to services.

[148] Joined Cases 110 and 111/78 *Ministère Public and Chambre Syndicale des Agents Artistiques et Impresarii de Belgique, ASBL v Willy van Wesemael and others* [1979] ECR 35.

[149] Case 155/80 *Oebel* [1981] ECR 1993 dealing with goods.

[150] Case 279/80 *Criminal Proceedings Against Alfred John Webb* [1981] ECR 3305 dealing with services.

[151] Case C-272/94 *Criminal Proceedings Against Michael Guiot* [1996] ECR I-1905 dealing with services.

[152] Case 302/86 *Commission v Denmark* (Danish bottles) [1988] ECR 4607 dealing with goods.

[153] Case C-368/95 *Vereinigte Familiapress Zeitungsverlags-und vertriebs GmbH v Heinrich Bauer Verlag* [1997] ECR I-3689 dealing with goods.

[154] Case C-120/95 *Nicolas Decker v Caisse de Maladie des Employés Privés* [1998] ECR I-1831 (goods) and Case C-158/96 *Raymond Kohll v Union des Caisses de Maladie* [1998] ECR I-1931 (services).

[155] Case C-384/93 *Alpine Investments BV v Minister van Financiën* [1995] ECR I-1141 dealing with services.

[156] Case C-275/92 *Her Majesty's Customs and Excise v Gerhart Schindler and Jörg Schindler* [1994] ECR I-1039 dealing with services.

[157] ibid.

[158] Case 62/79 *SA Compagnie Générale pour la Diffusion de la Télévision, Coditel, and others v SA Ciné Vog Films and others* [1980] ECR 881 dealing with services.

[159] Case C-288/89 *Collectieve Antennevoorziening Gouda* [1991] ECR I-4007 dealing with services.

[160] Case C-180/89 *Commission v Italy* [1991] ECR I-709 dealing with services.

[161] Case C-55/93 *Criminal Proceedings Against J G C van Schaik* [1994] ECR I-4837 dealing with services.

[162] Case C-3/95 *Reisebüro Broede v Gerd Sandker* [1996] ECR I-6511 dealing with services.

[163] ibid.

[164] Case C-254/98 *Schutzverband gegen unlauteren Wettbewerb v TK-Heimdienst Sass GmbH*, judgment of 13 January 2000, para 34.

d) Nature

The nature of the overriding requirements is not clear. How can justifications that are not mentioned in the EC Treaty and that only apply to indistinctly applicable national measures be explained?

The easiest way to account for the existence of overriding requirements is by reference to the idea of discrimination.[165] A national measure may apply equally to all goods and services but still bear more heavily on foreign than domestic ones. Such a measure only amounts to prohibited discrimination if it is not objectively justified. If there is a valid non-protectionist reason for the measure, it is not discriminatory in the first place and does not infringe Articles 28 or 49 (ex 30 and 59) EC.[166]

This approach explains why there was no need to include a mention of overriding requirements in the EC Treaty. The idea of justification for indistinctly applicable rules is already inherent in Articles 28 and 49 themselves and determines the scope of these provisions. It also explains why only express Treaty provisions can justify formally discriminatory rules. An existence of a justification cannot render them non-discriminatory. Therefore, they always fall foul of Articles 28 and 49 and, thus, require a specific derogation.

This reading is supported by the recent case law confirming that national measures having a discriminatory effect are equally applicable as long as they do not discriminate on their face. Additional support stems from the fact that the Court does not in practice examine the acceptability of the ground of justification. As long as the measure pursues a non-protectionist aim, it can be approved (unless it falls foul of the proportionality test).

This understanding of the overriding requirements is connected to the anti-protectionism reading of the free movement rules. Judge-made exceptions are not seen as true derogations but as a device filtering out non-protectionist measures. Even if a measure does have a protective effect, it is acceptable if it pursues a legitimate aim. The reading decentralises regulatory competence. As long as a Member State is not pursuing the forbidden aim, its measures will stand, and the centre will not interfere. The reading also promotes the power of legislative vis-à-vis judicial authorities. The Court is not substituting its judgment for that of a Member State's political process.

The discrimination reading is not sufficient to explain fully the existence of overriding requirements, however. It is unable to account for the need to

---

[165] This view has been adopted in Marenco (n 142 above) 321–324, Marenco (n 123 above) 148, N. Bernard, 'Discrimination and Free Movement in EC Law' (1996) 45 ICLQ 82, 93, and A.M. Arnull, A. Dashwood, M.G. Ross and D.A. Wyatt, *Wyatt and Dashwood's European Union Law* (2nd edn London 2000), 352. See also C. Hilson, 'Discrimination in Community Free Movement Law' (1999) 24 ELRev 445, 450.

[166] The Court has on occasion adopted a similar approach to Art 90 (ex 95) EC holding that a measure hindering imports is not discriminatory if it pursues a legitimate objective. See eg Case 46/80 *SpA Vinal v SpA Orbat* [1981] ECR 77.

justify truly non-discriminatory national measures.[167] According to this reading, only rules having a disparate impact are in need of justification.

Academic doctrine currently espouses three other major theories seeking to explain the development of overriding requirements.[168] The first sees them as a *rule of reason* which does not determine the substantive scope of the free movement provisions but amounts to 'a recognition by the Court, on essentially equitable grounds, that certain interests or values are deserving of judicial protection at the Community level pending the intervention of the Community legislator'.[169] The second view sees overriding requirements as a *concrete manifestation of residual competences* left to Member States. According to this view, overriding requirements determine whether the suspect measure falls within the scope of the free movement provisions in the first place.[170] The third view sees overriding requirements as a *general principle of Community law* protecting the general interest in connection with the achievement of the freedoms.[171] Whatever the theory that finally gains ascendancy, it is difficult to imagine that it would not apply both to goods and services.[172]

4. Proportionality

a) General

The balance between trade and other interests cannot be set in the abstract but needs to be determined in the light of the facts of an individual case. In some concrete situations it is sensible to give predominance to the Community interest in trade rather than, for example, to the protection of the environment, while in other factual circumstances the environmental interests should prevail. In the Community this balance *in concreto* is achieved through the principle of proportionality.

Proportionality is a familiar principle of administrative law, and has been particularly well developed in German law.[173] The principle is used in many different contexts across the whole area of Community law, and has been employed by the Court already in very early case law.[174]

---

[167] See Chapter 2 section 4 above.

[168] The view that overriding requirements are an extension of Arts 30 and 46 (ex 36 and 56) EC has fallen out of fashion.

[169] Gormley (n 42 above) 71 and 51–57.

[170] A. Mattera, *Le marché unique européen* (2nd edn Paris 1990) 274–275.

[171] See Hatzopoulos (n 40 above), 213–214, 227–228, 230–231, and 235–236. See also Weiler (n 99 above) 366.

[172] As my view is that the scope of the free movement provisions ought to be determined by a wide concept of discrimination, I still prefer the explanation based on the notion of objective justification of material discrimination.

[173] See eg Emiliou (n 73 above) 23–67, and J. Schwarze, *European Administrative Law* (London 1992) 685–692.

[174] See eg Emiliou (n 73 above) 134–139 and 166–169, and Schwarze (n 173 above) 708–709.

The application of the principle of proportionality in the context of Article 30 (ex 36) EC can easily be explained, as the provision requires that a measure be *justified* to protect one of the interests mentioned and not constitute *arbitrary discrimination or a disguised restriction on trade*. These words can be seen as an expression of the principle of proportionality.[175] Despite the lack of similar expressions in Article 46 (ex 56) EC, proportionality has been used in the area of services as well, and it is also applied to overriding requirements. This is due to the status of proportionality as one of the general principles[176] of Community law.[177]

The Court's approach to the principle of proportionality has not always been systematic.[178] It is therefore necessary to analyse closely both the content of the principle and the intensity of review by the Court. As the Court's approach to proportionality in the context of both the express Treaty exceptions and overriding requirements has been the same,[179] they will be examined together.

b) The nature of the test

The Court does not always clearly distinguish between different elements of the proportionality principle.[180] At its most extensive the principle entails three

---

[175] See eg Kapteyn and VerLoren van Themaat (n 20 above) 673, and A.R. Ziegler, *Trade and Environment Law in the European Community* (Oxford 1996), 97.

[176] Other general principles of Community law may also be relevant. The Court has stated in Case C-260/89 *Elliniki Radiophonia Tileorassi AE v Dimiotiki Etairia Pliroforissis and Sotirios Kouvelas* (ERT) [1991] ECR I-2925, concerning services and express EC Treaty exceptions, and in Case C-368/95 *Vereinigte Familiapress Zeitungsverlags-und vertriebs GmbH v Heinrich Bauer Verlag* [1997] ECR I-3689, concerning goods and overriding requirements, that justifications must be 'interpreted in the light of the general principles of law and in particular of fundamental rights'. This may cut two ways. On the one hand, a national measure constituting a prima facie restriction must be compatible with fundamental human rights to be justified. On the other hand, fundamental human rights, such as the freedom of expression, can serve as grounds of justification. See further on the first point J.H.H. Weiler and N.J.S. Lockhart, '"Taking Rights Seriously" Seriously: the European Court and its Fundamental Rights Jurisprudence' (1995) 32 CMLRev 51 at 74–78, and on the second Poiares Maduro (n 122 above) 311.

[177] See Emiliou (n 73 above) 134–138, and F.G. Jacobs, 'Recent Developments in the Principle of Proportionality in European Community Law' in E. Ellis (ed), *The Principle of Proportionality in the Laws of Europe* (Oxford 1999) 1–2.

[178] See Kapteyn and VerLoren van Themaat (n 20 above) 656, W. Van Gerven, 'The Effect of Proportionality on the Actions of Member States of the European Community: National Viewpoints from Continental Europe' in E. Ellis (ed), *The Principle of Proportionality in the Laws of Europe* (Oxford 1999) 60, Hatzopoulos (n 40 above) 205–206, and Notaro (n 138 above) 484–487.

[179] See Gormley (n 42 above) 69, Jarass (n 20 above) 721, Oliver (n 42 above) 181 and 185–189, and Tridimas (n 42 above) 137. See also the Opinion of AG Van Gerven in Joined Cases C-1/90 and C-176/90 *Aragonesa de Publicidad Exterior SA and Publivia SAE v Departamento de Sanidad y Seguridad Social de la Generalitat de Cataluña* [1991] ECR I-4151 para 14.

[180] See Schwarze (n 173 above) 854–855, T. Tridimas, 'Proportionality in Community Law: Searching for the Appropriate Standard of Scrutiny' in E. Ellis (ed), *The Principle of Proportionality in the Laws of Europe* (Oxford 1999) 68, and Van Gerven (n 178 above) 37–42.

tests: suitability, necessity and true proportionality of the measure. This is the structure of the test in German law.[181] Advocate General Van Gerven has supported the use of this formulation for both the free movement of goods and services.[182] Most often, however, the Court seems to use a two part test consisting of suitability and necessity. In *Gebhard*[183] it sought to develop a formula applicable to all four freedoms and stated that 'national measures liable to hinder or make less attractive the exercise of fundamental freedoms guaranteed by the Treaty... must be suitable for securing the attainment of the objective they pursue; and they must not go beyond what is necessary to attain it'.

i) Suitability

The first element of the principle of proportionality is suitability. This means that a national measure must be suitable or appropriate or pertinent for achieving the interest it pursues. There must be a connection between the means and the ends. This is a matter of causality. The measure must in actual fact be capable of attaining its purported objective.[184]

In the field of goods the judgment in *Schmit*[185] provides an example of the test in practice.[186] The case concerned French legislation providing that motor vehicle manufacturers and importers had to send to the Ministry of Transport a descriptive notice of the models that they envisaged putting on the French market in a given year, as well as the serial number from which vehicles were manufactured in accordance with the model. Vehicles conforming with these requirements could be designated with the model year of the following year provided they were sold after 30 June. Thus, a vehicle conforming with the relevant specifications sold between 1 July 1995 and 30 June 1996 was deemed a 1996 model.

The Court ruled that the measure constituted a prima facie restriction on the free movement of goods. In practice, during the second half of a year a vehicle manufactured in France or imported by an official importer could be marketed as the following year's model, while the same vehicle imported from another Member State by a parallel importer could only be sold as the current year's model, placing it at a competitive disadvantage.[187]

---

[181] See Schwarze (n 173 above) 687.

[182] Case C-312/89 *Union départementale des syndicats CGT de l'Aisne v SIDEF Conforama and others* [1991] ECR I-997 para 14 (goods) and Case C-159/90 *Society for the Protection of the Unborn Child v Grogan* [1991] ECR I-4685 para 35 (services).

[183] Case C-55/94 *Reinhard Gebhard v Consiglio dell'Ordine degli Avvocati e Procuratori di Milano* [1995] ECR I-4165 para 37.

[184] See in general Emiliou (n 73 above) 191–192, S. Laakso, 'Suhteellisuusperiaate yhteisöoikeudessa' (1999) 97 LM 1080 at 1082–1083, and Schwarze (n 173 above) 855–857.

[185] Case C-240/95 *Criminal Proceedings Against Rémy Schmit* [1996] ECR I-3179.

[186] See also eg Case 788/79 *Italian State v Gilli and Andres* [1980] ECR 2071, and Case C-362/88 *GB-INNO-BM v Confédération du commerce luxembourgeois* [1990] ECR I-667.

[187] See n 185 above, paras 10–22.

The French government in reply argued that the rules were designed to protect consumers and to ensure the fairness of commercial transactions. The Court, following Advocate General Elmer, gave short shrift to this argument, holding that the system was not suitable to protect those interests. First, the rules only provided for notification to the Ministry of Transport. There were no guarantees that customers would receive any of the information. Secondly, the system did not enable the customer to determine differences between vehicles on the basis of the model year if one of the vehicles was imported by a parallel importer. Two similar vehicles might have different model years, or two different vehicles might have the same model year. Thirdly, the legislation did not guarantee that a vehicle was a result of a recent product-run, as the manufacturers themselves specified which vehicles were given the new model year. Finally, there was nothing to prevent a manufacturer from modifying a vehicle during the course of the model year. Accordingly, the system was not capable of ensuring that the consumer was correctly informed.[188] It was not suitable for protecting consumers or the fairness of commercial transactions.

In the field of services the judgment in *Seco*[189] provides an example of the use of the suitability test.[190] The case concerned Luxembourg legislation requiring all employers to pay social security contributions for their workers. This legislation was applied to French companies Seco SA and Desquenne & Giral SA, which were providing services in Luxembourg. The undertakings were already paying contributions to the French social security scheme for the same workers and the same period of employment, and the workers could not gain any benefits from the Luxembourg system.

It was argued that the rules were justified by reasons relating to the enforcement of the Luxembourg minimum wage system. The Court did not accept the justification. The requirement that all service providers, irrespective of whether they had complied with Luxembourg minimum wage rules, pay social security contributions was not appropriate as it was 'by its nature unlikely to make employers comply with that legislation or to be of any benefit whatsoever to the workers in question'.[191] The measure was simply not suitable to achieve its purported aim.

The criterion of suitability is an indispensable part of the principle of proportionality on any reading of the EC Treaty.[192] It ascertains that a national

---

[188] ibid, paras 24–25 and paras 41–47 of the Opinion of AG Elmer.

[189] Joined Cases 62 and 63/81 *Seco SA and Desquenne & Giral SA v Établissement d'Assurance contre la Vieillesse et l'Invalidité* [1982] ECR 223.

[190] See also Case C-260/89 *Elliniki Radiophonia Tileorassi AE v Dimiotiki Etairia Pliroforissis and Sotirios Kouvelas* [1991] ECR I-2925 para 25, and Case C-211/91 *Commission v Belgium* [1992] I-6757.

[191] See n 189 above, para 14.

[192] The suitability test is also employed in the American commerce clause jurisprudence to flush out protectionism. See C.R. Sunstein, 'Protectionism, the American Supreme Court, and Integrated Markets' in R. Bieber, R. Dehousse, J. Pinder and J.H.H. Weiler (eds), *1992: One European Market? A Critical Analysis of the Commission's Internal Market Strategy* (Baden-Baden 1988) 134–135.

measure in actual fact does pursue the legitimate aim. It prevents Member States from adopting rules that ostensibly seek to protect a general interest but in reality have a protectionist purpose.

ii) Necessity

The second element of the principle of proportionality is necessity. The objective of the measure must not be capable of being achieved by alternative means that are less restrictive of intra-Community trade. Where there is a choice between several appropriate measures, the least onerous equally effective one must be selected.[193] This element of proportionality is dominant in the Court's case law in relation to the free movement of goods and services.[194]

In the field of goods the judgment of the Court in *de Peijper*[195] illustrates well the use of the necessity test. The case concerned Dutch legislation requiring inter alia that the importer of medicinal preparations possess certain documents which could only be obtained from the manufacturer. The Court examined whether the law could be justified on public health grounds. It stated that in relation to a specific batch of the imported product the authorities had a legitimate interest in being able to carry out checks. However, there were less restrictive means available as the objective could be equally well achieved by allowing the presentation of similar evidence more easily obtained by a parallel importer, by compelling the manufacturer to supply particulars, and by co-operating with the authorities of other Member States.[196] Thus, the measure was not necessary as public health could be protected by other means placing a lesser burden on intra-Community trade.

In the field of services the judgment in *Commission v Germany* (Insurance)[197] provides a good illustration of the necessity test.[198] The German Insurance Supervision Law stipulated inter alia that only insurers established in Germany could provide direct insurance services. The German government argued that supervisory authorities could only perform their tasks properly if insurers were permanently established in Germany. The Court held that the presence of the assets representing technical reserves could be verified even if the undertaking did not have any permanent establishment. The supervision of other conditions for the conduct of business could be effected on the basis of certified documents sent from the state of establishment. Thus, the Court ruled that the establishment requirement was not indispensable for the protection of policyholders

---

[193] See generally Emiliou (n 73 above) 192 and 250–251, Laakso (n 184 above) 1083, and Schwarze (n 73 above) 857–859.

[194] See on the free movement of goods Poiares Maduro (n 122 above) 306–309, and Tridimas (n 42 above) 133.

[195] Case 104/75 *Adriaan de Peijper* [1976] ECR 613.   [196] ibid, paras 23–29.

[197] Case 205/84 *Commission v Germany* [1986] ECR 3755.

[198] See also Case 33/74 *Van Binsbergen v Bestuur van de Bedrijfsvereniging voor de Metaalnijverheid* [1974] ECR 1299 para 16.

and insured persons.[199] Again, the objective could be achieved by less restrictive means, namely by requiring the insurers to provide certified documents. Therefore, the measure was not necessary.

An important aspect of the necessity test is that the requirements of another Member State may not be duplicated.[200] If, for example, the importing or host state demands that the good or service comply with its product rules, although the product is in conformity with equivalent standards of the exporting or home state, it is not employing the least restrictive means available.[201]

In the field of goods the judgment in *Biologische Producten*[202] provides an example of the requirement of non-duplication.[203] The case concerned Dutch legislation relating to the approval of plant protection products. The Dutch system required, on grounds of public health, laboratory tests of such products. The Court held that, while such rules were acceptable in principle, the Netherlands was 'not entitled unnecessarily to require technical or chemical analyses or laboratory tests where those analyses and tests have already been carried out in another Member State and their results are available'.[204] The importing state was not allowed to duplicate the conditions imposed by the exporting state.

In the field of services the judgment in *Webb*[205] illustrates well the non-duplication requirement. The case concerned Dutch legislation prohibiting the provision of manpower without authorisation. The Court held that the provision of manpower was a particularly sensitive matter directly affecting relations in the labour market and the interests of the workforce. Therefore, it was permissible for the Netherlands to impose a licensing regime. However, it had to take 'into account the evidence and guarantees already produced by the provider of the services for the pursuit of his activities in the Member State in which he is established'.[206] Again, the host state could not needlessly duplicate the requirements of the home state.

The search for the least restrictive alternative and the assessment of the equivalence of national requirements may be an onerous task for the European Court of Justice or a national court applying Community law.[207]

[199] See n 197 above, paras 52–56.

[200] This necessarily implies a view on which a Member State is competent to regulate a certain issue. See Chapter 2 sections 1 and 5civ above.

[201] See Dashwood (n 101 above) 149–150, Emiliou (n 73 above) 232–235 and 253, Tridimas (n 42 above) 230–234, and Weiler (n 99 above) 367.

[202] Case 272/80 *Criminal Proceedings Against Frans-Nederlandse Maatschappij voor Biologische Producten BV* [1981] ECR 3277.

[203] See also Case C-293/93 *Criminal Proceedings Against Ludomira Neeltje Barbara Houtwipper* [1994] ECR I-4249 paras 15 and 19.

[204] See n 202 above, para 14.

[205] Case 279/80 *Criminal Proceedings Against Alfred John Webb* [1981] ECR 3305.

[206] ibid, para 21.

[207] See Chalmers and Szyszczak (n 42 above) 319, A.T.S. Leenen, 'Recent Case Law of the Court of Justice of the European Communities on the Freedom of Establishment and the Freedom to Provide Services' (1980) 17 CMLRev 259, 267–268, and Tridimas (n 42 above) 140–142. See also the detailed discussion in section 4biii below.

However, the test of necessity is a crucial part of proportionality on any reading of the free movement provisions. Without a rigorous application of this test Member States would be able to adopt even intentionally discriminatory rules.[208] Indeed, if a Member State has not selected the least restrictive of the appropriate measures, it has either been protectionist or incompetent.

iii) True proportionality

General　　The most difficult problem relating to the proportionality test is whether the European Court of Justice, or a national court applying the free movement provisions, ought to examine the 'true proportionality'[209] of national measures. The question is should the Court conduct a cost-benefit analysis of the regulation, balancing the value of the national rule against the Community interest in free trade.[210] An example of such an exercise would be the Court weighing the lives saved by a national health measure against the Community interest in free trade compromised due to the measure.[211]

　　True proportionality is connected to more fundamental problems. The first is whether the EC Treaty freedoms are to be read as only precluding protectionist national measures, or whether they go beyond that. As explained above, suitability and necessity tests are already needed to flush out intentionally protectionist Member State rules.[212] If the means employed are not connected to the ends or if there are equally effective but less restrictive alternatives, it is likely that a national measure having a restrictive effect is in fact the product of protectionist intent. However, true proportionality goes further and is tied to the economic freedom conception of the free movement provisions.[213] Under this test Member State provisions pursuing a legitimate aim can be found to infringe the free movement rules if their effect on trade is deemed excessive.

---

[208] See generally M. Poiares Maduro, *We The Court. The European Court of Justice and the European Economic Constitution. A Critical Reading of Article 30 of the EC Treaty* (Oxford 1998) 55, and Poiares Maduro (n 122 above) 308–309. In the USA the test of less restrictive alternatives is used to combat protectionism. See Sunstein (n 192 above) 134–135.

[209] Also known as proportionality in a strict sense.

[210] See Poiares Maduro (n 208 above) 52–58 on different forms of balancing and 170 on the interests to be taken into account.

[211] True proportionality still falls short of being a test of 'the right balance'. The test only tells whether the measure is excessive or not. It does not seek out other possible equilibria. Assume, for example, that there is an appropriate and necessary measure A leading to protection level B, and an appropriate and necessary measure X leading to a protection level Y. If the cost-benefit assessment of the measure A is positive, the Court will accept it as proportionate even if the measure X produced a better cost-benefit result. See Schwarze (n 173 above) 860.

[212] See section 4b above, Poiares Maduro (n 122 above) 307–309, and Sunstein (n 192 above) 134.

[213] See Poiares Maduro (n 208 above) 53, and Sunstein (n 192 above) 129–131. This reading has traditionally commanded a wide support in the academic doctrine in Europe. See Chapter 1 section 1 above.

Secondly, the test is connected to institutional issues. Under true proportionality, legislatures lose their positions as the final arbiters of costs and benefits of regulation. It thus empowers courts by giving them the final say.

Thirdly, the test is connected to the issue of vertical division of power in the Community. Under true proportionality the European Court of Justice, a central organ, uses the Treaty provisions on free movement, central rules, to strike down Member State measures. Therefore, the test empowers the Community vis-à-vis Member States and has a centralising character.

Disadvantages and advantages of the test   The problems and benefits of the test are associated with the merits and demerits of the different decision-makers, with the anti-protectionism and economic freedom readings of the EC Treaty, and with the economics of federalism.

The test of true proportionality is extremely problematic for any court, both in practice and in principle. A court is likely to lack expertise in the subject matter. The information it can gather is limited, as it must to a large extent rely on the parties represented in the case and, unlike the legislature or a specialist regulatory body, cannot easily conduct or commission extensive studies itself.[214] These practical problems are exacerbated in the case of the European Court of Justice, which may not be well versed in the nuances and subtleties of the national measures involved. In Article 234 (ex 177) EC proceedings the procedure does not cater for fact finding, and the Court is only competent to interpret Community law, not to apply it.[215]

The European Court of Justice faces an additional difficulty as the value given to a regulation may vary between Member States. Cultural factors may mean that certain risks[216] and values are taken very seriously in one country but not given as much importance in another. More objective factors may also play a part. Differences in infrastructure may, for example, influence the disutility attached to physical invalidity. In a country where all public and many private facilities have been modified to accommodate wheelchairs, the disutility of losing the use of one's legs is smaller than in a country where no such effort has been made. These cultural and objective differences would make it very difficult for the Court, a central organ, to conduct a cost-benefit analysis, as its result would depend on the Member State involved. After all, the value of the regulation is the legitimate value attached to it by the persons protected.[217]

---

[214] See G. de Búrca, 'The Principle of Proportionality and its Application in EC Law' (1993) 13 YEL 105, 108 and 127, and Poiares Maduro (n 208 above) 59.

[215] See Jarvis (n 72 above) 191–193 and 269–271, and more generally D.W.K. Anderson, *References to the European Court* (London 1995) 67–69 and 73–79.

[216] Regulation can be perceived as centrally concerned with offering protection against risks, be these injuries caused by unsafe products or losses caused by erroneous legal advice. See Baldwin and Cave (n 3 above) 138.

[217] For recognition of these concerns, see the Opinion of AG Gulmann in Case C-315/92 *Verband Sozialer Wettbewerb v Estée Lauder* [1994] ECR I-317. In Case C-220/98 *Estée Lauder Cosmetics GmbH & Co. OHG v Lancaster Group GmbH*, judgment of 13 January 2000, para 29 the Court held that it was for the national court to determine whether the name of a product, although accepted in other Member States, could mislead German consumers due to social,

A national court would of course be more familiar with local circumstances and could therefore in theory better conduct the inquiry.[218]

The determination of proportionality by a national court is not without problems, however. National courts may feel uncomfortable about balancing dissimilar competing interests; traditionally this has been regarded as a political matter best left to the democratically elected legislature.[219] In addition, national courts may come to widely different conclusions on proportionality, even within a single Member State.[220] Understandably, the courts in different Member States may reach even more dissimilar results,[221] although some divergence is clearly justified because of the different valuations by the citizens of different Member States. All these practical problems face the European Court of Justice and national courts equally in the case of goods and services.

There are also severe difficulties of principle, again applying both to goods and services. A regulation does not have a 'correct expert value' that the Court could find and weigh against the Community interest in free trade. First, experts and laymen can rationally differ on the valuation of risks the regulation seeks to control. For example, laymen can give widely differing values to life-threatening risks based on the nature of death. A gruesome death striking innocents has a very high disutility, while an instant death striking people who have somehow voluntarily exposed themselves to the risk has a significantly lower one.[222]

Secondly, commensurability of the value of regulation and the value of trade can be disputed.[223] It has been claimed that some values can only be

cultural or linguistic factors. See also Case C-405/98 *Konsumentombudsmannen v Gourmet International Products Aktiebolag*, judgment of 8 March 2001, paras 33 and 41 and the Opinion of AG Jacobs, para 48, and Poiares Maduro (n 208 above) 153.

[218] The divergences in valuation are bound to increase as the Community enlarges. Many of the new applicants are much poorer than the current Member States. In addition, some of them have a different cultural background and have even been described as not being a part of 'Western civilization'. See S.P. Huntington, *The Clash of Civilizations and the Remaking of World Order* (New York 1996) 157–163.

[219] See eg Hoffmann J in *Stoke-on-Trent and Norwich City Councils v B&Q* [1990] 3 CMLR 31 paras 46–52.

[220] For example, in Sunday trading cases English courts came to different conclusions about the proportionality of the legislation. See C. Barnard, 'Sunday Trading: A Drama in Five Acts' (1994) 57 MLR 449, 454.

[221] See AG Van Gerven in Case C-312/89 *Union dèpartementale des syndicats CGT de l'Aisne v SIDEF Conforama and others* [1991] ECR I-997 para 8 of his Opinion, and the extensive analysis of national case laws by Jarvis (n 72 above) 175–294, especially 219, 228–229, 251–255, 263–269, 272–278 and 292–293. Jarvis concludes on 293 that '[t]he single most important conclusion which emerges from the discussion . . . is that the application of proportionality principle by the national courts is extremely erratic'. See also A. Biondi, 'In and Out of the Internal Market: Recent Developments on the Principle of Free Movement' (1999–2000) 19 YEL 469 at 478–479.

[222] See generally R.H. Pildes and C.R. Sunstein, 'Reinventing the Regulatory State' (1995) 62 Univ of Chicago LR 1 at 48–64.

[223] See generally on incommensurability C.R. Sunstein, 'Incommensurability and Valuation in Law' (1994) 92 Michigan LR 779 at 795–812. See also Poiares Maduro (n 208 above) 54.

traded-off against certain other values.[224] This issue may be connected to different moral theories. If one subscribes to the Kantian notion that a human being ought to never be treated only as a means but always as an end, it becomes difficult to balance, for example, human life against anything that has a purely instrumental value, such as trade. From a utilitarian point of view it is easier to describe everything in the terms of utility or disutility.

The problem of incommensurability was neatly encapsulated by Mustill LJ, who was examining the proportionality of Sunday trading rules, in *W.H. Smith Do-It-All Ltd v Peterborough City Council*:[225]

how is the balance to be struck, given that the conflicting interests are so totally different in kind? How could (say) a desire to keep the Sabbath holy be measured against the free-trade economic premises of the Common Market? If this is what the *Cassis de Dijon* exception requires, it seems to me that the task would be difficult to the point of impossibility in any but the simplest case, where the balance is to be struck, not between two conflicting trade interests, but between the Community free trade interest on the one hand, and an elusive national moral, social or cultural norm on the other.[226]

Finally, regulation may also have a symbolic value. It can modify the preferences of the regulated. For example, the criminalisation of a certain activity sends a strong signal to individual citizens that the society views the activity in question as wrong and evil. The hope is that citizens will internalise the valuation and desist from the activity even if they earlier had a more neutral attitude towards it. In the same manner, regulation of prostitution or trade in human body parts has symbolic significance. It tells the citizens something about how the society sees sexual activities or the human body. It sends a message that these are perceived as something more than objects of normal commercial transactions.[227]

Altogether, it may be argued that the true value of a regulation can only be found through a proper process where the citizens participate. Cost-benefit analysis by 'experts' can be a helpful tool to inform the process but it cannot be decisive on its own.[228] It might even be said that solely trusting experts to value risks is somewhat akin to trusting experts to set prices. The correct value of a risk or a price of a product may be better revealed through

---

[224] As an extreme example, it might be argued that the right not to be subjected to torture is an absolute right which cannot be infringed in any circumstances.

[225] *W.H. Smith Do-It-All Ltd and Payless DIY Ltd v Peterborough City Council* [1990] 2 CMLR 577.

[226] ibid, paras 49–50.

[227] See Pildes and Sunstein (n 222 above) 66–72. See also J. Scott, 'On Kith and Kine (and Crustaceans): Trade and Environment in the EU and WTO' in J.H.H. Weiler (ed), *The EU, the WTO, and the NAFTA. Towards a Common Law of International Trade?* (Oxford University Press 2000) 144 for a discussion of the 'moral dimension'.

[228] See Baldwin and Cave (n 3 above) 94 and 334–336. See also Scott (n 227 above) 157–158 for an argument against technocratic assessment of risk in the context of WTO.

a decentralised democratic or market process than through any 'expert' evaluation.[229]

Regan, writing about the American Commerce Clause, has expressed many of these concerns succinctly: 'The whole point of having legislatures is to allow *them* to decide how [public goods] should be valued. . . And the whole point of having fifty separate state legislatures is to allow one state to value these effects differently than another'.[230]

However, total deference to the cost-benefit analysis of the national political process is not a satisfactory solution either. It may be that such a solution is not sufficient to bring about the integration of previously fragmented and highly regulated national markets not sharing a common language. This is the traditional objection to the anti-protectionism reading of the EC Treaty.[231] However, the argument has lost some of its force in recent years as the internal market and common currency have been established, and it seems that the Court has moved towards the anti-protectionism reading in *Keck*.[232]

Secondly, the national political process may not take fully into account the harm suffered by out-of-state interests.[233] Nationals of a Member State have a voice in the decision-making process. They can use all the mechanisms of political accountability to oppose measures detrimental to them. In contrast, out-of-state interests are not represented. They simply do not have a say in the national political process and are therefore unable to protect themselves. Hence, it seems that there is a need for a central organ that can give weight to the harm caused to the interests of the whole Community.[234]

Thus, there is a case for marginal review by the Court.[235] In most circumstances national measures should be allowed to stand. However, if the value of the Community interest in free trade manifestly exceeds the value of regulation, the national measure ought to be found disproportionate. This might be the case, for example, if the regulation has in fact been unduly influenced

[229] Thus, Baldwin and Cave (n 3 above) 78–82 list as criteria for good regulation the legislative mandate, accountability and due process, as well as expertise and efficiency. See also G. Majone, *Evidence, Argument and Persuasion in the Policy Process* (New Haven 1989) 17–18 who stresses the value of process.

[230] D.H. Regan, 'The Supreme Court and State Protectionism: Making Sense of the Dormant Commerce Clause' (1985–1986) 84 Michigan LR 1091, 1144. Chalmers, 'The Single Market: From Prima Donna to Journeyman' in J. Shaw and G. More (eds), *New Legal Dynamics of European Union* (Oxford 1995) 68 calls the Court's weighing of the values involved an 'impossible balancing act'.

[231] See eg Gormley (n 42 above) 14. From the American perspective, see Sunstein (n 192 above) 144–145.

[232] Joined Cases C-267/91 and C-268/91 *Criminal Proceedings Against Keck and Mithouard* [1993] ECR I-6097. Cf however Case C-384/93 *Alpine Investments BV v Minister van Financiën* [1995] ECR I-1141. See on these issues Chapter 2 section 5 above.

[233] See Poiares Maduro (n 208 above) 70–72 and also 171–173.

[234] By definition, if a voluntary transaction with a foreign economic agent is prevented, that agent suffers harm. After all, he would not have even contemplated the transaction, had it not been beneficial to him.

[235] For a similar suggestion, see Emiliou (n 73 above) 273. The 'grossly excessive' test has sometimes been used in the USA as well. See Sunstein (n 192 above) 136–137.

by national private interest groups,[236] or if the host state regulation offers only slightly better protection than the home state one, but creates a very high barrier to trade. Additionally, to enable the European Court of Justice, or a national court, to make this complex assessment, it is crucial that the procedural rules allow all interested parties to be heard.[237] These arguments apply both to goods and services.

The economics of federalism teaches us that competition between legal orders created by free trade can be beneficial but is not an optimal solution in all circumstances.[238] Therefore, in its investigation the Court ought to adopt different solutions for different market failures.

In the case of trans-frontier externalities[239] competition between legal orders would be inappropriate. Each Member State would have an incentive to lower the level of its regulation as it would reap the benefits but the costs would be borne by other Member States. Therefore, the Court should respect national measures if they remedy this market failure.[240] The correct way to advance integration may well be to regulate at the Community level.[241]

The problem of cross-border externalities is alleviated by the principle established in *Van Binsbergen*[242] which allows the host state to apply its rules to activities entirely or principally directed towards its territory.[243] In these situations the home state does not have much incentive to regulate and supervise the activity. However, the Court has recently emphasised that the economic operator must be guilty of abusive or fraudulent conduct,[244] which reduces the usefulness of this doctrine in controlling cross-border externalities.

In the case of asymmetric information[245] competition between legal orders would be more desirable.[246] The crucial requirement is that the customers are alerted to the applicable regulatory regime. As long as they are aware of the

---

[236] This gives rise to an interesting question whether the Court ought to examine the integrity of the national political process. In theory such an investigation might be called for. In practice the Court would be faced with formidable political difficulties.

[237] I am grateful to Professor Van Gerven for this point made at a PhD Seminar of the Centre of European Law, King's College London, in November 1999. See further on the proceduralisation of proportionality Van Gerven (n 178 above) 63.

[238] See Chapter 2 section 1d above.   [239] See section 1 and Chapter 2 section 1d above.

[240] It might be argued that in the case of cross-border trade there are almost always externalities as the risks of defective products are carried by the host state. However, if the same products are marketed in the home state and there are proper product liability rules in place, these externalities are reduced to a minimal level.

[241] See Kay and Vickers (n 3 above) 243–244.

[242] Case 33/74 *Van Binsbergen v Bestuur van de Bedrijfsvereniging voor de Metaalnijverheid* [1974] ECR 1299 para 13. See also Case C-148/91 *Vereiging Veronica Omroep Organisatie v Commissariaat voor de Media* [1993] ECR I-487, and Case C-23/93 *TV 10 SA v Commissariaat voor de Media* [1994] ECR I-4795.

[243] On the goods sector see Case 229/83 *Leclerc and others v 'Au Blé Vert' and others* [1985] ECR 1 para 27.

[244] See Case C-212/97 *Centros Ltd v Erhvervs- of Selskabsstyrelsen* [1999] I-1459 paras 24–30. See also Commission Interpretative Communication, *Freedom to Provide Services and the General Good in the Insurance Sector* [2000] OJ C43/3, 8.

[245] See section 1 and Chapter 2 section 1d above.

[246] See Kay and Vickers (n 3 above) 244.

legal system regulating the goods or services, they can assess the (minimum) quality of the product. It can of course be argued that consumers are not necessarily aware of the contents of foreign rules. This argument does not apply to business customers, however. In addition, a rational private individual will know that he lacks the necessary information and therefore cannot assess the quality of the foreign goods or services. Thus, he will continue to purchase from domestic producers unless and until the price differences grow so wide that it becomes worthwhile to invest in acquiring additional information. The foreign producers of course have an incentive to provide this information by advertising. Different Member States may specialise in different quality products. Different regulations acquire trademark-like functions as they indicate a certain minimum quality. If certain price-quality combinations prove very popular, it is likely that other Member States will adapt their regulations accordingly. Whether the regulatory systems converge or not, general welfare is enhanced. In the case of specialisation, there is more to choose from. In the case of convergence, customers in one Member State are not stuck with sub-optimal regulation. Thus, competition between legal orders can lead to efficient regulation.[247]

The following example illustrates this point. Assume a customer has difficulties in assessing the quality of a service. If in Member State A the regulatory system is very strict while in Member State B it is very lenient, it is likely that the customer will be offered expensive but high quality services from A and cheap but low quality services from B. As long as the customer is aware that the services have been subjected to different regulations, he can make an informed purchasing decision. Only if he is not aware of this or does not understand its significance, is there a problem. The Member States have specialised in different segments of the service market. Their regulations act to guarantee a certain minimum quality. If in time services from A prove much more popular, B is likely to try to emulate A's successful system.

The practice of the Court   In practice, the Court's approach to balancing has been somewhat erratic. On occasion, it has indicated its willingness to assess the true proportionality of national measures constituting restrictions on trade. The best example[248] in the field of the free movement of goods is *Commission v Denmark* (Danish bottles).[249] The case concerned a Danish deposit-and-return system for beer and soft drink containers. Manufacturers could only use containers approved by the national environmental agency. As an exception, a producer could use non-approved containers for up to 3,000 hectolitres a year.

---

[247] See generally H. Hauser and M. Hösli, 'Harmonization or Regulatory Competition in the EC(and the EEA)?' (1991) 46 Aussenwirtschaft 497, 509–510.
[248] See also eg Case C-169/91 *Stoke-on-Trent and Norwich City Councils v B&Q* [1992] ECR I-6457 para 15.
[249] Case 302/86 *Commission v Denmark* (Danish bottles) [1988] ECR 4607.

The Court held that the national measure could in principle be justified by the mandatory requirement of environmental protection. It accepted that the deposit-and-return system was essential for ensuring the reuse of containers. It then turned to examine the requirement of approval of containers by the national agency. Denmark had argued that the deposit-and-return system would not work without the approval requirement, since the retailers could not accept too many different types of bottles due to the costs of handling and storage. The Court accepted that there was some force in the argument but then stated:

It is undoubtedly true that the existing system for returning approved containers ensures a maximum rate of re-use and therefore a very considerable degree of protection since empty containers can be returned to any retailer of beverages. Non-approved containers, on the other hand, can be returned only to the retailer who sold the beverages, since it is impossible to set any such comprehensive system for those containers as well.

Nevertheless, the system for returning non-approved containers is capable of protecting the environment and, as far as imports are concerned, affects only limited quantities of beverages compared with the quantity of beverages consumed in Denmark owing to the restrictive effect which the requirement that containers should be returnable has on imports. In those circumstances, a restriction of the quantity of products which may be marketed by imports is disproportionate to the objective pursued.[250]

Thus, the Court held that the Danish system ensured a maximum rate of reuse and a high level of environmental protection. However, it then held that the Danish measure was disproportionate, as a lower level of environmental protection could be achieved without the requirement of approved containers. The higher level of environmental protection was deemed excessive.[251]

In the field of services a good illustration of the true proportionality test is the judgment of the Court in *Säger*.[252] The case concerned German law that required persons providing patent renewal services to hold a licence. The Court decided that the rules were intended to protect the recipients of services but were disproportionate. This was due to the straightforward nature of services and the limited consequences that a failure by the service provider would cause, as the German patent office would send an official reminder two months after the date of renewal, although in these cases the fee was increased by a surcharge of 10 per cent.[253] The German measure was simply excessive.

An even clearer example is the Opinion of Advocate General Van Gerven in *Grogan*.[254] He stated that 'even if the national rule is useful and indispensable in order to achieve the aim sought, the Member State must nevertheless drop the rule, or replace it by a less onerous one, if the restrictions caused to

---

[250] ibid, paras 20–21.
[251] The judgment has been subjected to fierce criticism. See eg Chalmers and Szyszczak (n 42 above) 335, and L. Krämer, *EC Environmental Law* (4th edn London 2000) 77–78.
[252] Case C-76/90 *Manfred Säger v Dennemeyer & Co. Ltd* [1991] ECR I-4221.
[253] ibid, paras 16–20.
[254] Case C-159/90 *Society for the Protection of the Unborn Child v Grogan* [1991] ECR I-4685.

intra-Community trade by the rule are *disproportionate*, that is to say if the restrictions caused are out of proportion to the aim sought by or the result brought about by the national rules'.[255]

Despite these indications of the willingness to examine the true proportionality of national measures, in recent years the Court has shied away from the test. In *Gebhard*,[256] where the Court laid down a general formula applicable to all freedoms, the only requirements mentioned were suitability and necessity:

national measures liable to hinder or make less attractive the exercise of fundamental freedoms guaranteed by the Treaty must fulfil . . . conditions: . . . they must be suitable for securing the attainment of the objective which they pursue; and they must not go beyond what is necessary in order to attain it.[257]

In the recent cases where the Court has conducted a thorough examination of proportionality, it has tended not to analyse the true proportionality of national measures. In the field of goods in *Familiapress*[258] the Court placed emphasis on the test of necessity, ie the availability of less restrictive alternative means, and did not conduct a true balancing exercise.[259] The Court has also declined to apply the true proportionality test in the field of services. In *Läärä*[260] the Court held that, in the context of gambling, Member States had the power to determine the extent of protection necessary and could either totally or partially prohibit the activities or restrict them by establishing a more or less strict control mechanism. National rules could only be assessed by reference to the level of protection which they were intended to provide.[261]

It could be argued that the same reticence to engage in the review of true proportionality is evidenced by the refusal of the Court in cases such as *Aragonesa*[262] and *Alpine Investments*[263] to take into account the lower level of protection granted by another Member State. If the Court was conducting a true balancing exercise, more lenient rules of another Member State could be

---

[255] Case C-159/90 *Society for the Protection of the Unborn Child v Grogan* [1991] ECR I-4685, para 27 of AG Van Gerven's Opinion.

[256] Case C-55/94 *Reinhard Gebhard v Consiglio dell'Ordine degli Avvocati e Procuratori di Milano* [1995] ECR I-4165.

[257] ibid, para 37.

[258] Case C-368/95 *Vereinigte Familiapress Zeitungsverlags-und vertriebs GmbH v Heinrich Bauer Verlag* [1997] ECR I-3689.

[259] See Poiares Maduro (n 122 above) 306–309 who sees this move as fitting well 'with an underlying rationale of non-discrimination'.

[260] Case C-124/97 *Markku Juhani Läärä, Cotswolds Microsystems Ltd, Oy Transatlantic Software Ltd v Kihlakunnansyyttäjä (Jyväskylä), Suomen Valtio*, judgment of 21 September 1999.

[261] ibid, paras 35–36. See also Case C-67/98 *Questore di Verona v Diego Zenatti*, judgment of 21 October 1999, paras 33–34.

[262] Joined Cases C-1/90 and C-176/90 *Aragonesa de Publicidad Exterior SA and Publivia SAE v Departamento de Sanidad y Seguridad Social de la Generalitat de Cataluña* [1991] ECR I-4151 paras 16 and 17. The case concerned the free movement of goods.

[263] Case C-384/93 *Alpine Investments BV v Minister van Financiën* [1995] ECR I-1141 para 51. The case concerned the free movement of services.

used to demonstrate the excessive nature of the national measure under examination.[264]

While mostly declining to assess overtly the true proportionality of national measures, the Court has, however, in fact engaged in covert marginal review under the guise of the necessity test. The clearest illustration of this approach is the well-known line of cases where the Court has held that national product composition requirements are not necessary as the consumers can be protected by proper labelling.[265] The Court adopted this reasoning already in *Cassis de Dijon*.[266] It held that the German rule setting a minimum alcohol content was not necessary to ensure that consumers were not mislead into buying a liqueur expecting it to have a higher alcohol content. It decided that there was a less restrictive means available, namely labelling.

The reasoning based on necessity was not totally convincing. Although many consumers were adequately protected by product labels, the consumers who either did not or could not read the labels were liable to be misled.[267] Labelling was not a less restrictive means achieving an equal level of protection; the level of consumer protection provided by labels was lower.[268] In fact, the Court was examining the true proportionality of the national measure.

The Court's review in these cases corresponds to the marginal review advocated above. The added value of composition requirements, when compared with labelling, is relatively small, at least in the cases where the products do not endanger the health of the consumers. At the same time, the disintegrative value of composition rules is great, as they may significantly hinder trade in many products and deny the consumers the opportunity to experiment with goods produced in accordance with other rules and traditions.[269]

It has been argued that in cases such as *Webb*[270] and *Commission v Germany* (Insurance)[271] the Court has been unwilling to extend a similar review into the field of services.[272] It is true that in these judgments the Court

---

[264] However, it has been convincingly argued by Poiares Maduro that in actual fact the Court has been willing to take into account the view of the *majority* of Member States. It seems that the Court has been engaging in 'majoritarian activism' and 'judicial harmonisation' and deferred to the policy choices of the majority of Member States. See Poiares Maduro (n 208 above) 68–78. See also Weatherill (n 141 above) 69–70.

[265] See on this line of case law Oliver (n 42 above) 227–228, and Poiares Maduro (n 208 above) 72–73. On recent developments see Weatherill (n 141 above) 54–70.

[266] Case 120/78 *Rewe Zentrale AG v Bundesmonopolverwaltung für Branntwein* [1979] ECR 649. See also eg Case 178/84 *Commission v Germany* (Reinheitsgebot) [1987] ECR 1227.

[267] Naturally many consumers do read the labels. However, not every consumer reads every label of every purchase he ever makes.

[268] See Poiares Maduro (n 122 above) 307–308, H.-C. von Heydebrand u.d. Lasa, 'Free Movement of Foodstuffs, Consumer Protection and Food Standards in the European Community: Has the Court of Justice Got It Wrong?' (1991) 16 ELRev 391 at 408–409, and Weiler (n 99 above) 368.

[269] See Chalmers and Szyszczak (n 42 above) 327.

[270] Case 279/80 *Criminal Proceedings Against Alfred John Webb* [1981] ECR 3305.

[271] Case 205/84 *Commission v Germany* [1986] ECR 3755.

[272] See N. Reich, *Europäisches Verbraucherrecht* (3rd revised edn Baden-Baden 1996) 138.

did allow the host state to rely on its regulation as long as it did not demand the service providers to fulfil exactly the same requirements twice. However, the Court did this only after having referred to the 'particularly sensitive nature' of the provision of manpower and insurance services. In the same manner, in the field of goods the Court has been more generous towards Member State measures when the issue has been risks that are greater than getting a bottle of weak liqueur or strange-tasting beer.[273] For example, in *Kaasfabriek Eyssen*[274] the Court accepted that unknown potential health risks associated with preservatives justified a national ban of nisin in cheese. Labelling was not considered an equally effective less restrictive means. Additionally, the Court's trust in the wisdom of consumers has not been infinite in the goods sector either. For example, in *Oosthoek*[275] and *Buet*[276] it accepted national measures which were aimed at preventing consumers from being misled or making ill-considered purchases.

Moreover, in recent years in the field of services the Court seems to have become more critical towards Member State measures, at least in cases concerning the protection of employees of the service provider.[277] In *Vander Elst*[278] France wished to apply its labour laws to the employees of a Belgian service provider. The Court held that the rules could only be applied in so far as the general interest was not safeguarded by Belgian rules.[279] After examining the relevant circumstances, the Court stated that 'the application of the Belgian system in any event excludes any *substantial* risk of workers being exploited'.[280] *Guiot*[281] concerned the application of Belgian rules to the staff of Climatec SA, a service provider from Luxembourg. The Belgian system required Climatec to pay contributions to a Construction Workers' Subsistence Fund, even though the company was already liable to make similar contributions for the same workers and the same period of work in Luxembourg. The Court again held that the rules could only be applied if the public interest was not protected by the home state.[282] The protection did not have to be identical, however. It was sufficient that it was 'similar or in any event comparable'.[283]

---

[273] See also Poiares Maduro (n 208 above) 73–74, and the analysis of the Court's case law on public health justification in L. Hancher, 'The European Pharmaceutical Market: Problems of Partial Harmonisation' (1990) 15 ELRev 9 at 18–21.

[274] Case 53/80 *Officier van Justitie v Koninklijke Kaasfabriek Eyssen BV* [1981] ECR 409. See more recently Case C-220/98 *Estée Lauder Cosmetics GmbH & Co. OHG v Lancaster Group GmbH*, judgment of 13 January 2000, para 28 where the Court distinguished between the use of proportionality to protect consumers from being misled and the use of proportionality to protect public health.

[275] Case 286/81 *Oosthoek Uitgeversmaatschapij BV* [1982] ECR 4575.

[276] Case 382/87 *Buet v Ministère Public* [1989] ECR 1235.

[277] See also Joined Cases C-369/96 and C-376/96 *Jean-Claude Arblade, Arblade & Fils SARL and Bernard Leloup, Serge Leloup, Sofrage SARL*, judgment of 23 November 1999.

[278] Case C-43/93 *Raymond Vander Elst v Office des Migrations Internationales* [1994] ECR I-3803.

[279] ibid, para 16.   [280] ibid, para 25 (emphasis added).

[281] Case C-272/94 *Criminal Proceedings Against Michael Guiot* [1996] ECR I-1905.

[282] ibid, para 11.   [283] ibid, para 17.

In both cases the reasoning of the Court revolved around one aspect of the necessity test, namely whether the home country legislation ensures the protection of workers, but in reality the Court was also examining the question of true proportionality. Even if the levels of protection afforded by the home and host country rules were different, the latter rules could not be applied as long as the differences were not 'substantial' or the rules were 'comparable'. Thus, the relatively small, 'non-substantial', value added by the host country rules was outweighed by the relatively great disintegrative value of the application of two sets of rules.[284] The Court was once again conducting a marginal review of the true proportionality.

Marginal review of true proportionality was also evident in *Mazzoleni*.[285] A manager of a French company was prosecuted for breaking Belgian minimum wage rules. The French undertaking had provided services in Belgium, sending security officers over the border to a nearby shopping mall in Messancy, but had paid them according to the French minimum wage rules. The Court accepted that the application of host state minimum wage rules could be justified by the overriding reason of worker protection. However, it held that the application of the rules might not be proportionate if the application of Belgian minimum wage rules to a service provider resulted in a 'disproportionate administrative burden including, in certain cases, the calculation, hour-by-hour, of the appropriate remuneration for each employee according to whether he has, in the course of his work, crossed the frontier'.[286] The application of proportionality to the facts of the case was left to the national court, which had to take into account that some of the security officers had worked in Belgium only for a limited time in order to avoid being easily identified.

The Court was again engaging in a marginal review of true proportionality. Clearly the aim of worker protection would be compromised if the minimum wage rules were not applied in all cases, such as those where workers visited a country only occasionally for a brief period, as some workers would as a result receive less than their minimum wage. Yet the Court was prepared to see the rules waived when the administrative burden imposed on the service provider would outweigh the increase in the level of worker protection. The interest of service trade was balanced against the general interest in circumstances where the burden on free movement could be great and the benefit to workers slight.

Finally, for the sake of completeness, there is a discrete line of case law dealing with sanctions and penalties accompanying national provisions that restrict free movement of goods or services.[287] The Court has consistently

---

[284] In fact, the application of home country rules might have seriously compromised the competitive position of the foreign service providers. They would have had to pay twice, while their domestic competitors were subject only to a single payment.

[285] Case C-165/98 *André Mazzoleni*, judgment of 15 March 2001.   [286] ibid, para 36.

[287] See Emiliou (n 73 above) 166–169, and Tridimas (n 42 above) 157–160.

held that, even if the national measure itself is justified, sanctions attached to it cannot be so disproportionate to the gravity of the infringement that they become an obstacle to free movement.[288] This may be seen as a review of true proportionality. A very strict penalty creates a very high deterrent effect. When the Court disallows a disproportionate sanction, it is in fact conducting a balancing exercise where the benefits of the high level of deterrence are weighed against the costs of the penalty.[289]

Altogether, in recent years the Court seems to have steered away from overtly examining the true proportionality of national measures. It has, however, consistently engaged in a marginal review of costs and benefits, although its reasoning has been conducted under the necessity test.

The arguments for marginal review apply equally in the field of goods and services. The case law has followed similar patterns in both fields. It seems that in this area the unified approach is both the ideal and (at least close to) the reality.

c) The intensity of the review

In addition to the content of proportionality, the intensity of the review must be examined. It is necessary to analyse the approach of the Court in relation to different grounds of justification and in relation to Community acts as opposed to Member State measures. I will also conduct an empirical study of the results of the proportionality review.

The Court does not always conduct its proportionality inquiry with the same rigour. The intensity of the review may vary greatly, across a whole spectrum of responses. Many different factors affect the approach of the Court, but again the proper division of competence between Member States and the Community, and the relative strengths of the original decision-maker when compared with the Court, are of paramount importance.[290]

The ground of justification involved has an impact on the intensity of the review.[291] Concerns such as public morality, public policy, public security, and the related overriding reasons are primarily within Member State competence. The Court may be unfamiliar with the issues and there is often no consensus,

---

[288] In the field of goods see eg Case 41/76 *Suzanne Criel, née Donckerwolcke and Henri Schou v Procureur de la République au Tribunal de Grande Instance, Lille and Director General of Customs* [1976] ECR 1921 paras 36–38. See also, more recently, Case C-23/99 *Commission v France*, judgment of 26 September 2000, para 48. In the field of services see eg Case 118/75 *Lynne Watson and Allessandro Belmann* [1976] ECR 1185 paras 20–21.

[289] In the same manner, national authorities imposing penalties for breaches of Community law have to ensure that the sanctions are at the same time effective, proportionate and dissuasive. See Case 326/88 *Anklagemyndigheten v Hansen & Søn I/S* [1990] ECR I-2911 para 17. See also Case C-193/94 *Criminal Proceedings Against Sofia Skanavi and Konstantin Chryssanthakopoulos* [1996] ECR I-929 paras 29–39.

[290] See generally de Búrca (n 214 above) 111–113, 126–127 and 146–149.

[291] See ibid, 111 and 147, Handoll (n 23 above) 183, J.M. Fernández Martín and S. O'Leary, 'Judicial Exceptions to the Free Provision of Services' (1995) 1 ELJ 308 at 314, and Tridimas (n 180 above) 77.

scientific or otherwise, the Court could draw on.[292] These factors affect goods and services in the same way. Thus, in the field of goods the Court has shown deference to Member State measures in cases such as *Henn and Darby* (public morality)[293] and *Campus Oil* (public security),[294] and has treated national rules in the area of services similarly in, for example, *Schindler*,[295] *Läärä*,[296] and *Zenatti*[297] (social order). This can be contrasted with a more stringent approach towards national measures purporting to protect consumers, both in the field of goods[298] and services.[299] Consumer protection is more closely connected to the core competences of the Community, the Court has more expertise in the area, and there may well be a general consensus that the Court may draw upon.

The intensity of the review may also vary depending on whether the Court is examining a Community act or a Member State measure.[300] When compared with Member States, the Community has the advantage that all affected interests are represented in the decision-making process but the disadvantage that democratic control may not be sufficiently robust, in particular if the co-decision procedure of Article 251 (ex 189b) EC is not used. In general the Court has adopted a less stringent approach towards Community measures.[301]

In the goods sector, a comparison of the judgments in *Fietje*[302] and *Piageme*[303] with *Meyhui*[304] illustrates well the different standards of review.[305] The two former cases concerned national measures restricting the

[292] See de Búrca (n 214 above) 112, 127–128, 132–133 and 147.

[293] Case 34/79 *R v Henn and Darby* [1979] ECR 3795. See Arnull (n 76 above) 245–251 and de Búrca (n 214 above) 128–130. Note, however, the stricter standard in Case 121/85 *Conegate Ltd v Her Majesty's Customs and Excise* [1986] ECR 1007.

[294] Case 72/83 *Campus Oil v Minister for Industry and Energy* [1984] ECR 2727. See Weatherill and Beaumont (n 20 above) 535. See also Case C-83/94 *Leifer* [1995] ECR I-3231 analysed by Tridimas (n 42 above) 151–152.

[295] Case C-275/92 *Her Majesty's Customs and Excise v Gerhart Schindler and Jörg Schindler* [1994] ECR I-1039. See Fernández Martín and O'Leary (n 291 above) 321–329, L. Gormley, 'Pay Your Money and Take Your Chance?' (1994) 19 ELRev 644 at 651–652, and V. Hatzopoulos, 'Case C-275/92, Her Majesty's Customs and Excise v. Gerhart and Jörg Schindler, [1994] ECR I-1039 (1995)' 32 CMLRev 841, 850.

[296] Case C-124/97 *Markku Juhani Läärä, Cotswolds Microsystems Ltd, Oy Transatlantic Software Ltd v Kihlakunnansyyttäjä (Jyväskylä), Suomen Valtio*, judgment of 21 September 1999.

[297] Case C-67/98 *Questore di Verona v Diego Zenatti*, judgment of 21 October 1999.

[298] See eg Craig and de Búrca (n 103 above) 631, Weatherill and Beaumont (n 20 above) 581, and the cases analysed therein.

[299] See eg Case C-76/90 *Manfred Säger v Dennemeyer & Co. Ltd* [1991] ECR I-4221, and Fernández Martín and O'Leary (n 291 above) 315–321 and 324–329.

[300] See generally P. Eeckhout, 'The European Court of Justice and the Legislature' (1998) 18 YEL 1 at 4 and 24–28.

[301] See Jacobs (n 177 above) 21, Poiares Maduro (n 208 above) 76–78, and Tridimas (n 180 above) 66.

[302] Case 27/80 *Criminal Proceedings Against Anton Adriaan Fietje* [1980] ECR 3839.

[303] Case C-369/89 *Piageme and others v BVBA Peeters* [1991] ECR I-2971.

[304] Case C-51/93 *Meyhui NV v Schott Zwiesel Glaswerke AG* [1994] ECR I-3879.

[305] See also de Búrca (n 214 above) 114 contrasting Case 178/84 *Commission v Germany* (Reinheitsgebot) [1987] ECR 1227 with Case C-331/88 *R v Minister for Agriculture, Fisheries and Food, ex parte FEDESA and others* [1990] ECR I-4023.

use of certain expressions in the marketing of goods. In *Fietje* the Court examined Dutch rules prescribing the use of the word 'likeur' in relation to certain alcoholic beverages. *Piageme* concerned a Belgian measure providing that foodstuff labels had to use at least the language of the linguistic region where the products were marketed. In *Fietje* the Court ruled that the Dutch rules were a prima facie restriction on the free movement of goods. The Netherlands government countered by arguing that the measure was justified on grounds of consumer protection. The Court held that a requirement of informing consumers of the nature of the product was acceptable in principle, but that 'there is no longer any need for such protection if the details given on the original label of the imported product have as their content information on the nature of the product and that content includes at least the same information and is just as capable of being understood by consumers of the importing States, as the description prescribed by the rules of that State'.[306] In *Piageme* the Court ruled that Article 28 (ex 30) EC precludes 'a national law from requiring the exclusive use of a specific language for the labelling of foodstuffs, without allowing for the possibility of using another language easily understood by purchasers or of ensuring that the purchaser is informed by other methods'.[307] The Court was applying a strict necessity test to the measures.[308] The requirement of specific words or language was not the least restrictive means of consumer protection if consumers could be informed by using another language or other methods. An example might be the use of a language closely resembling the language of the consumers or a picture indicating the nature of the product.[309]

In contrast, in *Meyhui* the Court was dealing with a Community act, Council Directive 69/493/EEC of 15 December 1969 on the approximation of the laws of the Member States relating to crystal glass.[310] The Explanatory Notes in the Annex to the Directive stated that in the marketing of crystal glass and crystalline: 'Only the description in the language or languages of the country in which the goods are marketed may be used'. The validity of this provision was challenged on grounds of the free movement of goods. The Court accepted that the Explanatory Notes amounted to a prima facie restriction. However, it then stated that the argument of another language being easily understood was 'of only marginal importance' and that the requirement was 'necessary for the protection of consumers and the Council has, therefore, not exceeded the limits of its discretion'.[311] Therefore, it found the measure to be justified and proportionate and, thus, valid. Yet here the obstacle was more restrictive than in *Fietje* or *Piageme*: not only was the language

---

[306] See n 302 above, para 12. The final determination of proportionality was left to the national court.

[307] See n 303 above, para 17.

[308] Explicitly in *Fietje* (n 302 above), implicitly in *Piageme* (n 303 above).

[309] This line of case law has been recently reconfirmed in Case C-33/97 *Colim NV v Biggs Continent Noord NV* [1999] ECR I-3175.

[310] [1969] OJ Spec Ed II 599.   [311] See n 304 above, paras 19 and 21.

of the country of marketing prescribed but also the use of any other language was forbidden. Clearly the Court adopted a significantly lower standard of review towards a Community measure.[312]

An equally striking example cannot be found in the services sector, but in relation to the right of establishment *Germany v Parliament and Council*[313] provides an illustration of the tolerance of the Court towards Community acts.[314] In this case the Court adopted a low level of scrutiny in the context of a challenge to the validity of Directive 94/19/EC of the European Parliament and Council of 30 May 1994 on deposit guarantee schemes.[315] It accepted an export prohibition that a Member State clearly could not have adopted.[316] As there is no reason to treat services differently from goods and establishment[317] in this respect, it is likely that the deferential approach toward Community acts applies to the free movement of services as well.

Poiares Maduro has convincingly argued that in actual fact the Court has practised 'majoritarian activism' in the field of goods. It has compensated for the lack of Community legislative action by engaging in 'judicial harmonisation' of national rules in areas where a majoritarian view can be ascertained. This entails a strict assessment of measures diverging from the practice of the majority of Member States, and, in contrast, a more lenient approach in areas where there is no consensus.[318]

Evidence of a similar approach can be found in the field of services as well. As observed above, the Court has adopted a more stringent line in areas where consensus exists, such as consumer protection, in contrast to a tolerant attitude towards national measures in sectors characterised by an 'absence of common ethical or moral standards'.[319] Sometimes majoritarianism appears even in the Court's reasoning. For example, in *Messner*[320] the Court examined the necessity of an Italian rule requiring that a declaration of residence be made within three days of entering Italian territory. It held that the time limit was unreasonable. There was no reason to suspect that the Member State interest in obtaining information of population movements would be compromised by a longer period. It then stated: 'Moreover, that view is confirmed by the fact that the majority of the Member States of the

---

[312] See also Tridimas (n 42 above) 142.

[313] Case C-233/94 *Federal Republic of Germany v European Parliament and Council of the European Union* [1997] ECR I-2405.

[314] See Eeckhout (n 300 above) 12–14, and Jacobs (n 177 above) 5.   [315] [1994] OJ L135/5.

[316] See W.-H. Roth, 'Case C-233/94 *Federal Republic of Germany v European Parliament and Council of the European Union*, Judgment of 13 May 1997, [1997] ECR I-2405' (1998) 35 CMLRev 459 at 472–479.

[317] The legal basis of the Directive was Art 47(2) (ex 57(2)) EC, which is also applicable to services by virtue of Art 55 (ex 66) EC.

[318] See Poiares Maduro (n 208 above) 68–78. See also de Búrca (n 214 above) 127–128, and Weatherill (n 141 above) 69–70.

[319] Fernández Martín and O'Leary (n 291 above) 329.

[320] Case C-265/88 *Criminal Proceedings Against Lothar Messner* [1989] ECR 4209. It is not clear whether Mr Messner was in Italy as an employed person or as a supplier of services. See the Opinion of AG Mischo, para 9. The Court made no distinction between different freedoms.

Community imposing a similar obligation allow those concerned appreciably longer periods'.[321] In contrast, in *Commission v Germany* (Insurance)[322] the Court permitted a national authorisation procedure in the direct insurance sector stating it had been shown 'that considerable differences exist in the national rules currently in force concerning technical reserves and the assets which represent such reserves'.[323] In the former case the Court referred to the common practice of Member States when disallowing a diverging rule, in the latter the lack of consensus argued for the acceptance of the restriction.

It has now been argued that the level of scrutiny varies in the same way both in the field of goods and services. The final question to be answered is whether the intensity of the review is the same for both freedoms. Based on earlier case law it has sometimes been argued that the Court is more tolerant in the services sector.[324] The fact that information asymmetries are more common in relation to services than goods would point to a less rigorous scrutiny, but on the other hand it can be argued that this market failure should not automatically exclude free movement.[325]

The issue of justification is always closely connected to the facts of a case. Therefore, it is very difficult to draw any firm conclusions from comparing single judgments with each other. However, statistical analysis can reveal something about the level of scrutiny. I have examined the decisions in these two fields,[326] beginning from 25 July 1991, when the doctrine of overriding requirements was given its current shape also in the field of services,[327] and finishing on 30 April 1998.

During this period, in cases concerning Article 28 (ex 30 *et seq*) EC that proceeded to the level of justification, the European Court of Justice:

- held the measure(s) to be permissible in 20 judgments (30%);
- held the measure(s) to be not permissible in 30 judgments (45%);
- came to mixed results in 16 judgments (24%).[328]

During the same period, in cases concerning Article 49 (ex 59 *et seq*) EC that proceeded to the level of justification, the European Court of Justice:

[321] ibid, para 11. See also the importance given to international medical science in Case C-157/99 *Geraets-Smits v Stichting Ziekenfonds VGZ and Peerbooms v Stichting CZ Groep Zorgverzekeringen*, judgment of 12 July 2001, paras 92–98.

[322] Case 205/84 *Commission v Germany* [1986] ECR 3755.   [323] ibid, para 39.

[324] See Reich (n 272 above) 136, and W. Bratton, J. McCahery, S. Picciotto and C. Scott (eds), *International Reglatory Competition and Coordination. Perspectives on Economic Regulation in Europe and the United States* (Oxford 1996) 37. See also Barnard (n 143 above) 56–57. See on this also section 4biii above.

[325] See section 4biii above.

[326] Excluding decisions that did not proceed to the level of justification, where only secondary legislation was of relevance, or where the free movement provisions were only used in conjunction with the provisions on public undertakings.

[327] See section 3a above.

[328] Either the European Court of Justice set out conditions and referred the issue back to the national court, or the result was partly permissible/impermissible for the national court and partly permissible/impermissible for the national court.

- held the measure(s) to be permissible in seven judgments (23%);
- held the measure(s) to be not permissible in 19 judgments (63%);
- came to mixed results in four judgments (13%).[329]

The figures should of course be approached with caution and too much cannot be read into them. They can only give a general indication of the level of scrutiny, as it is conceivable that cases brought in one field during this time have been inherently more 'justifiable',[330] and there is also an element of subjectivity involved in the assessment of the judgments.[331] Yet, even with these caveats, it seems that the recent case law does not support a claim of less intense review in the field of services.

d) Conclusion

The examination of proportionality has shown that the principle is very flexible in its application. It has been applied differently in different contexts to protect different interests and entails varying degrees of judicial review.[332] It has even been said: 'The usefulness of the proportionality test lies in the fact that it gives the courts maximum flexibility in reviewing administrative discretion within acceptable limits'.[333]

What appears as flexible to some is 'unsystematic' or 'vague' to others.[334] This is especially problematic from the national courts' point of view. It will be very difficult for a national court to decide a case concerning the free movement of goods or services if it is unclear 'how to define the concept [of proportionality], whether it contains two or three elements and whether (and, if so, to what extent) it has a different content depending on the situation, that is to say, primarily on the nature of interests involved'.[335] Jarvis, after exploring the difficulties national courts have encountered when applying the principle, suggests that the European Court of Justice ought to give the referring court guidance on which aspect of the proportionality test to emphasise.[336] In my view this is not enough. If national courts are to fulfil their function as

[329] Either the European Court of Justice set out conditions and referred the issue back to the national court, or the result was partly permissible/impermissible for the national court and partly permissible/impermissible for the national court.

[330] For example, in the goods sector there are three Sunday trading cases in which the Court found the measure to be permissible.

[331] In direct actions brought by the Commission or a Member State the Court decides on the issue of proportionality itself. In preliminary rulings, however, the final judgment is delivered by the referring national court. Often the Court gives such clear guidelines that no doubts remain, but in some instances conflicting interpretations are possible. Therefore, the Appendix below lists the cases and the interpretation given to them.

[332] Jacobs (n 177 above) 20, and Tridimas (n 180 above) 69.

[333] Emiliou (n 73 above) 273.

[334] Kapteyn and VerLoren van Themaat (n 20 above) 656, and van Gerven (n 178 above) 60. See also Hatzopoulos (n 40 above) 205–206.

[335] van Gerven (n 178 above) 60.   [336] Jarvis (n 72 above) 229–230.

Community courts, they have to be able to decide cases themselves, without always resorting to the Article 234 (ex 177) EC procedure. An excessively flexible and nuanced proportionality test will prevent this. If a national court always has to refer a case to simply find out what is the content of and how to apply the proportionality test, something is not right.

5. Conclusion

The Court has balanced free trade against other values using a system of justifications and proportionality. Despite the fact that information asymmetries are more common in the services sector and the different wordings of Articles 30 and 46 (ex 36 and 56) EC, the Court has adopted an essentially uniform approach to both freedoms. It has interpreted express EC Treaty derogations in the same way, developed a similar system of overriding requirements, and adopted a common interpretation of proportionality in both areas.

The Court's case law in relation to justifications is by and large to be commended. It has developed a flexible system that is capable of achieving a sensible balance between the different interests in individual cases. Its approach has fallen between anti-protectionism and economic freedom readings of the EC Treaty. In practice, it does not evaluate the aims of the Member State measures, as long as the purpose is not economic, but concentrates on the means employed. It usually conducts a fairly robust assessment of suitability and necessity of the national rules, thus flushing out protectionist measures, but also engages in marginal review of true proportionality. The most problematic part of the Court's approach to justifications is the confused case law on the definition of distinctly and equally applicable measures. Additionally, the sheer complexity of the doctrine, in particular as regards the proportionality test, may make it difficult for national courts to decide cases correctly without a reference to the European Court of Justice.

5

Conclusion

1. Introduction

The point of departure in this study has been the desirability of a uniform interpretation of the EC Treaty provisions on the free movement of goods and services. There are both economic and legal arguments for a similar approach in the two fields.

The economics of trade in goods and services is the same. The theory of comparative advantage applies in both fields. Both goods and services are part of product markets, not factor markets. The same trade policy goals, principles, procedures and techniques can be used in both sectors. The differences examined, such as the different modes of the supply of services, the greater intensity of regulation in the services sector, the regulation of service suppliers instead of the product, and the intangible character of services, do not necessitate a fundamentally different approach. The migration and investment issues that create difficulties for the global liberalisation of trade in services do not apply to a Community which is committed to the movement of the factors of production, and in any case would mainly influence the approach to the free movement of persons and capital, not the freedom to provide services. Economically, it makes little sense to have distinct approaches to goods and services.

It is true that the two freedoms are governed by different EC Treaty provisions with differing wordings. However, the freedoms are based on the same general provisions of the Treaty, such as Article 14 (ex 7a) EC on the internal market. A common approach would contribute to the development of Community law into a legal system where the law is not just a group of particular rules but a coherent whole based on generally accepted principles.

Goods and services are closely related, particularly when services are provided, for example, by telecommunications, and persons do not move. The only difference is between the material and non-material nature of the product, and in practice it may even be difficult to decide on the classification of the activity. However, even the movement of persons providing or receiving services does not change the equation. The activities are only temporary, and in any event Community citizens should not lightly be deprived of their right to move freely. In *Gebhard*[1] the Court explicitly recognised the need for a

---

[1] Case C-55/94 *Reinhard Gebhard v Consiglio dell'Ordine degli Avvocati e Procuratori di Milano* [1995] ECR I-4165 para 37.

parallel interpretation of all four freedoms. Thus, there is a prima facie case for a uniform approach.

In this section I will offer the results of my study, seeking to answer three questions: Has the approach of the Court been the same in the two fields? What are the reasons for any differences? Can a sensible uniform solution be found?

2. The approach of the Court

a) Restriction

The interpretation given to the notion of restriction has fluctuated over time, in both the fields of goods and services. In general, it can be said that originally the European Court of Justice adopted a wider reading of Article 28 than of Article 49 (ex 30 and 59) EC, but that in the mid-1990s the positions were dramatically reversed.

The approaches to goods and services diverged from the very beginning. Unlike Article 28 (ex 30) EC, the Treaty provisions on services refer to the idea of non-discrimination, and Commission Directive 70/50/EEC on goods seemed to go further than the 1961 General Programme on Services. In the early cases of *Dassonville*[2] on goods and *van Binsbergen*[3] on services in 1974 the Court took a somewhat different approach to the two freedoms. Although neither decision went very far on the facts, the language of the Court in *Dassonville* could be interpreted very expansively. In contrast, *van Binsbergen* seemed to place the main emphasis on the existence of discrimination.

The problem of disparity between national rules and dual regulatory burden was tackled in the goods sector in *Cassis de Dijon*[4] in 1979. The Court confirmed the wide effects-based test of *Dassonville*, and created a principle of mutual recognition, entailing a presumption that goods 'lawfully produced and marketed in one of the Member States' had to be admitted to the markets of the other Member States.

The Court was more cautious in the services sector. Although from 1979 it used similar principles as in *Cassis*, full equality was only achieved in the cases decided on 25 July 1991[5] when both the language and the methodology of the Court in services cases were brought into line with the case law in the goods sector.

---

[2] Case 8/74 *Procureur du Roi v Dassonville* [1974] ECR 837.
[3] Case 33/74 *Van Binsbergen v Bestuur van de Bedrijfsvereniging voor de Metaalnijverheid* [1974] ECR 1299.
[4] Case 120/78 *Rewe Zentrale AG v Bundesmonopolverwaltung für Branntwein* [1979] ECR 649.
[5] Case C-288/89 *Collectieve Antennevoorziening Gouda* [1991] ECR I-4007, Case C-353/89 *Commission v Netherlands* [1991] ECR I-4069, and Case C-76/90 *Manfred Säger v Dennemeyer & Co. Ltd* [1991] ECR I-4221.

Neither *Cassis* nor the 1991 cases on services went so far as to establish that also truly non-discriminatory national rules fell foul of the free movement provisions. Material discrimination was still involved. The importing or host country applied its legislation to goods or services that had already complied with the requirements of the exporting or home country. The language of the cases referred to goods or services lawfully produced and marketed or provided in the exporting or home state. The idea was that the activities could be governed by one—and only one—regulatory system.

Truly non-discriminatory rules were sometimes found to fall within the scope of Article 28 (ex 30) EC. The clearest example of this were the Sunday trading cases, such as *Torfaen*,[6] where the Court stretched the scope of Article 28 as far as possible. All measures diminishing the volume of imports, regardless of their even-handed nature, were seen as obstacles to the free movement of goods. This was an economic freedom reading of the free movement rules. The Court did not go quite this far in the field of services, and soon changed its mind also as regards Article 28.

The judgment of the Court in 1993 in *Keck*[7] represented an important shift in the interpretation of Article 28. 'Re-examining and clarifying' its previous case law, the Court distinguished between product rules and rules regulating selling arrangements. It held that the latter fell within the scope of Article 28 only if they did not 'affect in the same manner, in law and in fact, the marketing of domestic products and of those from other Member States'.

This judgment established a wide concept of discrimination as the determinant factor in limiting the notion of a measure having an equivalent effect. Product rules created a double burden, and therefore always fell within the scope of Article 28, while rules concerning market circumstances did not normally impose a heavier burden on imports, and therefore were not automatically included. The approach of the Court was a move away from the economic freedom approach towards anti-protectionism, and also a step towards legal formalism. A standard-based test was partially replaced by a rule-like one with the capacity to provide greater legal certainty.

However, the Court did not follow this approach in the field of services. In *Alpine Investments*[8] the Court ruled that a Dutch measure preventing Dutch undertakings from cold-calling potential customers in other Member States fell within the scope of Article 49 (ex 59) EC. *Alpine Investments*, when read alone, could be reconciled with *Keck*. An equally applicable marketing rule was considered a prima facie restriction when it was adopted by the exporting home state. The principle could be that the importing host state regulated market circumstances and the exporting home state dealt with products and production. Therefore, a non-discriminatory host state rule on selling

---

[6] Case 145/88 *Torfaen BC v B&Q* [1989] ECR 3851.
[7] Joined Cases C-267/91 and C-268/91 *Criminal Proceedings Against Keck and Mithouard* [1993] ECR I-6097.
[8] Case C-384/93 *Alpine Investments BV v Minister van Financiën* [1995] ECR I-1141.

arrangements would not constitute a restriction, but the application of a similar rule by the home state had to be justified. Conversely, the application of host state product and production rules would amount to a prima facie restriction, while the home state was free to regulate in a non-discriminatory manner, in accordance with *Cassis* and *Groenveld*.[9] Regulatory competence would be divided between Member States to ensure that one, and only one, rule always applied. However, when read together with the judgment in *Bosman*,[10] *Alpine Investments* has to be seen as constituting the birth of a new doctrine. National rules creating a direct impediment to market access were scrutinised by the Court. Cross-border measures could be attacked even if they were truly non-discriminatory.[11]

With *Alpine Investments* the Court's case law on services overtook that on goods. While in the past the approach to services had been more cautious and conservative, the Court was now aggressively expanding the scope of Article 49 (ex 59) EC, although at the same time retreating in the goods sector. Whether the expansion and the retreat are permanent, remains to be seen. *Alpine Investments* and *Bosman* have been confirmed by *Pro Sieben Media*,[12] *Gourmet International Products*,[13] and *Graf*.[14] In the majority of its recent decisions on the free movement of goods the Court has applied the *Keck* formula, but there are some judgments where it seemed to be employing a broader test based on impediment to market access.

b) Persons bound

Another fundamental difference has developed in the interpretation of the addressee of Articles 28 and 49 (ex 30 and 59) EC. Both provisions apply to restrictions created by the Community legislature, but the approach to private measures has diverged significantly.

The wording of the Treaty indicates that Article 28 (ex 30) EC is aimed at state activities. The Commission has also been of this opinion. The Court has shared this view and has held in many judgments that the provisions on the free movement of goods concern only public measures.

---

[9] Case 15/79 *Groenveld v Produktschap voor Vee en Vlees* [1979] ECR 3409.

[10] Case C-415/93 *Union Royale Belge des Sociétés de Football Association ASBL and others v Jean-Marc Bosman* [1995] ECR I-4921.

[11] It would be tempting to explain *Bosman* away as a judgment limited to the movement of natural persons, as a case can be made for a greater protection being given to the movement of citizens. The reasoning did not turn on this factor, however, and in general citizenship has been of limited importance in the Court's interpretation of the free movement rules.

[12] Case C-6/98 *Arbeitsgemeinschaft Deutscher Rundfunkanstalten (ARD) v PRO Sieben Media AG*, judgment of 28 October 1999.

[13] Case C-405/98 *Konsumentombudsmannen v Gourmet International Products Aktiebolag*, judgment of 8 March 2001.

[14] Case C-190/98 *Volker Graf v Filzmoser Maschinenbau GmbH*, judgment of 27 January 2000.

It has sometimes been argued that in its judgments dealing with intellectual property rights and unfair competition the Court has in fact prohibited private measures restricting the free movement of goods, and seems to have given weight to the subjective behaviour of private parties. However, the early decisions of the Court can be interpreted in another way. It can be argued that the Court was not seeking to widen its interpretation of Article 28 (ex 30) EC, but was simply influenced by the dichotomy between the existence and exercise of intellectual property rights developed in the field of competition law. In addition, the Court sometimes employed conflicting language, even within a single decision. In the light of the more recent case law, it is clear that the obstacle attacked by the Court is not private behaviour but national legislation granting private parties the right to exercise their intellectual property rights in certain circumstances. The subjective behaviour of private parties has proven to be irrelevant.

The Court has interpreted the concept of Member State widely in this context. The involvement of private parties does not make Article 28 inapplicable if the private body is controlled by the state or has been granted special powers. A state cannot escape the EC Treaty provisions on the free movement of goods by using a private party as a medium through which a measure is brought into effect.

By contrast, despite the wording of the Treaty provisions in the Chapter on Services and the opinions of the Council and the Commission, the Court has held that Article 49 (ex 59) EC applies at least to some private restrictions. It has so far extended this doctrine only to rules aimed at collectively regulating services, but it has not ruled out an even wider interpretation.

Doctrinally, the Court's case law on private restrictions differs fundamentally in the two sectors. However, the practical impact of the differences is not great, as the concept of Member State has been interpreted widely in the field of goods. In addition, the Court has held that a Member State may be responsible for private restrictions.

In contrast, the approach to measures adopted by the Community seems to be the same in both the goods and the services sectors. Provisions in Part One of the EC Treaty, Principles, make it clear that the Community cannot escape the four freedoms. The Court has recognised in its case law that both the free movement of goods and the free movement of services bind the Community, and can serve to guide the interpretation of, or even invalidate, Community legislation. The concept of restriction seems to have the same meaning for both the Community and Member States.

c) Justification

The approach of the Court to the justification of measures falling within the scope of the provisions on the free movement of goods and services has been

similar in both fields. Exceptions found in the EC Treaty or developed by the
Court have been treated in the same way and the principle of proportionality
has played the same role in both sectors.

Articles 30 and 46 (ex 36 and 56) EC, which permit derogations from the
free movement of goods and services, have the same function but are worded
very differently. Nevertheless, the Court has interpreted the two provisions in
the same way. Neither provision reserves matters to the exclusive jurisdiction
of Member States, and they cannot be used once the Community has taken
action. The provisions are construed strictly, and purely economic justifications are not accepted.

Article 30 (ex 36) EC contains many more grounds of justification than
Article 46 (ex 56) EC. However, the development of overriding requirements
in general interest in the case law has narrowed the discrepancy. In practice,
there do not seem to be many measures that could be justified in the field of
goods under Article 30 but not in the field of services.

Article 46 does not contain a statement equivalent to the second sentence
of Article 30. Nonetheless, this does not create any significant differences
between the freedoms. The second sentence may lack independent value
and may in any event also be applied in the field of services. This reflects the
general trend. Despite the textual differences, the Court has interpreted the
provisions in a similar manner.

The Court has in its case law created additional exceptions. These developments have taken place in both sectors and have gone hand in hand with the
widening of the scope of the freedoms. They also reflect changes in societal
attitudes.

Overriding requirements are currently used in the same manner in both sectors. They cannot be employed if the field is occupied by the Community, and
purely economic reasons are not accepted. They may only justify equally
applicable measures, but the distinction between distinctly and equally
applicable measures remains unclear. Overriding requirements are not a
closed class but the Court may accept new grounds of justification.

The Court has applied the principle of proportionality both in the field of
goods and in the field of services. The principle is of relevance in relation to
EC Treaty exceptions as well as to overriding requirements. It entails at least
the tests of suitability and necessity, which have been employed in both the
goods and the services sectors.

The most controversial aspect of the principle is the test of 'true proportionality', or proportionality in the strict sense. The Court has on occasion
indicated its willingness to assess the true proportionality of national measures both in the field of goods and services. However, in recent years the
Court seems to have steered away from overtly examining the true proportionality, but has consistently engaged in a marginal review of costs and benefits under the guise of the necessity test. The case law has followed similar
patterns in relation to both freedoms.

The Court does not always conduct the proportionality inquiry with the same rigour. Many different factors, such as the ground of justification invoked and whether the Court is examining a Member State or a Community measure, affect the intensity of the review. The level of scrutiny varies in the same way in both the fields of goods and services. It has sometimes been argued that on the whole the Court is more tolerant in the services sector. The results of an empirical study of recent judgments do not support this argument.

The Court has balanced free trade against other values using a system of justifications and proportionality. It has adopted an essentially uniform approach to the free movement of goods and services. It has interpreted EC Treaty provisions in the same way, developed a similar system of overriding requirements, and adopted a common interpretation of proportionality in both areas. The case law is by and large to be commended. The Court has developed a flexible system that is capable of striking a sensible balance between the different interests in individual cases.

3. Reasons for the differences

The reasons for the differences in the Court's approach to the free movement of goods and services have been only briefly examined in the course of this study. This is due to the fact that the Court has never explained the reasons for the divergences. In general, it has seldom discussed its case law on services in a judgment on the free movement of goods, or vice versa. In this section I will offer a brief, necessarily speculative, theory of the reasons for the differences.

It may be that the freedom to provide services was originally seen as a less important adjunct to the free movement of persons, in particular the right of establishment. Certainly there was not much cross-border trade in services, and when such transactions did take place, the movement of natural persons was usually involved, as telecommunications were not terribly advanced. In many important cases the Court even declined to decide whether the activities involved ought to be classified as falling under the provisions on the free movement of workers, the right of establishment, or the freedom to provide services. It simply held that identical principles applied to all of these freedoms.[15]

In addition to the general tendency to view services together with persons rather than with goods, there may be more specific reasons for the differences. The non-application of *Keck*[16] to services may be connected to the lack of a

---

[15] See eg Case 36/74 *Walrave and Koch v UCI* [1974] ECR 1405 (workers and services) and, more recently, Case C-106/91 *Ramrath v Ministère de la Justice* [1992] ECR I-3351 (workers, establishment and services).

[16] Joined Cases C-267/91 and C-268/91 *Criminal Proceedings Against Keck and Mithouard* [1993] ECR I-6097.

tendency of traders to invoke Article 49 (ex 59) EC to challenge rules that limit their commercial freedom. As the provisions on the free movement of services only apply to cross-border situations, Article 49 cannot be used as a basis for a test case or as a general defence against the application of national rules as easily as Article 28 (ex 30) EC prior to *Keck*. The wider circle of addressees of the free movement of services may be connected to the more aggressive use of competition rules in the goods sector, which meant that there was less need to apply the provisions on the free movement of goods to private parties.

Since the early years services have become economically ever more important and international trade in services has increased dramatically. The legal situation is also changing. The provisions on the free movement of services have gained independent importance, and there are more connections to the goods sector. Perhaps the best illustrations are provided by the decisions of the Court on 25 July 1991,[17] together with the many recent Opinions of Advocates General where judgments on the free movement of goods are discussed in cases dealing with services.[18]

Yet even today the similarities between services and persons cannot be ignored. *Alpine Investments*[19] and *Bosman*[20] employ the same notions of restriction and both Articles 49 and 39 (ex 59 and 48) EC apply to the activities of private parties.

4. Proposed solutions

It has been seen that the Court's approach to the free movement of goods and services has not been identical. In the light of the arguments for a uniform approach, it has to be asked whether sensible solutions treating the two freedoms in the same way can be found. If such solutions cannot be devised, the case for uniformity cannot be made.

---

[17] See n 5 above.
[18] See eg AG Jacobs in Case C-76/90 *Manfred Säger v Dennemeyer & Co. Ltd* [1991] ECR I-4221, Case C-384/93 *Alpine Investments BV v Minister van Financiën* [1995] ECR I-1141 and Case C-405/98 *Konsumentombudsmannen v Gourmet International Products Aktiebolag*, judgment of 8 March 2001, AG Cosmas in Joined Cases C-51/96 and C-191/97 *Christelle Deliège v Asbl Ligue Francophone de judo et disciplines associées and others*, AG Elmer in Case C-111/94 *Non-contentious Proceedings Brought by Job Centre Coop. arl* [1995] ECR I-3361, AG Fennelly in Case C-266/96 *Corsica Ferries France SA v Gruppo Antichi Ormeggiatori del Porto di Genova Coop. arl and others* [1998] ECR I-3949, and AG Gulmann in Case C-275/92 *Her Majesty's Customs and Excise v Gerhart Schindler and Jörg Schindler* [1994] ECR I-1039. See also AG Tesauro in Case C-368/95 *Vereinigte Familiapress Zeitungsverlags-und vertriebs GmbH v Heinrich Bauer Verlag* [1997] ECR I-3689.
[19] Case C-384/93 *Alpine Investments BV v Minister van Financiën* [1995] ECR I-1141.
[20] Case C-415/93 *Union Royale Belge des Sociétés de Football Association ASBL and others v Jean-Marc Bosman* [1995] ECR I-4921.

a) **Restriction**

It is submitted that the notion of restriction ought to be the same for both freedoms. The scope given to the freedoms ought to be based on the principles behind the Court's recent case law in the field of goods.

A very wide reading of the free movement provisions leads to excessive centralisation. When the Court finds that a Member State measure falls within the scope of Article 28 or 49 (ex 30 and 59) EC, it allocates the competence to regulate to the Community. The measure is seen as a restriction, and harmonisation becomes the natural solution. If the Court, a central organ applying central rules, goes further and finds the national measure to be unjustified, it dictates policy choices to Member States and engages in negative harmonisation.

A centralised system has many disadvantages. It prevents competition between legal orders, restricts the possibilities for international specialisation, and ignores varying national preferences. It may produce inertia and fail to control the expansionist tendencies of the public sector and the rent-seeking of private interest groups.

To achieve the benefits of a decentralised system, in particular competition between regulations, the Court ought to guarantee that products from other Member States are able to compete on truly equal terms with domestic products and can maintain their competitive advantage, but go no further. Free movement should be safeguarded, but at the same time national measures should be respected as far as possible and Member States should be given freedom to discover efficient rules suited to the preferences of their citizens. In general, for the competition between regulatory systems to be maintained, the importing host country should not be required to mutually recognise the exporting home country's rules regulating market circumstances, and the exporting home country should not be forced to mutually recognise the importing host country's production rules.

A system based on a wide concept of discrimination would fulfil these criteria well. To avoid a double burden, the competence for the regulation of market circumstances would be allocated to the importing host state and the competence for product and production rules to the exporting home state. These measures would not fall under the free movement provisions, unless they discriminated. The exception to this division of competence would be the power of states to impose justified measures. In these situations the co-ordination of regulatory competences would not be sufficient and harmonisation would become necessary.

An excessively wide reading of the free movement rules also creates problems relating to the role of the courts in the system. It forces national courts to deal with situations they are ill-equipped to handle and strains the resources of the European Court of Justice. It undermines the legitimacy of the whole system and may endanger good relations between national courts and the European Court. A narrower, rule-like approach, such as that based on discrimination, is to be preferred.

The advocated approach would lead to a decentralised, federal Community where the Member States' regulatory competences are preserved. Market forces would be given the principal responsibility for bringing about the integration of national markets. The desired result would not be imposed by the public intervention of a central authority but would come about through the operation of the invisible hand of the market.

Thus, an approach based on the principles behind *Keck*[21] is appropriate for the two freedoms. The arguments apply equally in both sectors. The same system is optimal.[22]

b) Private parties

It is submitted that the approach of the Court to private measures is not fully satisfactory in either field. The interpretation of Article 28 (ex 30) EC is too narrow, while the interpretation of Article 49 (ex 59) EC is too extensive. The best solution is to be found between the two approaches.

The issue should be viewed from the perspective of the EC Treaty as a whole. Import and export restrictions created by undertakings are to be dealt with under competition rules. The application of the free movement rules would amount to inefficient, unnecessary and unfeasible public intervention. Additionally, individual or group exemptions of the Commission would be put in doubt by the use of the free movement provisions. The actions of a single non-dominant firm or agreements between firms having an insignificant effect on the market, which fall outside the scope of competition rules, do not constitute a threat to market integration, due to the lack of power to create a protectionist effect.

Nevertheless, the rules on the free movement of goods and services should be applicable to the actions of private non-undertakings. They fall outside of competition rules, but may have the means and the motive to create serious obstacles to intra-Community trade. The application of the free movement rules to these entities would also safeguard the uniform application of Community law. The actions of a private non-undertaking would need to have a protective effect, in the sense of being capable of hindering trade, for Articles 28 and 49 (ex 30 and 59) EC to apply.

Thus, a reinterpretation of both Articles 28 and 49 is needed. The provisions on the free movement of goods should be applicable to the activities of

---

[21] Joined Cases C-267/91 and C-268/91 *Criminal Proceedings Against Keck and Mithouard* [1993] ECR I-6097.

[22] The development of citizenship could in the future lead to a privileged position being given to the movement of EU citizens, however.

non-undertakings, while the provisions on the free movement of services should not be applied to undertakings. The principle of Member State responsibility for private restrictions is a useful addition to Community law but does not remove the need for this reinterpretation.

Again, the same arguments apply equally to goods and services. Here, as elsewhere, the optimal solution is the same for both freedoms.

Appendix
Cases analysed in the study

The following is a list of cases analysed in the empirical study on the intensity of review, whether they concern goods or services, and the result of the case.

Case C-288/89 *Collectieve Antennevoorziening Gouda* [1991] ECR I-4007; services; not permissible.

Case C-353/89 *Commission v Netherlands* [1991] ECR I-4069; services; not permissible.

Joined Cases C-1/90 and C-176/90 *Aragonesa de Publicidad Exterior SA and Publivía SAE v Departamento de Sanidad y Seguridad Social de la Generalitat de Cataluña* [1991] ECR I-4151; goods; permissible.

Case C-76/90 *Manfred Säger v Dennemeyer & Co. Ltd* [1991] ECR I-4221; services; not permissible.

Case C-18/88 *Régie des télégraphes et des téléphones v GB-Inno-BM SA* [1991] ECR I-5941; goods; not permissible.

Case C-204/90 *Hans-Martin Bachmann v Belgian State* [1992] ECR I-249; services; mixed result.

Case C-300/90 *Commission v Belgium* [1992] ECR I-305; services; permissible.

Case C-235/89 *Commission v Italy* [1992] ECR I-777; goods; not permissible.

Case C-30/90 *Commission v United Kingdom* [1992] ECR I-829; goods; not permissible.

Case C-62/90 *Commission v Germany* [1992] ECR I-2575; goods; not permissible.

Case C-106/91 *Ramrath v Ministère de la Justice* [1992] ECR I-3351; services; mixed result.

Case C-360/89 *Commission v Italy* [1992] ECR I-3401; services; not permissible.

Joined Cases C-13/91 and C-113/91 *Criminal Proceedings Against Michel Debus* [1992] ECR I-3617; goods; not permissible.

Case C-47/90 *Établissements Delhaize Frères et Compagnie Le Lion SA v Promalvin SA and AGE Bodegas Unidas SA* [1992] ECR I-3669; goods; not permissible.

Case C-137/91 *Commission v Greece* [1992] ECR I-4023; goods; not permissible.

Case C-2/90 *Commission v Belgium* [1992] ECR I-4431; goods; permissible.

Case C-95/89 *Commission v Italy* [1992] ECR I-4545; goods; permissible.

Case C-293/89 *Commission v Greece* [1992] ECR I-4577; goods; permissible.

Case C-344/90 *Commission v France* [1992] ECR I-4719; goods; permissible.

Case C-191/90 *Generics (UK) Ltd and Harris Pharmaceuticals Ltd v Smith Kline and French Laboratories Ltd* [1992] ECR I-5335; goods; not permissible.

Case C-3/91 *Exportur SA v LOR SA and Confiserie du Tech* [1992] ECR I-5529; goods; permissible.

Case C-279/89 *Commission v United Kingdom* [1992] ECR I-5785; goods; not permissible.

Case C-235/91 *Commission v Ireland* [1992] ECR I-5917; goods; not permissible.

Case C-280/89 *Commission v Ireland* [1992] ECR I-6185; goods; not permissible.

Case C-306/88 *Rochdale Borough Council v Stewart John Anders* [1992] ECR I-6457; goods; permissible.

Case C-304/90 *Reading Borough Council v Payless DIY Ltd and others* [1992] ECR I-6493; goods; permissible.

Case C-169/91 *Stoke-on-Trent and Norwich City Councils v B&Q* [1992] ECR I-6635; goods; permissible.

Case C-211/91 *Commission v Belgium* [1992] I-6757; services; not permissible.

Case C-148/91 *Vereiging Veronica Omroep Organisatie v Commissariaat voor de Media* [1993] ECR I-487; services; permissible.

Case C-375/90 *Commission v Greece* [1993] ECR I-2055; goods; permissible.

Case C-17/92 *FEDECINE v Spain* [1993] ECR I-2239; services; not permissible.

Case C-126/91 *Schutzverband gegen Unwesen in der Wirtschaft e. V. v Yves Rocher GmbH* [1993] ECR I-2361; goods; not permissible.

Case C-228/91 *Commission v Italy* [1993] ECR I-2701; goods; not permissible.

Case C-271/92 *LPO v UNSOF and others* [1993] ECR I-2899; goods; permissible.

Case C-373/92 *Commission v Belgium* [1993] ECR I-3107; goods; not permissible.

Case C-243/89 *Commission v Denmark* [1993] ECR I-3353; goods, services; not permissible.

Case C-20/92 *Anthony Hubbard v Peter Hamburger* [1993] ECR I-3777; services; not permissible.

Joined Cases C-46/90 and C-93/91 *Procureur du Roi v Jean-Marie Lagauche and others* [1993] ECR I-5267; goods; permissible.

Case C-317/91 *Deutsche Renault AG v AUDI AG* [1993] ECR I-6227; goods; permissible.

Joined Cases C-277/91, C-318/91 and C-319/91 *Ligur Carni Srl and others v Unità Sanitaria Locale No XV di Genove and others* [1993] ECR I-6621; goods; not permissible.

Case C-315/92 *Verband Sozialer Wettbewerb v Estée Lauder* [1994] ECR I-317; goods; not permissible.

Case C-45/93 *Commission v Spain* [1994] ECR I-911; services; not permissible.

Case C-375/92 *Commission v Spain* [1994] ECR I-923; services; not permissible.
Case C-80/92 *Commission v Belgium* [1994] ECR I-1019; goods; mixed result.
Case C-275/92 *Her Majesty's Customs and Excise v Gerhart Schindler and Jörg Schindler* [1994] ECR I-1039; services; permissible.
Case C-272/91 *Commission v Italy* [1994] ECR I-1409; services; not permissible.
Case C-9/93 *IHT Internationale Heiztechnik GmbH and Uwe Danziger v Ideal-Standard GmbH and Wabco Standard GmbH* [1994] ECR I-2789; goods; permissible.
Case C-317/92 *Commission v Germany* [1994] ECR I-2039; goods; not permissible.
Case C-426/92 *Germany v Deutsches Milch-Kontor GmbH* [1994] ECR I-2757; goods; mixed result.
Case C-314/93 *Criminal Proceedings Against Francois Rouffeteau and Robert Badia* [1994] ECR I-3257; goods; permissible.
Case C-131/93 *Commission v Germany* [1994] ECR I-3303; goods; not permissible.
Case C-17/93 *Criminal Proceedings Against J.J.J. Van der Veldt* [1994] ECR I-3537; goods; not permissible.
Case C-43/93 *Raymond Vander Elst v Office des Migrations Internationales* [1994] ECR I-3803; services; not permissible.
Case C-51/93 *Meyhui NV v Schott Zwiesel Glaswerke AG* [1994] ECR I-3879; goods; permissible.
Case C-146/91 *KYDEP v Council and Commission* [1994] ECR I-4199; goods; permissible.
Case C-293/93 *Criminal Proceedings Against Ludomira Neeltje Barbara Houtwipper* [1994] ECR I-4249; goods; mixed result.
Case C-249/92 *Commission v Italy* [1994] ECR I-4311; goods; not permissible.
Case C-23/93 *TV 10 SA v Commissariaat voor de Media* [1994] ECR I-4795; services; permissible.
Case C-55/93 *Criminal Proceedings Against J.G.C. van Schaik* [1994] ECR I-4837; services; permissible.
Case C-323/93 *Société Civile Agricole du Centre d'Insémination de la Crespelle v Coopérative d'Élevage et d'Insémination Artificielle du Département de la Mayenne* [1994] ECR I-5077; goods; mixed result.
Case C-320/93 *Lucien Ortscheit GmbH v Eurim-Pharm Arzneimittel GmbH* [1994] ECR I-5243; goods; permissible.

Case C-359/93 *Commission v Netherlands* [1995] ECR I-157; goods; not permissible.
Case C-324/93 *R v Secretary of State for the Home Department, ex parte Evans Medical Ltd and Macfarlan Smith Ltd* [1995] ECR I-563; goods; mixed result.
Case C-384/93 *Alpine Investments BV v Minister van Financiën* [1995] ECR I-1141; services; permissible.

Case C-470/93 *Verein gegen Unwesen in Handel und Gewerbe Köln e. V. v Mars GmbH* [1995] ECR I-1923; goods; not permissible.

Case C-51/94 *Commission v Germany* [1995] ECR I-3599; goods; not permissible.

Case C-484/93 *Svensson, Gustavsson v Ministre du logement et de l'urbanisme* [1995] ECR I-3955; services; not permissible.

Case C-272/94 *Criminal Proceedings Against Michael Guiot* [1996] ECR I-1905; services; not permissible.

Case C-101/94 *Commission v Italy* [1996] ECR I-2691; services; not permissible.

Case C-293/94 *Criminal Proceedings Against Jacqueline Brandsma* [1996] ECR I-3159; goods; mixed result.

Case C-240/95 *Criminal Proceedings Against Rémy Schmit* [1996] ECR I-3179; services; not permissible.

Joined Cases C-71/94, C-72/94 and C-73/94 *Eurim-Pharm Arzneimittel GmbH v Beiersdorf AG and others* [1996] ECR I-3603; goods; mixed results.

Case C-232/94 *MPA Pharma GmbH v Rhône-Poulenc Pharma GmbH* [1996] ECR I-3671; goods; mixed results.

Case C-313/94 *F.lli Graffione SNC v Ditta Fransa* [1996] ECR I-6039; goods; mixed results.

Joined Cases C-267/95 and C-268/95 *Merck & Co. Inc. and others v Primecrown Ltd and others* [1996] ECR I-6285; goods; mixed result.

Case C-3/95 *Reisebüro Broede v Gerd Sandker* [1996] ECR I-6511; services; permissible.

Case C-358/95 *Tommaso Morellato v Unità Sanitaria Locale (USL) No 11, Pordenone* [1997] ECR I-1431; goods; not permissible.

Case C-272/95 *Bundesanstalt für Landwirtschaft und Ernährung v Deutsches Milch-Kontor GmbH* [1997] ECR I-1905; goods; mixed result.

Cases C-321/94, C-322/94, C-323/94 and C-324/94 *Criminal Proceedings Against Jacques Pistre* [1997] ECR I-2434; goods; not permissible.

Case C-105/94 *Ditta Angelo Celestini v Saar-Sektkellerei Faber GmbH & Co. KG* [1997] ECR I-2971, goods; mixed results.

Case C-398/95 *Syndesmos ton en Elladi Touristikon kai Taxidiotikon Grafeion v Ypourgos Ergasias* [1997] ECR I-3091; services; not permissible.

Case C-114/96 *Criminal Proceedings Against René Kieffer and Romain Thill* [1997] ECR I-3629; goods; permissible.

Case C-368/95 *Vereinigte Familiapress Zeitungsverlags-und vertriebs GmbH v Heinrich Bauer Verlag* [1997] ECR I-3689; goods; mixed results.

Joined Cases C-34/95, C-35/95 and C-36/95 *Konsumentombudsmannen v De Agostini (Svenska) Förlag AB and TV-Shop i Sverige AB* [1997] ECR I-3843; goods, services; mixed results.

Case C-222/95 *Société Civile Immobilière Parodi v Banque H. Albert de Bary et Cie* [1997] ECR I-3899; services; mixed results.

Case C-316/95 *Generics BV v Smith, Kline & French Laboratories Ltd* [1997] ECR I-3929; goods; permissible.

Case C-189/95 *Criminal Proceedings Against Harry Franzén* [1997] ECR I-5909; goods; not permissible.

Case C-337/95 *Parfums Christian Dior SA and Parfums Christian Dior BV v Evora BV* [1997] ECR I-6013; goods; mixed results.

Case C-349/95 *Frits Loendersloot, trading as F. Loendersloot Internationale Expeditie v George Ballantine & Son Ltd and others* [1997] ECR I-6227; goods; mixed results.

Case C-265/95 *Commission v French Republic* [1997] ECR I-6959; goods; not permissible.

Case C-1/96 *R v Ministry of Agriculture, Fisheries and Foods, ex parte Compassion in World Farming* [1998] ECR I-1251; goods; not permissible.

Case C-120/95 *Nicolas Decker v Caisse de Maladie des Employés Privés* [1998] ECR I-1831; goods; not permissible.

Case C-118/96 *Jessica Safir v Skattemyndigheten in Dalarnas Län* [1998] ECR I-1897; services; not permissible.

Case C-158/96 *Raymond Kohll v Union des Caisses de Maladie* [1998] ECR I-1931; services; not permissible.

Bibliography

G.A. AKERLOF, 'The Market for "Lemons": Quality Uncertainty and the Market Mechanism' (1970) 84 QJ Econ 488.

M. ANDENAS, 'The Interplay of the Commission and the Court of Justice in Giving Effect to the Right to Provide Financial Services' in P. Craig and C. Harlow (eds), *Law Making in the European Union* (London 1998).

D.W.K. ANDERSON, *References to the European Court* (London 1995).

K.A. ARMSTRONG, 'Regulating the Free Movement of Goods: Institutions and Institutional Change' in J. Shaw and G. More (eds), *New Legal Dynamics of European Union* (Oxford 1995).

K.A. ARMSTRONG and S.J. BULMER, *The Governance of the Single European Market* (Manchester 1998).

A. ARNULL, *The European Union and its Court of Justice* (Oxford 1999).

A.M. ARNULL, A.A. DASHWOOD, M.G. ROSS and D.A. WYATT, *Wyatt and Dashwood's European Union Law* (2nd edn London 2000).

J.-Y. ART, 'Legislative Lacunae, the Court of Justice and Freedom to Provide Services' in D. Curtin and D. O'Keeffe (eds), *Constitutional Adjudication in European Community and National Law. Essays for the Hon. Mr. Justice T.F. O'Higgins* (Dublin 1992).

K. BACON, 'State Regulation of the Market and E.C. Competition Rules: Articles 85 and 86 Compared' (1997) 18 ECLR 283.

R. BALDWIN and M. CAVE, *Understanding Regulation. Theory, Strategy, and Practice* (Oxford 1999).

J. BAQUERO CRUZ, 'Free Movement and Private Autonomy' (1999) 24 ELRev 603.

R. BARENTS, 'New Developments in MEEs' (1981) 18 CMLRev 271.

C. BARNARD, 'Sunday Trading: A Drama in Five Acts' (1994) 57 MLR 449.

C. BARNARD, 'Social Dumping and the Race to the Bottom: Some Lessons for the European Union from Delaware?' (2000) 25 ELRev 57.

C. BARNARD, 'Fitting the Remaining Pieces into the Goods and Persons Jigsaw?' (2001) 26 ELRev 35.

P. BEHRENS, 'Die Konvergenz der wirtschaftlichen Freiheiten im europäischen Gemeinschaftsrecht' (1992) 27 EuR 145.

D.W. BELLAMY and G. CHILD, *Common Market Law of Competition* (4th edn by V. Rose, London 1993).

N. BERNARD, 'Discrimination and Free Movement in EC Law' (1996) 45 ICLQ 82.

N. BERNARD, 'The Future of European Economic Law in the Light of the Principle of Subsidiarity' (1996) 33 CMLRev 633.

N. BERNARD, 'La libre circulation des marchandises, des personnes et des services dans le traité CE sous l'angle de la competence' (1998) 34 CDE 11.

J. BHAGWATI, 'Splintering and Disembodiment of Services and Developing Nations' (1984) 7 *The World Economy* 133.

J. BHAGWATI, 'Services' in J.M. Finger and A. Olechowski (eds), *The Uruguay Round. A Handbook on the Multilateral Trade Negotiations* (Washington 1987).

A. BIONDI, 'In and Out of the Internal Market: Recent Developments on the Principle of Free Movement' (1999–2000) 19 YEL 469.

F. BLUM and A. LOGUE, *State Monopolies under EC Law* (Chichester 1998).

W. BRATTON, J. McCAHERY, S. PICCIOTTO and C. SCOTT (eds), *International Regulatory Competition and Coordination. Perspectives on Economic Regulation in Europe and the United States* (Oxford 1996).

M. BREALEY and M. HOSKINS, *Remedies in EC Law. Law and Practice in English and EC Courts* (2nd edn London 1998).

L.N. BROWN and T. KENNEDY, *The Court of Justice of the European Communities* (5th edn London 2000).

F. BURROWS, *Free Movement in European Community Law* (Oxford 1987).

R.M. BUXBAUM, G. HERTIG, A. HIRSCH and K.J. HOPT (eds), *European Business Law. Legal and Economic Analyses on Integration and Harmonization* (Berlin 1991).

P. CABRAL, 'Cross-border Medical Care in the European Union—Bringing Down the First Wall' (1999) 24 ELRev 387.

P. CABRAL and P. CUNHA, 'The Internal Market and Discriminatory Taxation: Just How (Un)steady is the Ground?' (1999) 24 ELRev 396.

D. CHALMERS, 'Repackaging the Internal Market—The Ramifications of the *Keck* Judgment' (1994) 19 ELRev 385.

D. CHALMERS, 'The Single Market: From Prima Donna to Journeyman' in J. Shaw and G. More (eds), *New Legal Dynamics of European Union* (Oxford 1995).

D. CHALMERS, 'Book Review on We the Court' (1999) 115 LQR 148.

D. CHALMERS and E. SZYSZCZAK, *European Union Law. Vol II. Towards a European Polity?* (Aldershot 1998).

D. CHARNY, 'Competition among Jurisdictions in Formulating Corporate Law Rules: An American Perspective on the "Race to the Bottom" in the European Communities' (1991) 32 Harvard Int LJ 423.

P. CRAIG, 'Once Upon a Time in the West: Direct Effect and the Federalization of EEC Law' (1992) 12 OJLS 453.

P. CRAIG, 'The Nature of the Community: Integration, Democracy, and Legitimacy' in P. Craig and G. de Búrca (eds), *The Evolution of EU Law* (Oxford 1999).

P. CRAIG and G. DE BÚRCA, *EU Law. Text, Cases, and Materials* (2nd edn Oxford 1998).

M.M. DABBAH, 'The Dilemma of *Keck*—The Nature of the Ruling and the Ramifications of the Judgment' (1999) 8 IJEL 84.

J.L. DA CRUZ VILAÇA, 'An Exercise on the Application of Keck and Mithouard in the Field of Free Provision of Services' in M. Dony and A. De Walsche (eds), *Mélanges en hommage à Michel Waelbroeck* (Bruxelles 1999).

L. DANIELE, 'Non-Discriminatory Restrictions to the Free Movement of Persons' (1997) 22 ELRev 191.

A. DASHWOOD, 'The *Cassis de Dijon* Line of Authority' in St.J. Bates, W. Finnie, J.A. Usher and H. Wildberg (eds), *In Memoriam J. D. B. Mitchell* (London 1983).

A. DASHWOOD, 'The Limits of European Community Powers' (1996) 21 ELRev 113.

G. DE BÚRCA, 'The Principle of Proportionality and its Application in EC Law' (1993) 13 YEL 105.

G. DE BÚRCA, 'The Role of Equality in European Community Law' in A. Dashwood and S. O'Leary (eds), *The Principle of Equal Treatment in EC Law. Papers Collected by the Centre For European Legal Studies, Cambridge* (London 1997).

G. DE BÚRCA, 'The Institutional Development of the EU: A Constitutional Analysis' in P. Craig and G. de Búrca (eds), *The Evolution of EU Law* (Oxford 1999).

R. DEHOUSSE, C. JOERGES, G. MAJONE and F. SNYDER, *Europe after 1992—New Regulatory Strategies* (EUI Working Paper Law No. 92/31, 1992).

K.S. DESAI, 'E.C. Competition Law and Trade Unions' (1999) 20 ECLR 175.

J.P.H. DONNER, 'Articles 30–36 EEC in General' (1982) 5 SEW 362.

M. DOUGAN, 'Minimum Harmonization and the Internal Market' (2000) 37 CMLRev 853.

S. DOUGLAS-SCOTT, 'In Search of Union Citizenship' (1998) 18 YEL 29.

O. DUE, 'Dassonville Revisited or No Cause for Alarm?' in A.I.L. Cambell and M.Voyatzi (eds), *Legal Reasoning and Judicial Interpretation of European Law. Essays in Honour of Lord Mackenzie-Stuart* (Gosport 1996).

F.H. EASTERBROOK, 'Antitrust and the Economics of Federalism' (1983) 26 Journal of Law and Economics 23.

F.H. EASTERBROOK, 'Federalism and European Business Law' (1994) 14 International Review of Law and Economics 125.

P. EECKHOUT, *The European Internal Market and International Trade. A Legal Analysis* (Oxford 1994).

P. EECKHOUT, 'The General Agreement on Trade in Services and Community Law' in S.V. Konstadinidis (ed), *The Legal Regulation of the European Community's External Relations after the Completion of the Internal Market* (Aldershot 1996).

P. EECKHOUT, 'Recent Case Law on Free Movement of Goods: Refining Keck and Mithouard' (1998) 9 EBLR 267.

P. EECKHOUT, 'The European Court of Justice and the Legislature' (1998) 18 YEL 1.

N. EMILIOU, 'Subsidiarity: An Effective Barrier Against "the Enterprises of Ambition"?' (1992) 17 ELRev 383.

N. EMILIOU, *The Principle of Proportionality in European Law. A Comparative Study* (London 1996).

J. FEENSTRA, 'Case C-288/89, *Stichting Collectieve Antennevoorziening Gouda and others* v. *Commissariaat voor de Media*, Judgment of 25 July 1991, [1991] ECR I-4007; Case C-353/89 *Commission of the European Communities* v. *Kingdom of the Netherlands*, Judgment of 25 July 1991, [1991] ECR I-4069' (1993) 30 CMLRev 424.

G. FEKETEKUTY, *International Trade in Services. An Overview and Blueprint for Negotiations* (Cambridge Massachusetts 1988).

G. FEKETEKUTY, 'Trade in Professional Services: an Overview' reprinted in J.H. Jackson, W.J. Davey and A.O. Sykes Jr, *Legal Problems of International Economic Relations. Cases, Materials and Text on the National and International Regulation of Transnational Economic Relations* (3rd edn St.Paul Minn 1995).

J.M. FERNÁNDEZ MARTÍN, 'Re-defining Obstacles to the Free Movement of Workers' (1996) 21 ELRev 313.

J.M. FERNÁNDEZ MARTÍN and S. O'LEARY, 'Judicial Exceptions to the Free Provision of Services' (1995) 1 ELJ 308.

B.S. FREY and R. EICHENBERGER, 'FOCJ: Creating a Single European Market for Governments' in D. Schmidtchen and R. Cooter (eds), *Constitutional Law and Economics of the European Union* (Cheltenham 1997).

T.J. FRIEDBACHER, 'Motive Unmasked: The European Court of Justice, the Free Movement of Goods and the Search for Legitimacy' (1996) 2 ELJ 226.

D. GERADIN, 'The Belgian Waste Case' (1993) 18 ELRev 144.

D. GERADIN, 'Trade and Environmental Protection: Community Harmonization and National Environmental Standards' (1993) 13 YEL 151.

D. GERADIN, *Trade and the Environment. A Comparative Study of EC and US Law* (Cambridge 1997).

D. GERADIN, 'L'overture à la concurrence des entreprises de réseau. Analyse des principaux enjeux du processus de libéralisation' (1999) 35 CDE 13.

R. GIESEN, 'Case C-120/95 *Nicolas Decker* v. *Caisse de Maladie des Employés Privés*, Judgment of 28 April, [1998] ECR I-1831; Case C-158/96 *Raymond Kohll* v. *Union des Caisses de Maladie*, Judgment of 28 April 1998, [1998] ECR I-1931' (1999) 36 CMLRev 841.

L. GORMLEY, *Prohibiting Restrictions on Trade within the EEC* (Amsterdam 1985).

L. GORMLEY, '"Actually or Potentially, Directly or Indirectly"? Obstacles to the Free Movement of Goods' (1989) 9 YEL 197.

L. GORMLEY, 'Pay Your Money and Take Your Chance?' (1994) 19 ELRev 644.

L. GORMLEY, 'Reasoning Renounced? The Remarkable Judgment in *Keck & Mithouard*' (1994) 5 EBLR 63.

L.W. GORMLEY, 'Two Years after Keck' (1996) 19 Fordham Int LJ 866.

D.G. GOYDER, *EC Competition Law* (3rd edn Oxford 1998).

R. GREAVES, 'Advertising Restrictions and the Free Movement of Goods and Services' (1998) 23 ELRev 305.

N. GREEN, T.C. Hartley, and J.A. Usher, *The Legal Foundations of the Single European Market* (Oxford 1991).

L. HANCHER, 'The European Pharmaceutical Market: Problems of Partial Harmonisation' (1990) 15 ELRev 9.

L. HANCHER, 'Community, State, and Market' in P. Craig and G. de Búrca (eds), *The Evolution of EU Law* (Oxford 1999).

J. HANDOLL, *Free Movement of Persons* (Chichester 1995).

T.C. HARTLEY, 'The European Court, Judicial Objectivity and the Constitution of the European Union' (1996) 112 LQR 95.

T.C. HARTLEY, *The Foundations of European Community Law* (4th edn Oxford 1998).

V. HATZOPOULOS, 'Case C-275/92, *Her Majesty's Customs and Excise* v. *Gerhart and Jörg Schindler*, [1994] ECR I-1039' (1995) 32 CMLRev 841.

V. HATZOPOULOS, 'Case C-384/93, *Alpine Investments BV* v. *Minister van Financiën*, Judgment of 10 May 1995, nyr' (1995) 32 CMLRev 1427.

V. HATZOPOULOS, 'Case C-484/93, *Svensson, Gustavsson* v. *Ministre du logement et de l'urbanisme*, Judgment of 14 November 1995, [1995] ECR I-3955' (1996) 33 CMLRev 569.

V. HATZOPOULOS, 'Case C-250/95, *Futura Participations SA & Singer* v. *Administration des Contributions (Luxembourg)*, Judgment of 15 May 1997, [1997] ECR I-2471' (1998) 35 CMLRev 493.

V. HATZOPOULOS, 'Exigences essentielles, impératives ou impérieuses: *une* théorie, *des* théories ou pas de théorie du tout?' (1998) 34 RTDE 191.

V. HATZOPOULOS, 'Recent Developments of the Case Law of the ECJ in the Field of Services' (2000) 37 CMLRev 43.

H. HAUSER and M. HÖSLI, 'Harmonization or Regulatory Competition in the EC (and the EEA)?' (1991) 46 Aussenwirtschaft 497.

B. HAWK, 'System Failure: Vertical Restraints and EC Competition Law' (1995) 32 CMLRev 973.

G. HERTIG, 'Imperfect Mutual Recognition for EC Financial Services' (1994) 14 International Review of Law and Economics 177.

I. HIGGINS, 'The Free and Not so Free Movement of Goods since *Keck*' (1997) 6 IJEL 166.

T.P. HILL, 'On Goods and Services' (1977) 23 *Review of Income and Wealth* 315.

C. HILSON, 'Discrimination in Community Free Movement Law' (1999) 24 ELRev 445.

B. HINDLEY and A. SMITH, 'Comparative Advantage and Trade in Services' (1984) 7 *The World Economy* 369.

K. HØEGH, 'The Danish Maastricht Judgment' (1999) 24 ELRev 80.

S.P. HUNTINGTON, *The Clash of Civilizations and the Remaking of World Order* (New York 1996).

L. IDOT, 'Case C-412/93, *Société d'Importation Édouard Leclerc-Siplec* v. *TF1 Publicité SA and M6 publicité SA*, Judgment of 9 February 1995, [1995] ECR 179' (1996) 33 CMLRev 113.

J.H. JACKSON, 'Constructing a Constitution for Trade in Services' (1988) 11 *The World Economy* 187.

J.H. JACKSON, W.J. Davey and A.O. Sykes Jr, *Legal Problems of International Economic Relations. Cases, Materials and Text on the National and International Regulation of Transnational Economic Relations* (3rd edn St.Paul Minn 1995).

F.G. JACOBS, 'Recent Developments in the Principle of Proportionality in European Community Law' in E. Ellis (ed), *The Principle of Proportionality in the Laws of Europe* (Oxford 1999).

J.P. JACQUÉ and J.H.H. WEILER, 'On the Road to European Union—a New Judicial Architecture: An Agenda for the Intergovernmental Conference' (1990) 27 CMLRev 185.

H.D. JARASS, 'Elemente einer Dogmatik der Grundfreiheiten' (1995) 30 EuR 202.

H.D. JARASS, 'Elemente einer Dogmatik der Grundfreiheiten II' (2000) 35 EuR 705.

M.A. JARVIS, *The Application of EC Law by National Courts. The Free Movement of Goods* (Oxford 1998).

M.A. JARVIS, 'Case C-265/95, *Commission* v. *French Republic*, Judgment of the Court of Justice of 9 December 1997, [1997] ECR I-6959' (1998) 35 CMLRev 1371.

C. JOERGES, 'European Economic Law, the Nation-State and the Maastricht Treaty' in R. Dehousse (ed), *Europe after Maastricht. An Ever Closer Union?* (München 1994).

E. JOHNSON and D. O'KEEFFE, 'From Discrimination to Obstacles to Free Movement: Recent Developments Concerning the Free Movement of Workers 1989 1994' (1994) 31 CMLRev 1313.

R. JOLIET, 'Der freie Warenverkehr: Das Urteil Keck und Mithouard und die Neuorientierung der Rechtsprechung' (1994) GRUR Int 979.

P.J.G. KAPTEYN, 'The Court of Justice of the European Communities after the Year 2000' in D. Curtin and T. Heukels (eds), *Institutional Dynamics of European Integration. Essays in Honour of Henry G. Schermers. Vol II* (Dordrecht 1994).

P.J.G. KAPTEYN and P. VERLOREN VAN THEMAAT, *Introduction to the Law of the European Communities. From Maastricht to Amsterdam* (3rd edn by L.W. Gormley London 1998).

J. KAY and J. VICKERS, 'Regulatory Reform: An Appraisal' in G. Majone (ed), *Deregulation or Re-regulation? Regulatory Reform in Europe and the United States* (London 1990).

P. KENNEDY, *The Rise and Fall of Great Powers. Economic Advantage and Military Conflict from 1500 to 2000* (London 1988).

T. KENNEDY, 'First Steps Towards a European Certiorari?' (1993) 18 ELRev 121.

E. KITCH, 'Business Organization Law: State or Federal? An Inquiry into the Allocation of Political Competence in relation to Issues of Business Organization Law in a Federal System' in R.M. Buxbaum, G. Hertig, A. Hirsch and K.J. Hopt (eds), *European Business Law. Legal and Economic Analyses on Integration and Harmonization* (Berlin 1991).

C. KOENIG, 'Some Brief Remarks on Interjurisdictional Competition between EU Member States' (1999) 10 EBLR 437.

T. KOOPMANS, 'The Future of the Court of Justice of the European Communities' (1991) 11 YEL 15.

V. KORAH, *An Introductory Guide to EC Competition Law and Practice* (7th edn Oxford 2000).

L. KRÄMER, *EC Environmental Law* (4th edn London 2000).

S. LAAKSO, 'Suhteellisuusperiaate yhteisöoikeudessa' (1999) 97 LM 1080.

P.H. LANE, *A Manual of Australian Constitutional Law* (6th edn Sydney 1995).

D.W. LEEBRON, 'Lying Down with Procrustes: An Analysis of Harmonization Claims' in J. Bhagwati and R.E. Hudec (eds), *Fair Trade and Harmonization. Prerequisites for Free Trade? Vol I. Economic Analysis* (London 1996).

A.T.S. LEENEN, 'Recent Case Law of the Court of Justice of the European Communities on the Freedom of Establishment and the Freedom to Provide Services' (1980) 17 CMLRev 259.

K. LENAERTS, 'Constitutionalism and the Many Faces of Federalism' (1990) 38 AJCL 205.

K. LENAERTS, 'Some Thoughts about the Interaction between Judges and Politicians in the European Community' (1992) 12 YEL 1.

A. MCGEE and S. WEATHERILL, 'The Evolution of the Single Market—Harmonisation or Liberalisation' (1990) 53 MLR 578.

I. MAHER, 'Competition Law and Intellectual Property Rights: Evolving Formalism' in P. Craig and G. de Búrca (eds), *The Evolution of EU Law* (Oxford 1999).

G. MAJONE, *Evidence, Argument and Persuasion in the Policy Process* (New Haven 1989).

G. MAJONE, 'Regulatory Federalism in the European Community' (1992) 10 Government and Policy, Environment and Planning C 299.

G. MAJONE, *Regulating Europe* (London 1996).

F. MANCINI and D. KEELING, 'From *CILFIT* to *ERT*: The Constitutional Challenge Facing the European Court' (1991) 11 YEL 1.

G. MARENCO, 'Pour une interprétation traditionelle de la notion de measure d'effet équivalent à une restriction quantitative' (1984) 19 CDE 291.

G. MARENCO, 'Competition between National Economies and Competition between Businesses—A Response to Judge Pescatore' (1987) 10 Fordham Int LJ 424.

G. MARENCO, 'The Notion of Restriction on the Freedom of Establishment and Provision of Services in the Case-law of the Court' (1991) 11 YEL 111.

G. MARENCO and K. BANKS, 'Intellectual Property and the Community Rules on Free Movement: Discrimination Unearthed' (1990) 15 ELRev 224.

G. MARKS and L. HOOGHE, 'Optimality and Authority: A Critique of Neoclassical Theory' (2000) 38 JCMS 795.

D. MARTIN, '"Discriminations", "entraves" et "raisons imperieuses" dans le traité CE. Trois concepts en quête d'identité' (1998) 34 CDE 261.

D. MARTIN and E. GUILD, *Free Movement of Persons in the European Union* (London 1996).

A. MATTERA, *Le marché unique européen* (2nd edn Paris 1990).

A. MAUNU, 'Jäsenvaltion vastuu yksityisen oikeussubjektin aiheuttamasta sisä-markkinakaupan esteestä' (1998) DL 358.

W. MOLLE, *The Economics of European Integration. Theory, Practice, Policy* (3rd edn Aldershot 1997).

K. MORTELMANS, 'Article 30 of the EEC Treaty and Legislation Relating to Market Circumstances: Time to Consider a New Definition?' (1991) 28 CMLRev 115.

K. MORTELMANS, 'The Common Market, the Internal Market and the Single Market, What's in a Market' (1998) 35 CMLRev 101.

J. MÜLLER, 'An Economic Analysis of Different Regulatory Regimes of Transborder Services' in D. Friedmann and E.-J. Mestmäcker (eds), *Rules for Free International Trade in Services* (Baden-Baden 1990).

K. MUYLLE, 'Angry Farmers and Passive Policemen: Private Conduct and the Free Movement of Goods' (1998) 23 ELRev 467.

U.B. NEERGAARD, 'Free Movement of Goods from a Contextual Perspective, A Review Essay' (1999) 6 MJ 151.

P. NICOLAIDES, 'Economic Aspects of Services: Implications for a GATT Agreement' (1989) 23 JWT 125.

P. NICOLAIDES, *Liberalizing Service Trade. Strategies for Success* (London 1989).

P. NICOLAIDES, 'Competition Among Rules' (1992) 16 World Competition 113.

P.R. NIELSEN, *Services and Establishment in European Community Banking Law* (Copenhagen 1994).

P. NIHOUL, 'Do Workers Constitute Undertakings for the Purpose of the Competition Rules?' (2000) 25 ELRev 408.

N. NOTARO, 'The New Generation Case Law on Trade and Environment' (2000) 25 ELRev 467.

J.E. NOWAK and R.D. ROTUNDA, *Constitutional Law* (5th edn St. Paul Minn 1995).

A. OGUS, *Regulation. Legal Form and Economic Theory* (Oxford 1994).

A. OGUS, 'Competition between National Legal Systems: A Contribution of Economic Analysis to Comparative Law' (1999) 48 ICLQ 405.

D. O'KEEFFE, 'Is the Spirit of Article 177 under Attack? Preliminary References and Admissibility' (1998) 23 ELRev 509.

D. O'KEEFFE and A. BAVASSO, 'Four Freedoms, One Market and National Competence: In Search of a Dividing Line' in D. O'Keeffe and A. Bavasso (eds), *Liber Amicorum in Honour of Lord Slynn of Hadley. Vol I. Judicial Review in European Union Law* (The Hague 2000).

D. O'KEEFFE and P. OSBORNE, 'L'affaire Bosman: un arrêt important pour le bon fonctionnement du Marché unique européen' (1996) RMUE 17.

S. O'LEARY, 'The Free Movement of Persons and Services' in P. Craig and G. de Búrca (eds), *The Evolution of EU Law* (Oxford 1999).

P. OLIVER, 'La législation communautaire et sa conformité avec la libre circulation des marchandises' (1979) 15 CDE 245.

P. OLIVER, *Free Movement of Goods in the European Community* (3rd edn London 1996)

P. OLIVER, 'Goods and Services: Two Freedoms Compared' in M. Dony and A. De Walsche (eds), *Mélanges en hommage à Michel Waelbroeck* (Bruxelles 1999).

P. OLIVER, 'Some Further Reflections on the Scope of Articles 28–30 (ex 30–36) EC' (1999) 36 CMLRev 783.

G. ORLANDINI, 'The Free Movement of Goods as a Possible "Community" Limitation on Industrial Conflict' (2000) 6 ELJ 341.

J. PELKMANS, 'Regulation and the Single Market: An Economic Perspective' in H. Siebert (ed), *The Completion of the Internal Market* (Tübingen 1990).

P. PESCATORE, 'Public and Private Aspects of European Community Competition Law' (1987) 10 Fordham Int LJ 373.

F. PICOD, 'La nouvelle approche de la Cour de justice en matière d'entraves aux échanges' (1998) 34 RTDE 169.

R.H. PILDES and C.R. SUNSTEIN, 'Reinventing the Regulatory State' (1995) 62 Univ of Chicago LR 1.

J.-C. PIRIS, 'Does the European Union have a Constitution? Does it Need One?' (1999) 24 ELRev 557.

M. POIARES MADURO, 'The Saga of Article 30 EC Treaty: To Be Continued. A Comment on Familiapress v Bauer Verlag and Other Recent Episodes' (1998) 5 MJ 298.

M. POIARES MADURO, *We The Court. The European Court of Justice and the European Economic Constitution. A Critical Reading of Article 30 of the EC Treaty* (Oxford 1998).

M. POIARES MADURO, 'Striking the Elusive Balance Between Economic Freedom and Social Rights in the EU' in P. Alston (ed), *The EU and Human Rights* (Oxford 1999).

A.M. POLINSKY, *An Introduction to Law and Economics* (2nd edn Boston 1989).

M.A. POLLOCK, 'The End of Creeping Competence? EU Policy-Making Since Maastricht' (2000) 38 JCMS 519.

M.E. PORTER, *The Competitive Advantage of Nations* (London 1990).

G. PROSI, 'Comments on Horst Siebert, "The Harmonization Issue in Europe: Prior Agreement or a Competitive Process?"' in H. Siebert (ed), *The Completion of the Internal Market* (Tübingen 1990).

M. QUINN and N. MACGOWAN, 'Could Article 30 Impose Obligations on Individuals?' (1987) 12 ELRev 163.

D.H. REGAN, 'The Supreme Court and State Protectionism: Making Sense of the Dormant Commerce Clause' (1985–1986) 84 Michigan LR 1091.

N. REICH, 'Competition between Legal Orders: a New Paradigm of EC Law' (1992) 29 CMLRev 861.

N. REICH, 'The "November Revolution" of the European Court of Justice: *Keck*, *Meng* and *Audi* Revisited' (1994) 31 CMLRev 459.

N. REICH, *Europäisches Verbraucherrecht* (3rd revised edn Baden-Baden 1996).

N. REICH, 'Europe's Economic Constitution, or: A New Look at Keck' (1999) 19 OJLS 337.

G.C. RODRÍGUEZ IGLESIAS, 'Drinks in Luxembourg. Alcoholic Beverages and the Case Law of the European Court of Justice, in D. O'Keeffe and A. Bavasso (eds), *Liber Amicorum in Honour of Lord Slynn of Hadley. Vol I. Judicial Review in European Union Law* (The Hague 2000).

M. ROSS, 'Article 59 and the Marketing of Financial Services' (1995) 20 ELRev 507.

W.-H. ROTH, 'The European Economic Community's Law on Services: Harmonisation' (1988) 25 CMLRev 35.

W.-H. ROTH, 'Case C-76/90 *Manfred Säger* v. *Dennemeyer & Co. Ltd.*, Judgment of 25 July 1991 (not yet reported)' (1993) 30 CMLRev 145.

W.-H. ROTH, 'Joined Cases C-267 and C-268/91, *Bernard Keck and Daniel Mithouard*, Judgment of 24 November 1993, [1993] ECR I-6097; Case C-292/92, *Ruth Hünermund et al.* v. *Landesapothekerkammer Baden-Württemberg*, Judgment of 15 December 1993, [1993] ECR I-6787' (1994) 31 CMLRev 845.

W.-H. ROTH, 'Drittwirkung der Grundfreiheiten?' in O. Due, M. Lutter and J. Schwarze (eds), *Festschrift für Ulrich Everling* (Baden-Baden 1995).

W.-H. ROTH, 'Wettbewerb der Mitgliedstaaten oder Wettbewerb der Hersteller? Plädoyer für eine Neubestimmung des Art. 34 EGV' (1995) 159 ZHR 78.

W.-H. ROTH, 'Case C-233/94 *Federal Republic of Germany* v. *European Parliament and Council of the European Union*, Judgment of 13 May 1997, [1997] ECR I-2405' (1998) 35 CMLRev 459.

G.P. SAMPSON and R.H. SNAPE, 'Identifying the Issues in Trade in Services' (1985) 8 *The World Economy* 171.

A. SAPIR, 'The General Agreement on Trade in Services. From 1994 to the Year 2000' (1999) 33 JWT 51.

U. SCHEFFER, *Die Marktfreiheiten des EG-Vertrages als Ermessensgrenze des Gemeinschaftgesetzgebers* (Frankfurt 1997).

H. SCHMIDT, 'Economic Analysis of the Allocation of Regulatory Competence in the European Communities' in R.M. Buxbaum, G. Hertig, A. Hirsch and K.J. Hopt (eds), *European Business Law. Legal and Economic Analyses on Integration and Harmonization* (Berlin 1991).

J. SCHWARZE, *European Administrative Law* (London 1992).

R.-O. SCHWEMER, *Die Bindung des Gemeinschaftsgesetzgebers an die Grundfreiheiten* (Frankfurt 1995).

J. SCOTT, 'On Kith and Kine (and Crustaceans): Trade and Environment in the EU and WTO' in J.H.H. Weiler (ed), *The EU, the WTO, and the NAFTA. Towards a Common Law of International Trade?* (Oxford 2000).

J. SHAW, 'The Interpretation of European Union Citizenship' (1998) 61 MLR 293.

H. SIEBERT, 'The Harmonization Issue in Europe: Prior Agreement or a Competitive Process?' in H. Siebert (ed), *The Completion of the Internal Market* (Tübingen 1990).

H. SIEBERT and M.J. KOOP, 'Institutional Competition. A Concept for Europe?' (1990) 45 Aussenwirtschaft 439.

H. SIEBERT and M.J. KOOP, 'Institutional Competition versus Centralization: Quo Vadis Europe?' (1993) 9 *Oxford Review of Economic Policy* 15.

L. SIEDENTOP, *Democracy in Europe* (London 2000).

J. SNELL, 'De Agostini and the Regulation of Television Broadcasting' (1997) 8 EBLR 222.

E. SPAVENTA, 'Casenote on TK-Heimdienst' (2000) 37 CMLRev 1265.

E. SPAVENTA, 'Casenote on Belgium v. Spain' (2001) 38 CMLRev 211.

E. STEINDORFF, 'Freedom of Services in the EEC' (1987–1988) 11 Fordham Int LJ 347.

J. STEINER, 'Drawing the Line: Uses and Abuses of Article 30 EEC' (1992) 29 CMLRev 749.

J. STEINER, 'Subsidiarity under the Maastricht Treaty' in D. O'Keeffe and P.M. Twomey (eds), *Legal Issues of the Maastricht Treaty* (Chichester 1994).

J. STEINER and L. WOODS, *Textbook on EC Law* (7th edn London 2000).

M.E. STREIT and W. MUSSLER, 'The Economic Constitution of the European Community: From "Rome" to "Maastricht"' (1995) 1 ELJ 5.

J. STUYCK, 'Joined Cases C-34/95, C-35/95 and C-36/95 *Konsumentombudsmannen (KO)* v. *De Agostini (Svenska) Förlag AB* and *Konsumentombudsmannen (KO)* v. *TV-Shop i Sverige AB*, Judgment of 9 July 1997, nyr' (1997) 34 CMLRev 1445.

J.-M. SUN and J. PELKMANS, 'Regulatory Competition in the Single Market' (1995) 33 JCMS 67.

C.R. SUNSTEIN, 'Protectionism, the American Supreme Court, and Integrated Markets' in R. Bieber, R. Dehousse, J. Pinder and J.H.H. Weiler (eds), *1992: One European Market? A Critical Analysis of the Commission's Internal Market Strategy* (Baden-Baden 1988).

C.R. SUNSTEIN, *After the Rights Revolution. Reconceiving the Regulatory State* (Cambridge Massachusetts 1990).

C.R. SUNSTEIN, 'Incommensurability and Valuation in Law' (1994) 92 Michigan LR 779.

J. TEMPLE LANG, 'The Duties of National Courts under Community Constitutional Law' (1997) 22 ELRev 3.

G. TESAURO, 'The Community Internal Market in the Light of the Recent Case-law of the Court of Justice' (1995) 15 YEL 1.

C.M. TIEBOUT, 'A Pure Theory of Local Expenditures' (1956) 64 Journal of Political Economy 416.

M. TISON, 'What is "General Good" in EU Services Law?' (1997) 24 LIEI 1.

A. TORGERSEN, 'The Limitations of the Free Movement of Goods and the Freedom to Provide Services—in Search of a Common Approach' (1999) 10 EBLR 371.

J.P. TRACHTMAN, 'International Regulatory Competition, Externalization, and Jurisdiction' (1993) 34 Harvard Int LJ 47.

N. TRAVERS, 'Rental Rights and the Specific Subject-matter of Copyright in Community Law' (1999) ELRev 171.

L.H. TRIBE, *American Constitutional Law* (2nd edn Minneola New York 1988).

T. TRIDIMAS, 'The Court of Justice and Judicial Activism' (1996) 21 ELRev 199.

T. TRIDIMAS, *The General Principles of EC Law* (Oxford 1999).

T. TRIDIMAS, 'Proportionality in Community Law: Searching for the Appropriate Standard of Scrutiny' in E. Ellis (ed), *The Principle of Proportionality in the Laws of Europe* (Oxford 1999).

A. TÜRK, 'Recent Case Law in Services and Establishment' (1998) EBLR 193.

R. VAN DEN BERGH, 'Economic Criteria for Applying the Subsidiarity Principle in the European Community: the Case of Competition Policy' (1996) 16 Internatonal Review of Law and Economics 363.

R. VAN DEN BERGH, 'The Subsidiarity Principle and the EC Competition Rules: the Costs and Benefits of Decentralisation' in D. Schmidtchen and R. Cooter (eds), *Constitutional Law and Economics of the European Union* (Cheltenham 1997).

R. VAN DEN BERGH, 'Subsidiarity as an Economic Demarcation Principle and the Emergence of European Private Law' (1998) 5 MJ 129.

R.J. VAN DEN BERGH and P.D. CAMESASCA, 'Irreconcilable Principles? The Court of Justice Exempts Collective Labour Agreements from the Wrath of Antitrust' (2000) 25 ELRev 492.

S. VAN DEN BOGAERT, 'The Court of Justice on the Tatami: Ippon, Waza-Ari or Koka?' (2000) 25 ELRev 554.

A.P. VAN DER MEI, 'Cross-Border Access to Medical Care within the European Union—Some Reflections on the Judgments in *Decker* and *Kohll*' (1998) 5 MJ 277.

M. VAN EMPEL, 'The Visible Hand in Invisible Trade' (1990) 17 LIEI 23.

W. VAN GERVEN, 'The Effect of Proportionality on the Actions of Member States of the European Community: National Viewpoints from Continental Europe' in E. Ellis (ed), *The Principle of Proportionality in the Laws of Europe* (Oxford 1999).

S. VAN RAEPENBUSCH, 'La libre choix par les citoyens Européens des produits médicaux et des prestaires de soins, conséquence sociale du marché intérieur' (1998) 34 CDE 683.

T.C. VINJE, 'Magill, Its Impact on Information Technology Industries' (1992) 14 EIPR 397.

H. VON DER GROEBEN, J. THIESING and C.-D. EHLERMANN (eds), *Kommentar zum EU-EG-Vertrag* (5th revised edn Baden-Baden 1997).

H.-C. VON HEYDEBRAND U.D. LASA, 'Free Movement of Foodstuffs, Consumer Protection and Food Standards in the European Community: Has the Court of Justice Got It Wrong?' (1991) 16 ELRev 391.

P. WATSON, 'Freedom of Establishment and Freedom to Provide Services: Some Recent Developments' (1983) 20 CMLRev 767.

S. WEATHERILL, 'Discrimination on Grounds of Nationality in Sport' (1989) 9 YEL 55.

S. WEATHERILL, 'After *Keck*: Some Thoughts on How to Clarify the Clarification' (1996) 33 CMLRev 885.

S. WEATHERILL, 'Free Movement of Goods' (1999) 48 ICLQ 217.

S. WEATHERILL, 'Recent Case Law Concerning the Free Movement of Goods: Mapping the Frontiers of Market Deregulation' (1999) 36 CMLRev 51.

S. WEATHERILL and P. BEAUMONT, *EU Law* (3rd edn London 1999).

J.H.H. WEILER, 'The Transformation of Europe' (1991) 100 Yale LJ 2403.

J.H.H. WEILER, 'The Reformation of European Constitutionalism' (1997) 35 JCMS 97.

J.H.H. WEILER, 'The Constitution of the Common Market Place: Text and Context in the Evolution of the Free Movement of Goods' in P. Craig and G. de Búrca (eds), *The Evolution of EU Law* (Oxford 1999).

J.H.H. WEILER and N.J.S. LOCKHART, '"Taking Rights Seriously" Seriously: The European Court and its Fundamental Rights Jurisprudence' (1995) 32 CMLRev 51 and 579.

F. WEISS, 'The General Agreement on Trade in Services' (1995) 32 CMLRev 1177.

R. WESSELING, 'Subsidiarity in the Community Antitrust Law: Setting the Right Agenda' (1997) 22 ELRev 35.

R. WHISH, *Competition Law* (3rd edn London 1993).

R. WHISH and B. SUFRIN, 'Article 85 and the Rule of Reason' (1987) 7 YEL 1.

E. WHITE, 'In Search of the Limits to Article 30 of the EEC Treaty' (1989) 26 CMLRev 235.

H. WILLGERODT, 'Comment on Jaques Pelkmans, "Regulation and the Single Market: An Economic Perspective"' in H. Siebert (ed), *The Completion of the Internal Market* (Tübingen 1990).

W.P.J. WILS, 'The Search for the Rule in Article 30 EEC: Much Ado About Nothing?' (1993) 18 ELRev 475.

W.P.J. WILS, 'Subsidiarity and the EC Environmental Policy: Taking Peoples' Concerns Seriously' (1994) 6 JEL 85.

S. WOOLCOCK, *The Single European Market. Centralization or Competition among National Rules?* (London 1994).

A.R. ZIEGLER, *Trade and Environmental Law in the European Community* (Oxford 1996).

Index